Poverty Amidst Prosperity

Essays on the Trajectory of Development in Gujarat

Edited by

Atul Sood

AAKAR

Poverty Amidst Prosperity:
Essays on the Trajectory of Development in Gujarat
edited by Atul Sood

First Published, 2012

Published by
AAKAR BOOKS
28 E Pocket IV, Mayur Vihar Phase I, Delhi 110 091
Phone : 011 2279 5505 Telefax : 011 2279 5641
aakarbooks@gmail.com; www.aakarbooks.com

Printed at
Arpit Printographers, Delhi 110 032
arpitprinto@yahoo.com

Acknowledgements

At the outset, my most sincere thanks to all the contributors of this book. Without the detailed and painstaking work of the chapter authors, the trajectory of Gujarat development would have remained hidden from history. If the authors had not spent months to scrutinize data, analyze trends and clarify facts, it would not have been possible for me to build a larger generalization about the path of development in Gujarat. I gratefully acknowledge the team work of the contributors.

In our endeavor to isolate each sector or dimension of Gujarat's development (in different chapters), from the whole, to comprehend the details, we have tried not to lose the vast interconnections between them. We have also tried to examine the dynamics of growth, as it changed and evolved, and hopefully, we have not missed the wood for the trees. This work is not meant to be a balance sheet account of the growth experience. It is our belief that in order to understand the experience of development and attempt to change it for the better, what we need is not just mute facts and descriptive statements, but a larger explanatory theory too. This volume has tried to answer the 'whys' of this path of development.

For the truth about the whole, for explanations that take us behind appearances, the reality of things under capitalism, this work recognizes and is aware of the larger processes that have propelled growth in Gujarat. A society, which is class divided, unequal, socially exclusionary and oppressive; a society where growth is for the few at the cost of the rest. This work speaks without apologies from the vantage point of the poor and the oppressed.

I cannot emphasize enough the contributions of Dr. Pramod Kumar, Director, Institute of Development Communication, Chandigarh. He is the lead motivator of this work. Our daily conversations about the larger purpose of social science research, and his immense support to deal with the challenges of doing such a volume is the only reason that this book got completed. Navsharan, Bhupendra and Rajinder as always, have been the sounding boards and guides for course correction, whenever I went astray. I owe a special thanks to them for assuring me that all of this is worth sharing with others. I also thank my students, who keep me going and their occasional nods in agreement makes this research a worthwhile experience. Mr. K.K. Saxena of Aakar Books has been a member of the team rather than just a publisher of this book. My sincere thanks to him for completing the task of publishing this volume in such a short time. Sangeeta, Nidhi and Pankaj deserve special mention for working long hours and doing the difficult job of coordinating with the contributors and the publisher. Central University Gujarat, Gandhinagar, provided the first platform to test the ideas of this book. I gratefully acknowledge the contribution of all those who were present there. A special thanks to Prof. Y.K. Alagh, Chancellor of the University, for his encouragement and critical engagement with the subject of the book.

Finally, this work is being shared with the hope that it will contribute to challenging the myth of a 'vibrant' Gujarat and thinking development beyond the Gujarat model.

October, 2012 **Atul Sood**
New Delhi,

Preface

Societies in transition like ours, are forced to rearrange their policies and rechart the course of their journey. There is a near consensus on nature, path and strategy of development. Consequently, efforts to realize 'other utopias' are negligible. Even the desire to speculate about 'other possibilities' has been tamed. This has posed a challenge to the researcher to build alternate knowledge. These are difficult times, but impregnated with ample opportunities. These opportunities are shaped by globalization of ideas, technological revolution and pressing need for holistic knowledge.

Globalization through integration of markets and the global process of capital expansion and accumulation has always been part of capitalist development. Once we recognise the historical continuity of the current model of development, the nature and the role of the state becomes very significant in understanding the current model of development. The state may become 'subservient' to capital, or it may moderate its impact or it may play role to accelerate the process of global integration; privatize public utilities, amend labour laws and deregulate natural resources like land, energy, coal, etc. And it may coin new catch phrases like Private-Public Partnership (PPP) which in actual practice means leveraging Public resources for Private Profit (PPP) and assign ethical value to social security programmes with prescriptions like 'nothing comes free' or 'there are no free lunches' and consequently dismantle welfare protections.

The consensus on nature of development is having variant implications at the regional level. The regional political parties have their own politics and corresponding economic priorities. Therefore, an evaluation of growth experience at the regional level shall help to draw appropriate lessons for pro-people and environment-friendly growth dynamics. There is an understanding that regions which are more knowledge rich, innovative, enterprising and outgoing may perform better. Therefore, variations in existing knowledge, development thinking, economic growth models, political economy approach – makes a strong case for studying regional outcomes. Not only this, the existing political coalitions define the limits and scope of policy-making and institutional change. This makes it urgent to understand development strategy and its outcomes at the regional levels in India.

The existing state of knowledge on regional studies is fairly limited. In order to meet this knowledge gap; we intend to come out with state specific studies. The studies are primarily based on careful analysis of secondary data and examine development outcomes in a comparative perspective. The larger understanding from literature on causal linkages that explain developmental outcomes – sectoral strategies, infrastructure, public and private investment, human capital, social inclusion and exclusion, governance and political practices are all examined in some detail in these studies.

In the first phase, we have covered Gujarat experience followed by Punjab and Haryana. The second phase shall be capturing other north-western states' development story to arrive at a comparative picture. The present study is on Gujarat conducted by a team of young scholars from JNU, under the leadership of Dr. Atul Sood. Following papers are part of this study: Rousing Growth Amidst Ragging Disparities – Atul Sood; Dynamics of Growth in Gujarat – Ruchika Rani; Sources and Patterns of Private Investment in Gujarat – Santosh Kumar Das; Public-Private Partnership: Insights from Infrastructure Development – Pankaj Vashisht And Gaurav Arya; Selective Development in Gujarat: A Study of the Manufacturing Sector – Sangeeta Ghosh; Understanding Gujarat's Agricultural Growth in a Liberalizing Environment: Signs of a Redefined Margin – Sucharita Sen and Chinmoye Malik; Galloping Growth Stagnant Employment: Mapping Regional and Social Differences – Ruchika Rani and Kalaiyarasan A.; Growth with Limited Outcomes: Poverty and Inequality in Gujarat – Nidhi Mittal; An Analysis of State of Education in Gujarat – Sourindra Ghosh ; and Rich State with Poor Health: Disappointing Status of Public Health in Gujarat – Sandeep Sharma.

Why Gujarat?

The model of development in Gujarat, which is very often other Indian states want to emulate. So, whatever impact and consequences of growth and development that Gujarat has experienced can be seen as a precursor by other states given the choices exercised by the political stakeholders' active at the regional level. This process can be altered only if the states attempt to change the policy orientation and develop new metrics to measure development other than the growth rates. The purpose of this effort is to understand the nature of the 'success' of Gujarat (in particular in the last decade or so) in its many dimensions and second, to evaluate lessons, if any, for other states of the Indian subcontinent. The main focus is to look beyond the GDP growth rates and per capita incomes to comprehensive measures of citizens' well-being.

Outcomes

Gujarat has experienced faster economic growth and the drivers of growth are infrastructure development, capital-intensive industrialization and high investment. Has this growth been inclusive? Who are the main beneficiaries of this high growth?

Are outcomes of the existing model of development just an unintended consequence? Are growth rate and citizen well-being divergent claims in terms of entitlements and rights? Are institutions, norms and the procedures predominantly functioning as instruments of private interest causing a visible disconnect between the people and the state policy? Can this model of governance in Gujarat ensure full citizenship for common people in spite of the fact that sovereignty continues to be located in privatization and free market?

These are some of the issues which have been addressed in this book.

Pramod Kumar
(Director IDC)

Contents

1

Rousing Growth Amidst Raging Disparities

Atul Sood

A myth, said the British philosopher Gilbert Ryle (1900-76), is not a fairy story. Instead, a myth is the presentation of facts belonging to one category in the idiom appropriate to another. To unravel the myth, therefore, we should not deny the facts but reallocate them (Ryle, 2002). India is growing and some of its regions are growing faster. The rousing growth is accompanied by furious inequalities between Indians and raging disparities between some regions of India. Gujarat is the lucky star rising on the Indian horizon and yet, Gujaratis have more to worry about today than they had to some decades back. Good governance can deliver targets set in boardrooms by matching available resources with feasible plans. But goals like social equality, justice and peace can be missed by such governance in high-speed lane. In developed parts of India, human beings in the 21st century care more for the goals, ethics and sustainability of development. It is here that there exists a myth of Rising Gujarat which waits to be exploded by, what Ryle called above, some reallocation of hard economic facts. This collection of research papers tries to understand the core features of Gujarat's growth and evaluate what implications it has for the poor and marginalized in other states of the Indian subcontinent, which are eager to replicate the Gujarat 'model'.

In this introduction, we first draw out the lessons from the studies examining growth experience of India. After having identified the factors around which we need to evaluate and understand the developmental outcomes in any region, we provide an integrated narrative of the development story of the state of Gujarat, focussing particularly on the last two decades. The evidence is drawn from various papers published in this volume, that specifically look at growth performance, employment situation, status of poverty and inequality, investment, infrastructure, agriculture, industry and the state of health and education in the state of Gujarat. This paper then goes on to draw some general lessons and suggest a framework to understand the experience of development in India and Gujarat in particular.

Studies on Growth and Its Outcomes in India

A lot of studies in India, in the recent years, that examine the driving forces behind growth, especially at the sub national level, relate economic and social outcomes to the market led economic changes and the effects of globalization. The reason for this connect with globalization or economic reforms is that the post 1980s superior growth performance of the Indian economy, compared to the pre 1980s, is attributed to liberalization of the 1990s (Panagariya, 2004). Two broad issues that are explored in these studies are: one, whether the growth differences across states have sharpened or diminished, and, secondly, what has been the impact of openness and trade liberalization on production structures, poverty, inequality and social sectors.[1]

Studies examining long-run growth performance and regional divergence in per capita income across major Indian states during the pre- and post-reform periods suggest that the gap between rich and poor states (divergence) has increased in the post-reform period. The overall evidence in the literature points to increasing growth differences between the rich and the poor states in India, following the initiation of economic reforms, along with the reality that in some cases rich states are coming closer to each other.[2] The differences in growth rates is most often attributed to inter-state variations in production structures (share of agriculture, industry and services in income), levels of private and public investment, differences in human capital, availability of infrastructure or a result of policy failures like centre-state government transfers.[3] The literature on difference in regional growth also relates household consumption expenditure with levels of income or the pace of development. It suggests that there is perhaps something in the economic structure and the pattern of development) which influences the income distribution (Hashim, 1998).

Given the importance of 'deep determinants' of growth, irrespective of whether we use GDP or consumption inequalities as a measure for growth performance, the focus of comparative growth literature has now shifted from pace or rates of growths to sector specific strategies, role of support programs, human capital and social sector programs (Gajwani and Kanbur, 2006). Pace of growth is still considered significant for its role in reducing headcount poverty (Ahsan et. al, 2010). However, it is the characteristics of growth which is considered more significant, in impacting the quality of life and welfare of the large majority, because of its more widespread and sustainable impact on the rates of poverty reduction, gains in nutritional security and for creating opportunities of 'decent work' to meet the needs of the growing labour force (Ghosh and Chandrashekar, 2007). Production structures, social outcomes, and human development outcomes have emerged as the more significant indicators in the recent discussions on growth, both as factors inhibiting growth and in other parts as an unacceptable consequences of growth. It is this understanding of growth dynamics that makes a compelling case for further examining social and economic outcomes at the sub national level in India. The importance of analysing growth dynamics at the sub regional level becomes even greater when the region for study happens to be 'beacon' of success in India's recent growth story. Given the fast pace of growth in Gujarat, in the last two decades, studying contemporary Gujarat can additionally help us to come up with more robust conclusions about the gains and challenges of the current strategy of growth. The conclusions drawn in this section from the literature on growth, and its outcomes, in India, will inform the discussion of this study to examine the growth experience in Gujarat.

The Unquestioned Development Paradigms

The recent model of development in Gujarat, which other Indian states want to emulate, is an extension of, and, a more committed implementation of the model that the ruling classes of India have chosen in particular, since the mid 1980s. This model, most simply can be characterized in terms of deregulation of the domestic economy and greater integration with the global markets. So whatever impact and consequences of growth and development that Gujarat has experienced are in a way a precursor for things to come in other parts of India unless something drastically changes in the policy orientation at the centre or, the states begin to negotiate the growth agenda in a substantially different manner.

The investor friendly, globally integrating, model of development adopted in Gujarat is not something that is new which has been brought along with 'economic reform' or 'globalization'. The state has been an active player in promoting private initiative in Gujarat since the past many decades. In fact, even at the national level, to see the current growth trajectory as a historical break from the past is perhaps not the best reading of the current model of development. Integration of markets and the global process of capital expansion and accumulation has always been part of India's development. Integration of national economies, the increasing significance of private investors and owners of capital in policy making and globalization of trade and investment is not something new to the present times but only a 'new phase in the normal existence of capitalism as a global system' (Singh, 2006, p. 693). Therefore, at a particular moment, in order to understand the characteristics and consequences of this integration, it is important to identify the specificities of this global system at the national or sub national level. This is what we will attempt in the sections that follow.

Gujarat, because of its high growth record in the recent years, provides one of the best case studies to examine the growth dynamics in India. Gujarat's success in growth is one of the important contributors to India's successful growth story of recent years. Gujarat has been amongst the top three states of India in the growth of per capita income in the last three decades. Recently, in the decade of 1990s and 2000s, GSDP growth in Gujarat has been faster than the national average and this growth has been quite robust. Growth in Gujarat has come from diverse sectors, including agriculture, manufacturing and services. In India, bulk of growth, in recent years has come from the services sector, while in Gujarat there is a healthy balance between the three sectors. Gujarat is often cited as a miracle where growth has been highly impressive. But what is the reality of Gujarat's current growth model? If the Gujarat growth model is unpacked, what do we find? What are the reasons, sources and drivers of growth in Gujarat?

Gujarat's success is not recent and historically, Gujarat's success is located in many factors including its history, its people's entrepreneurial skills, its farmers and their strong agrarian base, its artisans and their global recognition and the legacy of social reform and cooperative movement (Shah et. al., 2002). But is the contemporary dynamics of growth in the state in any way different?. What can the current success of growth in the state attributed to? Has the 'success' of growth brought investment and investor so much to the centre stage that the 'other' influences (farmers, artisans, cooperative movement) and their priorities been lost to the chorus of growth? When we think of the state of Gujarat today the images around growth that flash in our minds are that of successful entrepreneurs; 'grass root' participation in the stock markets; and money-making as involuntary intuition. Is there any objective basis to this 'new' image of the state, compared to the story of cooperative movement and social reform before? Where do the underclass, the poor, the landless, minorities, tribal's and other minority social groups fit in this story? Is Gujarat all a story of success? An investor's paradise!

State Initiatives on Investment

Numerous initiatives that the state has taken in the recent years confirm that rulers in Gujarat have unqualified faith in the workings of the market and the private investor to meet the development needs of the state. Public investment has taken a back seat, both in terms of quantity and its location to meet the developmental priorities.[4] In fact, the unqualified faith on private investor has often meant that the investor is no longer the source for resources but one who is deciding even the priorities of development. The implication of this model are serious in terms of sustainability and distributive justice.

In private investment (measured through intentions and proposals both) Gujarat is the third most popular destination for investors, after Odisha and Chhattisgarh. Between 1990 and 2011, Gujarat attracted 12 per cent of total investment proposals in the country, and remained a preferred destination in comparison to other states like Maharashtra, Andhra Pradesh and Tamil Nadu. In 2012 more than 26 per cent of Industrial Entrepreneur Memorandum (IEMs) submitted in India were based in Gujarat.[5] The high share of IEMs in Gujarat reflects the popularity of the state amongst investors. On its ability to actualize investment intentions, where the role of government and governance becomes more prominent, the performance of the state has also been reasonably good in comparison to other states. In terms of projects implemented, from amongst the proposed projects, close to 15 per cent came to Gujarat, and in case of investments which require license approval, the share of the state between 1991 and 2011, was highest in the country, around 20 per cent.

It is pertinent to point out that, though the share of investment in Gujarat is reasonably high, its ranking in employment associated with this investment is relatively low. Gujarat ranks first in terms of direct industrial license, but ranks seventh in employment; Tamil Nadu ranks seventh in investment in IEMs but tops in the country in its share of creating employment from this investment. The relationship between investment and employment becomes clear when we look at the sectors in which investment is flowing in Gujarat. Out of the total investment, between 1983 and 2010, 30 per cent projects, 42 per cent investment and 26 per cent employment is in the chemical and petrochemical sector alone. If we add textiles and pharmaceuticals, the two other historically well-known sectors in the state, their combined share in projects is close to sixty per cent. Combined share of these sectors in investment is more than 54 per cent and they contribute 55 per cent of total employment. Thus, in Gujarat, the investment trends reflect continued dependence on few sectors for most of its impetus to investment led growth. This investment pattern is bound to pose major challenges for accessing gains from growth across skills, social and economic classes and different regions of the state.

Even though the diversity of investment across sectors is limited in the state, still the volume remains impressive. The question that is often asked, and is also addressed in this volume is what is that which is unique in the state that explains this 'success story' of investment? Many researchers and the mainstream media suggest that since Gujarat's infrastructure is not extraordinarily different from other industrially competitive states, the substantial difference in investment levels can possibly be explained as a result of favourable government policy, in particular the investor friendly governance structure. The 'Vibrant Gujarat Global Investors Summit' held every two years is often highlighted as an example of state's proactive role. The recent summit in 2011 announced MOUs worth rupees 21 lakh crores from over eight thousand MOUs. However, to see these summits as long-term motivation or reasons for investor to flock to the state, does not appear to be very convincing. The success of these summit appears to be waning out after the initial euphoria. Out of the MOUs signed every year, the share of projects implemented and under implementation have continuously declined over the last few years. The share of projects implemented and under implementation has come down from 73 per cent in 2003 to 13 per cent in 2011 (numbers for 2005, 2007 and 2009 are 62, 63, 31 respectively). Ministry of Commerce data also suggests that the states share in investment intentions in terms of IEMs, LOIs and DILs has steadily declined from early 20's in 2005 to less than 10 per cent in 2011. In other words the failure rate of promised or projected MOUs and the states share in national investment is decreasing. What explains this 'investment fatigue' then? The explanations could perhaps range from the slowdown in overall investment climate; saturation of best investment opportunities in the state; or a more realistic assessment of the 'efficiency' of the state administration by the investors.

One important factor that supposedly strengthens investor confidence is 'peace' in the industrial relations or less 'labour unrest' and the belief in the state's administrative capacity to 'control' any undue disturbance, as and when it arises, and maintain industrial harmony at all times. Interestingly, *The Economic Survey of 2011*, listed Gujarat on the top, as the 'worst' state for labour unrest—'Gujarat witnessed the highest number of strikes and other forms of labour unrest in recent times on account of various financial and disciplinary issues' (*Economic Times*, February 25, 2011). The survey suggested that though overall the strikes and lockouts are declining in the country, currently 'maximum incidences were recorded in the state of Gujarat.[6] Wage and allowance, bonus, personnel, indiscipline and violence and financial stringency were the major reasons for these strikes and lockouts'. (*Indian Express*, February 25, 2011). How do we reconcile to the reality of industrial disputes and Gujarat being favourite destination for investment? It appears that the investors consider these incidents as aberrations in the otherwise happy story of growth of Gujarat. Capital is known to have contempt for labour, and historically labour is also known to fight the domination of capital. It is not unusual for capital to strengthen and defend their economic power through what they like to term as the 'rule of law'. This 'rule of law' in Gujarat, has meant more of 'political culture of authoritarianism' (Mukta, 2002) and in taking 'brash pride to demonstrate brute force', and in defending and 'worshipping inequalities' (Mukta, 1990). Gujarat has stripped itself bare of Gandhian humanism, liberal welfare programmes and democratic social engineering of the *KHAM* (an attempted alliance between Kshatriyas, Harijans, Adivasis and Muslims in the 1980s) days. This might explain the high incidence of 'labour unrest' in Gujarat, but interestingly, it is this culture of authoritarianism, which gives faith and belief to the investor, to invest in Gujarat, even when this authoritarianism has manifested itself more recently in spectacular form in acts of violence against religious minorities, scheduled tribes and lower castes. The harnessing of state resources towards crushing resistance, has been seen in the state around the days of resistance to development projects like Narmada dam, under the Congress rule, which was given cultural depth, and later a *Hindutva* tilt, through the involvement of preachers from Swaminarayan tradition and Morari Bapu, who mobilized symbols of religiosity associated with river goddess in order to espouse the dream of aggrandizement of rich farmers and industrialists of the area (Mukta, 1990). It appears that the legal and judicial power of the state in defense of the financial, commercial and industrial interests, has worked in favour of consolidating the globalizing development paradigm of the state and the faith of the investors in Gujarat.

The consequences and impact of this proactive investment policy of the state government can be understood and analysed by looking at infrastructure development and manufacturing sector in some detail. Literature in India on explaining differences in regional income often attributes it to difference in infrastructure spending and development. On aggregate parameters Gujarat appears to have done well in the last few years in ports, road, rail and power. The 'real' story lies in grasping the details!

Ports, Roads, Rail, Power, Corporate Agriculture and Industrialization: Giant Corporate Agglomerates Control Development

The essence of private investment led growth strategy is most discernible through what is happening to the development of infrastructure in the state of Gujarat. The unqualified faith on the private investor often gets reflected in the policy decisions that have been taken to facilitate infrastructure development. There have been legislative changes in the land use norms that have reinforced the speculation in land in the name of development of infrastructure. Priority in infrastructure development has been towards those projects that strengthen investments and profitability of the investor, rather than creating infrastructure to meet the needs of the ordinary people. Human habitations have been neglected in improving access through rail and road; facilitating access of SEZ, SIRs and other private investment has been the prime mover of investment in road and rail. Dependence on private initiative in deciding the priorities of infrastructure sector in general has also meant neglecting public expenditure in the creation of social infrastructure.

The introduction of Investor Support System (ISS); the Public Private Partnership Model (PPP) for infrastructure; establishment of Special Economic Zones (SEZ) and Special Investment Regions (SIR) for attracting investment and expanding industrial development are part and parcel of this dependence on private initiative. The strength of these SEZs and SIRs, it is believed, will be 'world-class infrastructure and civic amenities'; encouraging mega projects (units with investment of at least Rs. 1000 crores in core industrial sectors and Rs. 5000 crores in infrastructure projects). The industrial policy of 2009 in Gujarat locates all of these initiatives within the larger framework of the central government to create Delhi-Mumbai Industrial Corridor (DMIC). The state government believes in playing a supportive role to the private sector as reflected in the various PPP initiatives for specific sectors; for example textile, gems and jewellery parks in PPP mode, etc.[7]

The infrastructure development strategy of Gujarat involves two main components, encourage private sector for intergraded investment in port, rail, road and power and secondly, develop large enclaves for industrial and service sector growth (green field sites) where world class infrastructure is available. The crisis of Indian infrastructure planning is generally located in both these elements . To turn to the private sector to rescue the poorly performing state systems (at the national level this strategy is considered successful for the telecom sector but not for rest of the infrastructure, like power and roads), and secondly, not face the difficult problem of strengthening infrastructure where it exists and preferring to establish development enclaves in 'green field sites' are the two components of infrastructure development strategy that have been much critiqued in India.[8] The idea of green field sites has been combined with privatization in the SEZ policy, and this combination is characterized by some as 'thinly guised land grab for urbanization by the private sector' (Levein, 2011). The mega project of Delhi-Mumbai Industrial Corridor (DMIC) also incorporates these two elements in its approach. A project built around the proposed High Speed Freight Corridor between two cities promoted by the Japanese. The DMIC plan is full of references to public private partnerships and setting up industrial areas and infrastructure in green field sites, at Dhar, Pune, Surat, Alwar, Rewari and Muzaffarnagar. All of this is part and parcel of infrastructure and development strategy in Gujarat. The problematic that this approach poses can be seen in the project proposal itself. The prospective plan for the DMIC, in the case of Gujarat on groundwater says, 'Major uses for domestic and irrigation from groundwater are likely to leave hardly any balance for industrial use. The state policy of Gujarat would need to allocate water for industrial use from the resources for irrigation, depending upon the priority and requirement in the investment regions of Gujarat'. Further, if doubling of employment potential happens, as the prospective plan wants to believe, in the groundwater scarce regions of Haryana, UP, Gujarat, and Rajasthan as a result of implementation of this project, then the urban demand for water will multiply. What will happen then to the scarce water resources? Who will be taken care of? Also, the projected migration figures of 94 million migrants by 2039 (if it all happens), as a result of concentration of economic activity in and around the project area, is it desirable? There has not been much discussion in Gujarat or anywhere else on such issues. The grandeur of the project seems to have helped overcome the challenges associated with unleashing growth through such a strategy. How has this strategy been specifically implemented in Gujarat?

Since the mid 1990s, Gujarat made some proactive efforts to develop the non major ports under its jurisdiction. Ports are listed under the concurrent list and hence they fall under the jurisdiction of both federal as well as state government. The 12 major ports in India come under the jurisdiction of federal government, while state governments are responsible for the development of non major ports. In 1995, Gujarat formulated a comprehensive port development strategy which integrated development of ports facilities with industrial development, power generation and development of rail and road network in hinterland. It identified ten green field sites for the development of deep water ports. The port policy introduced in the state not only allowed private investment in ports but also announced various incentives to attract private players both from India as well as from abroad. The initiative of port privatization was further strengthened in 1997, when Gujarat introduced Build Own Operate and Transfer (BOOT) policy, which restricted the role of government to minimum and provided a complete operational and tariff freedom to the private developers for the entire BOOT period of 30 years. As a result of these measures, Gujarat witnessed a huge inflow of private investment in ports. From 1995 to 2010-11, its maritime sector received the private investment proposal of worth Rs.39147 crores, out of which Rs. 15500 crores have been already realized while rest of the projects are at different stage of development. So far, four private ports have commenced their operations in Gujarat while another seven private ports are expected to start their operations by end of 2015. In line with these developments, the total traffic handling capacity of non major ports in Gujarat has increased from 135 MTPA in 2001-02 to 273 MTPA in 2010-11 and by the 2020 it is expected to reach 919 MTPA which would be around 30 per cent of total traffic handling capacity of major and non major ports of India put together. Gujarat is positioning itself, in its port capability, in the long run, to utilize is coastal proximity to the Delhi-Mumbai Industrial Corridor (see the chapter on infrastructure development in this book). This driver for future growth is completely dependent upon and will be led from the front by the large private large consortiums (conglomerates like Essar and Cargo motors; commodity trading group Adani, Belgium's port of Antwerp, Israel Port Company, Europe based companies like Aegis - all involved in the development of private ports in Gujarat). The Gujarat Maritime Board has made special provisions to attract the private sector like giving royalty holiday to investors instead of revenue sharing of the royalty; permission to investors to adjust the royalty against capital costs; freedom to developers to charge any other service charge except wharfage and waterfront charges; land acquisition by Maritime Board on behalf of the private investor; permission for private and captive jetties; 30 year window to make profits before these ports may be handed over to the maritime Board; permission to create rail connectivity in PPP mode; and special arrangements of forward linkages for these private consortiums to special industrial regions (out of 13 SIRs 9 are based on ports located on the coast) and SEZs (out of 60 SEZ 29 are port based and 38 are under the influence of Delhi-Mumbai Industrial Corridor). Each of these measures caters to the needs of the large private sector, making Gujarat a 'favourite destination' for infrastructure investors. Infrastructure investment by its very nature is capital-intensive and in Gujarat this is reflected in the fact that around 37 per cent of total investment has been in infrastructure in the last two and half decades but this sector's share in employment is less than half percentage point.

The faith in the private sector to rescue the road sector is also strongly reflected in Gujarat's infrastructure strategy. Gujarat started exploring private funding for road projects as early as 1990s, and in 1994, it amended the section 9 of Bombay Motor Vehicle Act, 1958. The amendment permitted the levy of toll on either new construction or strengthening of road and bridge projects (emphasis added) and thus paved the way for public private partnership in road infrastructure. In 1996, Gujarat formulated a comprehensive road policy which announced various incentives to attract the private participation. Since then the government has borrowed resources from the World Bank for construction and improvement of roads, State Highways Development Project, to improve the quality of existing state highways, to connect the extremes of the state with high speed corridor, and to improve the connectivity for transporting farm products to the major Agriculture Products Market Committees. Gujarat Infrastructure Development Act, 1999 popularly known as BOT Law was enacted in and later on amended as Gujarat Infrastructure Development (Amendment) Act, 2006. It is the first of its kind institutional arrangement in India for private sector participation. A concession period of maximum 35 years is allowed under this act. It provides three modes for private sector participation in infrastructure projects: competitive bidding; comparative bidding and direct negotiation. There is also a provision for financial support for the development of infrastructure projects, with a subsidy up to 40 per cent (GoG-20 per cent & GoI-20 per cent) of the total project cost for the developers under the Viability Gap Funding (VGF) Scheme.

Interestingly, together with this extraordinary thrust to encourage the private investment in infrastructure, the per capita budgetary outlays on roads and bridges have been less than some of the other fast growing reform oriented states like Tamil Nadu and Haryana. The gains in road length in Gujarat in the 2000s can be largely attributed to the role of private sector. The implications of this on the structure of road length in Gujarat are worth elaborating.

First, Gujarat has not constructed any new state highways in last one and half decade, it has improved in a big way the existing highways only. The state highways development program alone has improved the quality of 1850 kms of state highways, while a loan from HUDCO resulted in an improved of another 254 km of state highways. Apart from this, the entire private investment of more than Rs.7000 crores, has only improved the condition and quality of existing highways.

Secondly, between 1995 to 2008, the combined length of national highways and state highways in Gujarat has increased by just 4 per cent, while the overall road length has increased by more than 60 per cent. This suggests that Gujarat has developed a large network of roads other than national and state highways, which includes PWD roads, rural roads and other project roads. It may appear that a huge inflow of private investment in state highways has allowed Gujarat to use its budgetary allocation for the improvement of roads other than state highways. However, even today 3380 habitations in Gujarat are not connected with road. In 1996, out of 18028, only 16932 revenue villages in Gujarat were connected with pucca road. Noticeably, within a decade, the number of revenue villages connected with pucca road increased to 17822, which improved the rural connectivity in Gujarat from less than 94 per cent in 1996 to 98.86 per cent in 2006. In spite of this very high rural connectivity, out of a total of 34187 human habitations, only 26767 human habitations were connected with road till the end of year 2000 in the state. The gains to connectivity from the vantage point of human settlement in the recent years has come from the central funds (in the last decade more than four thousand habitations have been connected, under the central government's flagship program of PGSY) whereas the state allocations seem to have improved rural connectivity in general. This could mean that the focus of state expenditure on roads has been to improve the access of the new ports, SEZs and SIRs, most of which fall in the rural areas and not towards improving access of human habitations. This approach to infrastructure development will further consolidate the power of the private investor/sector, perhaps at the cost of the right to services of the ordinary citizens of Gujarat. Dynamics of growth of rail infrastructure has further strengthened the private sector orientation of port and road development.

The main lead in Gujarat to upgrade the already existing high density of rail track has come from ports, who have joined hands with Ministry of Railways to upgrade the existing rail tracks. The first PPP project for track up gradation was launched in 2001, another one in 2004 and recently in 2010. These three projects taken together have upgraded a total rail track of more than 630 km from narrow & meter gauge to broad gauge, all of which is meant to improve the connectivity of ports—Surendranagar to Rajula to Pipavav; Palanpur to Gandhidham and Bharuch to Dahej.

The boost to the power sector in Gujarat has also come from captive (private) power plants. In the last five years installed capacity of electricity generation has grown tremendously in Gujarat, by close to 34 per cent as a result of private sector participation in generation. This is very high compared to the other states. Large encouragement has been given in Gujarat to captive power plants through legislative changes addressing wheeling of power; wheeling tariffs; supply of surplus power to the group companies (parent company); supply of surplus power to the state utilities (GEB); supply of surplus power to AEC (licensee), etc. in 1998. In 2002, the new industrial units which generate electricity for captive requirements have been exempted from payment of excise duty for the first five years and in 2005, the transmission service agreement have been streamlined by introducing intrastate availability based tariff. All this has given big boost to the power sector in Gujarat; where in large part of its industrial load is being met by captive power plants. This is Gujarat's unique response to the larger 'national' failure of the private sector led infrastructure strategy in the power, of not getting response of the private investment in generation. The tariff structure in Gujarat is also in favour of commercial and industrial use, the average tariff in these sectors is not very high than the national average and lower than some of the other industrially developed states, while in case of agriculture the average tariff is much higher than the national average.

What the Gujarat model of infrastructure development, as reflected above, in the story of ports, roads, rail and power, tells us is that private sector investment happens around the needs of investors and profiteers. There is nothing new in this! What is interesting and special is, how in the name of growth and development large conglomerates have got access to infrastructure projects to strengthen their own investments and profitability in other sectors. Road and rail expansion is less focussed on increasing access of human settlements but more about improving and strengthening those rural roads or rails that increase the access to SEZs and the minor ports. Private sector has not created many new roads, expansion of state and national highways is not their priority, but improving, broadening and strengthening the existing ones is more profitable venture for earning revenue under the PPP mode. In addition the private investment in infrastructure is dovetailed and integrated with the industrial corridor, which itself is suspect in terms of gains it will bring to the local people and its implications for groundwater in water scarce regions. The approach of the state government to achieve growth is clearly to attract large capital as of now and hope that the growth in the future that will be driven by large private investment-manufacturing-infrastructure conglomerates will benefit its citizens in the long run. Gujarat seem to have internalized, the two 'falsehoods' mentioned earlier, to turn to the private sector for addressing infrastructure and second to give preference to 'green field sites' rather than address the aggregative challenges of infrastructure inadequacy.

Agriculture Corporatized

Agriculture sector has not been left far behind in getting corporatized. In the political and social discourse in the state, as elaborated in the chapter on agriculture in this book there has been an overarching and increasing emphasis on the need for corporatizing the state's agricultural policy. The result of this approach has resulted in unprecedented growth in agriculture in Gujarat, making it a much more profitable activity in the state. In the decade of 90s, growth in agriculture in Gujarat was higher than the national average (4.44 per cent compared to 3.15 for all India). However, in the last ten years agriculture growth in Gujarat has been nearly two and half times faster than the national average (7.64 per cent compared to 2.96 percent). There are crop specific and area specific challenges that this growth has thrown up for agricultural economists. The share of non food crops has increased in Gujarat in terms of acreage and value added. Given this agricultural boom and the growing need of land for non-agricultural purposes, especially infrastructural development, agricultural land has acquired immense importance in the state. The aggregate numbers do not capture a distinct shift in the distribution of land in the state. However, what is found is that average size of marginal holdings are becoming smaller in the state compared to the national average, suggesting more than average leasing out or selling of land in the state by the smallest land owning classes. On the other hand, the largest size category (above 20 hectares) has gained in terms of area, suggesting, perhaps, leasing in or purchase of land in the last ten years. This is further reinforced by the fact that the average size of holding for the largest land owningclasses has increased over the years. The literature attributes this change in the land market to the legislative changes brought about in the state related with land use (especially the lifting of 8 km ban on purchase of land and allowing non-local, non-farming groups to enter the rural land market) and the overall dynamics of 'profitable' agriculture through corporatization of agriculture. The changes in control over land for the marginalized social groups in Gujarat is also distinctly different than the national trend. Over time, the access to land to the scheduled castes and tribes has worsened in the state, contrary to the national average and also in relative terms worsening of inequalities within the marginalized groups. Changes in the access to land notwithstanding, it is true that in the state of Gujarat many more small and marginal farmers have found it profitable to continue to cultivate, compared to the national average in terms of land cultivated.

The over arching environment created by the state in the last few years has undoubtedly facilitated liberalization and corporatization of Gujarat agriculture. While these policies appear to benefit the agricultural community at large, the supporting land policies that makes way for the entry of the corporate agro-industry much more explicitly, result in rolling back elements of 'land to the tiller' in land policies. There has been a shift in Gujarat's land policy from ideas of 'land to the tillers' to those of 'land de regulation and liberalization' over the past two decades. Such modification, on one hand, has and is likely to encourage speculative land transactions in the prospective canal commands and urban peripheries, and on the other hand, facilitate conversions of common wastelands lands to private cultivated land.[9]

The 'Success' of Manufacturing: Gujarat Way

Infrastructure development in Gujarat for the private sector, and by the private sector, along with the overall investor oriented governance has influenced and impacted the industrial growth in Gujarat. The government of Gujarat has taken many additional steps to support industrial growth in the state. These include, initiatives of the Gujarat Industrial Development Corporation to provide facilities in their locations, simplification of procedures to register small and tiny units with a proviso that units with a investment of up to Rs. 40 lakh can register without inspection, and the unique measure taken by the Gujarat government in 1997, is to grant permission to convert agricultural land to non-agricultural (NA) uses up to the limit of 10 hectares almost automatically.

As the chapter on industrial growth in the state in this book highlights, industrial development in Gujarat is biased in favour of developed regions; it has weak backward and forward linkages of the unorganized sector with the organized sector after the decline in the traditional textile sector in the state; and there has been massive growth of capital-intensive industries in the state leaving little scope for ancillarization and sub contracting. Concentration of chemical and plastic industries in the state has also raised serious concern in the state of severe environmental degradation.

Gujarat accounts for a substantial share of India's manufacturing gross value added, employment in the organized manufacturing sector, share in fixed capital and number of factories.[10] Manufacturing sector in Gujarat has done exceedingly well, the sector has grown at a faster pace than other states in the country.[11] The share of the state's manufacturing sector in the national gross value added has doubled between the 80s and 2000s, however, such high growth in this sector has not brought about commensurate benefits of employment. The contribution by this sector in the overall employment in the state is much lower compared to the share of manufacturing employment in total employment in India. Gujarat's contribution in India's manufacturing employment remains almost stagnant over the three decades, while Maharashtra's has actually declined. Tamil Nadu has seen a significant rise in its share in manufacturing employment over the years. This has happened when the share of the state in value added has doubled during this period. And its share in fixed capital has trebled since the 1980s and has surpassed even that of Maharashtra whose contribution to gross value added is double of Gujarat. What this implies is that growth of manufacturing sector in Gujarat in the last three decades has been accompanied by increasing capital intensity in the sector.

The source of this increased capital intensity can be located in the changing structure of the manufacturing sector in the state. There has been a significant shift in the structure of Gujarat since the 1980s in favour of the refined petrochemicals and chemical products, at the cost of the textile sector.[12] In 2000s, these two sectors together accounted for 60 per cent of the GVA, while the contribution of these sectors to employment was much less. Refined petrochemicals, a high capital intensive sector has negligible contribution in employment while chemical sector accounts for 23 per cent of employment. The importance of the employment generating textile sector has diminished in India by half since the 1980s. In Gujarat, it's share in value added has come down from 37 per cent in the 1980s to a mere 7.5 per cent in 2000s, though its contribution to employment was still 21 per cent in the 2000s. The recent initiative to encourage textile sector to come back to the state could help regain the employment generating role of the textile sector, provided the new investments in this sector, retain its technological character. The distributive value of the industrial process gets further minimized because of dismally low share of wages in the manufacturing value added. The share of wages in gross value added during the decade of 2000 was very low in the state and has fallen in comparison to its share in the 80s and 90s. In addition the growth rate of per employee wage was also very low in Gujarat. During the last decade, employee wages in the organized sector have grown at a mere 1.5 per cent, which is no match to the increase in the cost of living during this period.

In addition to these dismal feature of Gujarat's 'success' in the manufacturing sector from the vantage point of workers, the state has experienced a very low employment elasticity of output and lowest shares of wages in GVA in India, one of the highest use of contract workers in the organized manufacturing in the country and rising trends of casualization of the workforce. There has been fast growth in the non-establishment enterprises in the unorganized sector in the state. This has happened when the state's share in the nation in value added and fixed capital has substantially increased. It appears that the recent success of Gujarat industrialization appears to be at the cost of workers.

The structure and pattern of manufacturing growth in Gujarat can be closely associated with the thrust of infrastructure development in the state. As mentioned above, during last two decades, refined petroleum, chemical products and industries related to basic metal and fabricated metal product have been the prime drivers of aggregate manufacturing growth in the state. Both refined petroleum and chemical products industries have large import content. The crude oil which is the main input for these industries is primarily imported. Thus, a well-developed port sector is an essential prerequisite for the development of these two industries and this is where the success of the state in developing small ports in the last few years comes in handy. The other two industries, basic metal and fabricated metal products, which have done well in Gujarat, are relatively more energy intensive. Since Gujarat is the only power surplus state in India, the exceptional growth of these industries in Gujarat could possibly be associated with the development of power sector in the state.

The low employment generation, slow growth in wages, increasing use of contract workers and overall reduced position of workers in the manufacturing sector, accompanied by increasing profitability and growing investment in the sector is indicative of the characteristics of the industrialization trajectory chosen by the state. Low employment generating and high capital intensive growth, though witnessed in India's industrialization trajectory as well, is only intensified in the reform oriented state of Gujarat. The recent 'success' of growth and hype about governance has done nothing to address these regional, structural and employment imbalances. This selective development in the industrial sector has major repercussions on the distributional implications of growth in the state. The current direction and orientation of manufacturing growth is likely to push more and more of state's population into dependence for low paid jobs in the service and manufacturing sector and into greater uncertainty for sustainable livelihoods.

Facilitating Profits for Capital or Improving Quality of Life

The discussion above, clearly reflects the faith and commitment of Government of Gujarat to bring about growth by favouring the market and the private sector. The connect between 'this type' of growth and poverty and inequality is seldom highlighted either by those who 'celebrate' the success of this growth nor by those who provide leadership to this growth. What does all this investment, infrastructure and manufacturing growth mean for poverty, consumption and inequality?

Dynamics of Growth, Poverty and Inequality

Gujarat has achieved a lot in terms of growth of the economy but still nearly a third of its population lives below the poverty line.[13] As we have seen above, the main focus in Gujarat is has been on increasing economic growth and there is general hope that its trickle down effects will help reduce poverty. Gujarat has been consistently maintaining impressive growth in income since the last decade. The growth rate is higher than all India level and even other developed states like Tamil Nadu and Maharashtra. Unlike other states and all India level where the growth is driven mainly by service sector, the growth in Gujarat is driven by both industry and service sector. This is also reflected in the structure of economy too where for Gujarat the share of both industry and service sector is a significant factor contributing to the state income. The diverse sources of growth create a good potential for reducing poverty and inequality in Gujarat.

Unfortunately, Gujarat lags behind its competing states like Maharashtra and Tamil Nadu in terms of growth in consumption expenditure, poverty reduction as well as decrease in inequality (see for details chapter in this book on poverty and inequality in Gujarat). With respect to growth in consumption expenditure it's an average performing state. Between 2005 and 2010, growth in consumption expenditure was very good (2.54%) compared to the national average (2.41%) but substantially less than states like Tamil Nadu (2.95%) and Maharashtra (3.42%). This is also true for rural consumption expenditure. In urban areas, growth of consumption expenditure in Haryana (3.50%) and Maharashtra (3.56%) was higher than that of Gujarat (2.13%) during this period. Interestingly, in the previous decade, from 1993 to 2004-05, Gujarat did much better in terms of its growth in consumption expenditure compared to other states, in particular the state did better in urban areas compared to rural areas. The superior performance in the 1990s, compared to the last five years suggests that the much hyped recent growth has now petered out in its impact on growth in consumption expenditure of the people in the state of Gujarat.

How has the 'spectacular' growth fared for the poor? In 2009-10 around 18 per cent households in urban areas and 27 per cent in rural areas were poor. This is of course better than the national average (21 per cent in urban and 34 per cent in rural) but there is nothing 'superior' in these outcomes compared to other high growth states like Tamil Nadu (13 per cent in urban and 22 per cent in rural) and Haryana (23 per cent in urban and 19 per cent in rural). If we look at the changes in poverty, the decline in urban poverty in Gujarat has been much slower in the last five years (the period of high investment in 'vibrant Gujarat') compared to the national average, as well as other high growth states. The decline in rural poverty has been much better in the last five years compared to the national average but less than states like Maharashtra and Tamil Nadu.

The story is even more disconcerting when we look at the distribution of income, instead of the levels of income. Overall, level of inequality in Gujarat is very high and not distinctly different from the national average (33 per cent for Gujarat and 36 is the national average). In fact, the gap between the national average and state's own level has declined during the last decade. In the early 1990s, the state was better placed in relation to the national average. The change in inequality has been insignificant in the last five years (in fact it has marginally increased), which raises serious concern about the 'growth experience' of the state. The change in inequality, even though of very small magnitude, has been better in rural areas compared to the urban, once again reinforcing the conclusions drawn from the changes in the levels of poverty.

Thus, overall, the capital-intensive manufacturing and corporatization of agriculture and infrastructure, in the Gujarat in the last decade has not contributed much to benefit people in addressing their absolute deprivation (changes in poverty) as well as their relative deprivation (changes in the inequality). It may be added further that since the 1990s onwards, the rural areas of the state have done better than urban in terms of both poverty reduction and reduction in inequalities. In order to compete with other states and to achieve higher long term growth along with significant reduction in poverty Gujarat perhaps needs to rethink its growth dynamics and explore alternative drivers of growth for the future. The rural urban differences in terms of gains to the poor, suggests that the much 'exhibited' manufacturing and service sector growth of the state is not bringing in the desired outcomes. On the other hand, some shift of manufacturing activities to the peri urban or rural areas coupled with the high growth in agriculture has relatively benefitted poor people more in the rural areas. The exclusionary nature of growth in the urban areas is further reinforced by the fact that gap in average MPCE between Hindus and Muslims has increased between 2005-10 in the urban areas and the poverty levels for the households of the Muslim religious group has hardly changed in the urban areas in the last five years, while poverty in urban areas for households of the Hindu religious group has declined by around four percentage points.

The sub regional story in Gujarat around poverty and inequality and the difference in poverty and inequality across social groups further adds to the skeptical mood about the 'success' of growth in the state.[14] The differences across regions in terms of mean per capita expenditure, Gini coefficient and headcount ratio can either be explained due to high variation in the physical features across the state. Or as Hirway (1995) mentions, to the policy of selective development that the state has chosen for itself, development which can be characterized as 'hi-tech industrialization, in a few well-endowed areas, coupled with neglect of the backward aras'. We believe that the selective nature of development, in turn, is rooted in the very path of development, that the state is currently pursuing. Dubey (2009) also found that Gujarat has a fairly high level of regional disparities in all three indicators; mean per capita expenditure, Gini coefficient and Headcount ratio and explained that it may be on account of high variation in the physical features of the state and the very characteristics of growth that has been initiated in Gujarat since 1990s. The findings in this book suggest that across regions gains in mean expenditure are diametrically opposite to gains in reduction in poverty or reduction in inequality. Over the last five years, Saurashtra and Kutch regions, have attracted bulk of the investment in the state (around 56 per cent) and it is in these regions that average monthly per capita expenditure has increased the highest, compared to the other regions of Gujarat. At the same time the inequality has also increased in these regions, during this period, in comparison to other regions of Gujarat. This is an important point to be kept in mind when the evaluating the 'success' of growth in contemporary times in the state.

The social groupwise differences in mean per capita expenditure, Gini coefficient and headcount ratio provide a shocking description of the experience of growth in Gujarat. Overall, per capita expenditure has grown by 2.5 per cent per annum in the last five years, but the increase for scheduled tribes, who form 17 per cent of the population in Gujarat, is just 0.14 and for scheduled castes (who are 11 per cent of the population) the per capita income increased by 2.8 per cent per annum. The gap between the rate of change in income for the scheduled tribes and others has increased exponentially in the last five years compared to the decade before that. This tells us a lot about who has gained from the growth in the last few years. What is even more disturbing is that in the urban areas the income has declined, for both the scheduled tribes and castes in the last five years. When we look at changes in headcount ratio and inequality the difference in gainers and losers become even more sharper and clearer. In the urban areas poverty has increased for both the dalits and scheduled tribes, while in the rural areas there are significant gains in reduction of poverty, even though the extent of poverty still is nearly two and half times for the scheduled tribes compared to others. In terms of reduction in poverty scheduled castes have gained more than the tribes, but in terms of changes in inequality in the last five years inequality has increased sharply amongst them in both rural and urban areas. The trade-off between poverty reduction and inequality is again an important characteristic that needs to associated with the current strategy of growth.

As an initiative towards inclusive growth Gujarat has already launched programs like, Vanbandhu Kalyan Yojana for tribal areas and Sagarkhedu Sarvangi Vikas Yojana for development of coastal areas and has also tried to decentralize the decision-making process for effective grass roots planning. But still no big changes are visible in the poverty situation of the state. It clearly signifies the need to identify and design more specifically targeted policies and programs accompanied by more substantial shift in the growth strategy that brings better results for the people at the margin.

Jobless Growth

The high growth in Gujarat has been accompanied by a dismal growth in employment, for the state as a whole. Overall, in the last five years aggregate employment has remained stagnant in Gujarat, in spite of its high growth performance.[15] In India, which represents an average of large variations in economic performance across diverse Indian states, there has been a small decline in employment in this period. Unfortunately, the exceedingly high growth of Gujarat has not been able to do anything substantially better. The details of employment outcomes, discussed in this book, further reinforce the critical questions on the nature of development.

First, the structural shift in the income structure that Gujarat has experienced does not get reflected in the changes in the structure of employment. There is mismatch between the sources of income and employment across all sectors. Between 1993-94 and 2005-10, income from agriculture has fallen by nearly 50 per cent; contribution by industry has been nearly stagnant (close to 40 per cent now), and service sector contribution to income has increased from by nearly 10 percentage points (currently it is 47 per cent). The changes in employment in the corresponding period in the agriculture has declined only by seven percentage points.[16] It is pertinent to point out here, that in the last five years, the average annual agricultural growth rate in Gujarat has doubled, while the employment growth has been negative. Based on the experience of last five years, the possibility, if any, of absorbing labour in more productive activities within the agricultural sector, appear to be bleak.

This negative growth rate in the employment in the agriculture and industrial sectors has mainly been on account of the rural sector. The rural sector in Gujarat has experienced this negative growth in employment in all the three production sectors. The sharp decrease in rural employment growth rate, seen in the latter half of the decade (2005-10) is mainly on account of decrease in female employment. Whatever little growth of employment of male rural workforce has happened, it has been only in the agriculture and communication sector. Overall, rural non-farm employment has not changed much in Gujarat.

Service sector growth in the last years of the decade of 2000, in Gujarat was 11 per cent and 48 per cent of growth in Gujarat comes from this sector. However, whatever employment growth (it was around five per cent during 2005-10) has been achieved in this sector has happened in the urban areas and this employment has happened on account of massive growth of casual workers.[17] It seems that the expected benefits of the service sector boom, in terms of jobs, has not happened in the state so far. By 2009-10, the SC workforce shows more participation in the service sector, which as mentioned above has essentially meant employment gains through casual employment. What has happened to the secondary sector employment? If we compare the growth of employment in industry and manufacturing sector in Gujarat, with the all India average, we find that Gujarat's performance has not been impressive, compared to the level of growth it achieved. Employment in the organized sector rose just by 48.6 thousands between 1980 and 2004 in Gujarat after all the efforts at attracting investments. Since 2004, there have been increase in employment in the organized sector employment, both in Gujarat (around seven percent) and at the national level. Contract workers, in the organized manufacturing sector constituted 37 per cent of the total workers in 2007-08, from the already high 27 per cent in 2000-01. The growth rate of contract workers in Gujarat has been slower than the other states in the 2000s, but this needs to be seen in the context of the already high levels of contract workers in total workers in the state.

The dependence of the ST workforce on agriculture has increased. From 1993-94 to 2004-05, the participation of ST population in industry had seen an improvement, however, by 2009-10, their participation in the industrial sector decreased to levels that are half of that of 2004-05 levels. Those who have lost jobs in the industrial sector, got absorbed by agriculture. The changes in the employment structure of STs is diametrically opposite to the direction of change in the growth structure. It is to be noted here that nearly, 80 per cent ST population lives in the southern region of the state, and this region was not distinctly different from other regions in its employment structure before. The explanation for this reversal in employment structure, therefore, for the scheduled tribes, perhaps lies in lack of requisite skill and capacity to take benefits of the changing growth drivers of the Gujarat economy.

Education and Health Outcomes

An review of health outcomes in the state of Gujarat indicates that mere economic growth is not sufficient for improvements in the health outcomes of the population. High level of growth in the state has not necessarily led to progress in the health sector. As mentioned above, the State of Gujarat has been the front runner in the overall economic development of the country. But whether this impressive growth has transformed to overall socio-economic development especially in case of health of the people is something that needs to be examined. On aggregate parameters of health, overall, Gujarat is close to the national average, but lower than comparable states that are at par with the it in terms of per capita income. The levels of male and female life expectancy is close to the national average. States like Haryana, Tamil Nadu and Maharashtra are far ahead than Gujarat in these indicators. What is disturbing to note that even today Gujarat lags behind the national average in infant mortality rates and under five mortality rates and far behind the comparable states. In reach of vaccination and antenatal care Gujarat is better than national average but much behind the comparable states. Over time, from 1990 to 2010, the rate of decline in infant mortality rate has been slower than the national average and even slower than some states, which had lower levels of IMR in the beginning compared to Gujarat. Generally, it is expected that rates of catching up is faster for states at higher levels of IMR, as you reach lower levels of IMR, further decline becomes tougher. Ranking of Gujarat in IMR has not changed, in comparison to other states of India, in the last two decades. The disadvantage of rural areas and women in mortality rates has not been reduced over the years in Gujarat, in fact in the last five years these difference in Gujarat have exceeded the national average. It should be pointed out here that IMR as an indicator captures influence of large number of factors, such as the quality of food and water, the quality of housing and clothing, the quality of the health care and the quality of the education in the population group. Given the low achievement of Gujarat in IMR, failure on which fronts explains these outcomes in Gujarat?

The performance of Gujarat's growth in reducing social disparity in health is also not impressive. In fact, in many instances, this growth has had regressive impact on health indicators for the scheduled tribes and castes. Comparison of many indicators between scheduled tribes/castes and others between 1998-99 and 2005-06, reveals that the marginalized groups have lost out during this period, compared to their fellow beings, on an average, in the country. The data reveals clear deterioration for scheduled tribes during this period, while for the scheduled castes, there have been some gains. These differences have been seen in the health chapter in this book on mortality rates, access to vaccination and ante natal care and child undernutrition.

The dismal performance of changes in the health outcomes in the state of Gujarat in the last decade or so is also reflected in the pattern and trend of health expenditure. The neglect of the sector is much more serious in the last five years (2005-10) compared to the previous 10 years. This neglect is not in terms of fall in absolute levels of expenditure in health, absolute levels have increased, but in comparison to other states, the ranking of the state has fallen during this period. In the growth of per capita expenditure Gujarat is ranked the highest in the last two decades but in terms of public expenditure on health Gujarat ranks nineth in the first half of 90s; then it is ranked 4th in the second half of 90s; goes back to nineth rank in the first half of 2000 and falls to 11th rank amongst 15 major states between 2005-10. The share of health expenditure in total public expenditure follows the national pattern in the state, but the levels have remained behind the national average in Gujarat throughout the 90s and 2000s. The poor ranking of the state is further reinforced when we compare health expenditure as a percentage of NSDP. Between 1995 and 2010, this ratio has come down in the state of Gujarat, reflecting how the increase in NSDP has not given any gains to this sector. One of the consequences of this neglect of public health facilities is that out-of-pocket expense for hospitalization in public institutions has increased in both rural and urban areas. The increase in urban areas is more than the national average, and the increase in both rural and urban areas is more than the increase in comparable states like Maharashtra and Tamil Nadu. The neglect of health services is noticed and experienced by the people of the state of Gujarat. The utilization figure for hospitalization for private and public institutions reflect the lack of faith in public health institutions in Gujarat compared to the national average. The burden of going to these inadequately funded public institutions, as expected, has fallen more on the poor in Gujarat, compared to the better off sections. Tamil Nadu has done relatively much better in public expenditure than Gujarat. And this can be seen in utilization pattern of government health services in the state. Most of the Indian states, are gradually moving to greater privatization of health services, including Gujarat, Tamil Nadu comes out as an exception to this trend. In Tamil Nadu, there has been an increase in use of government health facility and the cost of health services also has been low in the state. Given the fact that advances in basic health indicators have been below par in the state of Gujarat there is a strong need to relook at the health policies of the state and there is a very urgent need for strong state intervention in the health sector of the state.

Education is one of the most important socio-economic parameter that impacts the quality of life of people both directly, in terms of livelihoods, but also indirectly through its impact on individual and household decision-making, that influences health and social outcomes. It is expected that the gains of growth in Gujarat will get reflected in the improvement of educational outcomes. The chapter on education in this book examines this question using the available secondary sources. Literacy is the most simple indicator to get a sense of aggregate characteristics in the field of education. It is no surprise to note that average levels of literacy in the state is higher than the national average. What is disturbing is the performance of the state in improving literacy between 99-00 and 2007-08 comparable to other Indian states. During this period, Gujarat's ranking, in comparison to 15 major states of India, has deteriorated in literacy levels, for both those above six years and those in the age group of six to 14. This sluggish growth in Gujarat is disconcerting since the gains in literacy at the national level have been much better. Another way to look at that state's achievement in the education sector is to examine the rate of current attendance. Here again, current attendance in the age group of six to 29 and six to 14 increased from 44.6 and 81.2 in 1999-00 to 45.8 and 86.9 in 2007-08. However, once again rank of the state has worsened during this time period from 23 to 30 in current attendance in the age group of six to 29 and 21 to 26 in current attendance in the age group six to 14 during this period. Not only in aggregative terms, but the educational outcomes in Gujarat across social groups further add to the gravity of the crisis in the education sector in the state. The gender difference in the state of 20 percentage points, which is higher than the gap in the literacy rate between men and women at the national level. In Gujarat, male literacy rate stands at 84.75 per cent as compared to 64.8 per cent for the females. This gap is also higher in Gujarat in comparison with comparable states like Haryana, Maharashtra and Tamil Nadu. Currently, the gender gap in Gujarat amongst those who are currently attending school, stands at 13.3 in the age group 11-14, which is more than two and a half times the difference at the national level. In the age group of six to ten, the gender gap amongst those currently attending school in the state, is not very different than the national average, but much larger than states like Maharashtra and Tamil Nadu. The gap in literacy outcomes between those belonging to general category and other marginal social groups was also greater than the national average in 2007-08. This gap in Gujarat is similar to the levels that exist in Tamil Nadu, but much higher than other faster growing states. For both 6-10 year age group and 11-14 year age group, caste gap in Gujarat is also higher than all the states under comparison and the national average. Thus, social disparities in education in the state of Gujarat are higher compared to other states in educational outcomes, and participation and access to education. The challenges in Gujarat are much more serious at the above primary stage. In rural Gujarat, access to upper primary and secondary school is less than the other states, and all India levels. Access of the lower castes, compared to the others, is also lower in Gujarat than the other states under comparison as well as all India levels, particularly at upper primary and secondary school stage.

One of the main reasons for such deterioration, perhaps, is the decline in expenditure on the education by the state government. There has been a general phenomenon of decreasing share of developmental expenditure in total expenditure, and on education in particular, since 1990s right up to 2003-04 in India. However, during this period, the rate of decline in Gujarat, as compared to all the states taken together, is very high. More importantly, post 1999-00, the decline in developmental expenditure in general, and on education in particular, as a proportion to GSDP is at a much higher rate in Gujarat, compared to the levels across all the states. Gujarat's expenditure on education, as a proportion to its GSDP was below the combined states level in 2000-01, and is falling at a higher rate since then. Thus, it is no surprise that Gujarat's educational indicators have deteriorated during this time period. It is important to point out here, that this relative neglect of public education in Gujarat is at the cost of people going to government institutions, especially the poor and those attending public institutions in the rural areas. The percentage of persons in rural Gujarat dependent on public education are more, as compared to the all India rural situation. Furthermore, the persons belonging to poorest 20 per cent household in urban Gujarat is significantly more dependent on public education than their urban all-India counterparts. This suggests that the poor and rural people are experiencing the neglect of public education in Gujarat the most. The relative neglect of public education has not meant, that private education has substituted the educational needs of the people in the state, even though government's efforts in the recent years has been to encourage the private sector. Overall, proportion of people going to government institutions or institutions run by local bodies is almost the same for Gujarat as at the all India level. In Gujarat, particularly in the urban areas, the cost of private education relative to public education is much higher than the corresponding all India levels. And in the urban areas, there are significantly larger proportion of people dependent on government-aided private institutions for education as compared to the all India situation. This suggests that there is a mismatch between the capacity of the population to afford private education and the governments own approach to neglect public education and encourage unaided private sector.

The crunch in resource allocation in the key sectors, and preference towards investor friendly growth has led to increased suffering for the deprived sections—the lower castes, minorities and women. What this book shows is that this mismatch between Gujarat's growth and its performance in key areas (such as education, health, poverty and employment) is integral to the 'phenomenal growth story' of Gujarat.

Where Do We Go From Here?

Study of Gujarat economy and society is a study in lessons of capitalist growth. It provides a window to understand the limits, constraints and achievements of market led growth, and also an insight into a policy regime 'that does not attempt to harness the most brutal consequences of a market led mode of capitalist production' (Breman, 2001). The growth experience of Gujarat in the last decade and a half, captured through secondary data sources reveals that the chief driver of growth in the state has been the private investor and the state has played a facilitating role for the market in a very significant manner. Public regulation to improve the quality of life of an average citizen and improve access to education, housing and health have been relegated to the background.

Some of the examples that are highlighted in this study and those that reflect complete dependence of the current regime on the private sector for growth and development are: legislative changes in the land use norms that have reinforced the speculation in land; identification of priorities in infrastructure development towards those project that strengthen investments and profitability of the investor, instead of creating infrastructure to meet the needs of the ordinary people; neglect of human habitations in improving access through rail and road and facilitating access of SEZ, SIRs and other private investment; dependence on private initiative in the social sector and neglecting public expenditure in the social sector; selective nature of manufacturing growth and reinforcement of capital-intensive manufacturing; neglect of employment and wages in the manufacturing sector; corporatization of agriculture, marginalization of small farmers and privatization of village commons; and neglect in public policy to remove poverty, increase consumption and reduce inequalities. Given this reality, it appears that very often policies drafted by the government are on behalf of the private sector. This study shows how over the last decade or so such regimes of governance have increased the deprivation and exploitation of people at the margins.

One important question that the findings of this book raise is: how do we explain the socially exclusionary outcomes of growth? What is the root cause of these uneven outcomes? Multiple explanations are possible. Unequal and unjust outcomes could be the result of neglect, and therefore by highlighting the plight of the neglected, we can try to achieve 'recognition' for them. If this is true, then once recognized, the remedy of their plight is a possible within the existing model of development. However, it is also possible that these unequal outcomes could be the result of unintended consequence of the existing model of development and not the result of neglect. If that was the case, then we will need to address the individual and group disadvantages (education, skills and social capital for better paid employment, stop overt discrimination, etc.) so that 'every one' could get equal access to gains from growth. Finally, we might argue that these exclusionary outcomes are rooted in the very nature of market led development and that structural change must occur to overcome these exclusions. This implies that the roots of inequalities are in the capitalism, in the neoliberal economy and the path of development inherently negates the possibility of a level playing field.

Where would Gujarat fall in these explanations? The overwhelming and widespread nature of worrisome evidence on the economic and social outcomes across sectors, in Gujarat, suggests that these outcomes cannot only be the result of neglect or non recognition of the socially and economically disadvantaged sections in the development strategy. Social exclusion in growth outcomes are very much rooted in the nature of economic models chosen by the state and the distribution of economic and social power inherent in the path of development. As the chapters in this book elaborate, the policy choices made by the political regimes in the state, at different points of time, reinforce and substantiate this understanding. This experience of Gujarat tells us that rest of India needs much more than just a 'governance fix', effective governance is often projected as a reason for Gujarat's growth success. Since path of development and orientation of development strategy is most important, we hope that the writings in this book will help construct an alternative development strategy. A strategy which recognizes that markets are not the only drivers of growth. Growth can also happen by limiting the power of markets and fostering growth with social justice.

NOTES

1. The issue of regional growth and spatial inequality did attract the attention of scholars for the period before the economic reforms too. The results of these studies are far from uniform. For example, analyzing the economic performance of 20 states over the period 1960/61–1989/90. Dholakia (1994) finds evidence of convergence of long-term economic growth rates for the states. He has identified 1980/81 as the year of break in the trend of real income, after which many lagging states started growing, while richer ones began to stagnate. Cashin and Sahay (1996a, 1996b) find that the dispersion in real per capita income has increased but there

has been absolute convergence across 20 states over the period 1961–91. Both Dholakia and Cashin and Sahay have not studied the impact of the economic reforms adopted in the early-1990s on regional convergence.

Analyzing the economic performance of Indian states during the post-reform vis-à-vis the pre-reform periods, Ahluwalia (2000) concludes that not all the rich states became richer relative to the poor ones and not all the poor states got poorer . His study includes only few early years of reform. Contrary to the findings of the aforementioned studies, Marjit et. al (1996) and Ghosh et. al (1998) find evidence of divergence in per capita income across Indian states over the period 1960/61–1994/95. Rao et. al (1999) observe that per capita incomes across 14 major states have diverged and inter-state disparities have accentuated during 1965/66–1994/95. The increases in divergence and dispersion have been much sharper since 1991. Dasgupta et. al (2000) observe a clear tendency of divergence in per capita income across 21 states during 1960/61–1995/96. For the period 1960-92 Trivedi (1992) finds that there is evidence of conditional convergence. Sachs et al (2008) also found an overall divergence in real per capita gross SDP across 14 major states during 1980–98 and they found this divergence particularly notable within the poorer group of states. For a detailed review on the subject see, Ghosh (2008).

Studies evaluating social progress after economic reform have followed very diverse patterns, ranging from accelerated progress in some fields to slow down and even regression in others. There has been much debate on Poverty in India but overall conclusion has been that India has seen some reduction in the poverty levels in the last two decades. Few studies examine the role of production structures on poverty reduction. Ravallion and Datt (1996) conclude that at the all India level, output growth in primary and tertiary sector reduced poverty in rural and urban areas but secondary sector growth did not help much in poverty reduction. Qadeer (2009) shows how the new growth strategy has restricted the improvement in outcomes in the social sector.

2. The conclusion associated with increase or decrease in growth differences in these studies is also sensitive to what measure of attainment are used, the time period of analysis, as well as the unit used for spatial measurement. For example, Singh et. al (2003) suggest, that if we look at consumption and credit indicators for regions disaggregated below the state level then the inequality trends may not be as bad as suggested by State Domestic Product data. Alternatively, on consumption inequality, there is also suggestion in the literature that regional disparities have increased in the 1990s, with the southern and western regions doing much better than the northern and eastern regions. Inequalities within states are highlighted by others (Deaton and Dreze, 2002), suggesting that economic inequality

also increased within states, especially within urban areas, and between urban and rural areas

3. Public investment is highlighted as an important factor influencing growth by World Bank (2008, page 31). The literature that finds reasons for differences in regional growth in investment also talks about the linkages between public and private investment and often associates public investment more strongly with growth differences because of its importance in creating social and economic infrastructure. Rao et. al (1999), and Nayyar (2008) highlight interstate transfers as important source of differences in regional growth. Role of infrastructure is highlighted by Ghosh and De (1998) and Nagraj et. al (1998) as an important factor influencing differences in regional growth. Production strategies of different sectors are considered important to explain differences in growth by Dholakia (2009).
4. Capital expenditure as a percentage of GDP has consistently fallen from 1985 onwards up to 2005 in Gujarat. After 2005 there has been some increase in capital expenditure, restoring it back to the 1985 levels. Within developmental expenditure outlay on social services, have declined, and there has been no change even after 2005.
5. IEMs are filed by industrial undertakings that are exempt from obtaining an industrial license, including existing units undertaking substantial expansion. Acknowledgement of IEM issued by the Department of Industry Policy and Promotion is purely for statistical purposes and is not in the nature of registration involving scrutiny of the memorandum.
6. One reason for high incidence of labour 'unrest' in Gujarat could be the neglect of labour department and labour services in the state. Even though state has been pioneer in launching the Unorganised Workers Board and Rural Labour Commissionerate, these offices have performed dismally in the state, in terms of staff hiring, enforcing labour laws, paying special attention to the chemical factories in the state or meeting their other statutory obligations. The situation has particularly worsened in the last two decades. See for details and a comparative perspective on changes labour laws in India, Hirway (2011).The study finds that Bhavnagar, Junagadh, Surat are the most neglected divisions, which also happen to be areas which have seen maximum growth in factory and non factory industrial units in the last few years.
7. The difference between supportive role of the government to the private sector and being subservient to the private sector is thin and depends on the terms at which the government and the private sector relate with each other. So far, the overwhelming evidence on PPP model in India is that it is less of public- private partnership but more of transfer of control and resources from public to private. See Sood (2007) for details.
8. For an critique of the current approach to infrastructure development

and some more details on DMIC project, see Desai (2012).

9. Gujarat Government brought about a significant policy change with respect to transfer of village commons to private parties on May 17, 2005, inviting big corporate houses and large farmers to initiate corporate farming in a significant way.
10. Gujarat accounts for only 5 per cent of the country's population, and 7 per cent of India's GDP. But its share in India's manufacturing gross value added is 14 per cent, 9 per cent in employment, 18.6 per cent in fixed capital and 10 per cent of total number of factories in India in the 2000s are located in Gujarat.
11. Gujarat's manufacturing sector has grown at a faster pace than all other states in India. Since 1990-91 it holds the first position in terms of the contribution of the manufacturing sector to GSDP. However, there is a distinct mismatch in the contribution of the secondary sector to GSDP and the employment generated by the sector.
12. Another important dimension of this structural shift is that the organized manufacturing activity is now heavily spatially skewed – Jamnagar, Vadodara and Surat alone account for 60 per cent of the gross value added and output, and 64 per cent of the fixed capital in 2005-06. The employment share of these three districts is 33.5 per cent. The districts of Jamnagar, Vadodara, Kutch and Rajkot were the main drivers of manufacturing growth in Gujarat in the 2000s. Vadodara and Jamnagar contribute very little to employment, with Vadodara having seen a fall in its employment share in the recent times.
13. GSDP growth in Gujarat has always exceeded the national average, since the 1980s. In the last three decades the average GSDP growth in the state has been 6.77 per cent compared to the national average of 6.12 per cent. In the last decade the difference in growth was of two and a half percentage points (10.5 compared to 8), while in the 90s the difference was of nearly two percentage points (8.3 and 6.2 per cent per annum respectively for Gujarat and India).
14. The discussion on sub regions in this study follows NSS. The NSS has classified Gujarat into five broad regions: South and South eastern, Plain Northern, Dry Areas, Kutch and Saurastra and this classification is based on the agro-climatic factors. Different NSS rounds (50th, 61st and 66th) have used, have different regional compositions. Unlike many other states, Gujarat displays considerable geographical heterogeneity in terms of agro meteorological and climatic conditions, and soil and water regimes. Therefore, to make the NSS regions meaningfully comparable for the successive rounds, has its limitations. For instance, in 50th round (1993-94) and 61st round (2004-05) there were five regions namely Eastern, Plain Northern, Plain Southern, Dry areas and Saurastra. However, the

regions for 66th round (2009-10) are different, where NSSO merged eastern and plain southern region in to one, but both regions exhibit different structure in terms of geography and economy. The eastern region is populated with tribal population and economically backward as inferred from the indicators of industrial development (see section on employment for details on this).

15. The main sources of data on employment in India are: National Sample Survey Organization (NSSO), Economic Census, Employment Market Information Programme of DGET, Registrar General of India, and the Labour Bureau. Economic Census, provides basic information by activity, type of ownership, rural/urban break up and employment size, in respect of each establishment, self owned or employing less than ten workers. So far five such Economic Census have been conducted by the CSO. The latest Economic Census was conducted in the year 2005. The data collected under the Employment Market Information Programme of DGET, covers only the organized sector of the economy , which inter-alia covers all establishments in the Public Sector irrespective of their size and non-agricultural establishments in the Private Sector employing 10 or more persons. This data is available quarterly and annually. Registrar General of India (Census), collects some key information on the workforce in the country after every ten years

    The surveys conducted by the NSSO are the main data source on employment and unemployment situation in the country.So far eight quinquennial surveys on employment and unemployment have been conducted by the NSSO. The latest such survey was conducted for the year 2009-10. The discussion in this book on employment is based on the NSSO surveys. Labour bureau conducts surveys on employment-unemployment on annual basis. Labour bureau has so far done two surveys. The first survey was conducted in 2009-10. It was a thin survey with a sample size of 46,000 households, which is less than the half of the NSSO sample conducted for the same year (66th Round). The second survey conducted in 2011-2012 has a sample of 1, 28,298 households, which is slightly bigger than the NSSO sample size. We do not have NSSO data for the same year to make comparison with the labour bureau survey. The last survey on employment by the NSSO was conducted in 2009-10

    Work Participation Rates in Gujarat for the year 2009-10, as per the labour bureau report (for persons of 15 years and above) was 48.9 per cent which is the sixth highest in the country. The WPR in the state is less than comparable states like Maharashtra and TN and some other states. For India, the WPR in 2009-10 is 45 per cent (Table 7.1, Page 77,Government of India, 2010)). The results on rural and urban sectors also shows that the work participation rates in the state are 52.8 per cent and 43.6 per cent respectively. The ranking of the state is not different if we look at the labour force participation ratios. Table 9.1 of the labour bureau report gives the unemployment rates in India. Unemployment rate in Gujarat, in 2009-10 was 9.9 per cent, compared to 9.3 for all India, and 5.8 per cent, 5.9 per cent and 8.6 per cent for the comparable states of Tamil Nadu, Maharashtra and Haryana. This report does not provide any temporal picture. The only temporal comparison of the findings of this report, if at all, can be with the same report for the year 2011-12, which is based on a much larger sample. The 2011-12 report does not report any significant change in the employment scenario in the state. Gujarat ranks seventh in WPR (52.2 per cent), seventh in LFPR (52.7 per cent) in the 2011-12 report amongst 15 major states of India and reports an unemployment rate of 10 per cent.

16. There is consensus about Gujarat that structural transformation has not occurred in Gujarat, and there is evidence of structural imbalance between employment and income Hirway and Shah (2011). Dholakia and Sapre (2011) argues that there is no theoretical prior to suggest that the shift in income and employment should move in tandem. He suggests that there is need to examine the compositional shift in employment within the primary sector. And that conceptually, it is possible to consider that the labour transformation from low productivity primary sector to high value commercial activity within the primary sector is a way out of for growth in the third world economies. The differences about appropriate strategy for labour transformation in the third world countries, notwithstanding, the fact remains that Gujarat has not been able to achieve more significant shift in its labour force, in spite of its high growth, in comparison to the shift in labour force from the primary sector to the other sectors at the all India level.
17. Overall, casual workers in Gujarat has marginally declined, in the last five years, this decline has happened mostly in rural areas. However, the share and growth of casual workers has increased in the last five years in the urban areas. This reflects the impact of changes in the service sector. The trend of changes in the casual workers has been somewhat different between 1993-94 and 2004-05.

REFERENCES

Ahluwalia MS. Economic Performance of States in the Post-Reform Period. *Economic and Political Weekly* 2000; 35(19): 1637–48.

Ahsan A, Gutiérrez C, Paci P, and Ranzani M. Jobless Growth and Poverty Trends in India: Unbundling the links. In *Fifth IZA/World Bank Conference on Employment and Development*, Cape Town, South Africa, May 3-4, 2010.

Breman J. The Impact of the Asian Economic Crisis on Work and Welfare in Village Java. *Journal of Agrarian Change* 2001; 1(2): 242-82.

Cashin P and Sahay R. Internal Migration, Centre-State Grants, and Economic Growth in the States of India. *IMF Staff Papers* 1996a; 43(1): 123–71.

Cashin P and Sahay R. Regional Economic Growth and Convergence in India. *Finance and Development* 1996b; 33(1): 49–52.

Dasgupta DP, Mukherjee MR, Sarkar S and Chakrabarti S. Growth and Interstate Disparities in India. *Economic and Political Weekly* 2000; 35(27): 2413–22.

Deaton A and Dreze J. Poverty and Inequality in India: A Re-examination. *Economic and Political Weekly* 2002; 37(36): 3729-48.

Desai N. This Corridor is Paved With Bad Policies. *Tehelka*, 11 August, 2012.

Dholakia R and Sapre A. Gujarat Growth Story. *Economic and Political Weekly* 2011; 46(32): 122-124.

Dholakia RH. Regional Sources of Growth Acceleration in India. *Working Papers*, No. 2009-03-06, Indian Institute of Management, Ahmadabad, March, 2009.

Dholakia RH. Spatial Dimensions of Accelerations of Economic Growth in India. *Economic and Political Weekly* 1994; 29(35): 2303–09.

Dubey A. Intra-state Disparities in Gujarat, Haryana, Kerala, Orissa and Punjab. *Economic and Political Weekly* 2009; 44(26/27), 224-30.

Gajwani K and Kanbur R. Patterns of Spatial Convergence and Divergence in India and China. In: *Annual Bank Conference on Development Economics (ABCDE)*, St. Petersburg, Russia, January, 2006.

Ghosh B and De P. Role of Infrastructure in Regional Development: A Study of India over the Plan Period. *Economic and Political Weekly* 1998; 33(47/48): 3039–48.

Ghosh B, Marjit S and Neogi C. Economic Growth and Regional Divergence in India, 1960 to 1995. *Economic and Political Weekly* 1998; 33(26): 1623–30.

Ghosh J and Chandrasekhar CP. Economic growth and employment generation in India: Old problems and new paradoxes, http://www.networkideas.org/feathm/mar2007/fa10_Jayati_Ghosh.htm (2007, accessed 15 July, 2012).

Ghosh M. Economic Reforms, Growth and Regional Divergence in India. *Margin: The Journal of Applied Economic Research* 2008; 2: 265.

Hashim SR. Economic Growth and Income Distribution: The Indian Experience of Development. *Economic and Political Weekly* 1998; 33(12): 661-666.

Hirway I and Shah N. Labour and Employment Under Globalization: The Case of Gujarat. *Economic and Political* Weekly 2011; 16 (22): 57-65.

Hirway I. Selective Development and Widening Disparities in Gujarat. *Economic and Political Weekly* 1995; 30 (41/42): 2603-18.

Levein M. Special Economic Zones and Accumulation by Dispossession in India. *Journal of Agrarian Change* 2011; 11(4): 454–83.

Marjit S and Mitra S. Convergence in Regional Growth Rates: Indian Research Agenda. *Economic and Political Weekly* 1996; 31(33): 2239–42.

Martin R and Datt G. How Important to India's Poor Is the Sectoral Composition of Economic Growth?. *The World Bank Economic Review* 1996; 10.1: 1-25.

Ministry of Finance. *Economic Survey, 2011-12*. February 2012. New Delhi: Ministry of Finance.

Ministry of Labour and Employment. *Report on Employment and Unemployment Survey 2009-10*, Labour Bureau, October 2010. New Delhi: Ministry of Labour and Employment.

Mukta P. On the Political Culture of Authoritarianism. In: Shah G, Mario R and Streekerk H (eds) *Development and Deprivation in Gujarat: In Honour of Jan Breman.* New Delhi: Sage Publications, 2002, pp. 59-73.

Mukta P. Worshipping Inequalities. *Economic and Political Weekly* 1990; 25(41): 2300-01.

Nagaraj R, Varoudakis A. and Veganzones MA. Long-run Growth Trends and Convergence across Indian States. *Technical Papers*, No. 131, OECD Development Centre, January, 1998.

Nayyar G. Economic Growth and Regional Inequality in India. *Economic and Political Weekly* 2008; 43(6): 58-67.

Panagariya A. Growth and Reforms during the 1980s and 1990s. *Economic and Political Weekly* 2004; 39(25): 2581–94.

Qadeer I. Political and Economic Determinants of Health: The Case of India. In: Cook H J., Bhattacharya S. and Hardy A. (eds), *History of the Social Determinants of Health.* Hyderabad: Orient BlackSwan, 2009, pp. 228-247.

Rao MG, Shand RT and Kalirajan KP. Convergence of Incomes across Indian States: A Divergent View. *Economic and Political Weekly* 1999; 34(13): 769–78.

Ryle G. *The Concept of Mind.* Chicago: Chicago University Press, 2002.

Sachs J, Bajpai DN and Ramiah A. Understanding Regional Economic Growth in India. *CID Working Paper*, No. 88, Centre for International Development, Harvard University, March, 2008.

Shah G, Rutten M and Streekerk H (eds). *Development and Deprivation in Gujarat: In Honour of Jan Breman.* New Delhi: Sage Publications, 2002.

Singh N, Bhandari L, Chen A and Khare A. Regional Inequality in India: A Fresh Look. *Economic and Political Weekly* 2003; 38(11): 1069-1073.

Singh R. *Crisis of Socialism.* New Delhi: Ajanta Publications, 2006.

Sood A. Deepening Disparities and Divides: Whose Growth is it Anyway?. In: *Citizen's Report on Governance and Development.* New Delhi: Social Watch India and Sage India, 2007.

Trivedi K. Regional Convergence and Catch-up in India between 1960 and 1992. *Working Paper,* No. 2003-W01, Nuffield College, University of Oxford, Oxford, December, 2003.

World Bank, India. *Accelerating Growth and Development in the Lagging Regions of India.* Poverty Reduction and Economic Management, South Asia, Report No. 41101-IN, 21 February, 2008.

2

Dynamics of Growth in Gujarat

Ruchika Rani

Gujarat is one of front runner states of India. With only 5 per cent of the country's population and 6 per cent geographical area of India, Gujarat contributes to approximately 16 per cent of the total industrial production and is a fast growing industrial hub. The people of Gujarat are well known for their entrepreneurial and industrial skills and nearly 40 per cent of the Gujarati population is residing in urban areas, which could positively impact the growth in the state. Gujarat has attracted high domestic investment, which has contributed to the industrial growth in the state and overall increase in the growth rate. The high growth of Gujarat is seen as an example by many other states of India. States want to emulate the development strategy of the Gujarat to achieve high growth rate. Ahluwalia (2002) argued that Gujarat has benefitted most in the post-reform period and called the Gujarat's growth rate as a 'miracle growth' which is the result of not of its geographical location but of its ability to provide a most favourable environment to new policies of the economic reforms. The chapters in this book evaluate this argument in great detail.

This paper tries to examine and understand the nature and structure of growth of the economy of the Gujarat. The main aim of this paper is to identify the key drivers of the growth of the economy by analysing sectorwise growth performance and their contribution to the growth. The paper has analysed the GDP growth trends since 1980s. The GDP data available at CSO is at different base periods. That has been used after making them consistent on same base period (1999-00 prices) using the splicing technique.

1. GDP Growth of the Economy

Figure 2.1: Sectoral Growth Rate of GDP in Selected States

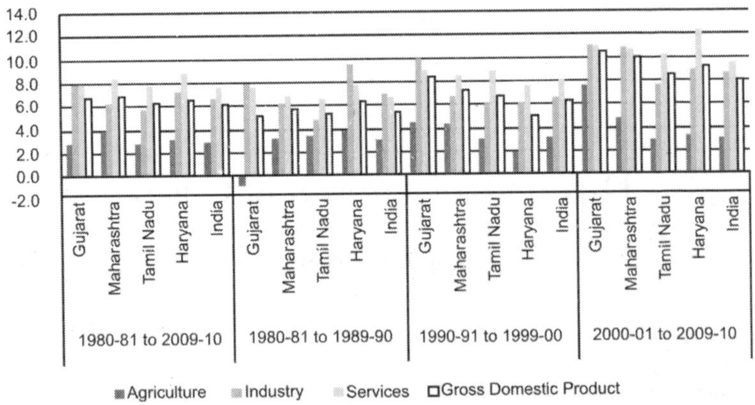

Source: Central Statistical Organisation, Mospi, GOI.

It may be seen from Figure 2.1 (Table 2.1, 2.2 and 2.3 in annexure) that Gujarat is performing well in terms of GDP growth rate in comparison to all India level and other three states, Maharashtra, Tamil Nadu and Haryana. The Gujarat has grown at a much faster rate than all India level and other three states in all decades except 1980-90. In the 1980s decade, Gujarat grows at a slower rate than all India and other three states. This was mainly because of the negative growth of agriculture sector during 1980s because of many droughts during this decade in Gujarat. In 1990s decade, Gujarat GDP grew at 8.3 per cent per annum compared to Maharashtra (7.1 per cent), Tamil Nadu (6.6 per cent), Haryana (4.9 per cent) and all India (6.2 per cent). In this decade, Haryana, which was growing at the faster rate of 6.2 per cent in 1980s compared to other three states and all India has reached to the lowest level. Again this was because of slow agricultural sector GDP growth in Haryana. In the 2000s decade, Gujarat maintained its first position by growing at 10.5 per cent per annum GDP growth rate. Haryana reached to third position and grew at 9.2 per cent per annum. Maharashtra grew at 10 per cent per annum and Tamil Nadu at 8.5 per cent per annum. All these four states were growing at a faster rate than all India GDP growth rate 8 per cent per annum. Over the 30 year period as a whole, Maharashtra is growing fast at 7 per cent per annum followed by Gujarat 6.8 per cent per annum, Haryana 6.5 per cent, Tamil Nadu

6.2 per cent and all India 6.1 per cent per annum.

During the last three decades, service sector has been an important driver of growth in India and has grown faster than the other two sectors. The only exception is the period 1980-90, when service and industrial sector growth was nearly at par with each other. However, in case of the state of Gujarat, industry and service have grown at par with each other, throughout the last three decades. The exception for the state is the 1990s, when the growth of the industrial sectoral was ahead of the service sector. For other fast growing states of India, the pattern is much closer to the national average and Gujarat appears to be the only exception. The lead of the service sector, over manufacturing can be seen, in the last three decades, for Maharashtra, Tamil Nadu and Haryana, and in many instances the difference between the two sectors is larger than the national average. The gap has sharpened mostly in the decade of the 1990s. Agriculture has grown at a dismal rate of 2.86 per cent in the last three decades at the national level. It is interesting to note here that in this decade of 2000s, the agriculture sector in Gujarat has also grown at an impressive rate of 7.6 per cent per annum, the fastest level of growth ever achieved by any of these four states. However, India's agriculture grew at only 3 per cent per annum and Tamil Nadu's agriculture could not achieve even 3 per cent growth. In the 2000s decade, Haryana's service sector grew at 12.2 per cent per annum, which is even faster than Gujarat service sector's growth rate (11 per cent).

At a more disaggregate level, it has been seen that in Gujarat, registered manufacturing has grown at faster rate compared to unregistered manufacturing and aggregate growth rate of industrial sector during all the three decades. Within the service sector, trade, hotels and restaurants and transport, storage and communication and banking & insurance have grown fast during all the three decades.

In Maharashtra also, the registered manufacturing has grown at a higher rate compared to the unregistered manufacturing except for 1990s decade. Within the service sector, banking & insurance have grown at a higher rate during all the three decades. During the last decade, trade, hotels and restaurants have grown at a higher rate. In Tamil Nadu and Haryana also the registered manufacturing has grown at a higher rate compared to the unregistered manufacturing except for 1980s decade in Haryana. Within the service sector, more or less these three sectors namely, trade, hotels and restaurants and transport, storage and communication and banking & insurance have grown at a higher rate. In Haryana during last decade the real estate and business services have also increased at a higher rate.

In all India, the pattern of growth at disaggregated level is more or less similar to these states. The registered manufacturing has grown at a higher rate compared to unregistered manufacturing. Also, within the service sector, trade, hotels and restaurants and transport, storage and communication and banking & insurance have grown at a higher rate.

2. Sectoral Contribution to GDP Growth

The service sector has comparatively larger contribution to GDP growth in all the four states and India. But in Gujarat, the industrial sector has also played an important role and the difference between the contribution of industry and service sector is minimal.

Figure 2.2: Sectoral Contribution to Growth

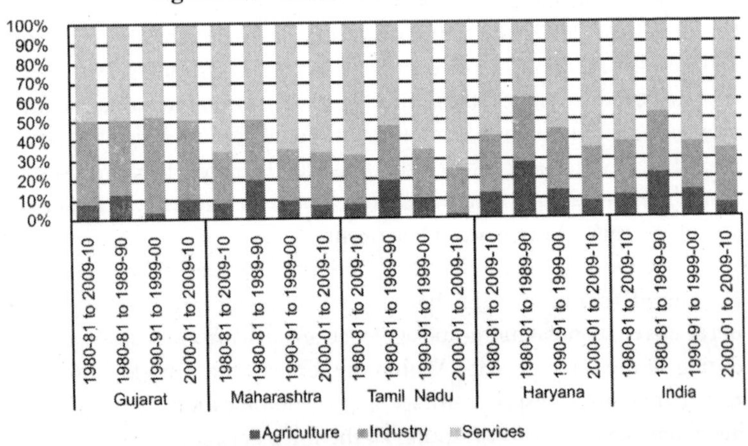

Source: Central Statistical Organisation, Mospi, GOI

However, at the all India level and in other three states, the contribution of service sector is much larger than the industrial sector. In other words, in the other three states and India, the service sector drives growth while in Gujarat both service and industrial sector drive the growth of the economy. Within industrial sector, registered manufacturing has contributed more to growth comparatively in both Gujarat and also at all India level. Within services sector the trade, hotels and restaurants and transport, storage and communication has contributed more to growth. In all the other three states, the largest contributor to growth is the service sector and over the years, its contribution has gone on increasing (Figure 2.2 and Table 2.1, 2.2 and 2.3 in annexure).

3. Changes in Structure of GDP of the Economy

Similarly, the structure of economy has also shifted away from agriculture to service sector at all India level, while it has shifted toward both industrial and service sector in Gujarat. The share of the service sector is not much higher than that of the industrial sector in Gujarat. At all India level, agriculture sector share in total GDP was 38 per cent in 1980-81 which decreased to 30.9 per cent in 1990-91 and further to 23.9 per cent in 2000-01 and 14.5 per cent in 2009-10. The share of industrial sector fluctuated between 25 per cent and 30 per cent during this whole period while the share of services sector has increased from 36 per cent to 57.2 per cent. Within the services sector, a sharp increase has been seen in transport, storage and communication and real estate and business services.

Figure 2.3: Structure of the Economy

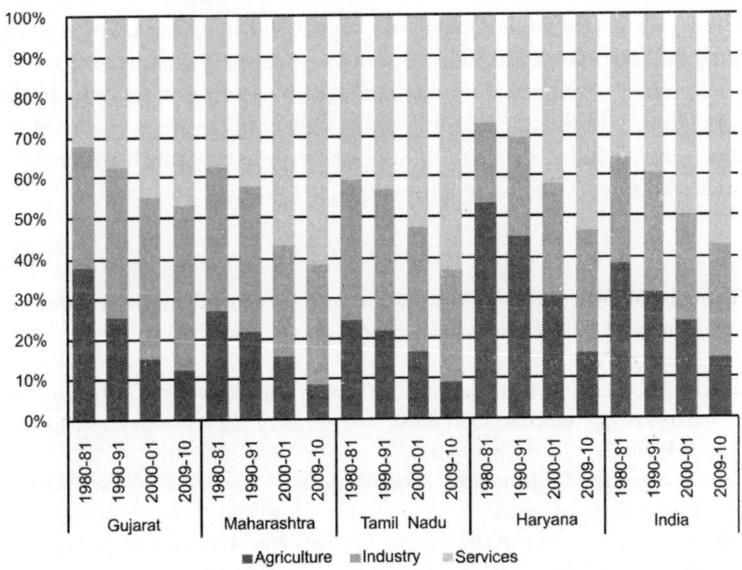

Source: Central Statistical Organisation, Mospi, GOI

In Gujarat, the share of agriculture has decreased from 37.3 per cent in 1980-81 to 15 per cent in 2009-10. While the share of industry and services both have increased, the share of industrial sector has increased from 30.4 per cent to 40.7 per cent and service sector share has increased from 32.3 per cent to 47.2 per cent.

All the other three states also follow the similar trend of shifting away from agriculture to service sector. In Maharashtra and Tamil Nadu, the share of industrial sector has also decreased from 36 per cent in 1980-81 to 29 per cent in 2009-10 in Maharashtra and 35 per cent to 28 per cent in Tamil Nadu while in Haryana, similar to Gujarat, the share of industrial sector has increased from 19.8 per cent in 1980-81 to 30.6 per cent in 2009-10 (Figure 2.3 and Table 2.4, 2.5 and 2.6 in annexure).

Conclusion

The growth rate of Gujarat is higher than all India level and other three states in all decades except 1980-90. This was mainly because of negative growth of agricultural sector during 1980s which happened because of many droughts in Gujarat during that period. Both the service and the industrial sectors drive the growth of the economy in Gujarat while in other states and all India; the service sector drives growth of the economy. The service sector has comparatively larger contribution to GDP growth in all the four states and India. But in Gujarat, the industrial sector has also played an important role. The economy is moving away from agriculture to both industrial and services sector in Gujarat while in other states and all India the share of service sector is very much larger than other two sectors of the economy.

REFERENCES

Ahluwalia M. State Level Performance under Economic Reforms in India. In: Kruegar A (eds) *Economic Policy Reforms and the Indian Economy.* University of Chicago Press, 2002.

Bagchi AK, Das P, Chattopadhyay S. Growth and Structural Change in the Economy of Gujarat, 1970-2000. *Economic and Political Weekly* 2005; 40(28): 3039-3047.

Central Statistical Organisation. *National Accounts Statistics.* 2005, New Delhi: Government of India.

Dholakia HR. Sources of Economic Growth and Acceleration in Gujarat. *Economic and Political Weekly* 2007; 42(9): 770-778.

Dholakia R. Growth acceleration and Potential in Gujarat. *Working Paper* No. 2006-02-02, Indian Institute of Management, Ahmedabad, 2006.

Ghosh M. Economic Growth and Human Development in Indian States. *Economic and Political Weekly* 2006; 41(30): 770-778.

3

Sources and Patterns of Private Investment in Gujarat

Santosh Kumar Das

Introduction

In recent years, the state of Gujarat has emerged as a preferred destination for investment, which has been one of the key sources of economic growth for the state. In terms of output growth, today Gujarat is distinctively placed as the fastest growing regional economy in India with an annual average growth rate of more than 10 per cent, in the last seven years. In a sense, Gujarat has been one of the key sources of India's economic growth, and in future Gujarat has to maintain its growth momentum to sustain India's GDP growth. Moreover, the growth momentum of the state has to be accelerated as it aims to transform its economy at par with the middle income economies. As the state is striving to transform its economy to bring its per capita income at par with the middle income economies by undertaking several economic activities that would require massive investment plans in the coming years, the paper aims to study the pattern of investment inflow and the factors that have made the state so unique from some other successful and industrialized states in India in terms of its ability in attracting higher volumes of investment. So far as investment intentions are concerned, since economic liberalization in 1991, Gujarat stands at number three position in terms of volume of investment with Odisha and Chhattisgarh at the top. Certain other states like Maharashtra, Andhra Pradesh, Tamil Nadu also seem to have emerged as preferred destinations for investment. However, the distinctness of Gujarat seems to be in converting those investment proposals into implementations. Gujarat accounts for more than one fourth of investments made through IEM (Industrial Entrepreneur Memorandum) in the country. It is important to mention here that Gujarat is the only state which attracts so much of investment without significant mining activities. The maximum share of the investment made in the state has gone to the electricity and the manufacturing sector. However, in the recent years, the infrastructure sector seems to have emerged as the preferred one for investment. More than 38 per cent of investment under implementation has gone to various infrastructure projects in the state. Perhaps, what makes Gujarat a leader as a destination for investment, is its approach to investment, which is so distinct from the rest. It has moved on from the traditional approaches to industrialization like industrial clusters, to certain innovative approaches like setting up Special Investment Regions, Investment Regions, SEZs (Special Economic Zone), etc. The state has successfully created industrial infrastructure and is striving hard to build world-class industrial infrastructure. Broadly, there seems to be four major factors that may have influenced the investment decisions. First, even though Gujarat is not a leader in physical infrastructure, it has successfully created world-class industrial infrastructure. Second, government policies and procedural reforms like single window system for industrial clearances, speeding up of investment projects on urgency basis, investor friendly administrative set-up, investment facilitation and monitoring system, and more importantly, the manner in which business and investment projects are valued. The above two factors make the investment climate friendlier and influences the investment decisions in favour of the state. Third, a strong industrial base and fourth, it also takes the advantage of the fact that several other states do not enjoy a favourable investment climate.

However, the two key factors that seem to have worked in favour of Gujarat in attracting huge volume of investment are favourable government policy and creation of world class industrial infrastructure. The key constituents of government policies include adherence to quality standards, proactive governance, project facilitation, simplification and rationalization of rules and removal of numerous beauracratic hurdles. However, among the above two factors, the former seems to be playing a critical role in attracting higher volumes of investment into the state. It is because regions with similar or better infrastructure facilities have not been as successful as Gujarat is. Therefore, there is sufficient reason to believe that the key components of investment climate like proactive governance, adherence to quality standards, project facilitation, simplification and rationalization of rule, and removal of numerous beauracratic hurdles play critical role in influencing the investment decisions.

Investment in Gujarat

In terms of investment proposals, since economic liberalization in 1991, Gujarat has been one of the top favoured destinations of private investment among the Indian states. As mentioned in Table 3.1 (see annexure), since 1991 till December 2011, in terms of investment proposals, Gujarat is ranked at third position with Odisha and Chhattisgarh at the top. The investment proposals made to the state of Gujarat is about 11.5 per cent of the total investment proposals. However, in terms of number of proposed projects, Gujarat is ranked at second position, with Maharashtra at the top.

In 2005, the share of investment intention, in terms of IEM (Industrial Entrepreneur Memorandum) filed and DIL (Direct Industrial Licence) issued in Gujarat was more than one fifth of total proposed investment in the country, which was highest for any individual state. In recent years also Gujarat continues to remain as a favoured destination for investors. Odisha and Chhattisgarh are ahead of Gujarat in terms of IEM (Industrial Entrepreneur Memorandum) filed. However, when it comes to IEM implementation, Gujarat out competes the rest of the states. In terms of actual investment made, Gujarat seems to be way ahead over the rest. Since 1991, Gujarat has been the destination for more than one fourth of investment made through IEM route in India. The state must be credited for being able to actualize the investment intentions so efficiently. That seems to be the striking feature, which is why Gujarat enjoys a distinct place among the states in India.

Another distinct feature that emerges from the investment story is that Gujarat is the only major state which attracts so much of private investment without any significant mining activities. Except Gujarat, all other states that are favoured investment destinations are mineral rich. And to a large extent, mining related activities have been a major source of investment for these states. The share of electricity and manufacturing together constitute more than half of the total investments made in Gujarat. Investment in mining is quite negligible.

While Gujarat remained as the most preferred destination for investment among the Indian states, it would be interesting to analyse the rate at which the proposed projects are implemented in the state. The number of projects implemented as a percentage of total proposed projects in Gujarat is 15.43 per cent, which is highest among the successful and industrialized states. However, the not so industrially developed states have been relatively more successful in implementing investment projects.[1] Similarly, in terms of volume of investment implemented as percentage of total proposed investment, the states those are industrially not so advanced are seem to be doing relatively better.[2] Among industrially advanced states, Haryana is at the top followed by Gujarat, Maharashtra, Tamil Nadu, Andhra Pradesh and Karnataka. Haryana has implemented 18.68 per cent of total proposed volume of investment over last two decades, while Gujarat has been able to implement 8.59 per cent of the total proposed investment which even less than half of Haryana. However, taking all major indictors like volume of proposed investment, actual volume of investment made, and the rate of implementation of projects and volume of investment, it is evident that Gujarat has been the most successful state as a destination for investment in India.

Industrial groupwise analysis of investment projects commissioned between 1983 and 2010, demonstrates a high degree of investment concentration in a few industry groups like Chemicals & Petrochemicals (42.19 per cent), Textile (10.28 per cent), Engineering Equipments (8.1 per cent), and Metallurgical Industry (8.07 per cent) (see Table 3.3 in annexure). Similarly, in terms of the number of investment projects, the maximum (1576) have gone to the Chemicals & Petrochemicals industries which are about 30 per cent of the total number of projects commissioned. Textile industry has also attracted a large number of investment projects which are about 22 per cent of the total commissioned projects. Chemicals & Petrochemicals and Textile industry, together constitute about half of the investment projects commissioned in Gujarat. However, in recent years, the investment seems to be concentrating in the infrastructure projects. Analysing investment projects under implementation across different industry groups, it is evident that the investment is shifting in favour of infrastructure projects, as there has been a significant decline in investment in Chemicals &

Petrochemicals and Textile industries. About 38 per cent of the total investment has gone into the infrastructure projects, while investment in Chemicals petrochemicals has significantly gone down, which is about 25 per cent of the total investment under implementation (see Table 3.4 in annexure). Similarly, Textile is another industry which has taken a beat and investment under implementation in the above mentioned industry, is less than 2 per cent of the total investment. On the other hand, Glass, Ceramic and Cement industry is experiencing an increase in its share of investment.

Investment in infrastructure projects seem to be highly capital intensive in nature. As it is evident, that with 80 projects which are about 3 per cent of the total number of projects under implementation, investment in infrastructure projects accounts for more than 37.59 per cent of the total ongoing investment and creates only about 21.5 per cent of total employment. However, it is important to mention here that the investment projects under implementation in Chemicals Petrochemical industry are less capital intensive in nature in comparison to the investments already commissioned in the same industry.

Districtwise distribution of investment demonstrates a high degree of concentration of investment in a few districts like Kutch (32.26 per cent), Jamnagar (13.94 per cent), Bharuch (13.52 per cent), Surat (10.74 per cent), and Ahmedabad (9.28 per cent). These five districts together constitute more than 80 per cent of the total investment under implementation in the state (see Table 3.5 in annexure). While investment projects under implementation in Kutch and Jamnagar are highly capital intensive in nature, Ahmedabad, Bharuch, and Surat seem to be the destination for less capital intensive projects. Hence, two striking features that can be identified from the analysis of districtwise project details are huge concentration of investment in certain districts, and districts that tend to receive higher volumes of investment are destinations for capital intensive activities.

Saurashtra region has been the destination for about 56 per cent of total investment under implementation in the state, followed by the Central & Southern Gujarat (37 per cent) & North Gujarat (7 per cent). Kutch and Jamnagar districts have emerged as the major destinations of investment that fall within the Saurashtra region. Within the Central & Southern region, Bharuch, Surat and Ahmedabad districts seem to have emerged as preferred destinations for investment. On the other hand, the Northern Gujarat region seems to be the least preferred destination for investors.

Figure 3.1: Distribution of Investment across Regions of Gujarat under Implementation

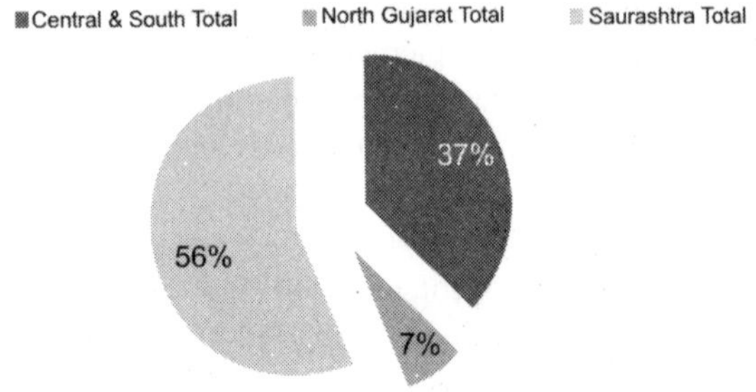

Source: Calculated from Industries in Gujarat, Statistical Information, 2010.

Figure 3.2: Distribution of Projects across Regions under Implementation

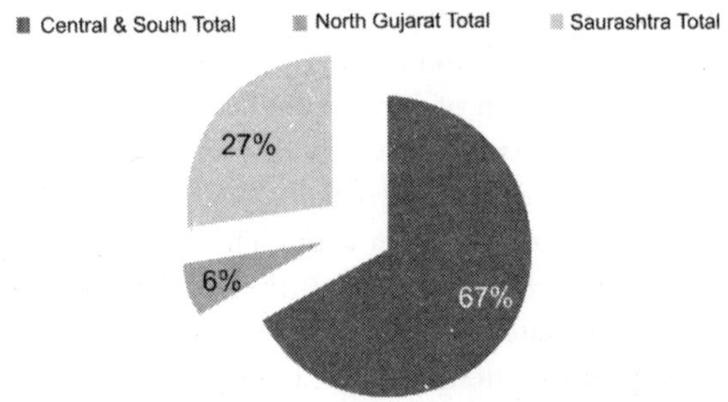

Source: Calculated from Industries in Gujarat, Statistical Information, 2010.

In terms of the number of investment projects, as seen from figure above, the highest number of projects is under implementation in the Central and Southern region. About 67 per cent of the total projects are under implementation in the above region, where as the Northern region is the destination for only 6 per cent of total ongoing projects. However, it is to be noted that while the Central & Southern region has emerged as the destination for the highest number of projects, in terms of volume of investment the Saurastra region is at the top of the list. With only 27 per cent of total projects, the Saurashtra region constitutes 56 per cent of total investment under implementation. On the other hand, the Central & Southern region constitutes only 37 per cent of total investment with

67 per cent of total number of projects under implementation.

Figure 3.3: Distribution of Employment Generated from Investment Projects under Implementation

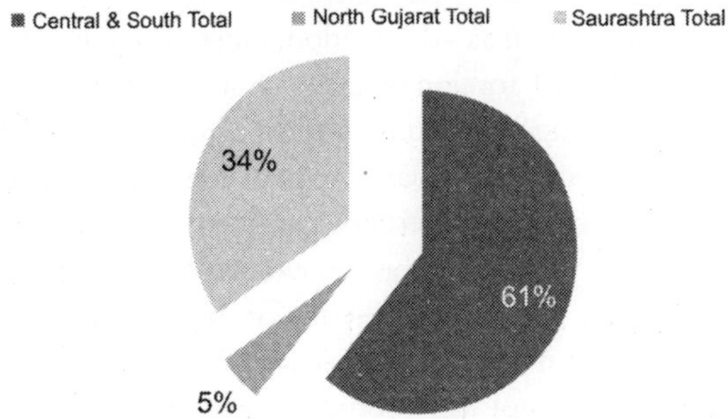

Source: Calculated from Industries in Gujarat, Statistical Information, 2010.

As discussed in the preceding section, the seeming contradiction continues to unfold as far as the generation of employment is concerned. The highest number of employment seems to be generating from the investment projects located in the Central & Southern region. With only 37 per cent of total investment, the region seems to be generating the largest amount of employment (61 per cent of total employment). Thus, it can be concluded from the above analysis that investment under implementation in the Saurashtra region is more capital intensive in nature; whereas investment under implementation in the Central & Southern Gujarat is less capital-intensive in nature.

The investment made in Gujarat, especially in the large scale industries is highly capital-intensive in nature. The capital intensity of investment made in the large scale industries in Gujarat is way above the all India level.[3] The capital per worker ratio is always higher in Gujarat. And in recent years, the capital intensity of investment has gone up significantly. Therefore, we can conclude that since the investment projects are more capital intensive, they tend to create lesser employment. The sectors those are highly capital-intensive include Chemicals & Petrochemicals and infrastructure. On the other hand, Textile industry is found to be less capital-intensive in nature.

Foreign Direct Investment (FDI) in Gujarat

Gujarat is also a preferred destination for foreign investment. Among Indian states, Gujarat is ranked at fifth position as a destination for foreign investment with Maharashtra at the top.[4] However, there seems to be a contradiction—why it is so that a state which attracts more than one fourth of domestic investment, witnessed a relatively lesser amount of foreign investment. While Maharashtra is at the top with about 35 per cent of foreign investment as a destination, Gujarat stands at fifth position with about 5 per cent of foreign investment since 2000. An independent evaluation of the foreign investment inflow figures of Gujarat may look satisfactory. However, a comparison between foreign and domestic investment in Gujarat would certainly make one inquisitive to explain such a contradiction. Broadly, there could be two explanations to the above contradiction. First, the presence of big industrial houses with huge domestic investment in certain sectors likes petroleum, electricity and manufacturing do not leave room for foreign investment. Second, India's experience with FDI shows that foreign investment is predominant in sectors like services and infrastructure. Therefore, Gujarat, predominantly being an industrially advanced state recorded lower volume of foreign investment in comparison to the top rankers like Maharstara, NCR, etc.

Investment Needs of the State

In order to build world-class infrastructure, the Government of Gujarat has come out with a report—BIG 2020, highlighting the investment requirements of the state in next few years. As discussed in BIG 2020, investment in infrastructure would create a robust infrastructure and it is expected that creation of a better infrastructure could further attract large volumes of investment in manufacturing and services activities.

The BIG 2020, which was prepared by the Gujarat Infrastructure Development Board (GIDB), is an integrated plan for infrastructure development which envisages an investment of Rs. 1180912 crore across 19 sectors over the next decade, till 2020. The BIG vision states, that it would attempt 'to make Gujarat a globally preferred place to live in and to do business through accelerated, balanced, inclusive and sustainable growth driven by robust social, industrial and physical infrastructure' (BIG 2020). Accordingly, the BIG 2020 document has fixed the timeline of proposed investment. By 2020, it envisages to achieve the proposed investment target which would be a catalyst in transforming the industrial and physical infrastructure at par with the global standards.

Why So Much Private Investment in Gujarat?

As mentioned in the preceding sections, Gujarat has been among the top three states in India in terms of investment proposals and is at the top when it comes to the realization of those proposed investment projects. It is the destination for more than one fourth of the private investment made through IEL route in India. Hence, in this context, the question which is so obvious is that why Gujarat has become a preferred destination for private investment? Broadly, the success of Gujarat in attracting so much of private investment can be attributed to its favourable investment climate and industry friendly policies.

Favourable Investment Climate

Favourable investment climate has been one of the key determining factors that has influenced the investment decisions. Several empirical studies have established that investment climate which includes favourable government policies and developed infrastructure, plays a critical role in attracting higher volumes of investment. However, what seems to be the key factor in attracting higher volumes of investment is favourable government policy. It is because there are several other states possessing similar or even better physical infrastructures yet they have failed to attract high volumes of investment. Port is the only sector where Gujarat is ahead of other states. Even though, Gujarat seems to have a sound infrastructure which has played an enabling role in attracting higher volumes of investment, in physical infrastructure it is certainly not the leader. States with similar or even better infrastructure facilities have not been able to attain the desired levels of investment. Therefore, it becomes interesting to find out that with similar kind of infrastructure facility why Gujarat has been more successful in attracting more investment in comparison to the other states. The obvious factor that comes to our mind is the favourable government policy including reforms in bureaucratic procedures and proactive governance that influence the investment decisions.

(a) Favourable Government Policy

Gujarat has been one of the highly industrialized and investment friendly states in India. Reflecting on the desire to transform the state economy to the next level, i.e., at par with the middle income economies through industrial development, the state industrial policy of 2009 emphasizes the need for domestic and global investment. The industrial policy of 2009, emphasizes on indentifying specific interventions that are required for different sectors in order to facilitate growth and attract global investment. The above policy was formulated with an objective of making Gujarat one of the most attractive destinations for domestic investment and one of the most preferred destinations for global investment. The three major objectives of the industrial policy are: (a) facilitation of investment, (b) generation of employment, and (c) adherence to high quality standards. As the industrial policy aims to create conducive environment for attracting high end investment, facilitation of investment projects through proactive governance has been identified as the core to the required intervention. Recognizing the importance of private players, the industrial policy declares to encourage the Public Private Partnership Model (PPP), especially in the infrastructure sector. In order to facilitate investment, the state industrial policy argues in favour of a strong information dissemination system and an administration which is investor friendly with the recognition of the fact that investment prefers to flow into regions that possess strong, efficient and transparent institutional set-up. The earlier industrial policies (2003), had also highlighted the issue of information dissemination and investment facilitation. At present, at district level, District Industries Centers (DICs) have been modernized for providing updated information on relevant aspects of industrial development and investment. The state government is also developing an Investor Support System (ISS) to speed up information dissemination mechanism. Creation of land banks as proposed in the new industrial policy for industry in industrial zones is another step forward in facilitation of investment.

In order to attract more investment projects and to showcase Gujarat as a possible destination for business to global business leaders, the state government has taken an initiative by organizing the Vibrant Gujarat Global Investors' Summit once in every two years. The Vibrant Gujarat Summit was organized for the first time in the year 2003. The last summit was organized in 2011 at Gandhinagar. A total of 8380 MoUs were signed or announced during the summit with a total proposed investment of Rs. 20.83 lakh crore. Since 2003, five summits have been organized and so far Rs. 3960148.01 crore of investment projects have been promised, of which several of them are at different stages of implementation.

(b) Developed Infrastructure

The state has moved on from the traditional approaches like developing industrial clusters to creation of industrial estates and establishment of Special Economic Zones in order to be able to provide world-class infrastructure facilities for further industrial development and expansion. The new industrial policy makes provision for private participation in creation of new industrial estates. Following this approach, the state has announced to build 60 SEZs and work on realizing the proposed special investment regions—huge in size, specially designed investment regions around the Delhi-Mumbai Industrial Corridor with world-class infrastructural facilities. So far as the availability of physical infrastructure is concerned, the state has 13 domestic airports which is the highest number in any state in the country, and one international airport along with extensive railway and road network. The state also has one major port at Kandla and 41 minor ports. In fact, in terms of port traffic, Kandla port happens to be the largest in India. In the year 2011-12, the Kandla port handled about 14.5 per cent of the total port traffic of the country. The new industrial policy envisages developing the port infrastructure of the state further, by expanding the private ports and upgrading capacity with the help of private players.

Special Investment Regions

In order to transform the state into a global destination for investment, the industrial policy highlights the need for establishing several mega projects which would be the hub of large scale economic activity. Several industries have been identified to be promoted as a part of those mega projects include auto and auto components, ship building and ship repairs, semiconductor fabrication and industries having nanotechnology applications, etc. It will also include several core infrastructure sectors like metro rail lines, logistic parks, railway lines, expressway, fast trains. It will also include residential and commercial projects. Around the Delhi-Mumbai Industrial Corridor (DMIC), six Special Investment Regions (SIRs) have been proposed by the state government through the SIR ordinance 2009. The ordinance makes provision for the creation of large investment regions and industrial areas in the state. The idea behind the creation of such investment regions is to facilitate the region with world-class infrastructure and civic amenities to develop it as a global hub of economic activity at par with advanced economies. Hence, as per the estimation, one third of the proposed investment of US$ 90 billion in DMIC is likely to be located in the state of Gujarat. The creation of Investment Regions (IRs) around the proposed Dedicated Freight Corridor (DFC) between Delhi and Mumbai has also been announced in consultation with the state government. Accordingly, in Gujarat, an investment region will be developed which would spread over more than 100 square kilometre and an industrial area would be of more than 50 square kilometre. In the first phase, Bharuch-Dahej Investment Region has been identified to be developed as a Petroleum, Chemical and Petrochemical Investment Region (PCPIR) hub. And, similarly, Vadodara-Ankleshwar Industrial Area has been identified to be developed as a hub for general manufacturing.

Box 1: Six Mega Investment Regions/Industrial Nodes (in the DMIC Area Focus)

Dholera	Ahmedabad Investment Region
Vadodara	Ankleshwar Industrial Area
Palanpur	Mehsana Industrial Area
Bharuch	Dahej Investment Region as PCPIR
Surat	Hazira Industrial Area
Valsad	Umergam Industrial Area

Source: Government of Gujarat Portal (http://www.gujaratindia.com/business/investment-regions.htm)

Strong Industrial Base

Gujarat is one of the highly industrialized states in India. With about 10 per cent of factories, Gujarat contributes about 18 per cent of output in value terms, and is responsible for more than 13 per cent net value addition. The state also accounts for 22 per cent of exports from India.[5] The state houses Asia's largest grass roots refinery, at Jamnagar and is the world's largest producer of castor and cumin. It is the largest producer of processed diamond in the world and world's third largest denim producer. The importance of industrial sector can be derived from the fact that the industry constitutes more than 40 per cent to the state's GDP which is quite high from the rest of the states. The level of Gujarat's industrial development is evident from the fact that the state has 83 industrial clusters, 257 industrial estates, 60 SEZs and several proposed investment regions.

Sector Specific Incentives

The new industrial policy 2009 makes sector specific provisions for promoting industrial development and investment. The sectors that have been identified to be promoted includes textiles and apparels, gems and jewellery, agri-business, fisheries, IT/ITES industry, port and related industry and non-conventional energy. The major incentives that might work in favour of investors include provision for interest subsidy in credit and provision for greater role of private sector through PPP (Public Private Partnership) mode. In most of the above mentioned sectors, a space has been created for active participation of the private sector. The industrial policy makes provision for setting up of textile and gems & jewellery parks in PPP mode. The industrial policy makes provision for greater private sector participation and recognizes the fact that investors need to be incentivized for greater inflow of investment into the state. The private sector has been provided with a greater scope for participating in the investment activities. In recent times, the majority of the investment projects in the infrastructure sectors are coming in PPP mode.

In terms of value of PPP projects, Gujarat is ranked fourth after Andhra Pradesh, Maharashtra and Karnataka. More than one tenth of the PPP projects in value term have gone to Gujarat. Though several other states have moved ahead of Gujarat in terms of both number and value of PPP projects, however, Gujarat had an advantage over the rest during initial years.

Geographical Location

Situated in the west coast of India with 1600 kms of coastline, thus providing numerous opportunities for development of several ports based industry in the state, the strategic location of Gujarat is the gateway to the landlocked northern and central region of the country. It has port connections to several industrial countries like UK, Australia, China, Japan, Korea and Gulf countries. Developed port infrastructure significantly reduces the transportation cost and thus, facilitates import and export activities.

Poor Investment Climate in Other States

Poor investment climate in many other states of India is also another key reason that might have worked in favour of Gujarat. The majority of the Indian states lack favourable investment climate. Though majority of the states adopt investment friendly industrial policies, however, in practice, most of them do not adhere to high quality standards. Industrial strikes, lockouts is a general feature in many of the states which keeps the investors away from investing. In addition to the above mentioned factor, lack of physical and industrial infrastructure in many of the states is another factor responsible for low level of investment in those states. Gujarat seems to be getting the full advantage of it by adhering to the best practices of quality standards, by adopting proactive governance system and by creating better industrial infrastructure. However, it would be worth mentioning that it is adherence to best quality practices and the urgency and sincerity with which the investment projects are handled; that makes it a different place from the rest.

Conclusion

The paper has attempted to explain the pattern of investment in the state of Gujarat and concomitantly, an attempt has been made to demystify the fact that why there are so many investment activities in the state. While explaining the pattern of investment, we come across a very interesting fact. In terms of investment intentions Gujarat is ranked at third position behind Odisha and Chhattisgarh. However, when it comes to implementation of investment projects, Gujarat is ahead of others. Since economic reforms, the state has been the destination for more than one fourth of total private investment made in India. Another striking feature that comes out of the investment analysis is that except Gujarat, all other major investment destinations (states) are endowed with rich mineral resources with significant mining activities. The sectors that have attracted investment the most in Gujarat are electricity and manufacturing. However, in recent years, the infrastructure sector has emerged as the preferred destination. More than 37 per cent of investment under implementation has gone into infrastructure projects. Sub regional analysis of investment demonstrates high degree of concentration of investment in a few districts and regions. The Saurashtra region has been the destination for maximum volume of investment (56%) in the state, followed by Central & Southern Gujarat (37%) & North Gujarat (7%). Districtwise distribution of investment demonstrates a high degree of concentration of investment in few districts like Kutch (32.26%), Jamnagar (13.94%), Bharuch (13.52%), Surat (10.74%) and Ahmedabad (9.28%). These five districts together constitute more than 80 per cent of total investment made in the state. Investment made and under implementation in the state is highly capital intensive in nature. The capital per worker ratio in Gujarat is way above the all India figure. Sub regional analysis shows that investment made in Saurashtra region is more capital intensive in nature. And, industrywise analysis shows that investment made in Chemicals & Petrochemicals industry and infrastructure sector is highly capital intensive in nature. On the other hand, Textile industry is found to be less capital intensive in nature. Attributing what makes Gujarat a preferred destination over the rest of the states, the favourable investment climate of Gujarat seems to be the major factors that influences the investment decisions. There are two core features that constitute the investment climate in Gujarat. First, adherence to quality standards, proactive governance, and friendly and simplified procedures to facilitate investment projects by doing away with numerous beaucratic hurdles. Second, Gujarat has been successful in creating world-class industrial infrastructure, which seems to be a major reason behind its success. However, between the above two features, the former feature seems to be the key factor as there are regions with similar or better infrastructure facilities have failed to do so. Therefore, there are strong reasons to believe that the adherence to quality stands and the way investment projects have been handled is the key factor which seemed to have influenced the investment decisions. Along with the above mentioned factors, certain other factors like strong industrial base, geographical location and unfavourable investment climate in several other states, seem to be influencing the investment decisions.

NOTES

1. The implementation rate of investment projects is highest in Sikkim (22.12%), followed by Assam (19.78%), Uttrakhand (17.33%), Manipur (16.27%) and Goa (16.27%).
2. In terms of volume of investment implemented as percentage of total proposed investment, industrially not so advanced states like Sikkim (39.39%), Jammu & Kashmir (13.37%), UP (10.43%) and Tripura (10.02%) are seem to be doing better than the industrially advanced states.
3. In 2009-10, the capital per worker in Gujarat was around Rs. 26 Lakhs, which was way above the all India average of Rs. 14.76 Lakhs.
4. After Maharashtra, the NCR seems to the preferred destination for foreign direct investment (20.72%), followed by Karnataka (6%) and Tamil Nadu and Pondicherry (5.27%).
5. See *Gujarat Economic Profile*, January 2012. Government of Gujarat.

REFERENCES

Department of Industrial Policy Promotion. *FDI Statistics,* Various Issues. New Delhi: DIPP, Ministry of Commerce, Government of India.

Department of Industrial Policy Promotion. *SIA Statistics*, Various Issues. New Delhi: DIPP, Ministry of Commerce, Government of India.

Dholakia RH. Sources of Economic Growth and Acceleration in Gujarat. *Economic and Political Weekly* 2007; 42(9): 770-778.

Directorate of Economics and Statistics. *Socio Economic Review 2011-12, Gujarat State.* Budget Publication No. 34, 2012. Gandhinagar: Government of Gujarat.

Government of Gujarat. Blueprint for Infrastructure in Gujarat 2020 (BIG 2020), http://www.gidb.org/downloads/news_BIG2020.pdf (accessed on 20th June, 2012).

Government of Gujarat. *Gujarat Industrial Policy*, 2009. Gandhinagar: Government of Gujarat.

Government of Gujarat. Industries in Gujarat – Statistical Information, 2010. http://ic.gujarat.gov.in/pdf/INDUSTRIES-IN-GUJARAT-2010.pdf (2010, accessed on 20th June, 2012).

Lall SV. The Role of Public Infrastructure Investments in Regional Development: Experience of Indian States. *Economic and Political Weekly* 1999; 34(12): 717-725.

4

Public-private Partnership: Insights from Infrastructure Development

Pankaj Vashisht and Gaurav Arya

Introduction

Over the last three decades, the relation between economic growth and infrastructure has emerged as one of the most researched area in the field of economics. The theoretical understanding has highlighted infrastructure development as an essential prerequisite for a sustainable economic growth. It has been argued that a well-developed infrastructure increases the effective size of labour and product markets as well as generates positive externalities which results in higher productivity of firms and makes them more competitive nationally as well as internationally (Prud'Homme, 2004). Despite this unanimous theoretical understanding, the empirical literature on a nexus between growth and infrastructure is full of contradictions. A large number of studies starting from Ratner (1983) to Sanchez-Robles (1998) have reported a positive effect of infrastructure on economic growth. In contrast, equally large numbers of studies have concluded that there is little evidence of an effect of infrastructure on growth (Tatom 1991, 1993a, 1993b, Holtz-Eakin, 1994, Holtz-Eakin and Schwartz 1995 and Garcia-Mila, McGuire and Porter, 1996). Canning and Pedroni (2008), provided an excellent explanation for these contradictory empirical findings. Using a panel data of 51 countries spanning over a period of 42 years, they asserted that there is a growth maximizing level of infrastructure above which the diversion of resources from other productive uses offsets the gain from having more infrastructure. However, below the growth maximizing level of infrastructure, any increase in infrastructure improves the long run per capita income.

Given the fact that India is ranked low in the world in terms of infrastructure availability (Kumar, 2008), it is hard to believe that India is anywhere close to the growth maximizing level of infrastructure. The 11th five year plan, therefore, rightly identified the poor infrastructure as the single most crucial constraint to economic growth and pegged the infrastructure investment requirement at Rs. 20,54,205 crore for 11th five year plan. Since India is a federal country, the responsibility of improving basic infrastructure facilities rests with central as well as state government. While centre government looks after railways, national highways and major ports, state governments are responsible for the development of state highways, non-major port and other local infrastructure facilities.

Over the last few years, the composition of infrastructure spending in India has witnessed a significant change. The share of central government in total infrastructure spending has declined while the share of state governments has gone up (Planning Commission 2010). Nonetheless, infrastructure development has not drawn equal importance from all states which according to Ghosh (2008), have led to an increase in income divergence among the Indian states in post-reform periods. It has been argued that with a better and continuously improving infrastructure facilities, some state have been able to sustain high growth by attracting more private investment while the laggard states have failed to catch them.

Since, Gujarat has also sustained an impressive rate of economic growth during last one and a half decade, it is imperative to examine its efforts and achievements in terms of infrastructure development. Against this backdrop, we try to analyse the performance of infrastructure development in Gujarat and compare it with three other developed and reform oriented states Tamil Nadu, Haryana and Maharashtra. The focus of this paper is on transport and power infrastructure. We are not including telecommunication as it exclusively comes under the jurisdiction of centre government. The chapter is divided in 6 parts. After introduction, section 2 provided an overview of port policy and development of ports in Gujarat. Section 3 deals with roads infrastructure, while section 4 highlights the development of rail network in Gujarat.

Finally, before making concluding remarks in section 6, section 5 provides a comprehensive analysis of power sector development in Gujarat.

1. Indian Port Infrastructure and Gujarat

In a globalized economy, where international trade holds a crucial significance, ports play a vital role in economic growth as it provides an interface between domestic and international market. With growing importance of intra industry trade (Virmani, 2004), a testimony growing global production network, well-developed ports enable a country or region to get the maximum advantage from the process of globalization. Fortunately, with 12 major and 199 non-major ports[1] (NMP) along a costline of 7,517 km, India always had a great potential of engaging with international production network. However, given the inward economic orientation and resultant low volume of international trade in pre 1990s, the maritime sector was grossly ignored in India. Consequently, the traffic handling capacity at Indian ports remained extremely low. The state governments were particularly more passive towards the development ports under their jurisdiction. Till 1990-91, with a very low level of cargo handling capacity, the share of NMP in total cargo handled remained in single digit (see annexure Table 4.1).

The government attitude towards the ports started changing after the adoption of liberal economic regime in 1991-92. Anticipating a huge turnaround in international trade, both federal as well as some state governments made conscious effort to increase the traffic handling capacity at Indian ports. Consequently, the traffic handling capacity of Indian ports increased manifolds. The combined capacity of 12 major ports, which are under the jurisdiction of federal government, went up from 152 million tons per annum (MMTP) in 1990-91 to 570 MMPT in 2010-11, registering a growth of more than 275 per cent in 20 years. However, it is the NMP which have shown a miraculous growth during the post-reform period. The total traffic handled at NMP has increased from less than 13 MTPA 1990-91 to 315 MMPT in 2010-11. In line with this, the share of NMP in total traffic handled at ports has increased vertically from less than 8 per cent in 1990-91 to more than 35 per cent in 2010-11 (see annexure Table 4.1).

The development of NMP in India has been extremely lopsided as the capacity expansion has primarily been led by Gujarat. Sensing a huge potential of port centric economic development in post-reform period

Gujarat made some proactive efforts to develop the NMP under its jurisdiction. In 1995, it formulated a comprehensive port development strategy which integrated development of port facilities with industrial development, power generation, and development of rail and road network in hinterland. It identified ten green field sites[2] for the development of deep water ports. In order to overcome the resource constraint, the port policy not only allowed private investment in ports but also and announced various incentives to attract private players both from India as well as from abroad. The initiative of port privatization was further strengthened in 1997, when Gujarat introduced Build Own Operate and Transfer (BOOT) policy, which restricted the role of government to minimum and provided a complete operational and tariff freedom to the private developers for the entire BOOT period of 30 years.

These efforts to attract private players started yielding desired results sooner than later as Gujarat witnessed a huge inflow of private investment in ports. From 1995 to 2010-11, its maritime sector received the private investment proposal of worth Rs. 39147 crore, out of which Rs. 15500 crore have been already realized while rest of the projects are at different stage of development (see annexure Table 4.2). So far, four private ports have commenced their operations[3] in Gujarat while another seven private ports are expected to start their operations by end of 2015. In line with these developments, the total traffic handling capacity of non-major ports in Gujarat has increased from 135 MTPA in 2001-02 to 273 MTPA in 2010-11 and by the 2020 it is expected to reach 919 MTPA (Figure 4.1) which would be around 30 per cent of total traffic handling capacity of major and non major ports of India put together.

Figure 4.1: Traffic Handling Capacity of Non-Major Ports in Gujarat

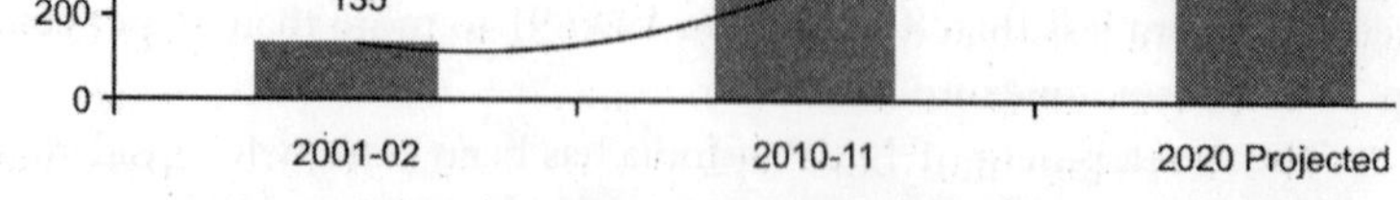

Source: Gujarat Maritime Board, http://www.gmbports.org/

Taking an inspiration from Gujarat, other maritime states have also formulated plans to develop their non-major ports through privatization. Maharashtra, Andhra Pradesh, Tamil Nadu, Kerala, Orissa all have allowed private participation in port and have also announced various incentives to attract private investors.[4] However, so far, these states have failed to replicate the success story of Gujarat. Andhra Pradesh is the only state which has registered a significant growth in its maritime sector. However, the rise of non-major ports in Andhra Pradesh has failed to make any dent in share of Gujarat. Gujarat still accounts for the lion's share of 73 per cent in total traffic handled at NMP while with a share of 13.5 per cent Andhra Pradesh is distance second (see annexure Table 4.3). Surprisingly, the performance of non-major ports in Maharashtra and Tamil Nadu has remained extremely disappointing. Despite being known to have a big appetite for reforms and privatization, these two states have almost failed to attract the private investment in their maritime sector. Both these states have completely failed to increase their share in total traffic handled at NMP. The share of Maharashtra in total traffic handled at NMP has actually declined over the last eight years while share of Tamil Nadu has remained virtually stagnant throughout the last decade (see annexure Table 4.3).

Box 1: Inventive and Policy for Private Investors in Maritime Sector in Gujarat and Maharashtra

Maharashtra	Gujarat
• Establishment of Maritime Board: 1996. Port Policy: 1996, 2000, 2002, 2010. Mode of Private Participation: Build Own Operate Share and Transfer (BOOST). Concession Period: 50 years. Exemption from payment of registration fee and stamp duty. Full freedom to fix tariff/rates for services provided at the port. State Equity Participation up to 11 per cent. Two directors of the MMB on the board of the company. Transfer of government-owned land to the developer at the prevalent market value.	• Established Maritime Board in 1986. Port Policy: 1995. Mode of Private Participation: Build Own Operate and Transfer. Concession Period: 30 years. Concession on Stamp Duty and registration fee. Full freedom to fix tariff/rates for services provided at the port. State Equity Participation: Zero. No involvement in management of Private developer. Land acquisition government responsibility.

Source: Maharashtra Maritime Board and Gujarat Maritime Board

In a nutshell, Gujarat has witnessed a phenomenal increase in port infrastructure during the last one and a half decade. The distance between port infrastructure in Gujarat and other maritime states reflects that Gujarat virtually has no competitor in maritime sector. At the same time, with a large number of ongoing projects, Gujarat is set to rule the maritime sector in India and other maritime states have no real hope to bridge the gap in near future. The phenomenal success of non-major ports in Gujarat could possibly be attributed to a blend of natural advantage and proper execution of policy. With a coastline of 1600 km and proximity to northern growth centre of National Capital Region (NCR) Gujarat always has a natural advantage over other maritime states. For northern states like Haryana, Punjab, Delhi, Himachal, Rajasthan, Jammu & Kashmir and western Uttar Pradesh, Gujarat is the nearest gateway to sea. Since these regions account for a large share in total imports and exports of India, they are natural costumers of Gujarat ports. Except Gujarat no other maritime state enjoys such a big customer base. Gujarat realized this fact soon after the implementation of liberal economic regime and formulated an investor friendly port policy to properly utilize its unique locational advantage.[5] These two factors taken together have persuaded private investors to invest a huge amount in the maritime sector of Gujarat, which has led to a phenomenal increase in port infrastructure.

2. Roads Network

The development of an efficient inland transport network is one of the primary requirements for rapid economic growth. Good transportation system improve connectivity, interlink potential growth centres and promote faster movement of goods and services at lower costs which are essential for providing an impetus to economic activity. Among the all types of transport system, road transport plays the most important role as it accounts for around 65 per cent of the freight and 80 per cent of the passengers' traffic. Though, with a total road length of 4.109 million kilometers, India has the second largest road network in the world, it suffers from problems like slow technological developments, low energy efficiency and slow movement of passenger and freight traffic. A great importance has, therefore, been given to the development of roads in recent time. Since 1998, central government has implemented policies for an all-round development of road network in India. While National Highways Development Project has revolutionized the condition of national highways, the Pradhan Mantri Gram Sadak Yojna has given a significant boost to the rural connectivity.

In line with this, Gujarat has also made some serious efforts to improve and strengthen the road infrastructure under its jurisdiction. Given the fact, that Gujarat had constructed a large network of state highways in 1980s and first half of 1990s,[6] the recent round of efforts have focused on upgrading the quality of existing highways and improving the rural connectivity. In view of the acute paucity of budgetary resources, Gujarat decided to explore all possible options for infrastructure finance. It not only approached international and national lenders such as World Bank, Asian Development Bank and Housing and Urban Development Corporation (HUDCO) for infrastructure loans but also started exploring private funding for road projects in early 1990s, much before any other state. In 1994, it amended the Section 9 of Bombay Motor Vehicle Act 1958. The amendment permitted the levy of toll on either new construction or strengthening of road and bridge projects and thus paved the way for public-private partnership in road infrastructure. In 1996, Gujarat formulated a comprehensive road policy which announced various incentives to attract the private participation. In 1999, Gujarat formulated an ambitious infrastructure development plan 'Gujarat Infrastructure Agenda Vision 2010', which predicted an investment of Rs. 19000 crores for construction and improvement of roads. In 2000, with a loan from World Bank, Gujarat initiated yet another ambitious project, Gujarat State Highways Development Project, to improve the quality of existing state highways. In order to connect extremes of state with high speed corridor, Gujarat introduced another ambitious scheme 'Pargtipath Yojana' in 2005. It identified nine corridors measuring a total road length of 3710 km to be developed under Pargatipath Yojna and set a time frame of three years to achieve this target. Apart from these schemes, Gujarat has also implemented Kisan Path Yojna to improve the connectivity for transporting farm products to the major Agri Products Market Committees.

Over the last one decade, the Gujarat government has tried to complement intentions with actions as the budgetary outlay on road and bridges has been continuously increased (Figure 4.2). From 2000-01 to 2011-12, Gujarat has allocated a total sum of Rs. 9669 crore for the construction of road and bridges. A comparison of Gujarat with other fast growing reform oriented states reflects that despite a continuous increase in budgetary allocation, per capital expenditure on road and bridges in Gujarat has remained significantly lower than Tamil Nadu and Haryana. Maharashtra is the only state in this club of four states where the per capita expenditure on roads and bridges has remained lower than Gujarat (Figure 4.3). Nonetheless, even with this lower per capita expenditure; Gujarat has outshined Tamil Nadu and Haryana when we look at the outcome in terms of increase in road length. From 1999 to 2008, the total road length in Gujarat has increased from 92043 km to 143630 km, an increase of 56 per cent.[7] In comparison to this Tamil Nadu has witnessed an increase of 24 per cent while Haryana has registered a growth of less than 5 per cent. The performance of Maharashtra has remained extremely poor as it has registered a negative growth in road length between 1999 to 2008 (see annexure Table 4.4).

A similar kind of trend could be seen in the case of surfaced road length. From 1999 to 2008, the surfaced road length in Gujarat has increased by 62.5 per cent, while in Tamil Nadu and Haryana it has increased by 61.9 per cent and 4.8 per cent respectively. A relatively higher growth of surfaced road as compared to the growth in total road length in Tamil Nadu reflects that Tamil Nadu has given a great emphasis on improving the quality of existing road, which was not at par with Haryana and Gujarat till 1999 (Table 4.4, see annexure). As a result, the share of surfaced road in total road length in Tamil Nadu has gone up from 76 per cent in 1999 to 98 per cent 2008. Noticeably, Maharashtra is the only state among these four states where the share of surfaced road in total road length is below 80 per cent. Apart from Maharashtra, all three states have a 90 plus share of surfaced road in their total road length.

Figure 4.2: Capital Outlay of Gujarat on Road and Bridges at 1999-00 Prices

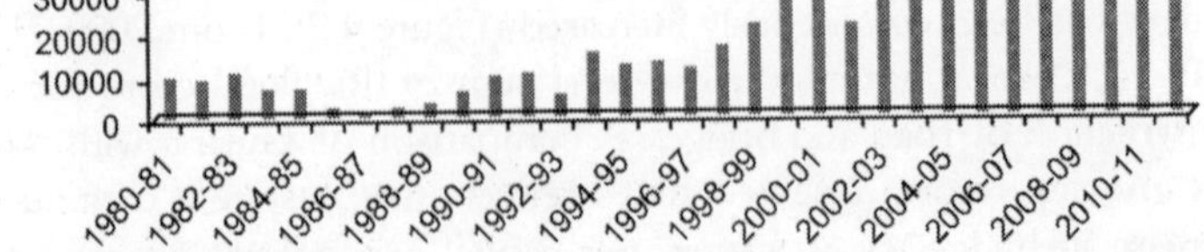

Source: Gujarat Annual Budget Documents, Various Issues

Figure 4.3: Per Capita Capital Outlay on Road and Bridges, from 2000-01 to 2009-10

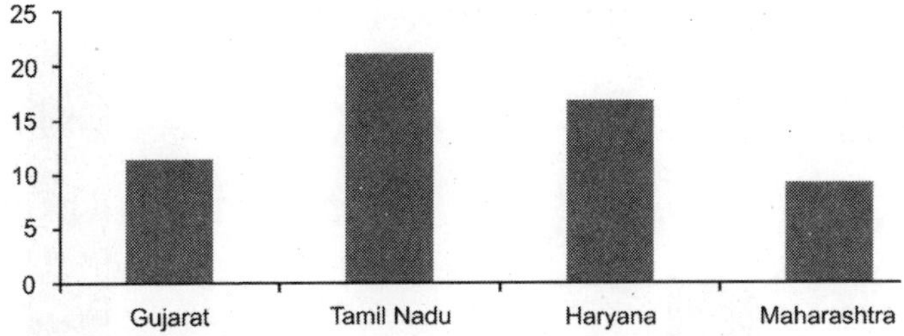

Source: Annual Budget Documents of States, Various Issues

The mismatch between per capita budgetary allocation and outcome of road infrastructure among the selected states could mainly be attributed to the involvement of private sector. A comparison of private investment in road infrastructure among Gujarat, Haryana and Tamil Nadu clearly shows that while Gujarat has successfully attracted a large amount of private investment in roads, both Haryana and Tamil Nadu have almost failed to do so (Figure 4.4).[8] While Gujarat has attracted a total private investment of more than Rs. 7000 crores in various road projects, Tamil Nadu has attracted only Rs. 3000 crores as private investment. The performance of Haryana in this regard has remained completely unsatisfactory as it has failed completely to attract any private investment. Interestingly, Maharashtra has attracted a huge amount of private investment in road sector. However, a major chunk of this investment is concentrated in Mumbai where private players have constructed some of the most expensive bridges and roads such as Mumbai Trans Harbor Link, Bandra-Worli Sea Link, etc.[9] A high concentration of private investment in selected cities along with a lower budgetary allocation for road and bridges probably explain the poor performance of Maharashtra in terms of addition and upgradation of road network from 1999 to 2008.

Figure 4.4: Private Participation in Roads Infrastructure, Value in Rs. Crore

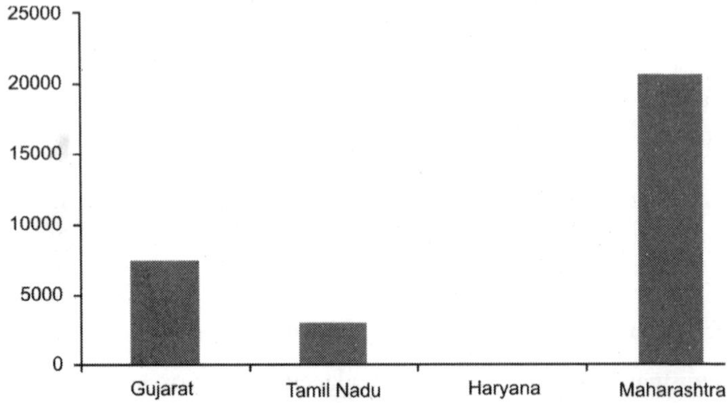

Source: PPP Data Base Ministry of Finance, GOI, available at: http://www.pppindiadatabase.com/Screens/frmSearch.aspx?AUTHORISEDUSER=N&ACTIONTAG=VIEW

A disaggregated analysis of road infrastructure in Gujarat shows an interesting fact. From 1995 to 2008, the combined length of national highways and state highways in Gujarat has increased by just 4 per cent, while the total road length has increased by more than 60 per cent. It underlines the fact that Gujarat has developed a large network of roads other than national and state highways, which includes PWD roads, rural roads and other project roads. It seems that huge inflow of private investment in state highways has allowed Gujarat to use its budgetary allocation for the improvement of roads other than state highways. An analysis of rural connectivity in Gujarat also collaborate this hypothesis. In 1996, out of 18028, only 16932 revenue villages[10] in Gujarat were connected with pucca road. Noticeably, within a decade, the number of revenue villages connected with pucca road has increased to 17822, which improved the rural connectivity in Gujarat from less than 94 per cent in 1996 to 98.86 per cent in 2006 (Figure 4.5). Nonetheless, in a state like Gujarat which has a significant share of tribal population, 99 per cent connectivity of revenue villages does not mean that 99 per cent of human habitations are connected with road. Gujarat has a total 34187 human habitations, out of which only 26767 human habitations were connected with road till the end of year 2000 (see annexure Table 4.5). Since 2000-01, central government has taken the responsibility to provide road connectivity to all human habitations under its flagship program of PGSY. From 2000-01 to 2009-10, PMGSY has improved the connectivity status in Gujarat to a great extent as it has provided connectivity to 4040 habitations. However, still 3380 habitations in Gujarat are not connected with road.

Figure 4.5: Rural Connectivity in Gujarat, % of Villages Connected with Pucca Road

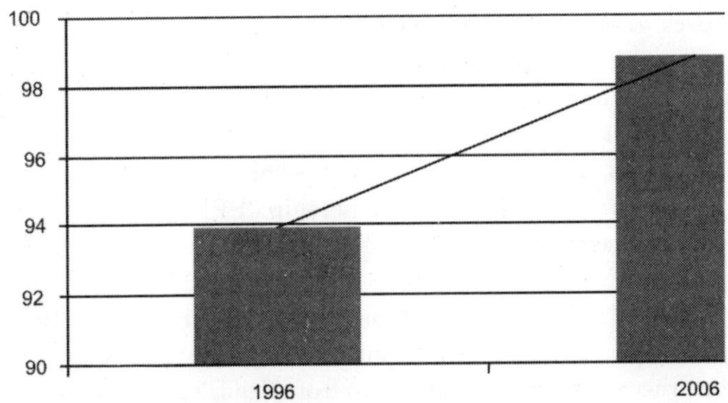

Source: Road and Building Department, Government of Gujarat

Though, as mentioned above, Gujarat has not constructed any new state highways in last one and half decade, it has improved the existing highways in a big way. The state highways development program alone has improved the quality of 1850 kms of state highways, while a loan from HUDCO resulted in an improved of another 254 km of state highways. Apart from this, the entire private investment of more than Rs. 7000, has also improved the condition and quality of existing highways. In a nutshell, we can say that road infrastructure in Gujarat has witnessed a significant improvement over the last one and a half decades. The rural connectivity has increased and quality of state highways has improved. However, despite this all-round development of road the road density in Gujarat is still very low which could be attributed to the low density of population in Gujarat.

3. Rail Network

Railway is the most affordable and efficient mode of long distance transportation. India has a total rail network of 64,460 km, of which

5,328 km fall in the territory of Gujarat. Though, Gujarat always had one of the high rail density among the Indian states (Figure 4.6), its rail network was very outdated till recently as almost 50 per cent of its total rail track consisted of narrow and meter gauge (Figure 4.7). From 2001 onward, Gujarat government along with some ports in Gujarat has joined hands with Ministry of Railways to upgrade the existing rail track in Gujarat. The main lead in this regard has been taken by various ports. After adding a massive traffic handling capacity, these ports have taken initiatives to improve their connectivity with industrial growth centre within as well as outside Gujarat. So far, three rail track upgradation projects have been successfully completed under an active partnership between ministry of railways, Government of Gujarat and different private players, while one project is in pipeline.

The first Public-Private Partnership (PPP) project for track upgradation was launched in 2001, when Pipavav port (then a joint venture between A. P. Moller-Maersk Group and GMB) and Ministry of Railways jointly formed a special purpose vehicle, to upgrade the rail track between Surendranagar to Rajula from existing meter gauge to broad gauge and to construct a new rail track of 21 km from Rajula to Pipavav port. This project involved a total cost of Rs. 370 crores and was completed in 2003. Another project of gauge conversion between Palanpur and Gandhidham was initiated in 2004. With a total cost of Rs. 500 crore, this project upgraded a total rail track of 301 km from meter gauge to broad gauge. Recently, in 2010, under a joint venture of Rail Vikas Nigam Ltd., Gujarat Maritime Board and some other private investors, the narrow gauge rail track between Bharuch and Dahej has also been upgraded. These three projects taken together have upgraded a total rail track of more than 630 km from narrow and meter gauge to broad gauge. Apart from completed projects, GMB have also conducted studies to connect Hazira, Sutrapada, Mahuva, Chhara, Maroli and Modhwa ports with rail track. Among these, the Hazira Kosad missing link project has already been negotiated and the process of land acquisition has started. Since, a large share of upgraded rail network fall in economically backward area of Kutch, these rail track upgradation projects could potential play a significant role in correcting the problem of growing regional inequalities in Gujarat.

Figure 4.6: Rail Density among Selected States

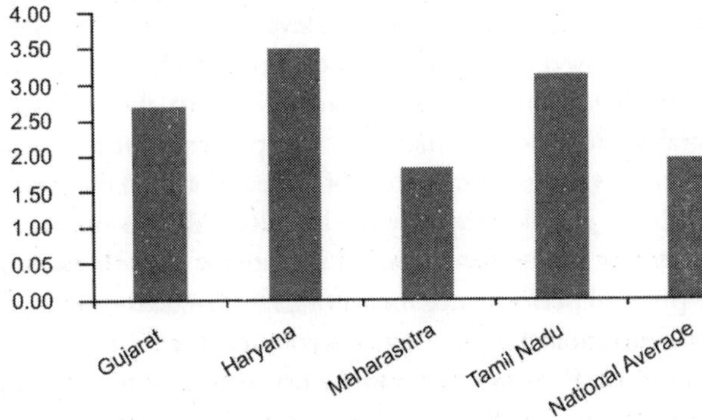

Figure 4.7: Composition of Rail Tracks in Gujarat

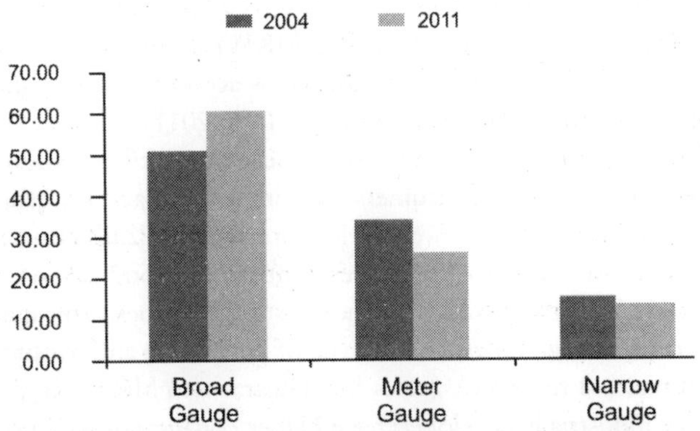

Source: Compiled from Ministry of Railways, GOI and Socio Economic Review of Gujarat State, Directorate Economics and Statistics, Government of Gujarat available:
1. *http://indianrailways.gov.in/railwayboard/uploads/directorate/stat_econ/yearbook10-11/Track_bridges.pdf*
2. *http://www.gujaratindia.com/*

A comparison of Gujarat with Maharashtra, Tamil Nadu and Haryana shows that Gujarat is the only state which has witnessed a significant growth in its rail infrastructure through PPP. Apart from Gujarat, Haryana is the only state in this group which has seen some sort of PPP in rail sector. However, the only PPP rail project in Haryana is related to the extension of Delhi Metro from Delhi to Gurgaon.[11]

4. Power

Electricity is central to the economic development of a country. The significance of power in a fast growing economy such as India can hardly be negated. Acting as a catalyst, particularly to the industrial and agricultural sector, development of the power sector is crucial to development of various other sectors of the economy. In the post-reform period, with the installed capacity of 173626.4 MW as on 31st March, 2011, the power sector has recorded impressive growth rates both in terms of physical performance indicators, i.e., installed capacity and the electricity generation. Of this states accounted for 47.49 per cent, the central sector for 31.34 per cent and the private sector for the remaining 21.34 per cent. Out of these combination hydel power accounts 21.64 per cent, RES (renewable energy source) for 13.38 and major portion comes through the thermal power which is 64.98 per cent. The electricity gross generation has reached 811056 MKWH, out of which centre accounts for 42.67 per cent, whereas, rest is accounted for by the state and private sources (Ministry of Power [MoP], 2011).

The major segments that consume electricity are industries, agriculture and domestic consumers. Industrial sector accounts for 33.11 per cent of total sale of power, agriculture around 22.62 per cent and domestic sector accounts for 24 per cent of the total sale of power (MoP, 2011). The major portion of the consumption goes to the industrial sector. There is huge variation, however, of generation and consumption of power across the states. States like Gujarat and Maharashtra which are highly industrially developed have higher consumption of power in industrial sector compared to others. Maharashtra has both conventional and non-conventional resources for the generation of power. On the other hand, Gujarat is lacking in both hydel as well as thermal power because the state has no hydro and coal resources for the generation of power.

A brief History of Gujarat Power Sector

Gujarat Electricity Board (GEB) was established along with the formation of Gujarat State in the year 1960 under Section 5 of the Electricity (Supply) Act 1948. At the time of formation of the state, the total generation of the capacity was only 315MW with meagre 1.40 million consumers. During the period 1960-1990, Gujarat Electricity Board (GEB) and Ahmedabad Electricity Company (AEC), which is a private licensee, were the main generators (Shukla, 2004). With the formation of Gujarat Electricity Board the major thrust was given on the supply of electricity in the rural areas. Due to these efforts, Gujarat achieved 100 per cent rural electrification very early compared to other states (Shah, 2006).

Gujarat Electricity Board (GEB) continues to focus on its key objectives concerning generation, transmission and equitable distribution of power to achieve all-round growth of the state. Keeping these objectives till the year 1998, Gujarat Electricity Board was one of the most profit-making and efficiently run boards in the country. After 1998, Gujarat power sector started incurring losses and reached at a high figure of Rs. 6,233 crores by end of 2002-03 (Government of India, 2006). Transmission and Distribution losses were at the peak. Palpably low levels of Plant load factor (below 65%) and auxiliary consumption (below 10%) in the state, which measures generating capacity of the power plant aroused the need for restructuring of the power sector which has already taken place in many Indian states like Orissa, Haryana, U.P., Andhra Pradesh, etc. With the enactment of Gujarat Electricity Industry Act, 2003 the unbundling of state electricity board took place with separate generation, transmission and distribution entities in March 2005.

Power Sector Policies in Gujarat

In Gujarat private sector participation in generation started very early but the real change came after the power sector reforms which took place late compared to other states like Haryana and Tamil Nadu. Gujarat has been arguably the most successful state in India in attracting and operationalizing the Independent Power Producers (IPPs) through relatively low cost of the projects. The state government provided good support for these steps and politics appeared to have played a comparatively lesser role in this state.

Gujarat, though a late reformer when compared to Haryana and Tamil Nadu, has been the most successful among the states in attracting private players and has the highest growth of installed capacity in the private sector. What seems to have driven the success of the state in attracting private players were relatively lower fixed costs of the projects and lower variable costs due to the availability of alternate fuel when the original fuel became relatively costly.

In India, private players came in generation sector only except Orissa and Delhi where distribution sector was also privatized. The main reasons for the large involvement of private sector in generation segments in Gujarat compared to other states were the vast possibilities for cooperative, complementary and participative ventures between private (both domestic and foreign) and state sectors in developing the power sector.

Specifically, the following steps were taken in this regard:[12]

- Identification of suitable location for the project.
- Creation/Upgradation of connecting infrastructure to the project site i.e. roads, etc.
- Arranging right of way.
- Obtaining clearances & approvals which are in the purview of the state.
- Recommending the project to avail benefits under any policy declared by the Government of India.

Larger encouragement was given to Captive Power Plants through two factors: macro level changes in policy environment and at the micro level economic and financial factors at the firm level. At macro level in 1998[13], '*Energy and Petroleum Department, Gujarat Government passed a resolution.' 'Resolution No. CPP 1197/2253/PP Cell, 1998' which was a policy for the Captive Power Projects. This resolution addressed issues like wheeling of power; wheeling tariffs; supply of surplus power to the group companies (parent company); supply surplus power to the state utility (GEB); supply of surplus power to AEC (licensee), etc.'* This policy farther enhanced the growth of the Captive Power Plants (CPPs) in Gujarat. At micro level, high industrial tariffs, multiple benefits and lower production cost of the outputs of industry were the major components.

To further attract the private players, with the enactment of Electricity Regulatory Commission, 1998 the Gujarat Electricity Regulatory Commission took over state government's power of deciding tariff. To rationalize the tax structure Gujarat has removed the sales tax on sale of electricity w.e.f. 1st April, 2002, thus extending relief to the extent of Rs. 260 crores per year to all categories of consumers. Further, the new industrial units which generate electricity for captive requirements are also exempted from the payment of excise duty for the initial period of 5 years (GoG).

With the enactment of Electricity Act, 2003 the road towards attraction of private sector got more cleared and in 2005 when the state got fully reformed, transmission services agreements have been signed by Gujarat Urja Vikas Nigam Limited (GUVNL) and the four Distribution Companies (DISCOMs) jointly with Gujarat Energy Transmission Corporation Limited (GETCO) on payment terms for transmission charges and for carrying out the function of load dispatch for interstate as well as intrastate dispatch. With a view to bring discipline in the operation of generating plant and the four DISCOMs, it has been decided to implement intrastate Availability Based Tariff (ABT). Gujarat was the first state in the country to have proceeded in adopting intrastate ABT mechanism (MoP, 2006).

The other factor which makes private participation in generation successful is the positive implementation of reforms in the whole power segment which is considered one of the most successful among Indian states. The most noteworthy feature of this exercise was immediate inclusion of representatives of the unions and associations of the staff in the restructuring process, right from initial stage after deciding on reforming the sector. The attitude of the staff in the entire restructuring process remained positive. In achieving the above schedule, Government of Gujarat's role was very positive and proactive. It also took stringent/ strict measures against theft of electricity by enacting the Anti-Theft Law, creation of dedicated police stations and special courts to deal with this menace (MoP, 2006).

To increase the generation and supply of power, Government of Gujarat has drafted its power policy according to which it envisages to utilize non-conventional sources and conserve energy. Other measures to improve the production and supply of power are to improve the quality of services, de-monopolize distribution of power and encourage involvement of private partners, rationalize tariff structure and make the best possible use of the available energy sources (GIDB, 2012).

These policy guidelines given above are the main differentiating factors between Gujarat and rest of the states which favoured Gujarat in attracting large private players in generation segment.

Current Installed Capacity and Generation of Electricity

The growth in total installed capacity of electricity in Gujarat and some selected states from 2001-02 to 2010-11 is given in Table 4.6 (see annexure). In Gujarat the total installed capacity has increased with a compound annual growth rate of 2.17 per cent in 2001-02 to 2005-06 which is very low compared to other states like Tamil Nadu, Haryana and all India except Maharashtra. The interesting fact is that during this period from 2001-02 to 2005-06 the private sector installed capacity has decreased, and growth in private sector was negative in Gujarat. States like Tamil Nadu, Maharashtra and all India show positive growth in installed capacity in private sector during the same period.

In the last five years from 2006-07 to 2010-11 the installed capacity has increased with a compound annual growth of 12.87 per cent. The growth in this period is very high compared to earlier period and from other states into consideration. The high growth in installed capacity in Gujarat is mainly contributed by the private sector whose participation has increased tremendously to 7178 MW and with growth at 33.24 per cent in the same period from 2006-07 to 2010-11, which is very high compared to private sector of other states and India. During this period, the growth of state sector in installed capacity has decreased compared to period 2001-02 to 2005-06. This explains that after 2005-06 the installed capacity addition in Gujarat was mainly from the private sector. The year 2005-06 was the year of power sector reforms in Gujarat which has given boost to private sector participation. This clearly explains that power sector policies of Gujarat have encouraged the private sector participation in Gujarat power sector.

In 2001-02, the share of private sector in installed capacity at 36.15 per cent was high when compared to other states such as, Maharashtra (25%), Tamil Nadu (23%) and Haryana (0%) (see annexure Table 4.6). The share of private sector has increased drastically in all the states in 2010-11 as given in Table 4.6 (see annexure) but Gujarat leads with 54.75 per cent of the total installed capacity, Tamil Nadu is closer to Gujarat with private share of 54.7 per cent.

If the different sources are considered then one can find that share of hydro power has decreased from 7.49 per cent in 2001-02 to 5.89 per cent in 2010-11 which is totally state owned power in Gujarat. Share of thermal which was 90.22 per cent in 2001-02 has come down to 78.85 per cent in 2010-11. Other states have also shown some decreasing trend in hydro as well as in thermal power in some state. But the interesting observation is that there has been a shift from the thermal and hydel in the total installed capacity to renewable energy sources, the share of which increased to 15.03 per cent for Gujarat in 2010-11 from 2.05 per cent in 2001-02 which is almost seven times in 10 years which is highest from other states. And the most important fact about Gujarat is that the whole share of renewable energy source (RES) is coming from the private sector only. Tamil Nadu also shows some interesting facts where the share of renewable energy resource (RES) has grown from 12.70 per cent in 2001-02 to 45.45 per cent in 2010-11 which is highest for any state in the country.

As discussed earlier, Gujarat lacks in hydro and thermal resources but has huge potential of wind power compared to other states (IREDA, 2011). There is net capacity addition in the installed capacity form 2001-02 to 2010-11 through private sector participation in India which is totally private owned renewable energy resource (RES) as given in Table 4.7 (see annexure). Gujarat shows a significant increase in wind power capacity addition after 2005, with total capacity addition of 2176.77 MW up to 2010-11.

Table 4.7 (see annexure) shows that Tamil Nadu has achieved highest capacity addition of 5867.16 MW but after 2005 the increment in the capacity addition in Gujarat is much higher than the Tamil Nadu which is around six times from the 2005 level.

Electricity Generation also shows increasing trend where states like Maharashtra and Tamil Nadu show negative annual growth rate, Gujarat and Haryana are the only states having positive growth rate of 2.83 and 7.05 per cent respectively (see annexure, Table 4.8). But in absolute terms Gujarat is leading in power generation.

In terms of gross generation, the private sector occupies a significant share of 45.78 per cent in 2010-11 in Gujarat which is higher when compared to the share of Maharashtra and Tamil Nadu but much higher than the all India and Haryana where private participation is negligible. Similar trends can be seen in the shifting of power generation from thermal to renewable in all the states as well as in India. But the interesting thing is that Gujarat has around 98 per cent renewable power supply form private sector with state occupying a negligible share.

If the growth rate of generation of power is considered after the reform of power sector in 2005 in Gujarat, one can find that it has grown at an annual rate of 8.66 per cent which is highest among Indian states like Haryana, Maharashtra and Tamil Nadu. States like Maharashtra and Tamil Nadu show sign of negative growth in all state and private power utilities. Gujarat shows a very high growth in electricity generation in private sector at around 17.63 per cent annually. The share of private sector has increased significantly from 33.33 per cent in 2006-07 to 45.78 per cent. On the other hand, the share of private sector declined in Tamil Nadu from 27.55 per cent in 2006-07 to 21.76 per cent in 2010-11 as shown in the Table 4.8 (see annexure).

Private Sector Involvement in Gujarat Power Sector

Gujarat is one of the most highly industrialized Indian states and continues to be the industrial base for chemical, fertilizer, petroleum, textiles and non-ferrous metal production. Private sector participation in Gujarat power sector generation started in early 1990's through the involvement of independent power producers (IIP's) (MoP, 2006). The policy changes of Government of India to attract private producer was the main factor for the encouragement of IIP's. But industrial sector in Gujarat was facing high shortages of power and higher tariff regulation so the Government of Gujarat introduced encouragement for the captive power plants (Shukla, 2004).

The high industrial tariffs have lead many large manufacturing plants to choose captive generation and leave the grid system, which acts to undercut the revenue of the state electricity boards (SEBs) even further. Gujarat has seen a rapid increase in captive power plant capacity, rising from less than 1 GW in 1996 to more than 2.7 GW in 2005 (Joshi, 2008). Gujarat was producing 50 per cent of its industrial load from captive power plant (CPP), while captive power plants (CPPs) exports were only 609 GWh, or 2 per cent of total industrial demand in 2004 as given in Table 4.9 (see annexure).

The share of captive power plants was much higher than the other states and all India. The use of captive power in Gujarat can be analysed from several viewpoints. The different industries used Captive Power Plant (CPP), in each case the use was more than 80 per cent of energy needs and for chemicals and petroleum, they were actively involved in the export of power to other sectors (i.e. above 100 per cent). For the state as a whole, captive power was 81 per cent of power used by industries with captive plants and was approximately 50 per cent of all power used in the state by all industrial units (Hansen, 2008). The overall picture of Gujarat Captive Power Plant (CPP) was one of fast growth in a highly industrialized state with poor service form the State Electricity Board (SEB) and high tariffs.

In 2005, the state power sector got unbundled and State Electricity Board (SEB) changed to just regulatory authority. With the enactment of reform process in power sector there has been a lot of private sector participation, with the delicensing of the generation sector. The participation is autonomous in the generation vertical, while some companies are regulated to participate in the transmission and distribution verticals.[14] In case of Ahmedabad, Torrent Power Limited is authorized to transmit and distribute electricity in the areas of Ahmedabad and Surat. The presence of private participation continues to be on the rise with participators like Essar, Adani group, Torrent Power Limited (GIDB, 2012).

But the tariff structure did not change yet and industrial tariff remained highest even after the reform process which is a door opener for the captive power plants in Gujarat. Higher tariffs as given in Table 4.10 (see annexure) shows that Gujarat has higher tariff charges from every category of consumers except commercial category but the tariff for industrial sector remained highest. These high tariffs charged from industrial sector clearly explained that the power sector policy in Gujarat was rural biased, it favoured rural areas by providing relatively cheap electricity to domestic and agriculture sector.

Due to higher tariff structure and policy incentives like identification for suitable location, better infrastructure facilities, low gestation period and many more, private sector participation has been increased through captive power plants (GoG, 2009).

Performance of Physical and Financial Parameters

Per capita consumption of electricity in Gujarat is one of the highest and more than double the national average. This highest per capita consumption is mainly due to the high industrial base of Gujarat state compared to other states in consideration. The per capita consumption of electricity is growing with compound annual growth of 4.99 per cent for 2001-02 to 2009-10 which is highest among all the states under consideration.

The power sector reforms in Gujarat were very successful for declining the Transmission and Distribution (T&D) losses which came down to 22.74 per cent in 2010-11 (Planning Commission, 2011). During the time period concerned, T&D losses gradually declined in the state from the peak of 30.43 per cent in 2004-5. This clearly marks towards the positive performance attained in the power sector due to the reforms undertaken.

Plant load factor of thermal power plants which determines the capacity of plants to utilize the power decreased in Gujarat from 68.14 per cent in 2001-02 to 67.32 per cent in 2010-11 (Planning Commission, 2011). Low plant load factor of thermal power station shows that the condition of the plant deteriorated in utilizing the power. The plant load factor reached its maximum in 2008-09 at 76.18 per cent. Technical factor, henceforth, is showing negative trend. Maharashtra shows the lowest plant load factor at around 59 per cent compared to the national average of 75.08 per cent.

Commercial losses without subsidies in the states has increased almost in all states except for Maharashtra and Gujarat where one can see the decreasing trend in the commercial losses during 2001-02 to 2010-11(MoP 2011). The commercial losses in the Gujarat state were very high after 2000 due to high T&D losses and low plant load factor of state power utilities but after the reform process in power sector of Gujarat in 2005, the losses started declining trend due to large participation of the private players in the power sector and low subsidy to the domestic and agriculture sector. Increased private sector participation after reforms has played a major role in easing the financial burden of the state. With subsidy the commercial profit of Gujarat state shows a positive sign compared to other states. Tamil Nadu even after huge subsidies shows very high commercial losses same is true for Haryana as given in Table 4.12 (see annexure). The subsidy to the agriculture and domestic sector further shows a declining trend in Gujarat as shown in Table 4.13 (see annexure).

Gujarat is the only state among the states into consideration which has given lowest subsidy to domestic and agriculture sector. The commercial losses are maximum in the Tamil Nadu at around Rs. 10426 crores which are maximum for any state in the India.

Aggregate technical and commercial losses have been declined for all the states in to consideration but Tamil Nadu shows very low aggregate technical and commercial losses due to better technical factors. Gujarat state has also low aggregate technical and commercial losses around 23.81 per cent in 2010-11 (Planning Commission, 2002, 2011). The losses have come down from a very high of 35 per cent in 2004-05. This improvement is mainly due to the large private sector participation in power generation after the reform process which has kept commercial losses at a low level. But still there is a need still need to focus on the technical drawbacks of the sector.

5. Conclusion

Over the last one and a half decades, Gujarat has given an overriding priority to infrastructure development. It has created special institution like GIDB and has increased budgetary outlays for infrastructure development. It also opened up its infrastructure sector for private investment and announced various incentives to attract private capital in key infrastructural activities like ports roads and power. All theses initiative taken together ensured a tremendous increase in basic infrastructure in Gujarat. The ports in Gujarat have emerged as the best in the country while road network has witnessed a significant growth. At the same time, rail network in Gujarat has also improved a lot. The power sector has also improved significantly, both in terms of quantity and quality of power. Noticeably, the growth of infrastructure in Gujarat has remained relatively better than some of the other well-developed and growth-orientated states of India. The difference between the infrastructure growth in Gujarat and other states could mainly be attributed to involvement of private investment. The private sector has invested a huge amount in Gujarat, while the private involvement in other states has remained limited. Given large coastline, well-developed industrial base and proximity to northern states, Gujarat has a locational advantage. It realized this advantage and allowed private investors in infrastructure, much before any other state. At present, it is reaping the benefit of first mover advantage which perhaps being enhanced by administrative ease of doing business. Thus the growth of infrastructure in Gujarat can be attributed to a blend of natural advantage and proactive execution of state policy.

NOTES

1. Ports are listed under the concurrent list and hence they fall under the jurisdiction of both federal as well as state government. The 12 major ports in India come under the jurisdiction of federal government, while state governments are responsible for the development of non-major ports.

2. In late 1990s, one more green field site was added to the list of ten green field site for the development of deep water ports; take the total number to 11.
3. The four private ports which have commenced operation are Pipava in 1996, Mundra in 1998, Dahej in 2004 and Hazira in 2005.
4. For a comparative analysis port policy and incentives provided to private sector in Maharashtra and Gujarat, please see Box 1.
5. Though Gujarat has been consciously using its proximity to northern growth centre of National Capital Region as a toll to attract the private investment in its maritime sector (see Gujarat port Policy, 1995 and Sinha 2010) since 1995, the announcement of Delhi-Mumbai Industrial Corridor (DMIC) has further increased the attractiveness of Gujarat's ports for private investors.
6. Gujarat constructed 10558 kms of state highways between 1980 to 1995.
7. This increase in road length also includes roads constructed under Pradhan Mantri Gram Sadak Yojana (PMGSY), which is a central government sponsored scheme. However, the contribution of PMGSY is not the prime driver of increase in total road length in Gujarat because from 2000-01 to 2007-08, only 5888 kms road length was constructed under PMGSY.
8. It should be noted that the incentives provided to private investors under BOT policy are almost same across Gujarat, Maharashtra and Tamil Nadu. All these states assist private developers in land acquisition, grants them the advertisement rights along the right of way and exemption from royalty on construction material. All these three states also provided financial support to ensure the project viability, if needed. However, the financial support varies from 33.33 per cent in Tamil Nadu to 40 per cent in Maharashtra and Gujarat. These states also allow commercial development along the corridor to increase the revenue the revenue by a stream of projects like hotels, restaurants, warehousing, etc.
9. For detail of PPP road project in Maharashtra, please see PPP Data Base Ministry of Finance, GOI.
10. Revenue village is an administrative unit which could include one and more than one hamlet.
11. For details of PPP projects, visit http://www.pppinindia.com/
12. Government of Gujarat, 'Power Generation Policy, 2009'.
13. Shukla P.R., Debashish Biswas, Tirthankar Nag, Amee Yajnik, Thomas Heller and David G. Victor (March 2004), 'Impact of Power Sector Reforms on Technology, Efficiency and Emissions: Case Study of Gujarat, India', Working Paper No. 21.
14. http://www.scribd.com/Leon_scorpio/d/31560516-Supply- and-Demand-Power-Gap-Case-study-of-Gujarat

REFERENCES

Asian Development Bank, India. *Gujarat Power Sector Development Program.* Project No. 29694, September 2008. New Delhi: Asian Development Bank.

Canning D and Pedroni P. Infrastructure, Long-run Economic Growth and Causality Tests for Cointegrated Panels. *Journal of Manchester School* 2008; 76: 504-527.

Central Electricity Authority. *Load Generation Balance Report 2011-12.* 2012. New Delhi: Central Electricity Authority, Government of India.

Central Electricity Authority. *Seventeenth Power Survey of India.* 2007. New Delhi: Central Electricity Authority, Government of India.

Central Statistics Organization. *Energy Statistics 2011.* 2011. New Delhi: Government of India.

Chetan Ghate. Understanding Divergence in India: A Political Economy Approach. *Journal of Economic Policy Reform* 2008; 11: 1-10.

CRISIL. *Gujarat Infrastructure Development Board (GIDB) - Review of Blueprint for Infrastructure in Gujarat (Big 2020).* Final Report, Volume 1- Summary and Vision, August 2009. New Delhi: CRISIL.

CRISIL. *State Power Sector Performance Ratings.* Final report to the Ministry of Power, 2006. New Delhi: Ministry of Power.

Dholakia R. Growth acceleration and Potential in Gujarat. *Working Paper* No. 2006-02-02, Indian Institute of Management, Ahmedabad, 2006.

Dholakia R. Macro-Economic Framework for Development in Gujarat. *Working Paper* No. 2004-02-02. Indian Institute of Management, Ahmedabad, 2004.

Garcia-Mila T, McGuire TJ and Porter RH. The Effect of Public Capital in State Level Production Functions Reconsidered. *Review of Economics and Statistics* 1996; 78: 177-180.

GETCO. *Annual Report for year 2009-10.* 2010. Government of Gujarat.

GETCO. *Annual Report for year 2010-11.* 2011. Government of Gujarat.

Ghosh M. Economic Growth and Human Development in Indian States. *Economic and Political Weekly* 2006; 41(30): 3321-3329.

Government of Gujarat. *Gujarat Industrial Policy 2009- Catalysing Robust, Sustainable and Inclusive Growth.* 2009. Government of Gujarat.

Government of Gujarat. *Gujarat State: Socio-Economic Review, 2010-11.* Budget Publication No. 34. 2011. Government of Gujarat.

Government of India. *Annual report (2001-02) on the Working of State Electricity Boards and Electricity Departments (Power and Energy Division).* 2002. New Delhi: Planning Commission, Government of India.

Government of India. *Annual report 2011-12 on the Working of State power utilities and Electricity Departments (Power and Energy Division),* 2011. New Delhi: Planning Commission, Government of India.

Government of India. *Report on Assessment of Investment Climate for Wind Power*

Development in India for Indian Renewable Energy Development Agency (IREDA). 2011. New Delhi: Government of India.

Government of India. *Study on 'Impact of Restructuring of SEBs.* 2006. New Delhi: Ministry of Power, Government of India.

Hansen Christopher Joshi. *Bottom-up Electricity Reform Using Industrial Captive Generation: A Case Study of Gujarat, India.* 2008. Oxford Institute for Energy Studies.

Holtz-Eakin D and Schwartz AE. Infrastructure in a Structural Model of Economic Growth. *Regional Science and Urban Economics* 1995; 25: 131-151.

Hulten CR and Schwab RM. Is There Too Little Public Capital?: Infrastructure and Economic Growth. In: *American Enterprise Institute Conference on Infrastructure Needs and Policy Options in 1990s,* Washington D.C, USA, February 4, 1991.

Kannan KP and Pillai NV. Plight of the Power Sector in India: SEBs and their saga of inefficiency. *Working Paper* No. 308. Centre for Development Studies, Thiruvananthapuram, November 2000.

Kumar N. East Asian Infrastructure Development in a Comparative Global Perspective: An Analysis of RIS Infrastructure Index. *RIS Discussion Paper* 2008; 135. RIS, New Delhi, 2008.

Menon VS. Drivers of economic growth in Gujarat. *MPRA* Paper No. 9233, ICFAI Business School, Ahmedabad, 2008.

Menon VS. Energy Sector in Gujarat: Performance and Prospects. *MPRA* Paper No.9502, ICFAI Business School Ahmedabad, 2008.

Ministry of Power. *Annual Report of Ministry of Power.* Various Years. New Delhi: Ministry of Power, Government of India.

Morris S. Regulatory Strategy and Restructuring: Model for Gujarat Power Sector. *Economic and Political Weekly* 2000; 35(23): 1915-1929.

Planning Commission. *Midterm Appraisal of Eleventh Five Year Plan.* 2011. New Delhi: Planning Commission, Government of India.

Prud'Homme R. Infrastructure and Development. In: *Annual Work Bank Conference on Development Economics.* Washington D.C, USA, May 3-5, 2004.

Rao MG, Shand RT and Kalirajan KP. State Electricity Boards: A Performance Evaluation. *The Indian Economic Journal* 1998-99; 46(2).

Ratner JB. Government Capital and the Production Function for U.S. Private Output. *Economic Letters* 1983; 13: 213-217.

Sanchez-Robles B. Infrastructure Investment and Growth: Some Empirical Evidence. *Contemporary Economic Policy* 1998; 16: 98-108.

Shukla PR, et al. Captive Power Plants: Case Study of Gujarat, India. *Working Paper* No. 22, Center for Environmental Science and Policy, Stanford University, California, 2004.

Shukla PR, et al. Impact of Power Sector Reforms on Technology, Efficiency and Emissions: Case Study of Gujarat, India. *Working Paper* No. 21, Center for Environmental Science and Policy, Stanford University, California, 2004.

Tatom JA. Paved with Good Intentions; the Mythical National Infrastructure Crisis. *Working Paper* No. 196. Cato Institute Policy Analysis, Washington D.C, 1993a.

Tatom JA. Public Capital and Private Sector Performance. *Federal Reserve Bank of Saint Louis Review* 1991; 73: 3-15.

Tatom JA. The Spurious Effect of Public Capital Formation on Private Sector Productivity. *Policy Studies Journal* 1993b; 21: 391-395.

Virmani A. Growing Intra Industry Trade in Manufacturing Implications for Policy. *Economic and Political Weekly* 2004; 39(41): 4556-4559.

5

Understanding Gujarat's Agricultural Growth in a Liberalizing Environment: Signs of a Redefined Margin?

Sucharita Sen and Chinmoyee Mallik

1. The Context

Located in the semi-arid western India, Gujarat has been the second most industrialized, third most urbanized and fifth richest state among the major states of India (Arya, et. al, 2011). Known for its entrepreneurial culture and a government that patronizes privatization, Gujarat nurtures a diversified economic structure with large industrial sector along with a highly commercialized agriculture (Arya, et. al, 2011). Although the share of agriculture in terms of output as well as workforce in Gujarat has been declining consistently over the last 30 years, what has set it apart from rest of the major states of India has been the unprecedented agricultural growth experienced by it against the dwindling agricultural scenario at the all India level.[1] Infact, in triennium ending 2009-10, Gujarat accounts for 6.14 per cent of India's value of total output from agriculture & allied sector which is the sixth rank among all the states. In the same decade, its rate of growth has been far higher than that observed at the national level.

Given the dramatic growth of agriculture in the state that has been fairly extensively covered in the literature in the recent years, this study sets itself three specific tasks:

1. Tracing the recent agricultural policy changes in the state with particular reference to land policy in their historical context.

2. Describing elements of agricultural growth in the state, specifically with respect to the major drivers of agricultural growth, and bringing out a regional distribution of the same.
3. Attempting to understand the way in which the benefits of this growth have percolated to different social and economic sections of the agricultural community.

2. Land and Agricultural Livelihoods: A Historical Perspective to the Current Policy Settings

Access to land has been known to have a strong association with incidence of poverty in rural India (Agarwal, 1994). The direction of the causality in this relationship, however, is not clear (Mearns, 1999). Holdings that are very small often derive a greater share of their livelihoods from their own labour than from their own land. The association between land and livelihood is deeper in rural areas for not only the obvious reasons that agriculture is the primary mainstay of rural livelihoods and that it is a far more land intensive activity than the activities in the non-primary sectors. In addition, land ownership also 'confers collateral in credit markets, security in the event of natural hazards or life contingencies and social status' (Mearns, 1999: p. 1). Those who control land tend to exert a disproportionate influence over other rural institutions, including labour and credit markets. Land control through leasing in is banned in the state of Gujarat, with a few exceptions, but as is the case in many other states, tenancy in the state continues to exist through informal and oral tenancies. There is evidence to show that operational area, which includes area cultivated by leasing in, is less skewed, when seen in comparison with ownership holdings in most states of India (Chadha, Sen and Sharma, 2004).

The issue of access to agricultural land in Gujarat has become all the more important, given the remarkable spurt of growth in agriculture in the last decade. Given the increased profitability of the sector driven by cotton, groundnut, horticultural crops and wheat, along with milk, access to cultivable land has become even more of a crucial element to boost rural livelihood now, compared to the decade of '90s. Land policies in Gujarat have undergone some changes in recent years and seen in their historical contexts, form an essential backdrop to the changes in access to land among different economic and social groups in recent years.

Since distribution of ownership holdings in India is more skewed than distribution of operational holdings, land reform policies, which are very varied in different states of India, provide useful insights to understand the pattern distribution of cultivated land. While the 1948 Land Tenancy Act in the Gujarat granted all land tenants the right to purchase the land they cultivated from the current landlords, the 1957 amendment to the act *simply banned the practice of land tenancy* outright. This ban effectively forced tenants to buy or quit the land, the outcome depending on the tenants' bargaining power with the landlords, which in turn, was influenced by the relative positions of both the landlords and the tenants in the rural socio-economic ladder of the state. Despite the land reform laws' overarching stated objective of the 'land to the tiller', early policies favoured the middle and upper caste farmers and the net effect of devolution of 'surplus' landholdings belonging to Brahmans and other upper castes benefitted the middle castes, and not the lower castes and dalits (McDougal 2007, Sud 2007). There is evidence to believe that the post-independence reforms actually encouraged the middle caste recipients of land to oust agricultural labourers and tenants from their land in order to reduce the latter's legal claim to it (Mohanty 2004 in McDougal 2007). In Gujarat, this process led to the economic dominance of the Patels that continues to this day (Navsarjan 2000 in McDougal 2007). Thus there emerged in the state significant caste and class overlaps in terms of access to agricultural land from the early years after independence, a phenomenon not uncommon in many other states in India.[2]

The 1960 Gujarat Agricultural Land Ceiling Act (ALCA) can be easily considered one among Gujarat's progressive land measures. The Act fixed the maximum land area tenable by a single owner in a rural sector at 132 acres (later reduced to 54 acres in the 1976 amendment) (Jindal 1985 in McDougal 2007) and dictated that the surplus be allotted to dalits, tribal peoples, and Other Backward Castes (OBCs). This act, was however, not a stand-alone measure in the state, but was among similar incentives taken in other parts of the country (Srivastava, 2006). The effect of this act worked towards its end to some degree, at least on paper. There are scholars that assess the implementation of ALCA as more or less a failure in the state (Sud, 2007). Even the less severe interpreters of the implementation of ALCA argue that the outcome was not uniformly positive, as while ALCA may have bolstered intercaste land ownership equity, it increased intracaste inequality (McDougal, 2007). McDougal also shows higher and increased inequalities among the scheduled castes, then among the scheduled tribes, followed by the OBCs and other social groups, in Gujarat, and argues that intracaste inequalities are probably inevitable, when a society adopts measures to convert a 'ranked' society to an 'unranked' one.[3] The more favoured among a marginalized socio-economic group probably commonly benefit disproportionately from a policy meant for the upliftment of the group as a whole.

Overall, the early land reforms did little to empower the landless agricultural labourer or the lower caste farmers, while the *khedut*s (tillers) who benefitted either from the tenancy or ceiling reforms were the state's socially and politically powerful rich and middle classes. The neo-urbanizing entrepreneurial classes have been seen as having their roots linked to the *khedut* identity and economic base of agricultural land (Sud, 2007). Agriculture and industry have been closely interwoven in terms of capital and management for a few decades now, as field evidences in South Gujarat sugarcane economy elaborates (Bremen, 1989).

It is significant that during the period of a full term Government of a Congress, backward caste leader, Madhavsing Solanki, government between 1980 and 1985, who was a KHAM (Kshatriyas, Harijans, Adivasis and Muslims) alliance representative, there was an attempt to review the land policy to make it pro-poor by setting up the Jinabhai Darji Commission (Shah, 2002). The Commission's report not only suggested land redistribution from large landowners, who had been subverting ceiling laws by dividing land among family members, to dalits, but also recommended expansion of the Tenancy Act to include within its scope the non-tiller landowners, who were to be made to surrender the land to their cultivating tenants. The report also emphasized that the existing rule of the owner-tiller residing within eight kilometers should be strictly enforced. This report was never tabled, however, a fact that has been seen as a failure of a pro-poor government to 'shake the entrenched dominant interests in Gujarat's land' (Sud, 2007: p. 617).

The last decade of 90s has seen attempts of land liberalization by all political parties. Scholars have seen a rightward shift of Gujarat's political economy and have characterized it as being more conservative compared to the environment after independence (Mukta 2002 in Sud 2007). There has been an overarching and increasing emphasis on the need for corporatizing the state's agricultural policy.[4] The actual implementation of a range of agricultural policies, that were directly or indirectly linked to agricultural land or use of such land, were however implemented by the Gujarat Government over the last two decade, many of which have been lauded for leading to Gujarat's remarkable agricultural growth in the last few years (Shah et. al, 2009). Among these are:

1. Amendment of Agricultural Produce Marketing Committee (APMC) Act, enabling farmers to directly sell to wholesalers.
2. Direct capital subsidy offers to set-up greenhouses.
3. Unbundling of Gujarat Agricultural University into four independent universities to reinvent agricultural extension model.
4. Setting up of a 'Krishi Rath' demonstrating latest agricultural technologies, using audio-visual aids.
5. Investments in Narmada Valley project to irrigate drought-prone areas of the state.
6. Promotion of a decentralized rainwater harvesting and groundwater recharge work.
7. Jyotigram providing villages 24-hour electricity while regulating electricity for agriculture

Much of the efforts mentioned above can be enjoyed by the agricultural community at large, though some of them benefit the richer farmers more than the smaller and poorer ones.[5] The Narmada Valley project, of course, has been the subject of extensive debates, which among other things focus on the benefits and costs of the project going to different sets of people (Turaga 2000, Rajagopal 2004, Khan 2012). Also, there is very little in this wave of policies that is directed towards the landless, but then, this element is not new in the state's land policy. While these policies appear to benefit the agricultural community at large, the supporting land policies that makes way for the entry of the corporate agro-industry much more explicitly, result in rolling back elements of 'land to the tiller' in land policies.

One of the major land policy shifts that have far-reaching consequences has its roots in the earlier norms of sale and purchase of agricultural land and the way in which 'personal cultivation' was defined by the Land Ceiling Act. The former is a product of the Bombay Tenancy and Agricultural Land Rules (section 2(6)) disallowing sale or purchase of agricultural land beyond a residential limit of 8 kilometers. Later, in the mid-70s, the Land Ceiling Act underwent five changes, most under the leadership of Chimanbhai Patel of the Congress Party between 1973 and 1974. While the more substantive element of the amendments dealt with defining cultivating units, and the way dependent male descendents were treated in this respect, a more innocuous norm that was to be followed in the Land Ceiling Act for defining personal cultivation (failing which land was to be declared surplus and handed over to the government for redistribution) was if a person resided at a distance of within 15 kms from the land, which subsequantly was revised to 8 kms. Significantly, too, an absolute ban was imposed on the purchase of land by a non-agriculturalist whose annual income from other sources exceeded rupees five thousand, even for the purpose of agricultural activities (Government of Gujarat, 1976). These rules that prevented participation of non-local and non-farming groups in agriculture in the '70s, protected the interests of the then landed *Patidars*. With their transition to urban high-end occupations, made smoother by the general environment of liberalization, this provision not only lost its significance for the same interest group/s, but actually went against their interests. Ironically, the first Adivasi Chief Minister, albeit due to pressure from upper and class BJP and Janata Dal, 'used the drought years of 1987-89 to change the 8 kilometer rule for drought affected areas' (Sud, 2007: p. 622). This change was made to ostensibly protect the interest of drought hit marginalized farmers, facilitating the process of sale of land for them. The more substantive benefit implicitly accrued to the previously land-owning and now urbanized entrepreneurs, who were interested in not only investing in agricultural land for evading taxes, but also in converting agricultural land to non-agricultural land and this change enabled them to achieve some of these ends. In addition, they got the benefit of purchasing these lands at low prices as a result of distress sale due to the natural disaster. This move set the tone for changes in policy directions for land markets much before the formal opening up of the economy in the country, and was a precursor to the actual liberalization of policies of agricultural land undertaken in the early 2000.

There were attempts to universalize the lifting of the 8 km rule in the early part of 1990, by both Janata Party-BJP and Janata Party-Congress Governments, but without success (Sud, 2007). The first BJP Government in 1995 in its very first Legislative Assembly scrapped the 8 km rule by proposing a Tenancy Bill amending the Bombay Tenancy and Agricultural

Land Act of 1956. The pressure to do so came from two sections, the rich farmers and agro-industrialists of the current times, whose identities were not necessarily distinctly separable a generation back. The specific reasons for this pressure, other than it being consistent with corporatization of agriculture were:

- Narmada project gave rise to speculative land markets in the proposed command area, and the lifting of the ban allowed the rich farmers from all across the state to purchase land relatively cheaply and sell it off at a high price later or use it for growing high value crops with the available irrigation.
- Demand from builders and agro-industrialists for purchasing agricultural land in the vicinity of urban areas which were growing fast leading to increased demands for residential and commercial purposes.

The land transfers were made possible at the cost of local cultivators, particularly those needing ready cash to non-local agriculturalists and agro-industrialists. A decade after lifting of the 8 km ban, the Gujarat Government brought about a significant policy change with respect to transfer of village commons to private parties, impacting the landless depending on livestock in a significant way. On May 17, 2005, Gujarat issued a Government Resolution[6] to bring wastelands under cultivation inviting big corporate houses and large farmers to initiate corporate farming in a significant way (Barwada and Mahajan, 2006). 'Wastelands' commonly constitutes pasture land in Gujrat, where the pressure of livestock is increasing faster than most other states in the country. Other than the facts that White Revolution brought the state into the reckoning for demonstrating successful operationalization of a sustainable rural livelihood model to the rest of rural India, and that milk has been a major driver of the recent spurt of agricultural growth in the state, livestock form an insurance for survival in semi-arid part of the state, where agriculture is uncertain and gives little return. This move of transferring commons is likely to impact a large number of landless and small farmers, dispossessing them of their limited supply of common property resource.

Changes in Gujarat's land policies have become explicitly consistent with a liberalized regime that is moving towards corporatization of agriculture. It has not only facilitated transfer through sale of agricultural land to non-locals and non-agriculturalists, the access of agro-industrial activities to common property land resources are being actively promoted by the state government, disposing the marginalized of their *defacto* and *dejure* rights to it. While these moves could have positive impacts on growth *via* private investment in agricultural infrastructure, it could also lead to distress of the land poor, particularly in unfavourable conditions. Privatization of commons, thus could lead to futher marginalization of the landless, specifically in areas with high incidence of poverty.

3. Agricultural Performance in Gujarat

This section attempts to assess the significance of the agricultural sector within the Gujarat economy in general and explore its nature and characteristics. The specific focus has been to look into the recent trends experienced by the agrarian economy and its probable linkages with recent changes in the policy frame.

3.1 Data and Methodology

Although there has been the problem of unavailability of recent data for comparable periods across all the variables employed in this analysis, attempts have been made to maintain consistency. Data on land use and cropping pattern have been obtained from the Department of Agriculture & Cooperation, Directorate of Economics and Statistics for the period spanning from 1990-91 to 2009-10 for the state level aggregates and upto 2006-07 for the sub-regional levels. The time series data on state domestic product by the industry of origin published by the Central Statistics Organization (CSO) pertaining to 1980-81 to 2009-10 and population figures provided by Census of India (various years) have been employed to look into the dynamics of the economy broadly. Further, the item-wise contribution of the various agricultural outputs in value terms published by CSO have been used pertaining to the period Triennium Ending (TE) 1992-93 to TE 2008-09 to analyse the shift in the contribution of the various sectors of the agricultural economy.

3.2 Dynamics of Agricultural Land-use

Changes in land use pattern has been conceived as the manifestation of the interplay of environmental factors, manner of resource utilization and policy frame that steer the direction of resource use. While natural forces are pervasive and often not very evident, the socio-political and economic factors are by far much more prominent and perceptible.

There has been a shift in Gujarat's land policy from ideas of 'land to the tillers' to those of 'land deregulation and liberalization' over the past two decades (Sud, 2007). Such modification, on one hand tacitly encouraged speculative land transactions in the prospective canal commands and urban peripheries, and on the other hand have facilitated conversions of common wastelands lands to private cultivated land. It is therefore relevant to account for the inventory of stock of land and understand the dynamics operative in the land use categories with a focus on livelihood. The nine-fold categories evolved by the Department of Agriculture and Cooperation in India have been grouped to have a meaningful appreciation of the emerging land use changes.[7]

The trends experienced by the stock of agricultural land is perhaps most valuable from the livelihood perspective as about a little less than half of total rural workers continue to depend upon agriculture. The forests, pastures and common grazing lands are also important for rural livelihoods, more so for the rural poor, as access to these common resources in some way compensate for the low asset ownership of the poor (Jodha, 1990). Clearly, reduced access of the rural population to either of Total Cultivable Land or de facto Common Property Resources (CPR) through any norm or institution or policy change would affect those dependent upon land resources for sustenance. On the other hand, cultivable wasteland may be conceived as a potential stock of agricultural land that through proper management may be brought under the plough. With rapid development of infrastructure and urbanization land under non-agricultural uses have been on the rise. The issue therefore lies in the study of the direction of transformation of the different categories of land uses. Any intervention that might lead to a decline in the share of land-use categories that bear critical implications for livelihoods has to be undertaken with caution. Within this frame of analysis in mind the pattern of land utilization in Gujarat in comparison to India has been analysed for the period pertaining to TE 1990-91 to TE 2008-09.

The share of total land not available for cultivation has been higher in Gujarat compared to India during all the time periods and this has been mostly on account of the share of barren land in Gujarat (Table 5.1). Though fallows have been remarkably low in Gujarat compared to that in India, underutilization of land has been very high, almost double that at all India level on account of culturable waste lands. Both the stock of cultivable land as well as land under productive agricultural uses has been higher in Gujarat relative to India. The shares of the different land use categories have not displayed any remarkable change during the study period and have essentially stagnated in Gujarat. However, the growth rates of the different categories display some variations. Total cropped area, net sown area and area under non-agricultural uses have registered increase (Figure 5.1) while there has been negative growth in the de facto CPR principally on account of decline in the long-term fallows. However, the pastures and grazing lands have revealed positive growth rates perhaps indicating transfers from the long-term fallow lands.

Figure 5.1: Growth Rate of Land Uses in Gujarat, 1998-99 to 2006-07

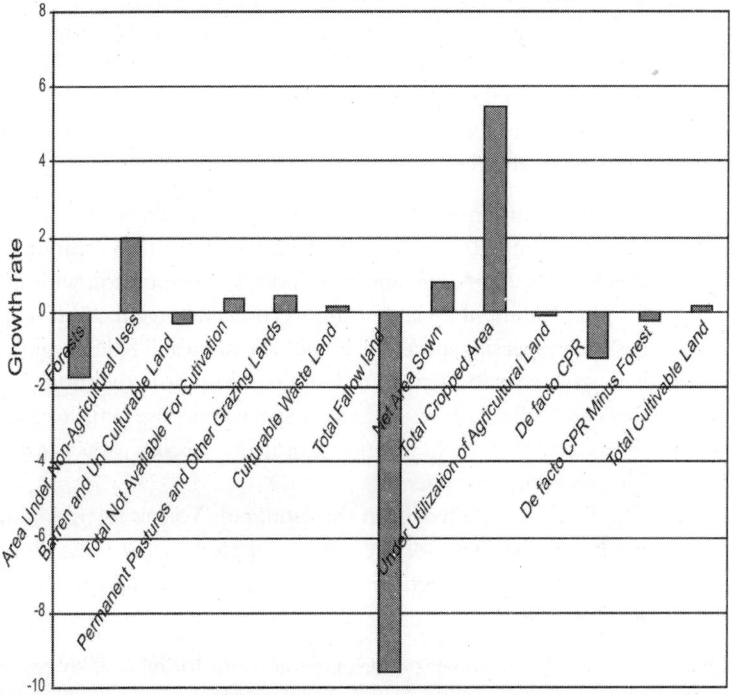

A study at the subregional levels has not reveled any notable trends in the pattern of land utilization in Gujarat. However, there have been changes in the area reported between 1998-99 to 2006-07 which is indeed confusing and calls for deeper probe.[8] This comes as somewhat surprising given that there have been remarkable changes in the land policies in addition to significant changes within the structure of the economy in terms of both workforce as well as state domestic product.

3.3 A Brief Overview of Irrigation

The priority of the Indian plan periods has been expansion of irrigation to tide over the instability of the rainfall that affects agriculture. Since the inception of the state of Gujarat, its state government has devoted substantial budgetary resources to the construction of major and medium canal irrigation projects. The Sardar Sarovar Project (SSP) on the Narmada has been hailed as the lifeline of Gujarat (Shah et. al, 2009). However, the share of NSA that is irrigated has been much lower compared to the India levels between TE 2001-02 and TE 2008-09 and the chief source of irrigation in Gujarat has been groundwater (Table 5.2). Keeping view of the heavy dependence upon wells and tubewells, the Gujarat Government have emphasized upon management of the groundwater economy. There have been three remarkable strategies undertaken for managing the groundwater economy (see Shah et. al, 2009):

(a) The government has encouraged decentralized rainwater harvesting and ground water recharge work through creation of check dams, *bori-bandhs* and farm ponds in association with the farming communities and non-governmental organization. This has been especially successful in the Saurashtra and Kutch regions.
(b) The government promoted micro-irrigation technologies through a subsidy-loan scheme. A special purpose vehicle called the Gujarat Green Revolution Company (GGRC) was created for executing this scheme.
(c) The final strategy has been the Jyotigram Yojana for rationing uninterrupted high voltage power supply to rural areas along separate feeders for agriculture, non-agricultural enterprises and for domestic uses.

The central and southern parts of Gujarat account for highest shares of net sown area irrigated and the Kutch and Saurashtra region account for lower shares of Net Sown Area (NSA) covered by irrigation (Figure 5.2). The central and southern parts are covered by the canal irrigation systems and the rest depends upon groundwater sources. In the recent years, the increase in the extent of irrigation has taken place primarily in the Saurashtra region (Figure 5.3). Even the irrigation intensity has been

Figure 5.2: Irrigation Extent in Gujarat: 2006-07

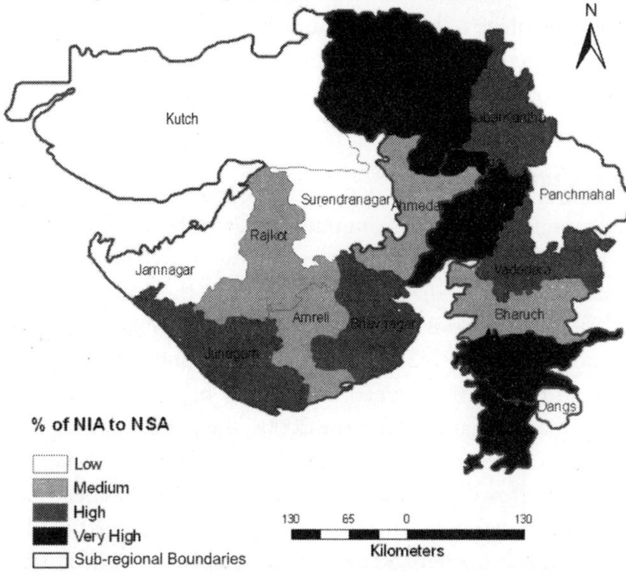

Irrigation Extend = Net Irrigated Area/Net Shown Area

Figure 5.3: Percentage Change in Irrigation Extent in Gujarat: TE 1998-99 to TE 2006-07

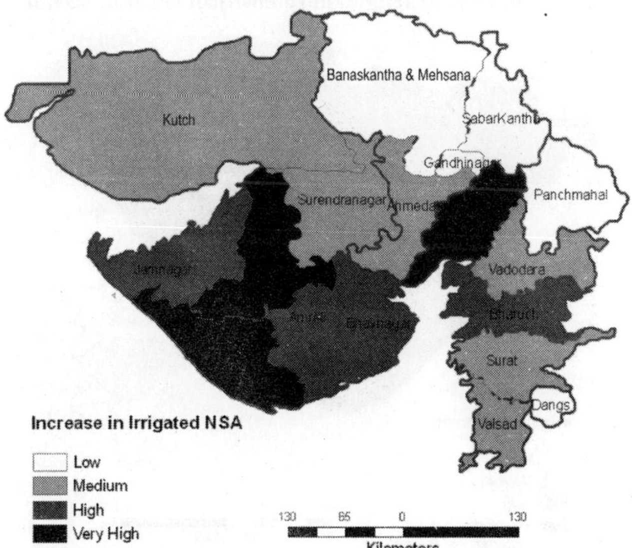

highest in the Kutch and Saurashtra region during the recent years (Figure 5.4). It may be observed that the Saurashtra and Kutch region although have been currently maintaining low irrigation level, the growth and intensity of irrigation use have been remarkably high in these parts of Gujarat.

3.4 Agricultural Growth

The per capita NSDP of Gujarat and its growth rate have been much higher than that of India and its rate of growth have been much higher compared to that of India ever since 1961 upt the recent times (Figure 5.5). Between the 1980-81 and the early 1990s in Gujarat the per capita NSDP and agricultural NSDP per rural population have moved almost parallely and then have diverged, the former beginning to increase at a rate higher than the latter. After the 2000s, the per capita state domestic product registered dramatic growth while agriculture sector have virtually stagnated. The growth rates of the agricultural NSDP has been extremely fluctuating in Gujarat much more than that experienced at the India level there by denoting remarkable in stability in Gujrat agriculture (Figure 5.6). Instability of agricultural production has been high in Gujarat due to low proportion of area under irrigation and high dependence on rain-

Figure 5.4: Gujarat Irrigation Intensity in Gujarat, 2006-07

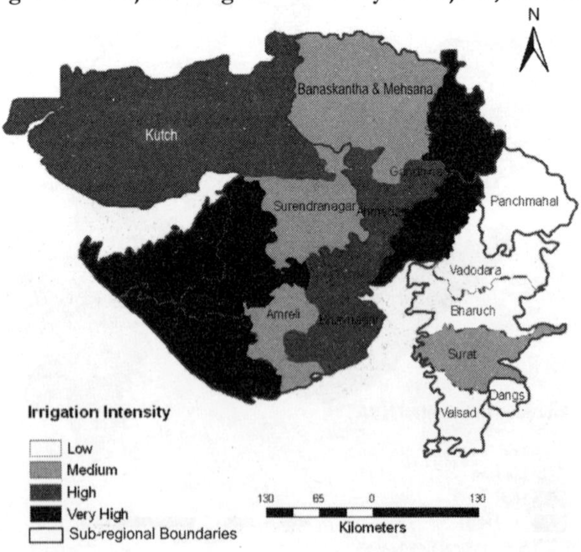

fed agriculture under semi-arid conditions. Nonetheless, the value of output of agriculture and allied sector has been increasing albeit negotiating fluctuations (Figure 5.7).

Figure 5.5: Per Capita Net Domestic Product (at 2004-05 constant prices) 1980-81 to 2009-10

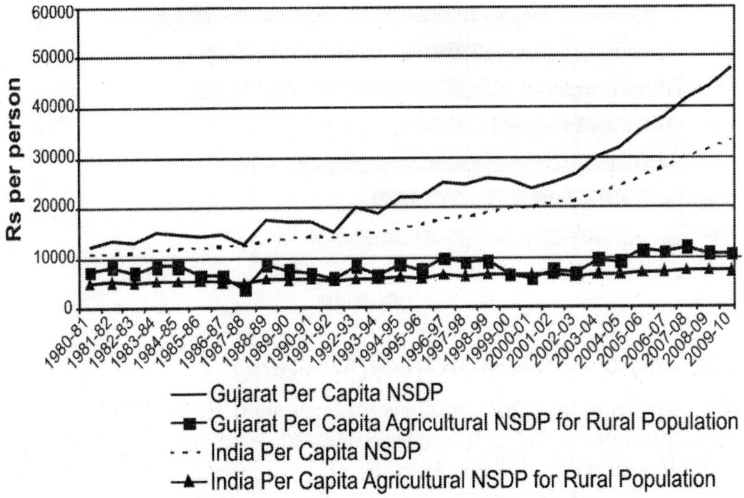

Figure 5.6: Growth Rate of Agricultural NSDP (at 2004-05 constant prices) 1980-81 to 2009-10

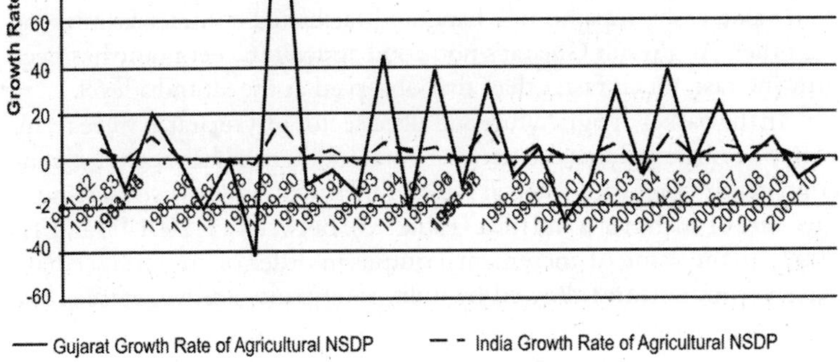

Figure 5.7: Value of Output of Agriculture & Allied (2004-05 Constant Prices): Gujarat

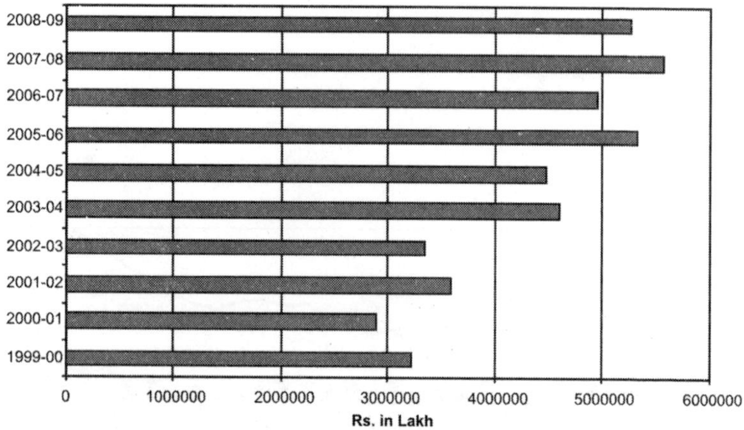

3.4a Chief Drivers of Agricultural Growth

The growth in the agricultural sector may stem from growth in area under plough or through enhancement of yield or both. Although technological revolution has been the pivot for any agricultural change, what has been a prerequisite for any of these to take place has been favourable policy frame that would in effect, directly or indirectly improve market access, disseminate affordable technology and provide proper infrastructure including road, irrigation and power. Studies tend to suggest that the nature of growth experienced by the agricultural sector in Gujarat has been largely the result of state intervention at various levels in facilitating and encouraging farmers. The market reforms undertaken by the state to enable farmers to directly sell their produce to wholesalers, exporters and large trading companies i.e., without operating through commission agents have acted as an inducement to farmers to cultivate high value cash crops on one hand and facilitated contract farming on the other. As a result Gujarat's non-food agricultural economy has been growing fast, much faster than that observed at the all India level.

In the basket of agriculture and allied sector of Gujarat in value terms it may be observed that the share of total food grains has been declining consistently from the 1990s till recent times with progressive increase in the share of cash crops and milk (Table 5.3). Between TE 2001-02 and TE 2009-10, the value of incremental output in order of importance have arisen from cotton followed by milk, total fruits and vegetables and groundnut which have emerged as the chief drivers of agricultural growth in the recent times (Table 5.4). Infact, milk constitutes one fifth of the value of total agriculture and allied and more than 80 per cent of total value of livestock. During the last seven years, growth of value has been highest for cotton followed by the horticultural crops, total oilseeds spearheaded by groundnut and milk.[9]

The share of total food grains to total area cultivated in Gujarat have been lower than the national averages through all the trienniums and the shares have been declining (Table 5.5). Non-food crops have been fast replacing the food crops in terms of acreage as well as value. Allocation of land for any particular crop is usually impacted by the minimum support price regulation besides trade policies related to the agricultural sector. Availability of irrigation as well as other technical support also guides the cropping pattern of any region. In Gujarat, among the food crops, while acreage of rice has remained almost unchanged, that of the coarse cereals, total cereals and pulses have declined remarkably. Only acreage under wheat has increased from 6.2 per cent in TE 1990-91 to 9.6 per cent in TE 2008-09.

Among the non-food crops, although the acreage under oilseeds has experienced a slight increase during the first period, it has declined to 24 per cent in TE 2008-09 and area under cotton has registered consistent rise (Table 5.6). Looking at the share of area under the broad categories of crops it is evident that total fruits & vegetables, total spices & condiments and fibres have been gaining while the other food crops have been declining (Table 5.7).

3.4b Pattern of Change in the Acreage under the Major Crops

It may be noted that the chief source of non- food crops has been the Kutch and Saurashtra area where the acreage under non-food crops has been the highest (Figure 5.8). This has been the region which accounts for highest area under both cotton (Figure 5.9) and groundnut (Figure 5.10). A high share of the Gross Croped Area (GCA) in the south-central districts of Vadodara and Bharuch also account for cotton cultivation. Recently, there has been slight outflow from area under cotton in the northern district of Panchmahal and Kutch, while there has been high positive growth in area under cotton in the Jamnagar in Saurashtra, Sabarkantha, Vadodara and Gandhinagar (Figure 5.12). In the main, except for Kutch and Panchmahal, the entire Gujarat has registered growth in area under cotton principally on account of improvements in

Figure 5.8: Area under Non-food Crops in Gujarat, 2006-07

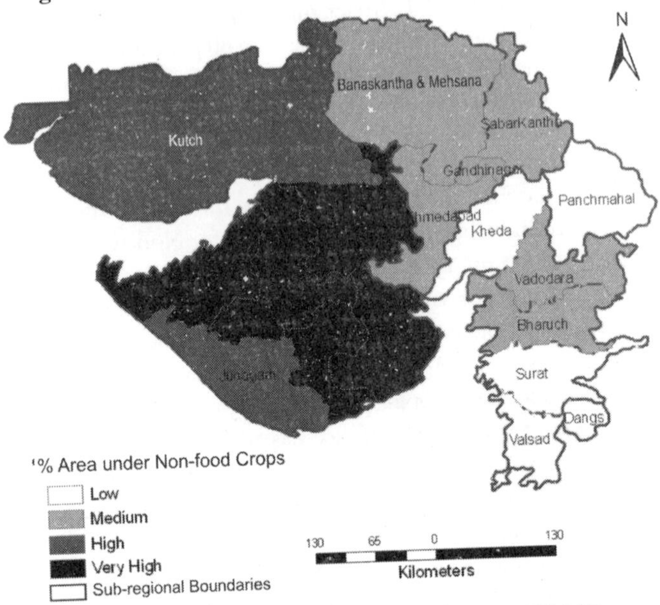

Figure 5.9 : Area under Cotton in Gujarat, 2006-07

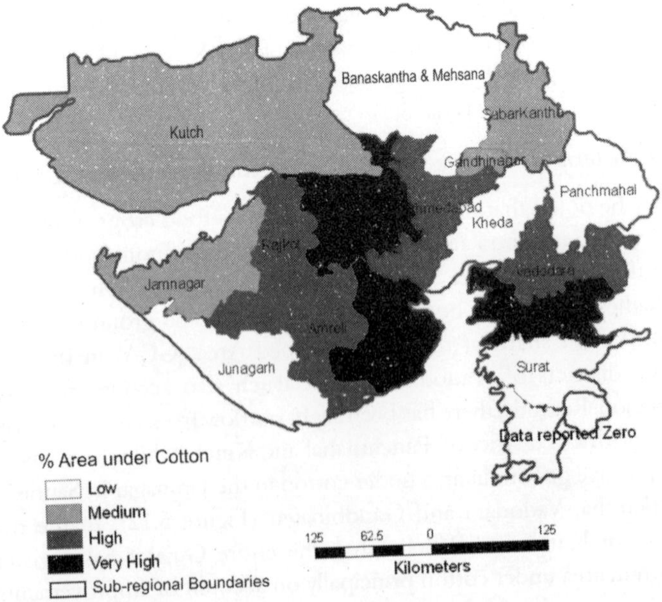

Figure 5.10: Area under Groundnut in Gujarat, 2006-07

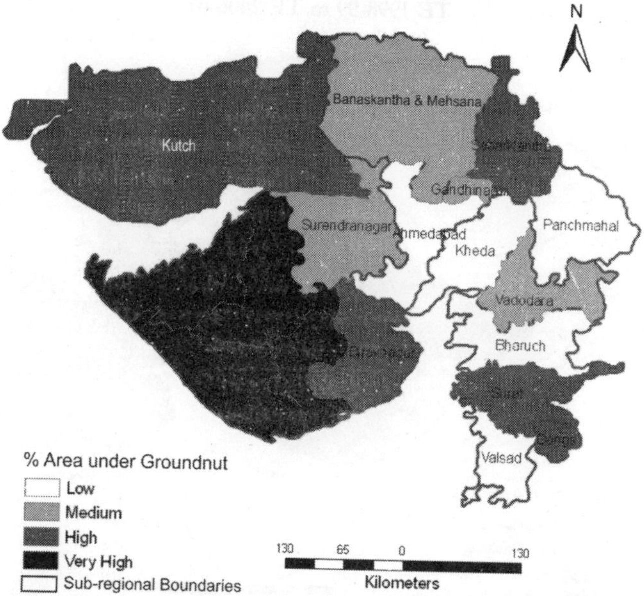

Figure 5.11: Area under Fruits & Vegetables in Gujarat, 2006-07

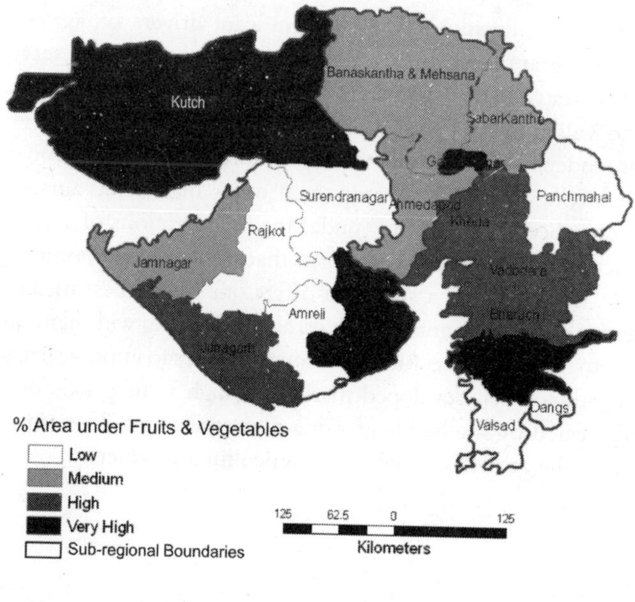

Figure 5.12: Growth Rate of Area under Cotton in Gujarat, TE 1998-99 to TE 2006-07

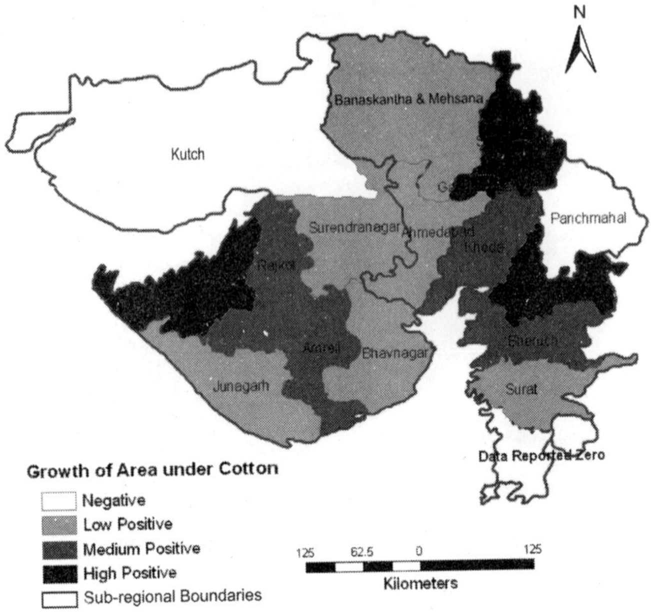

irrigation. The cultivation of other significant drivers of agricultural growth in Gujarat that is total fruits & vegetables has been observed to have concentrated in the Central and Southern districts of Gandhinagar, Surat and Valsad besides Kutch and Bhavnagar (Figure 5.11).

The tendency of the cropping pattern shifting away from food crops and diversifying toward cash crops and other high value agricultural products has been possible only under the preconditions of developed infrastructure and marketing conditions that would render its cultivation profitable. Gujarat being a state that offers one of the best maintained road networks in the country (Shah et. al, 2009) along with high quality electricity to the farming sector and various measures to improve irrigation situation besides well-developed market for high value goods through demand created by the highly growing non-agricultural economy have encouraged the growth of high value agricultural products.

3.4c Production of the Major Crops in Gujarat

In terms of production, while Gujarat's share in the national output of total food grains has remained unchanged, the share of wheat alone has registered an increase. Among the non-food crops, the shares of groundnut and cotton to the Indian total have increased remarkably from about 1/5th to 1/3rd of the national output (Table 5.8). The growth in cotton has taken place primarily owing to the spread of Bt cotton in Gujarat that has remarkably enhanced the yield levels besides area expansion under irrigated cotton. High procurement price of cotton coupled with high volumes of procurement from the state have also encouraged the farmers to shift in favour of cotton cultivation.

The fact that Cotton Corporation of India has a sizeable procurement of cotton from Gujarat and that cotton enjoys highly remunerative MSP from the centre serves as a further inducement to the farmers to allocate land in favour of cotton in Gujarat (Shah et. al, 2009). The production increase in wheat has been again due to both area expansion and yield increase although the yield fluctuation has been noteworthy. The improvements in the irrigation conditions promoted by the state through encouragement of decentralized water harvesting and micro-irrigation initiatives in the groundwater irrigated areas have been instrumental in the expansion of allocation of irrigated crops, especially cotton and wheat. The production of groundnut has been negotiating fluctuations owing to rainfall conditions but largely has remained a significant crop in Gujarat's agricultural basket through the last three decades.

The major crops of Gujarat have been compared with that of Maharashtra and Karnataka which share similar cropping pattern and agro-climatic characteristics. Production of total food grain in Gujarat has been lower than that in the other two states and the year to year fluctuation in output has been of moderate nature (Figure 5.13). The instability of production of foodgrain and cotton has reduced in the recent years as has been the case with Karnataka which is comparable with Gujarat in terms of agro- climate as well as cropping pattern (Table 9). The production of output of wheat (Figure 5.14) and cotton (Figure 5.15) has been higher in Gujarat compared to the other two states especially since 2004-05. In case of groundnut Gujarat has surpassed the other two states in terms of output. The most remarkable trend has been the high fluctuation in Gujarat's output levels. Comparing the coefficient of variation of production of cotton and total foodgrains

Figure 5.13: Production of Total Foodgrains

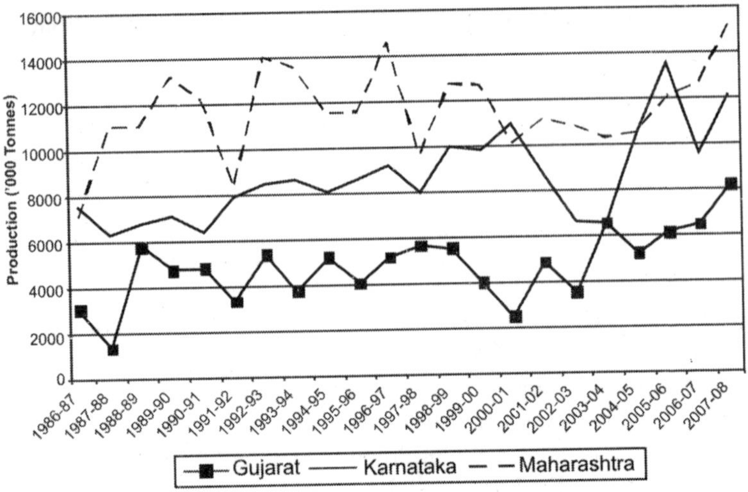

Figure 5.14: Production of Wheat

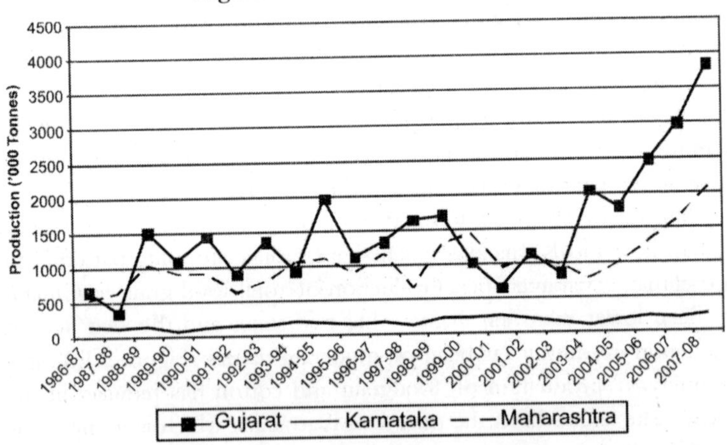

Figure 5.15: Production of Cotton

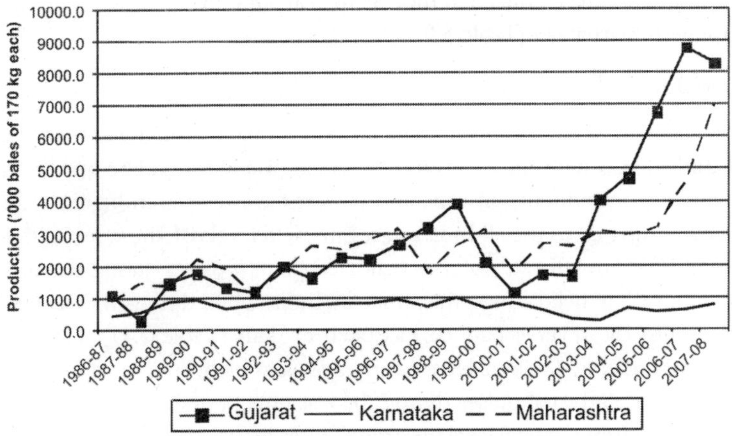

Figure 5.16: Production of Groundnut

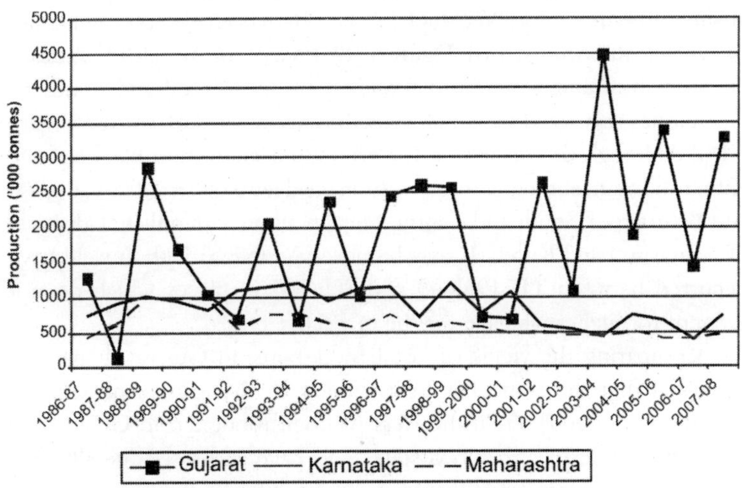

for Karnataka, India and Gujarat it may be observed that the instability of production has reduced in the recent years in Gujarat as has been the case with Karnataka (Table 5.9).

3.4d Yield of the Major Crops in Gujarat

The yield levels of total foodgrains in Gujarat have been lower than the all India levels with the exception of wheat (Table 5.10). The non-food grains like groundnut, oilseeds and cotton have registered higher yield levels compared to the all India aggregate yield levels of these respective crops. The growth rates of the major crops in Gujarat during the first triennium has been lower than that in India while during the second triennium the reverse pattern has been evident (Table 5.11). Growth rates of yield in Gujarat have been especially high in case of cotton, ground nut and total pulses during the last time period.

At the sub- regional level the growth rates of yield of total foodgrains have been negative in the Junagarh from Saurashtra region, Sabarkantha and Gandhinagar in the Northern districts and in Surat from among the Southern districts. Within Saurashtra however, there has been medium positive growth of yield. Very high growths have been observed in Dangs, Bhavnagar and Ahmedabad (Figure 5.18). Except for Amreli, the districts of Saurashtra and Kutch and few districts of Central and Southern Gujarat has registered very high growth rates of yield of cotton (Figure 5.18). Although the main area for groundnut cultivation has been the Kutch and Saurashtra region, growths in yield have occurred in Vadodara and Bharuch of South and Central Gujarat along with only few districts of Saurashtra and Kutch. It may be observed that growth in yield have occurred between TE 1998-99 and 2006-07 in places which do not account for highest acreage for the respective crops.

Comparing the yields of total foodgrains, in Gujarat, it may be observed that the trend has been similar to that of Karnataka and Gujarat and after 2005-06 the yield of total foodgrain in Gujarat has risen above that of other two states and have surpassed the all India levels hitherto not reached (Figure 5.20). Specifically, the yield of wheat in Gujarat that has surpassed the other two states throughout the study period and ever since 2003-04, its production of wheat has shot up in Gujarat (Figure 5.21).

Among the non-food crops, the production as well as yield of cotton has been high and increasing in Gujarat throughout the study period and

Figure 5.17: Growth Rate of Yield of Total Foodgrain in Gujarat, TE 1998-99 to TE 2006-07

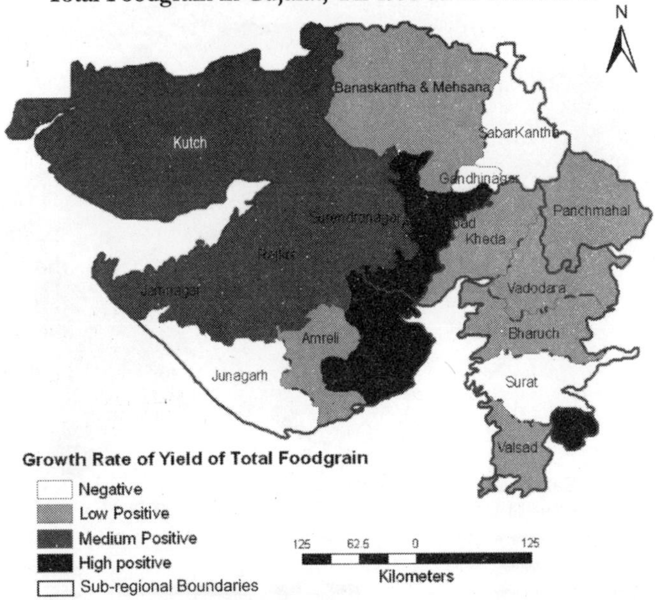

Figure 5.18: Growth Rate of Yield of Cotton in Gujarat, TE 1998-99 to TE 2006-07

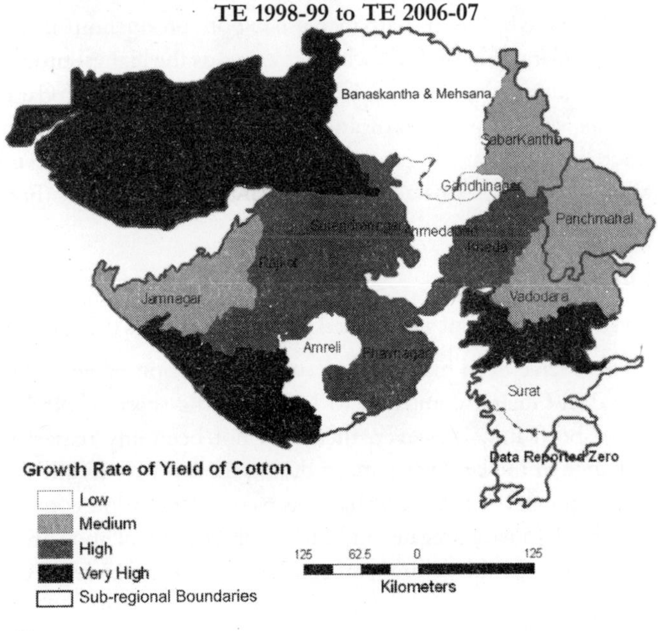

Fig 5.19: Gujarat Growth Rate of Yield of Groundnut TE 1998-99 to TE 2006-07

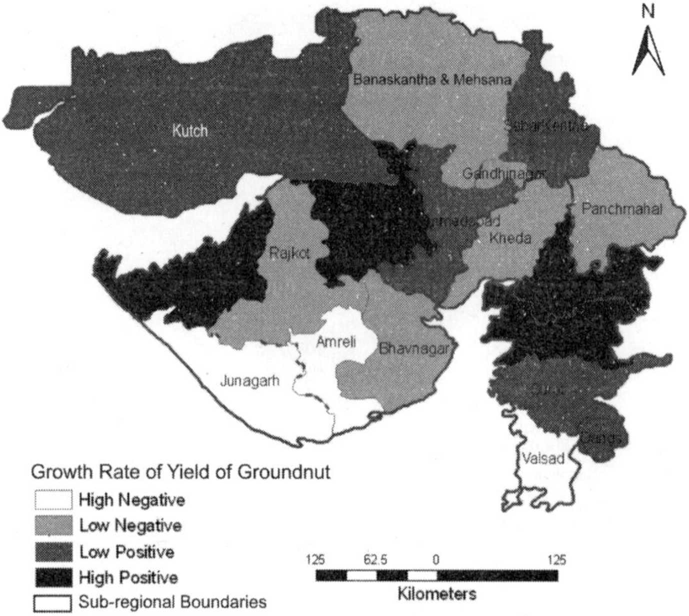

after 2003-04 there has been sharp increase in both production and yield of cotton in Gujarat (Figure 5.22) which emerged as the highest producer of cotton in India during 2007-08. The other important crop of Gujarat that accounts for 36.8 per cent of India's total output, groundnut, have maintained its high production as well as yield levels relative to Maharashtra as well as Karnataka, but reveals intense fluctuations (Figure 5.23).

3.5 Summing up

The analysis of the Gujarat agricultural parameters reveals the following:

- There have been high levels of under utilization of agricultural land in Gujarat compared to India and the share of NSA has also been low. However, there has not been any remarkable change in the land use pattern during the last two decades.
- Irrigation levels in Gujarat have been considerably low compared to the all India aggregates and it is heavily dependent upon ground water except the central and southern districts which are canal

Figure 5.20: Yield of Total Foodgrains

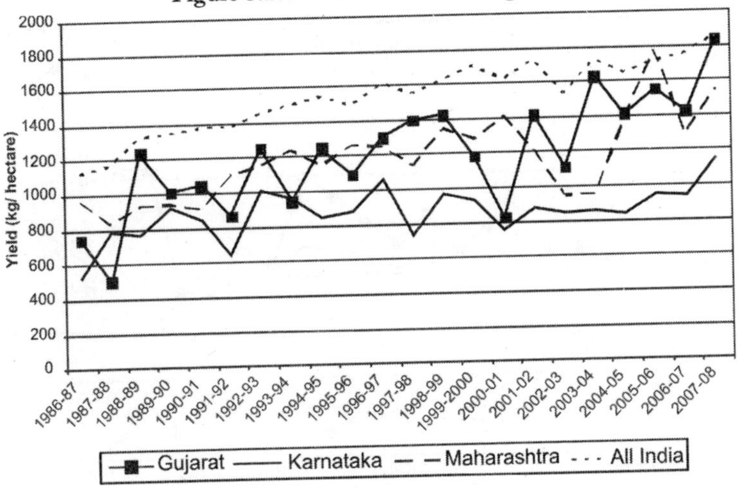

Figure 5.21: Yield of Wheat

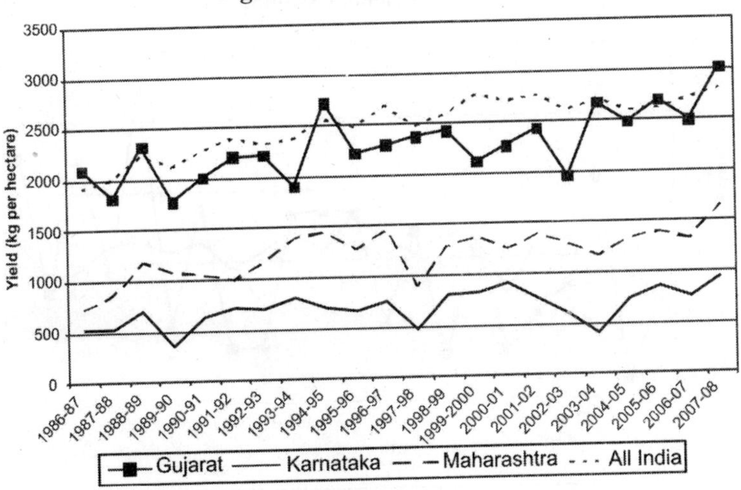

irrigated. However, the intensity of irrigation has been very high in the Saurashtra and Kutch region compared to the rest of Gujarat which indicates that this has been the region that needs to be included within the canal command to arrest groundwater depletion.

- There have been notable shifts towards cash crops and high value

Figure 5.22: Yield of Cotton

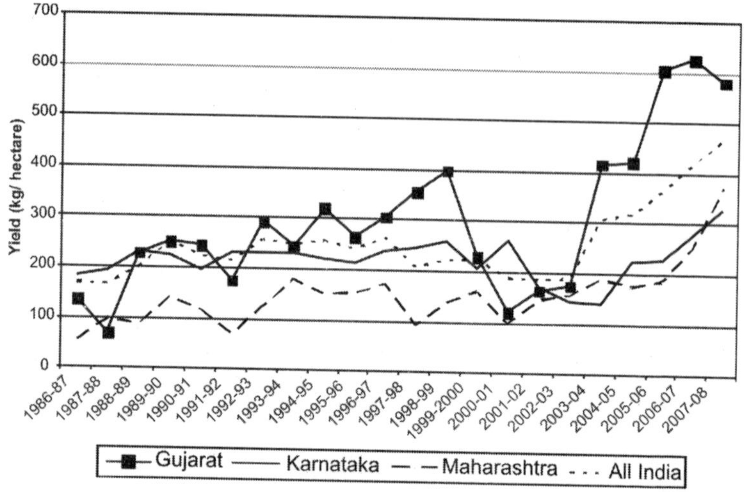

Figure 5.23: Yield of Ground Nut

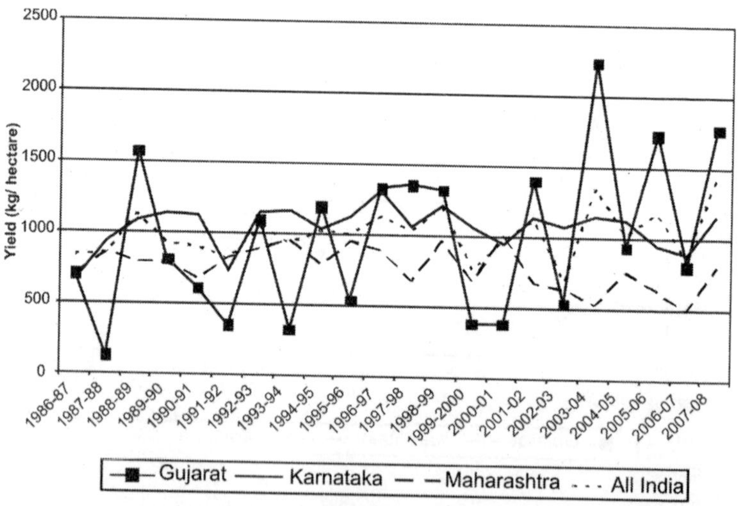

agricultural products at the cost of declining shares of foodgrains in terms of acreage, output and value.

- The recent growth in the agricultural sector has been primarily driven by both growth in area and high yield levels for cotton.

Milk, fruits & vegetables and groundnut have been the other drivers of agricultural growth.

- The chief agricultural region has been the Saurashtra and Kutch region that account for majority of the non-food crops. The central and southern districts have emerged as prominent areas cultivating fruits & vegetables.
- In the recent years, instability of production of foodgrain and cotton has reduced marginally but groundnut continues to register violent fluctuations in terms of both yield and production.

The most intriguing feature of the Gujarat economy especially the agricultural sector has been its intense instability. Many scholars argue that continued heavy dependence on rainfed agriculture in large parts of the state that still lack adequate irrigation has been one of the significant factors contributing to the unstable nature of the agricultural sector as Indian monsoon itself behaves erratically. Heavy dependence on groundwater sources perhaps has been another factor leading to volatility as these sources fail to yield irrigation water on the face of drought as the aquifers run dry. The cash crop driven growth of Gujarat agriculture has been yet another source of fluctuation as this feature essentially links the sector to the market fluctuations at both national and global levels.

4. The Spread Effects: An Inclusive Growth Story or Signs of an Unequal Beginning?

What emerges very clearly from the preceding section is that the unprecedented growth in Gujarat has made agriculture in the state much more profitable in recent years. This is probably even more remarkable given the semi-arid agro-climatic location of the state, as well as the rapid decline in importance of agriculture in the state. While the general consensus about a positive association between land and rural livelihood remains valid, there is no doubt that given the current context of agricultural boom in the state, access to agricultural land has become of crucial importance more than ever before. It is generally observed that when land productivity increases, inequalities in land distribution tend to increase, if not through sale or purchase of land, assuredly through the land lease market. Punjab and Haryana, where reverse tenancy is observed in recent years are cases in point. Gujarat's context is quite different, however, and among other things, tenancy is not legal in the state, where as in Punjab and Haryana, transfer through lease is not only legal, but almost completely done through cash exchanges. Incidence of tenancy in Gujarat is likely to be much lower to begin with and probably likely to decline further due to increased profitability of agriculture in recent years. In this context, it becomes important to understand the finer changes of access to agricultural land across economic and social groups. A related but somewhat different aspect of distribution of benefits of growth would be participation of various categories of farmers in crops that have driven the growth of agriculture in the state. Lastly, it would be relevant to look at not only changes in share of the landless in the state, i.e. those who the agricultural growth process may have by and large bypassed, but also at the changes in their economic status in relation to the landed in the larger context of growth and liberalization.

4.1 Data Sources and Limitations

The data sources that have been used for this section are Agricultural Census and National Sample Survey Organization (Employment Unemployment Rounds 50th, 61st and 66th rounds). There are a few limitations of this kind of analysis. Firstly, land markets are 'sticky' in India and do not show rapid changes over time. Concepts of operational holding and cultivated land have been thus used instead of ownership holding and owned land for the most part, which are somewhat more amenable to short spans of temporal analysis. However, tenancy is legally banned with a few exceptions in the state, and therefore the actual tenancy, which constitutes a part of operational holding, is likely to be under-reported. Secondly, while SC/ST access to agricultural land and participation in important crops across farm sizes depend on Agricultural Census data and span from 1995-96 to 2005-06, the NSSO data that analyse landlessness and its overlaps with poverty span for the most part from 2004-05 (61st round) to 2009-10 (66th round). Some comparisons had been done with 1993-94 (50th round), but they are restricted to the state level changes due to comparability problems at the sub-regional levels.

4.2 Inequality in Land Distribution

The land distribution of cultivated land in Gujarat is more equal than that of India (Table 5.12, see annexure). There has been little change in the period between 1995-96 and 2005-06 in terms of overall land distribution. The Lorenz curves reveal that the distribution of land has become marginally more unequal in 2005-06 compared to 1995-96 in the state, while the reverse is true for India.

A detailed analysis of the land distribution reveals some changes that are not drastic but still of some significance.

Due to population pressure, holdings have become smaller in India, with larger size classes losingout and smaller holdings gaining both in terms of shares of households and area. This change is visible for most parts of the country, and does not reflect any structural change in land relations. The changes in Gujarat, however, are notably different from those in India in two major ways (Table 5.12):

- The smallest size classes have gained far more in terms of shares of household than area.
- The largest size class has gained in terms of area, by over 1 per cent point.

The former deviation of the state from the country pattern implies that the average size of marginal holdings is becoming smaller, relative to India (Table 5.12, see annexure). This may be indicative of this smallest size classes leasing out or selling out parts of their land. On the other hand, the largest size category, above 20 hectares has gained in terms of area, though not in terms of number of holdings. Though this increase is by a little above 1 per cent of the land held by this category, it can be said with a fair degree of certainty that this trend implies accumulation of land through leasing in or sale over these ten years. This effect of this can be observed in terms of a substantial increase in the average size of holding (by more than 8 hectares) held by farmers having more than 20 hectares of land between 1995-96 and 2005-06. The above changes in the state's land distribution is significant on three counts; first, because it goes against the general wave of land-sizes becoming smaller due to population pressure in the country; second, in view of the 1995 lifting of the 8 km ban for purchasing land and third, in the backdrop of the recent growth in agriculture in the state that has made land more profitable than before (Shah et. al 2009).

Both Gujarat and India have lower share of SC households having access to agricultural land when compared with their respective shares in total population (Table 5.13). This pattern is consistent with the existing literature and general understanding of marginalization of scheduled caste population in the hierarchy of rural social order in the country (Mearns 1999, McDougal, 2007). This gap widens significantly as one moves to the higher size classes, both for the country and the state.

In terms of change in access of operational landholding of the SC population, there are two deviations in Gujarat's trend when compared with that of India (Table 5.13).

1. SCs have lost out both in terms of shares in households and area in the smaller size groups between 1995-96 and 2005-06 in Gujarat, while this group has gained during the same time period with respect to the two smallest categories in both respects in India.
2. SCs have gained in large size category in Gujarat while their counterparts have lost out in the same size category at the all India level over time.

The two above differences imply that the inequality among the SC group has increased more in relation to the other social groups. This finding is consistent with that of other studies (McDougal, 2007), which found increasing inequalities among SCs between 1982 and 1992. Though this trend has been explained by appropriation of disproportionate benefits by the better offs in socially marginalized groups, what is of greater concern here is increasing marginalization of a social group that were already in the margins.

The share of scheduled tribes having access to operational holding is lower when compared to their share in population in Gujarat for all size classes, particularly in the lowest size class (Table 5.14). This observation is not true of India. They further lose out somewhat over time (2005-06 over 1995-96) in the state over time, while the position of their counterparts remains constant in the country between the same periods.

The above observations point towards the fact that the marginalized social groups are more so with respect to access to cultivated land in Gujarat relative to that in the country. Over a period of time, their position has worsened in the state, whereas in India, SCs have become better off, and the STs have maintained a status quo. The only exception is with respect to the SCs in the highest size class, who have gained in the state. A more detailed analysis at the sub-regional as well as based on primary surveys is required to understand whether a political trade-off exists between the SCs losing out at the lower end and gaining in the higher end.

4.3 Participation of Farmers in the Cotton, Groundnut and Horticultural Crops across Farm-size Categories

The three major drivers of agricultural growth experienced by Gujarat in the last decade are cotton, groundnut and fruits & vegetables. Participation of the farmers in these crops can be treated as a proxy variable to the nature of profits earned across farm size categories. Also, their dependence on a crop that is associated with production or price risks could provide useful pointers for evaluating existing policies.

Cotton has registered a remarkably high growth in the state, and this can be explained, among other factors, by the increase under the area of irrigated cotton, and by increased adoption of BT cotton. Studies reveal that there is now negligible area under non BT cotton (Gandhi and Namboodiri, 2006). Gujarat has registered a fivefold increase in cotton yield and has in recent years surpassed the world average (Shah et. al 2009). The smaller farmers in the state have substantially lower area under cotton compared to the larger farm sizes (Table 5.15). This is true both of irrigated and unirrigated cotton. The difference across farm sizes is far more in terms of proportion of farmers participating in cotton cultivation than allocation of area under cotton. The above mentioned differences even out marginally over the period of 10 years under consideration.

The reasons for lower participation as well as lower allocation in cotton in spite of their profitability could be, among other things, the high cost of BT cotton cultivation as well as the production instabilities associated with the crop. The difference in cost of cultivation particularly with respect to paid out costs of BT and non BT cotton is significant in the state (Gandhi and Namboodiri, 2006). Also, though first in terms of growth, it is ranked 10th in terms of instability of production among 13 crops considered by a recent study of Gujarat agriculture (Arya and Mehta, 2011).

Similar analysis for groundnut reveals that the differences in both land allocation and participation in the crops cultivation is much less sharp across farm size categories compared with cotton (Table 5.16, see annexure). The difference that is significant is between the marginal and the small farmers' categories beyond which the increases are slow or insignificant for both parameters under consideration. The increase in area under groundnut is very high over the period under consideration for all farm size categories. Groundnut is the 4th crop in terms of growth but 13th in terms of instability, as per a state study on agricultural instability (Arya and Mehta, 2011). The small farmers' participation in this extremely unstable crop exposes these farmers to large risks, and this, along with the possibility of increased cost of accessing tubewell irrigation post Jyotigram scheme (Shah et. al, 2008), make them particularly vulnerable.

Together, fruits & vegetables are the third major driver of Gujarat agricultural growth after cotton and milk. Though the share in area under these two crop groups is small, their contribution in terms of value is substantial (Shah et. al, 2009). The difference of allocation of land and farmers' participation in cultivation of this group of crop is small across all farm size categories (Tables 5.17 & 5.18, see annexure). In case of irrigated vegetables, smaller size groups allocate somewhat higher percentage of land than their larger counterparts. Fruits & vegetables are associated with high price and production risks, and in addition have low shelf life. Marketing of these products usually require a certain threshold production and this is the reason smaller farmers often tend to allocate higher shares of land for their cultivation.

In sum, the smaller farmers do not benefit as much from cotton as the larger farm size categories, as they allocate smaller share of their land and participate in smaller proportion in cultivation of cotton. To some extent, the source of a major profit bypasses the smaller farmers, probably because of high costs of cultivation of BT cotton. Their participation in groundnut and fruits & vegetables is comparable with that of the larger farm size categories with a few exceptions, in spite of high instabilities associated with these crops.

4.4 Incidence of Landlessness and Poverty among the Landless in Gujarat

Two concepts of land access have been used here to consider landlessness. As per the NSSO definitions 'a plot of land is considered to be owned by household if the right of permanent heritable possession of the plot, with or without the right to transfer the title, is vested in some member or members of the household. Land held in owner-like possession under long-term lease or assignment is also considered as owned land.' Land owned include own homestead land too and hence does not only refer to own cultivated land. Land cultivated is the second concept that has been taken into account for this analysis; it is synonymous to operational holding and includes owned and leased in area under cultivation, but excludes leased out land.

Landlessness in India and in many other major states has been increasing in the last few years, and Gujarat is an exception in this respect. Table 5.19 reveals that particularly with respect to change in incidence of landlessness in terms of cultivated land, the difference between India and Gujarat is stark. Though there is not too much difference in the respective status of landlessness in terms of cultivated area in the terminal year 2009-10, the state has a reduced incidence over time, while in the country, the same has gone up by nearly eight percentage points. The reasons for the states performance are probably numerous, ranging from improved irrigation bringing in additional area under cultivation, to high profitability that has characterized the state in the recent years. The small and marginal farmers probably have found it worthwhile to stick to cultivation in the last five years, rather than leasing out or selling off their land.

The tribal area that includes Dangs Panchmahal and Dohad district, is the most underdeveloped region in the state and is characterized by first generation dairy and crop farmers. The region has low coverage of irrigation and has not benefitted from cotton cultivation, unlike the other regions. This is also the only region that has a higher incidence of landlessness in 2009-10 compared with the earlier period (Table 5.20). The other three regions are developed, though different in terms of sources of irrigation and crop mix. Saurashtra and Kutch have had the highest increase in irrigation coverage, driven by micro-irrigation. This region is also expected to benefit the most after completion of the Narmada Valley project. Though landlessness has declined in this region, it is still substantially high with 50 per cent of the households not having access to cultivated land.

It is well documented in literature that landlessness is associated with poverty in rural India (Aggarwal, 1994; Mearns, 1999). To see the change in relative poverty status among the landless compared to the smallest land size category and the largest land size categories, these land size classes were divided into quartile classes of monthly per capita consumer expenditures. The condition of the landless has significantly deteriorated both in Gujarat and in India (Tables 5.21 & Table 5.22, see annexure). The landless were significantly better off when compared to the smallest size class of cultivator in Gujarat in the year 2004-05. Gujarat being an industrial state, the non-farm sector wages might have been a better option than cultivating small plots of land. At the all India level, there was no significant difference between the poverty status of the landless and the smallest farm size category in the first period under consideration. There is a drastic decline in their poverty status in Gujarat with 80 per cent of the landless falling in the two bottom quartile expenditure groups in 2009-10 compared to a corresponding figure of around 58 per cent in the earlier period. These percentages are comparable to that of India. What is different for the state, though, is that both the smallest and the largest size classes have gained significantly over the five year period, particularly the latter. This is not surprising, given the high growth that the agricultural sector of the state is experiencing in recent years. In India, in contrast, the positions of both the smallest and largest size classes of cultivators are worse off, along with the landless in the terminal period. Thus over the last five years, being in agriculture in Gujarat has become associated with a far higher status of livelihood, and along with it the stake of being landed has increased significantly. The agricultural sector in Gujarat between the periods under observation has had gains for even the smallest of farmers. The reduced incidence of landlessness is good news for the state for the time being at least, and whether the same trend can be sustained in years to come that may have less than average rainfall and slower irrigation increases is still to be seen.

5. Conclusion

The current study attempts to look at the nature and components of agricultural growth in Gujarat in the recent years and does so in a backdrop set by the recent changes in the agricultural policy regime, particularly those pertaining to land. It also tries to understand the spread of benefits of the 'agricultural high' in the state and the extent to which these benefits may have percolated to households with limited or no access to the land, which constitutes the basis of agricultural livelihood. In other words, the question that we seek to answer is whether the recent agricultural growth spurt, backed by a liberalized policy regime, redefines the margins, to either include or exclude the socio-economically vulnerable from the benefits of growth.

The recent policy changes in agriculture in the state have been entirely consistent with the general environment of a liberalized regime. It is however fair to note here that these changes, by no means, represent a drastic deviation from the previous land policies, and they were a product of a smooth transition, which were always driven by the interests of the earlier dominant landed groups now becoming increasing urbanized, while retaining their roots and identities entrenched in the rural cores of the state. These visible changes in land policies explicitly articulates the will of the state to corporatize agriculture at a fairly fast pace through land transfers on the one hand, and a host of state-instituted measures in the areas of infrastructure, institutions and technology driven by the intent of enhancing efficiency and growth in the agricultural sector, on the other.

Even a critical review of the recent developments in the agricultural sector in the state would have to concede that the above-mentioned state initiatives have yielded remarkable results in boosting agricultural growth in the state in the past decade, albeit backed by good rainfall in all the years after 2001-02. The drivers of agricultural growth are distinct and easily identifiable, cotton being the leading force, effective more through yield than area expansion, though the increase in area is by no means meager. The only spot that disturbs this nearly perfect story of agricultural growth is the element of fluctuations of this growth over the years, which while becoming less violent than before, is still very much an integral part of the agricultural trend of the state. A further point of concern in the same area is that, the two major crops that have led the growth are characterized by high degrees of instability, groundnut more than cotton.

To state the obvious, farmers with greater access to agricultural land would get the bigger share of the incremental production, given the nature of agricultural growth in the state. Though the kind of land policy shifts that have occurred in the recent years could well influence the distribution of cultivated land, laying out exact directions of causality is outside the scope of this particular study. What is significant, though, that there are clear evidences of further marginalization of the already vulnerable economic and social groups in terms of access to cultivated land over the last five years in the state. Given the fact that tenancy is likely to be low and under reported in the state, such changes are causes for concern as the change may have partially come from dispossession of own land. In addition, the participation of the smaller farmers is appreciably lower in cultivation of cotton compared to their larger counterparts, which is further indicative of the fruits of the recent growth bypassing the former.

The change in incidence of landlessness, though starting from a higher base compared to India, has improved during the last decade and a half in Gujarat, while India and comparable states have showed a worsening status, some of them by a disturbingly high magnitude. While the decline in landlessness could be explained by better micro-irrigation facilities and extension of canal networks, these developments could have also had a reverse effect on landlessness. More detailed analyses are required to interpret such results. Landlessness, however, has increased in the tribal areas (Panchmalal, Dahod and Dangs) which is the most underdeveloped region in the state and has by and large remained outside the loop of the recent growth spurt. It may be pointed out here that the recent move of privatization of commons further makes the landless and the small farmers of these districts more vulnerable. The landless have moved down the ladder of relative poverty in the state when compared with even the smallest category of farmers over the last five years, while in India, these two categories have no difference in terms of their strength of clustering in the two lowest quartile groups of consumption expenditure. Land, therefore, by virtue of indications more than one, has increasingly become a means to sustain an acceptable livelihood in rural Gujarat, and this evaluated in context of policies that facilitate land transfers to non-locals agriculturists and non-agricultural corporates seem to entrench possibilities of unequal gains from agriculture in the future.

NOTES

1. According to Gulati et. al, (2009) and Shah et al, (2009) the average rate of growth of agricultural SDP between 2000-01 & 2006-07 for Gujarat and India has been 9.6 per cent and 2.7 per cent respectively.
2. It may be noted though, states permitting tenancy and ostensibly protecting the interest of tenants sometimes produced nearly similar outcomes. Maharashtra is a case in point, where there is no ban on tenancy and the tenants get a right to purchase the land after one year of the commencement of the tenancy contract (Deshpande, 2003). The effect of the tenancy laws indifferent states were more closely related to the intent and nature of grass roots support base of the party in power, rather than the policy per se.

3. Horowitz (2000), contends that a society having ethnic cleavages can be characterized by ranked hierarchies or cleavages running 'horizontally', thereby dividing society into hierarchical stratifications, or unranked in which the society is divided 'vertically', thereby dividing society into side-by-side, stand-alone pillars.
4. A book from Vishwa Samvad Kendra, a documentation centre of the Hindu right wing, comments on the need for corporatizing agriculture to make it commercially viable to encourage agro-industrialists, and water from the Narmada Dam reaching remote parts of Gujarat to facilitate irrigation to boost agricultural surpluses (Mehta, 2002 in Sud, 2007). It has been pointed out that the same document is silent about landless labourers, minimum wage rates, as well as the need to subsidize small farmers whose economic means do not permit them to lift canal water.
5. The marginal farmers and landless labourers were negatively impacted by the Jyotigram Scheme in several different ways: (a) groundwater markets declined, restricting the buyers' access to irrigation; (b) pump irrigation prices in cash sales increased by 40–60 per cent; (c) landless labourers cultivating leased land faced reduced availability of irrigation as well as lower returns on lease farming; (d) they also faced reduced opportunities for farm work as the irrigated area declined (Shah et. al, 2008).
6. As per this Government Resolution, 'lands will be given up to a maximum of 2000 acres (800 hectares) for 20 years' lease. The project must begin in the first five years and the required capital shall be arranged by the lessee. Rs. 500 will be charged as interest free security deposit. If the project does not take off in five years, the deposit will be forfeited and land shall be taken back. It is compulsory for the lessee to use the modern micro-irrigation methods. There shall be no rent for the first five years. Annual rent will be charged at Rs. 40 per acre from sixth to tenth year and Rs. 100 per acre from 11th to 20th year. When any value adding activities are taken up, there will be 50 per cent increase in the rent. The lessee can also mortgage this land to scheduled banks and RBI approved other banks. In case of any processing of agricultural produce from this land no NA (non-agricultural) permission is required'. GR No. JMN/3903/453/A (as quoted in Barwada and Mahajan, 2006).
7. The nine- fold categories evolved by the Department of Agriculture and Cooperation in India may be grouped to capture the following:

(a) Under utilization of agricultural land comprising of the culturable waste(CW) land and fallow lands other than the current fallows (FOCF),

(b) Land not available for cultivation comprising of area not under agricultural uses (ANUAU) and barren uncultivated lands (BUL).

(c) De facto rural common property resources (de facto CPR) comprising of the forests, pastures & grazing lands, land under tree crops & groves (not included in net sown area) and the fallow other than current fallows.

(d) Total cultivable land (TCL) comprising of net sown area, current fallows, fallow other than current fallows and culturable waste lands.

8. Among the 18 districts in Gujarat, 13 of them have been found to register either positive or negative growth rates between 1998-99 and 2006-07 due to which the analysis on land use change at the district level have not been possible.
9. The steady increase of milk in the share of Gujarat's agriculture has been once again supported by the good road and other infrastructure along with the Operation Flood programme launched by the National Dairy Development Board in the 1970s.

REFERENCES

Agarwal B. *A Field of One's Own: gender and land rights in South Asia.* New York: Cambridge, 1994.

Arya A and Mehta N. Performance of Gujarat Economy: an Analysis of Growth and Instability. *MPRA* Paper No 35712, 2011.

Balakrishnan R. Limits of law in Counter-Hegemonic Globalization: The Indian Supreme Court and the Narmada Valley struggle. *Working Paper,* CSLG/WP/04-04, Centre for the Study of Law and Governance, Jawaharlal Nehru University, New Delhi, 2004.

Bharwada C and Mahajan V. Quiet Transfers of Common. *Economic and Political Weekly* 2006; 4(4): 313-315.

Breman J. Agrarian Change and Class Conflict in Gujarat India. *Population and Development Review Supplement: Rural Development and Population: Institutions and Policy* 1980; 15: 301-323.

Chadha GK, Sen S, and Sharma HR. State of the Indian Farmer: A Millenium Study, Vol. 2: Land Resources, Report, Ministry of Agriculture, Government of India, 2004.

Gandhi VP and Namboodiri NV. The Adoption and Economics of Bt Cotton in India: and Preliminary Results from a Study. *Working Paper* No. 2006-09-04, Indian Institute of Management, Ahmedabad, 2006.

Government of Gujarat. *The Land Reforms Laws in Gujarat.* Gandhinagar: Central Government Press, 1976.

Horrowitz D. *Ethnic Groups in Conflict.* Berkey: University of California Press, 2000.

Jodha NS. Rural Common Property Resources: Contributions and Crisis. *Economic and Political Weekly* 1990; 25(26): A65-A78.

Khan TR. "Dam" the Irony for The Greater Common Good: A Critical Cultural Analysis of the Narmada Dam Debate. *International Journal of Communication* 2012; 6: 194–213

Kumar MD, Narayanamoorthy A, Singh OP, Sivamohan MVK, Sharma M and Bassi N. Gujarat's Agricultural Growth Story: Exploding Some Myths. *Occasional Paper* No. 2-0410, Institute for Resource Analysis and Policy, Hyderabad, 2010.

McDougal TL. *Law Of The Landless: The Dalit Bid for Land Redistribution in Gujarat, India.* Massachusetts: The Department of Urban Studies & Planning Master's Degree in City Planning, Massachusetts Institute of Technology, 2007.

Mearns R. Access to Land in Rural India: Policy Issues and Options. *Policy Research Working Paper*, 2123, World Bank, South Asia Regional Office, Rural Development Sector Unit, 1999.

Shah G. Caste and Land Reforms in Gujarat. In: Shah G and Sah DC (eds) *Land Reforms in India Performance and Challenges in Gujarat and Maharastra. Vol 8.* New Delhi: Sage Publications, 2002, pp. 127-43.

Shah T, et al. Groundwater governance through electricity supply management: Assessing an innovative intervention in Gujarat, western India. *Agricultural Water Management,* 2008; 95: 1233-1242.

Shah T, et al. Secret of Gujarat's Agrarian Miracle after 2000. *Economic and Political Weekly* 2009; 44(52): 45-55.

Srivastava RS. Land Reforms. Employment and Poverty in India. In: *International Conference on Land, Poverty, Social Justice and Development*, The Hague, Netherlands, 2006.

Sud N. From Land to the Tiller to Land Liberalization: The Political Economy of Gujarat's Shifting Land Policy, *Modern Asian Studies* 2007; 41(3): 603-637.

Turaga U. Damming waters and wisdom: protest in the Narmada River Valley. *Technology in Society*, 2000; 22(2): 237-253.

6

Selective Development in Gujarat: A Study of the Manufacturing Sector

Sangeeta Ghosh

Introduction

Gujarat's growth experience has been quite different from the rest of India as the driver of growth in the state has been both the secondary and the tertiary sector, while for most of India, the growth experience is that of a service sector led growth. Gujarat is hence seen as a 'model state' that has set an example for industrialization in India that has benefitted by not contradicting the centre's initiatives in liberalization and economic policy reforms by facilitating liberalization in its state and jurisdiction. At the beginning of the 2000s, Gujarat was the second most industrialized, third most urbanized and fifth richest state in terms of per capita income among the major states of India. It is a top destination for domestic investments (third in the country) and has attracted a large share of domestic investments for its electricity, manufacturing and infrastructural sector. It is the destination for more than one fourth of the private investment made through Industrial Entrepreneur Memorandum route in India.

Gujarat has encouraged the secondary sector through greater expenditures on physical capital than on human capital and has chosen the path of unbalanced and inequitable growth with emphasis on directly productive capital rather than creating social overhead capital (Dholakia R. 1994, 2000, Dholakia A. 1990). The Gujarat government has given an array of fiscal and financial incentives to attract industries. Most importantly, Gujarat developed its infrastructure for industries through initiatives involving chiefly private participation. From the second half of the 1990s, major liberalization initiatives were implemented in Gujarat. Major reforms in the power sector were initiated around 1995-96 following the recommendations of the Gujarat State Finance Commission (1994) report. In other infrastructural sectors like ports and roads also, private participation is encouraged. Using its geographical advantage of a long coastline, port infrastructure was strengthened by privatization through the Build Own Operate and Transfer (BOOT) policy in 1997, which gave private developers complete operational and tariff freedom for 30 years. The Gujarat Industrial Development Corporation (GIDC) has been providing facilities to the industrial units in selected locations in the state. Major simplifications were introduced since 1999 to speed up the registration of small and tiny sector units. Units with an investment up to Rs. 40 lakh in plants and machinery can now be registered without inspection. The drive to register small entrepreneurs, rural artisans, cottage industries, etc., aims to enable them to get incentives and also to strengthen the database in the sector.

Another major liberalization initiative is the abolition of urban land ceiling in the state from April 1999, with the hope that excess land locked up with several industrial units in the state can be released for sale and development purposes. It is expected that the sale of excess land with industries in deep trouble can provide a vital dose of fresh resources for their rehabilitation. For making land available to industries, the unique measure taken by the Gujarat government in 1997 is to grant permission to convert agricultural land to non-agricultural (NA) uses upto the limit of 10 hectares almost automatically (Dholakia, 2000). However, the effect of land related reforms is yet to be seen in Gujarat, as it might encourage land sharks and cause the land price to rise. Also, reform related to the conversion of agricultural land to non-agricultural uses may have repercussions on the marginal farmers.

Hirway (1995) and Awasthi (2000), concluded that the nature of industrial development in Gujarat is biased in favour of developed regions. Hirway (2000) further observed that though the economic growth in Gujarat was associated with a diversified economic structure during the 1980s and 1990s, the process is not sustainable as it has distorted the agricultural-industry linkage. Unni, Lalitha and Rani (2001) have observed that the structural changes in Gujarat's industrialization with declining textile shares has destroyed the backward and forward linkages that the unorganized sector had with the organized sector. The massive growth of capital-intensive chemical and related industries leaves little scope for ancillarization and subcontracting (Lalitha, 1999). Streefkerk (2001) has reported casualization and feminization of the workforce in Gujarat and has observed that liberalization has officially justified these long-term trends. Concentration of chemical and plastic industries in the state has caused severe environmental degradation in the state (Hirway 2000, Streefkerk 2001, Awasthi 2000).

Given this background, this paper critically evaluates the process of industrialization in Gujarat. It questions the imperative for industrialization in the state, which seems to have undergone a higher degree of concentration than the rest of India with declining distributive features. To get a comparative perspective, we have compared Gujarat's manufacturing performance with that of Maharashtra, Tamil Nadu and Haryana.

Data Source

For looking at the organized manufacturing sector, time series data from Annual Survey of Industry (ASI) (1980-81 to 2007-08) has been used after necessary concordance[1] to make a consistent series confirming to National Industrial Classification (NIC) 1998. We have used NIC industries from 15 to 36; these industries constitute the organized manufacturing sector (we excluded recycling, NIC 37 as data before 1998-99 was not available for this industry).[2] The manufacturing industries considered here constitute around 95 per cent of the total employment in the organized sector. The values of output and gross value added (GVA) have been deflated for all the states and India by the wholesale price index for manufactured products (1993-94 base year). For calculating real wages, wages have been deflated by consumer price index for industrial workers at the same base year. For calculating the net fixed capital stock, we have used the perpetual inventory method.[3]

For looking at some patterns in the districts of Gujarat, unit level data from ASI is seen for the years 2000-01 and 2005-06. These years are chosen as the unorganized manufacturing survey of NSSO (56th and 62nd round) are also conducted in the same years and helps us to construct a picture of the manufacturing sector in Gujarat at these two points in time. The 51st, 56th and 62nd round of the NSSO cover the unorganized manufacturing enterprises in the country exclusively. The

NSS reports (51st, 56th and 62nd) are looked at to study the unorganized manufacturing sector. The 62nd round unit level data is used for the unorganized manufacturing sector.

Gujarat's manufacturing sector has grown at a faster pace than all other states and since 1990-91, it holds the first position in terms of contribution of the manufacturing sector to GSDP. The contribution of manufacturing sector to Gujarat's GSDP is 27 per cent in 2009-10 of which registered manufacturing constitutes 21.6 per cent. However, as seen in Table 6.1 (see annexure), there is a distinct mismatch in the contribution of the secondary sector to GSDP and the employment generated by the sector. This mismatch is even more pronounced in the manufacturing sector. By 2009-10, the contribution of the secondary sector to Gujarat's employment is actually found to be lower than that of India, while its contribution to GSDP has increased marginally. In the manufacturing sector in Gujarat, the organized sector accounts for around 31 per cent of employment in 2005-06 while the bulk of manufacturing employment lies in the unorganized sector. The figure is an improvement over the national average of 20 per cent organized workers in the manufacturing sector and is marginally higher than Maharashtra and Tamil Nadu. However, given the high contribution of the registered manufacturing sector to Gujarat's GSDP, the corresponding employment contribution in the organized sector is starkly lower.

With only 5 per cent of the country's population, Gujarat accounts for 7 per cent of India's GDP, 14 per cent of India's manufacturing gross value added, 9 per cent of employment, 17.25 per cent of fixed capital and 10 per cent of total number of factories in India in the 2000s (Table 6.2, see annexure). The manufacturing sector in Gujarat has gained in the share of GVA in India's total GVA and the share has almost doubled from 1980s to 2000s. While Maharashtra has the highest share in manufacturing GVA, together the two coastal states in western India account for more than 35 per cent of India's manufacturing GVA in the 2000s. This is however, largely unmatched by their contribution in manufacturing employment which stands at 9 per cent for Gujarat and 14 per cent for Maharashtra in 2000s. In spite of the doubling in the share of GVA, Gujarat's contribution in India's manufacturing employment remains almost stagnant over the three decades, while Maharashtra's has actually declined. Tamil Nadu has seen a significant rise in its share in manufacturing employment over the years. Gujarat's share in fixed capital has almost trebled since the 1980s and is close to that of Maharashtra whose contribution to gross value added is double of Gujarat. This in itself indicates the path of industrialization chosen by Gujarat—a low employment generating and high capital intensive growth—which though witnessed in India's industrialization trajectory as well, is only intensified in the reform-welcome state of Gujarat.

The growth rate of GVA in manufacturing sector has been the highest in Gujarat as compared to the other states in India and growth rate has been much higher than the national growth rate for all the three decades. In the 1980s, Gujarat and Maharashtra saw negative employment growth mainly owing to the closure of textile mills in both the states. In fact, the negative growth rate of employment seen in India in the 1980s, has been mainly on account of these two states. Though Maharashtra has seen a much lesser growth rate of employment in the subsequent decades, the growth rate of employment in Gujarat picked up in the 1990s and 2000s and though it has lagged behind Tamil Nadu and Haryana; it has been more than that of India. For all the four states, as well as for India, growth rate of fixed capital has been very high in the 1990s, though for Gujarat, it has been the highest–nearly 20 per cent.

Employment in Organized Manufacturing

In India as for Gujarat, the 1980s were a decade of job loss in organized manufacturing (Figure 6.1). Between 1980 and 1989, 1.2 lakh workers lost their jobs in Gujarat mostly because of job loss in the textiles, food and beverages sector. In Maharashtra, the job loss was even higher and 3.4 lakh workers lost their jobs. As pointed out earlier, the jobless growth of the 1980s in India was mainly on account of these two states and was caused by widespread job loss in the textiles, food and beverages sector.

The first half the 1990s show significant efforts at liberalization in India and at the state level and investment boom in this period saw high growth rates of gross value added and employment in organized manufacturing increased both in India and in Gujarat. However, as the growth momentum fizzled out from the latter half of the 1990s, employment declined again to the levels of early 1990s. This means that employment in the organized sector rose by merely by 48.6 thousands between 1980 and 2004 in Gujarat after all the efforts at attracting investments. From 2004 onwards, employment is the organized sector

Figure 6.1: Employment in Organized Manufacturing in India and Gujarat

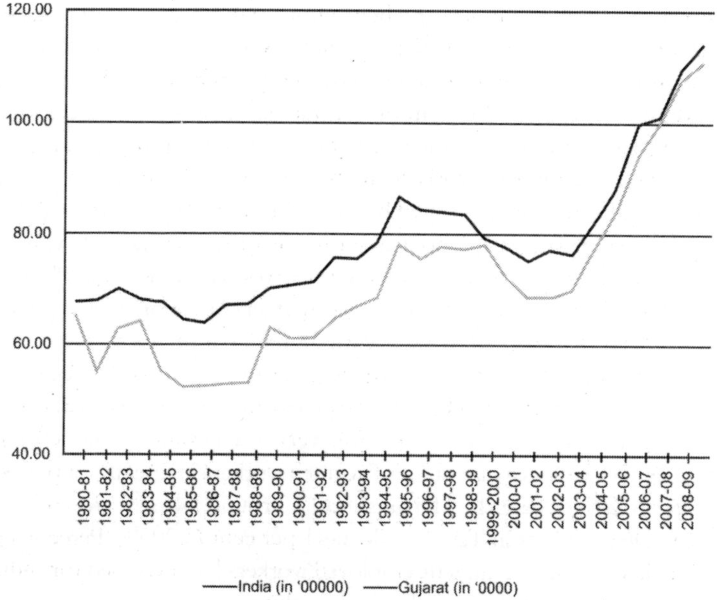

Source: Own Calculations from State Level Data, Annual Survey of Industry, 1980-81 to 2009-10.

*The figures for India are shown in lakhs and for Gujarat in ten thousands.

has increased significantly both in India and Gujarat and this holds a ray of hope for the organized manufacturing sector employment.

It is important here to talk of the quality of employment of the jobs that were created in the 2000s. As can be seen from Table 6.3 (see annexure) growth in employment has been accounted for to a large extent by contractual employment for all the states studies here, and for Maharashtra, the growth rate of directly employed workers has actually been negative in 2000s. In Gujarat, contract workers constituted 37 per cent of the total workers in 2007-08 from the already high 27 per cent in 2000-01. The growth rate of contract workers in Gujarat has been slower than the other states in the 2000s, but this needs to be seen in the context of the already high levels of contract workers in total workers in the state. This is the fourth highest in Indian states in terms of contractual worker proportion after Andhra Pradesh (which is high due to the presence of the tobacco sector), Orissa and Haryana. This is a striking feature as far as employment generation in organized manufacturing is concerned as this is one sector where labour rights are more protected, and workers have more rights than the large unorganized sector. Even in this sector, the production structure is becoming more and more flexible, as indicated by the employment of contractual workers.

ASI data reports the women workforce in directly employed workers alone. Directly employed workers are those workers in the factory sector that are relatively more protected by labour laws. However, reportedly in many sectors, particularly labour-intensive sectors, wage rate of women workers is lesser than that of the contract workers. Ghosh (2009) has studied the ratio of wage rate of type of workers in the organized sector and has seen that women workers earn 38 per cent of wages earned by men workers and 87 per cent of the wages earned by contract workers on an average in India in 2002-03. The proportion of women workers in Gujarat and Haryana's factory sector is very low (around 5 per cent) in 2000s. India's average percentage of women workers in directly employed workers is 20 per cent. In Maharashtra it's around 14 per cent and the percentage is highest in Tamil Nadu at 41 per cent in 2000s. Percentage of female workforce in directly employed workers has increased for India and for all other states except for Maharashtra.

Table 6.4 (see annexure) shows the employment elasticity in the manufacturing sector with respect to output. We see that Gujarat shows the lowest employment elasticity over the period of study, among all the states and it is lower than the national value as well. For Gujarat, the employment elasticity with respect to output has improved over the decades, but is only slightly higher than the national average and much lower than Tamil Nadu and Haryana.

Table 6.5 (see annexure) shows the capital intensity of the manufacturing process. We see that Gujarat's capital intensity has been more than that of India from the 1990s onwards, and it has become tremendously capital intensive in the last decade. In fact, it is often claimed that Gujarat's high capital intensity figure is mostly accounted for by the highly capital-intensive refined petrochemical industry, but even if we remove this industry from the analysis, Gujarat's manufacturing process is highly capital absorbing, in fact the highest among all states. The process of high capital-intensive manufacturing has been witnessed in Gujarat particularly post-reforms and it has increased phenomenally in the decade of 2000s.

When capital is substituted for labour it brings forth an increase in labour productivity as has been seen in the case of India as well as all the states. Gujarat's labour productivity levels are much higher than India and only second to Maharashtra. However, if the growth in labour productivity is equal to the growth of capital intensity with no decline in capital productivity then technological upgradation takes place. As seen in Table 6.5 (see annexure), this has not happened in India or in Gujarat in the 1980s and 1990s, which saw negative growth rates of capital productivity implying the substitution of labour for capital without any increased in capital productivity. However, in the 2000s, the situation has changed and capital intensification has been accompanied by technological upgradation in India as well as all the states studied here.

Labour Share

Even though employment has increased in 2000s, with increase in labour productivity, the share of wages in gross value added has been falling constantly in India, and it is the least among the four states seen here for Gujarat. Haryana, Maharashtra and Tamil Nadu have better share of wages in gross value added (product wages) than the national figure, while for Gujarat, it is a dismally low 20 per cent (Figure 6.2).

Figure 6.2: Share of Wages in GVA

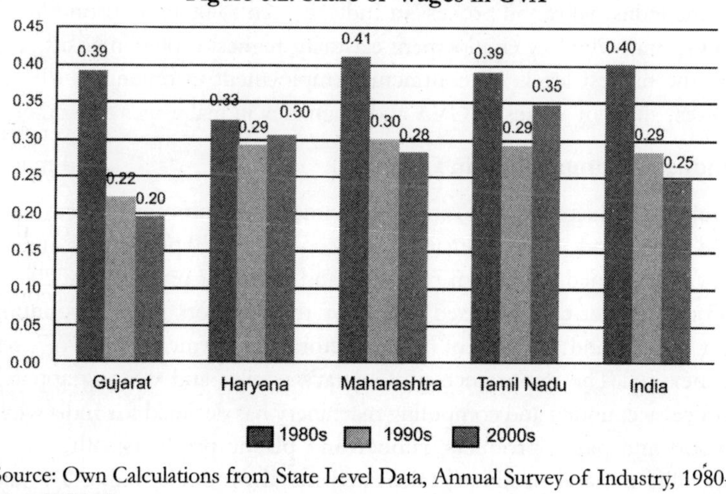

Source: Own Calculations from State Level Data, Annual Survey of Industry, 1980-81 to 2007-08.

The growth rate of per employee wages has been low in India in the 1990s, but has picked up in 2000s. However, all the four states seen here had much lower growth rate of wages than the national figure in the 2000s and for Haryana and Tamil Nadu—the wage growth rate has been near zero. In Gujarat, the growth rate of wages has been 1.5 per cent in 2000s. However, this wage rate includes the wages given to supervisory and managerial staff. If we look at the growth rate of wages to workers in the organized manufacturing (Table 6.6, see annexure), we see that the 1990s have witnessed a stagnant growth rate of 0.07 per cent and in the 2000s, the growth rate of wages to workers actually turned negative. In Gujarat, the higher growth rate of wages in throughout the period of study accrued to the supervisory and managerial staff while the worker wage rate grew at a little above one per cent.

So we see that as for India, as well as the advanced industrial states seen here, the labour benefiting or employment generating potential of the manufacturing sector has been extremely limited. Employment elasticity with respect to output remains very low and most of the employment generated has been in the form of contractual workers. Wage share in GVA has fallen to dismally low levels and there has been stagnancy in growth of wage rates, particularly for the blue-collared workers in organized manufacturing. This phenomenon, while prominent in the industrialization process in India, is seen to be more pronounced in Gujarat, with low employment elasticity, highest capital intensity, one of the highest levels of contractual employment in organized labour, lowest share of wages in GVA and stagnancy in real wages to workers.

Industry Composition in Gujarat

Gujarat's industrial composition has witnessed significant changes over the period under study. Gujarat now accounts for 30 per cent of India's GVA in refined petroleum products and chemical products by 2000s, 45 and 35 per cent of fixed capital of these sectors while accounting for only 18 and 22 per cent of the sectoral employment (Table 6.7, see annexure). The importance of Gujarat's textiles and wearing apparel, office, accounting and computing machinery has declined for India while wood and paper products, rubber and plastic products, other non-metallic mineral products, fabricated metal products, radio, TV and communication apparatus and gems and jewels have seen an increase in their shares. There has been a significant shift in the industrial structure of Gujarat since the 1980s, in favour of refined petrochemicals and chemical products, while textiles lost its share heavily. Looking at the structure of the manufacturing sector in Gujarat (Table 6.8, see annexure), we see that in 2000s, the two major industries in Gujarat which together account for 60 per cent of its GVA are refined petrochemicals and chemical products. Refined petrochemicals, a high capital intensive sector has negligible contribution in employment while chemical sector accounts for 23 per cent of employment. These industries also, leave little scope for ancillary or subcontracting activities (Lalitha, 1999) and have little to contribute to organized-unorganized sector linkages. The importance of the employment generating textile sector has diminished in India by half from the 1980s, while in Gujarat, it has come down from 37 per cent in the 1980s to a mere 7.5 per cent in 2000s, though its contribution to employment is 21 per cent in the 2000s.

The growth in Gujarat's manufacturing industry is strongly linked with the infrastructure development in the state. During the last two decades, refined petroleum, chemical products, basic metal and fabricated metal products, machinery and equipment, have seen impressive growth in Gujarat. These industries have been the prime driver of aggregate manufacturing growth in the state. The refined petroleum and chemical products industries have large import content. Crude oil is the main input for these industries and Gujarat has offered a well-developed port sector as infrastructural prerequisites. Basic metal and fabricated metal products, and machinery and equipment are relatively more energy intensive. Gujarat has offered huge power generation capacities and has a success in captive power plants based on private investments and the high growth of these industries in Gujarat can be largely attributed to the development of power sector in the state.

The share of rubber and plastics, chemical sector which are more polluting in nature have increased in Gujarat and these industries have seen high growth rates in the last two decades. This has raised concerns over severe environmental degradation in the state (Hirway 2000, Streefkerk 2001, Awasthi 2000). The share of mineral based industries has also increased in the state.

Gujarat has improved its share in textiles sector in India (as well as food and beverages sector) in 2000s than the 1990s if not the 1980s, indicating a slight betterment in the agriculture-industry linkage in this sector, which had deteriorated in the 1990s. It needs to be noted however, that the share of its employment in the textiles industry in India has declined in the 2000s in spite of an increase in the GVA share. The share in GVA of the wearing apparel sector has declined in the 2000s, though the employment has declined more. There is evidence to suggest that the textiles sector in Gujarat is turning a lot more capital-intensive and its capacity to generate employment will be far lesser.[4]

Gujarat accounts for 17 per cent of furniture, gems and jewels sector's GVA and 21 per cent of the employment the sector generates in India.

Spatial Concentration in Manufacturing Activity

Gujarat has witnessed a change in its manufacturing activity structure in the last decade not only in terms of its industrial composition but also in terms of the spatial distribution in its districts. The nine districts that account for most of the manufacturing activity are Jamnagar, Kutch and Rajkot (in Saurashtra region), Vadodara, Surat, Bharuch, Ahmedabad and Valsad (Central and Southern Gujarat) and Gandhinagar (North Gujarat).

The Saurashtra region has the most shares in investment which are capital-intensive in nature and this region has been the main drivers of manufacturing growth in Gujarat in the 2000s along with Vadodara, though Vadodara and Jamnagar contribute very little to employment, with Vadodara having seen a fall in its employment share in recent times. Jamnagar which accounted for only 3.22 per cent of GVA in Gujarat in 2000-01 has seen a massive increase in its contribution mainly on account of the refined petrochemical industry (Table 6.9, see annexure). Refined petrochemical industry is highly capital-intensive, thus reflected by the increase in share of fixed capital for Jamnagar, while its employment and factory share have increased only marginally. In Vadodara also, refined petrochemicals increased its contribution significantly by 2005-06, however, its employment growth turned negative with a significant fall in the number of units in chemicals, basic metals and electrical equipment industry. The food and beverage industry saw significant increase in employment in Kutch and new industries of basic metal and fabricated metals caused the employment and GVA growth to be very high.

The refined petroleum industry was completely moved out of Surat by 2005-06 and textiles and gems and jewelery industry contributed significantly to a rise in employment in this district. Bharuch, Ahmedabad and Valsad have seen negative employment growth owing mostly to the fall in employment in its textiles and chemical sectors.

The organized manufacturing activity is now heavily skewed in favour of three districts namely—Jamnagar, Vadodara and Surat which alone account for 60 per cent of gross value added and output, and 64 per cent of the fixed capital in 2005-06. However, the employment share of the three districts is 33.5 per cent (Table 6.9, see annexure). North Gujarat has a very low share of industrial activity.

For measuring the concentration of manufacturing activity in districts we have looked at two measures, namely the Herfindahl–Hirschman Index (HHI)[5] and Spatial Gini (G).[6] Looking at HHI (Table 6.10, see annexure), we see that for Haryana, Maharashtra as well as Tamil Nadu, the concentration of manufacturing activity in districts has increased both in terms of GVA and employment in 2005-06. Gujarat has seen a greater concentration of manufacturing activity by gross value added in 2005-06 than in 2000-01, although in terms of employment, manufacturing activity is more distributed in its districts in 2005-06. This kind of a pattern in Gujarat implies that the districts that have contributed to more GVA in the state in recent times have not brought forth much employment. This has an adverse effect on the share of labour in GVA as has been seen before.

Presence of Manufacturing Activity in Rural Areas

An interesting fact that gets revealed about the industrialization process in Gujarat, is the increasing presence of manufacturing activities in its rural areas (Table 6.11, see annexure). As much as 52 per cent of GVA and 57 per cent of output from the manufacturing sector and 42 per cent of manufacturing employment is located in rural areas in 2005-06. While the concentration of GVA, output, fixed assets, land assets is much higher in Gujarat's rural areas than the national figure, the employment percentage is nearly the same, while the percentage of units is lesser in the rural areas in Gujarat than the national figure. What is most interesting is that much of the land assets (in value terms) for Gujarat (as much as 48.5 per cent) are located in its rural areas—the figure is highest among all states. Whether this is a reflection of Gujarat's land policy of converting agricultural land to non-agricultural uses upto 10 hectares almost automatically is a matter of further research.

Among the nine districts where most of the manufacturing activity in Gujarat is located, Kutch, Gandhinagar, Rajkot, Jamnagar and Surat have large presence of industries in their rural areas. In Gandhinagar and Surat, the industrial activity has shifted more to urban areas, although it still remains high. Ahmedabad, Vadodara, Bharuch and Valsad too have seen a fall of manufacturing activity in rural areas.

Unorganized Manufacturing Sector

Gujarat accounted for as much as 9.6 per cent of unorganized manufacturing GVA of the country in 1994-95, this value had dropped to 6.9 per cent in 2000-01 and has picked up to 7.2 per cent by 2005-06 (Figure 6.3). The share of unorganized manufacturing workforce for Gujarat has increased marginally in the first half of 2000s (Figure 6.4). Maharashtra has the highest share in unorganized manufacturing GVA, again like in the organized sector, it is unmatched by employment share. Among the four states, Tamil Nadu has the highest share in unorganized workforce.

Most of the unorganized manufacturing activity in Gujarat is concentrated in six labour-intensive industrial sectors, namely food and beverages, tobacco, textiles and wearing apparel, wood products and gems and jewels. Together they account for around 80 per cent of unorganized employment. As witnessed in the case of organized manufacturing, unorganized manufacturing is also concentrated in select districts of Gujarat. Ahmedabad, Surat, Amreli and Bhavnagar account for more than 55 per cent of total unorganized employment and 70 per cent of GVA. Together with Vadodara, Rajkot, Bharuch, Jamnagar, Surendranagar and Patan they make up for more than 80 per cent of unorganized manufacturing activity both in terms of output and employment.

Between 2000 and 2006, the unorganized manufacturing workforce grew at 4.47 per cent in Gujarat. For most of the early years of this decade, the organized manufacturing saw a fall in employment. The total manufacturing sector saw a rise in employment in this period on account of the unorganized manufacturing sector which constitutes the bulk of the manufacturing employment in India as well as Gujarat (70 per cent in Gujarat in 2005-06). However, as the paper on employment in this book shows, the latter half of the 2000s saw a negative growth in employment in the manufacturing sector (at -2.61 per cent between 2004-05 and 2009-10). This happened in spite of the high growth rate of employment in the organized sector as we have seen before. It implies that employment in unorganized manufacturing has declined after 2005-06 for which NSS data on unorganized manufacturing sector employment is not available. The job loss in the diamond industry in Gujarat during the global financial crisis of 2009 is well documented (Hirway, 2011). The gems and jewels sector was the highest contributor to employment (30 per cent) in unorganized manufacturing sector in Gujarat in 2005-06. So the widespread job loss in this sector, must have adversely affected the aggregate manufacturing employment.

Among the unorganized enterprises, Gujarat and Maharashtra have a higher share of DMEs than the rest of the country. Non-directory establishments (NDMEs) and Directory establishments (DMEs) fall under establishments which run with the help of at least one hired worker (for DMEs its six or more workers). In 2000s, the share of non-establishment enterprises has increased in Gujarat while it has declined in all other states as well as for India (Figure 6.5). Own Account Enterprise (OAME) run without the help of any hired worker has grown at a faster rate in Gujarat than the rest of the county in 2000s (Table 6.12, see annexure). Both in terms of number of enterprises as well as employment, OAMEs in Gujarat have recorded the highest growth rate in 2000s among the states under comparison, and it's higher in the urban areas than in the rural areas. This indicates a higher degree of casualization of the work force in Gujarat.

Figure 6.3: Share of GVA of Selected States in India's Unorganized Manufacturing

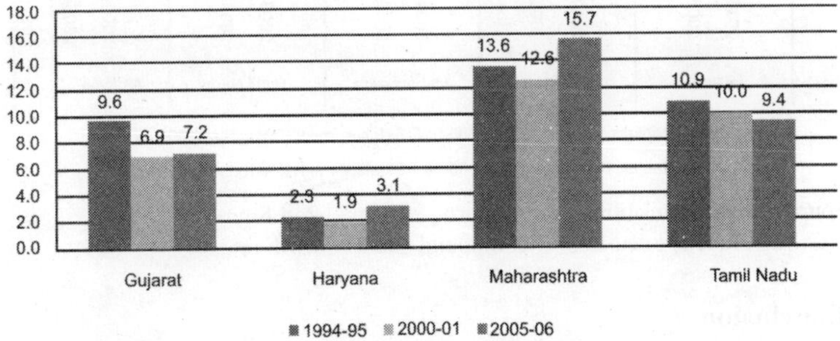

Source: NSS Report on Unorganized Manufacturing Enterprises, 62nd Round.

Along with casualization of the workforce, feminization of the workforce has occurred all over the country from the 1990s. All the states, as well as India, show higher female employment in the percentage of total workers. In Gujarat, female workers constitute 20 per cent of unorganized workforce, which is much lower than the rest of the country (Table 6.13, see annexure).

Figure 6.4: Share of Workforce of Selected States in India's Unorganized Labour

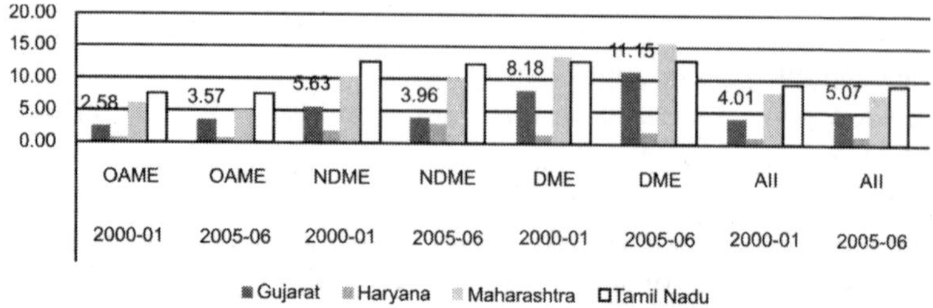

Source: NSS Report on Unorganized Manufacturing Enterprises, 56th and 62nd Round.

Figure 6.5: Share of Type of Enterprises in States Total Number of Enterprises

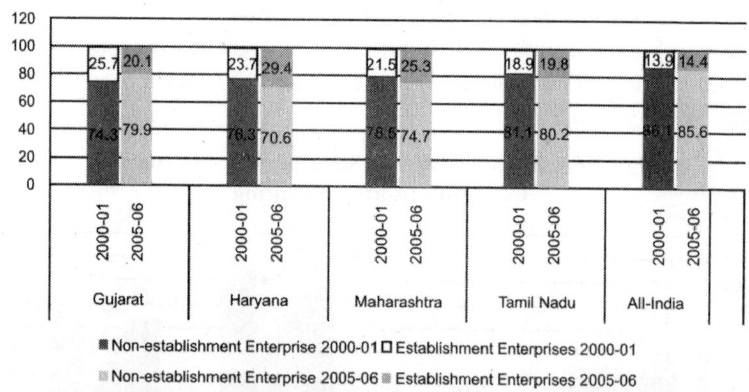

Source: Own Calculations, NSS Reports, 56th and 62nd Round.
* Growth Rate is calculated by compound annual growth rate

Conclusion

The paper concludes that the industrial experience in Gujarat is one that has witnessed high concentration in industrial sectors, incomes and regions. While the state holds the first position in terms of contribution of the manufacturing sector to GSDP, and this share has increased over the decades—there is a distinct mismatch in the contribution of the secondary sector to GSDP and the employment generated by the sector which has been low and has remained stagnant over the decades. The contribution of the manufacturing sector to GSDP is the highest in Gujarat compared to all states and much above the national average and yet the employment share is below the national average in recent years. Post-reforms, Gujarat's manufacturing sector has become tremendously capital-intensive and has the most capital-intensive manufacturing process in India. Gujarat has clearly chosen a low employment generating and high capital-intensive industrial strategy for itself—which though witnessed in India's industrialization trajectory as well, is only intensified in the reform-welcome state of Gujarat.

Gujarat's manufacturing growth performance has been impressive in the last two decades and a lot of this is on account of the infrastructure development in the state. Refined petrochemicals and chemical industry, basic and fabricated metal products, machinery and equipments and mineral products have been the main drivers of the aggregate manufacturing growth and this has had a lot to do with excellent infrastructural capacities of the state particularly in ports and power sector. Gujarat has seen a huge concentration of refined petrochemical and chemical industries and Jamnagar and Vadodara have seen increased shares in GVA mainly on account of refined petrochemical industry with stagnant or decreased (as in the case of Vadodara) share of employment. These industries have little to offer in terms of ancillary and subcontracting activities, the organized-unorganized linkages in the state have weakened. Gujarat has also concentrated more and more in its sectoral composition with high concentrations of refined petrochemicals and chemical industry as well as high regional concentrations in Jamnagar, Vadodara and Surat. The share of rubber and plastics, chemical sector and mineral based industries which are more polluting in nature have increased in Gujarat and these industries have seen high growth rates in the last two decades. This has raised concerns over severe environmental degradation in the state (Hirway 2000, Streefkerk 2001, Awasthi 2000). The share of mineral based industries has also increased in the state.

With the most capital absorbing industrial process in India, Gujarat has little to offer to the workforce in its factories. The growth rate of organized employment has increased in the recent years which holds a ray of hope for the employment scenario in this sector. However, given the loss of jobs in the unorganized sector, the contribution of employment from this sector to total employment in the state has deteriorated. The distributive value of the industrial process is at its minimum as employment and wage shares of the manufacturing industry have been dismally low. This has been witnessed through very low employment elasticity of output, and lowest shares of wages in GVA in India and stagnancy in growth of real wages to workers. In Gujarat, the higher growth rate of wages throughout the period of study accrued to the supervisory and managerial staff while the worker wage rate grew at a little above one per cent. Rising trends of casualization of the workforce is witnessed in Gujarat through much faster growth of non-establishment enterprises in the unorganized sector and high use of contract workers in organized manufacturing in the country. Gujarat has as much as 37 per cent of contract workers in its organized workers - one of the highest in the country.

This selective development has major repercussions on the state economy because it will widen regional disparities and shrink the overall size of the market while pushing more and more of its population into uncertainty and poverty. With calls for more economic reforms, particularly labour reforms, one wonders to what effect industrialization serves development and for whom precisely this development is meant. More casual workers mean an insecure effective demand. The recent reforms that have taken place in the state particularly with respect to land can have adverse affects on the poorer sections of the population. All this will affect the poor adversely since they will not get enough employment and the degraded environment due to concentration of chemical and plastic industries will affect them adversely.

NOTES

1. From 1980-81 to 2007-08 state level data from Annual Survey of Industries at 4 digit level of disaggregation was used for this study. Up to 1988-89, the classification used was NIC 70, up to 1997-98 it was NIC 87 and up to 2003-04 it was NIC 98 and thereafter NIC 2004. The data was converted to 3 digit level concordances at NIC 98 and then aggregated for 2 digit level for the study.
2. The reported value of aggregate employment data in the Annual Survey of Industries includes agriculture and related activities, mining and quarrying, recycling, electricity, gas and steam, collection, purification of

water, repairing services, retail trade, recreational, cultural and sporting activities and other service activities. Throughout this study, the data used is a summation of the manufacturing industries from NIC 15-36. From 1998-99, electricity undertakings were not covered under ASI data. The problem of non-coverage of sectors is overcome by the summation of manufacturing industries for the aggregate manufacturing sector for all the variables used.

3. For calculating India's total Net Capital Stock the benchmark year used is 1973-74. A factor load value of 1.8 is multiplied with the fixed capital to determine the benchmark value. The share of the industrial sectors in total fixed capital is determined and appropriate benchmark for each sector is calculated. Gross Investment in fixed capital is then calculated by subtracting the book value of fixed assets in the previous year from the current year and adding to that the reported depreciation in fixed assets in that year. This gross investment is then deflated by gross fixed capital formation deflators at 1993-94 prices. A constant depreciation of 5 per cent was assumed for obtaining net fixed capital. The ASI data for States is available from 1980-81. We use the share of fixed capital of selected states in India's total fixed capital and use this weight to determine the benchmark for each state at 1980-81.

   Then we use the same method as described to calculate the State Net Capital Stock.

4. The recent Textile Policy announced in Gujarat (*The Economic Times*, September 5, 2012) has offered an array of benefits to investors in the textile sector including interest subsidy for technology upgradation and purchase of plant and machinery, exemption on VAT on produce, power subsidy and assured lignite for captive power plant. The Gujarat government expects an investment of Rs. 20,000 crore over five years and hopes to create 25 lakh new jobs. Gujarat produces close to 30 per cent of country's cotton and the recent high growth of cotton crops along with the self-sufficiency of Gujarat's power sector has trigged this policy.

   The Rajasthan Spinning and Weaving Mills who are keen to invest 400 crores in Gujarat (i.e. one-fifth of the sought investment) want fully automated plants with minimum human intervention owing to labour issues in the sector. Their recently commissioned 52,000 spindles plant at Kharigram in Rajasthan has only 200 workers (*The Economic Times*, September 5, 2012). For jobs to be created in the textiles sector, Gujarat needs to be wary of the nature of investment in the sector. If capital-intensive investments such as these take place, the subsidies and incentives offered will have little to contribute in fostering employment in the textiles sector.

5. HHI $=\Sigma s^2$ for all districts, where s is the share of employment/GVA in each district
6. $G = 1 + 1/m - 2/m\ (\Sigma r_i\ p_i)$where m is the number of districts, r_i is the ranking of district and p_i is the share of employment/GVA in the district

BIBLIOGRAPHY

Awasthi DN. Recent Changes in Gujarat Industry – Issues and Evidence. *Economic and Political Weekly* 2000; 35(35/36): 3183-3192 .

Bagchi AK, Das P and Chattopadhyay S. Growth and Structural Change in the Economy of Gujarat, 1970-2000. *Economic and Political Weekly* 2005; 40(28): 3039-3047.

Dhandeo K. Gujarat government announces textile policy; targets Rs 20,000 crore investment, 25 lakh jobs. *The Economic Times,* 5 September, 2012.

Dholakia RH. Liberalisation in Gujarat – Review of Recent Experiences. *Economic and Political Weekly* 2000; 35(35/36): 3121-3124.

Dholakia RH. Spatial Dimension of the Acceleration of Economic Growth in Gujarat in India. *Economic and Political Weekly* 2000; 29(35): 2303-2309.

Ghosh S. *Sub-contracting in Organised Manufacturing Sector in India,* MPhil Disseration, Jawaharlal Nehru University, 2009.

Hirway I and Shah N. Labour and Employment under Globalisation: The Case of Gujarat. *Economic and Political Weekly* 2011; 46(22): 57-65.

Hirway I. Dynamics of Development in Gujarat: Some Issues. *Economic and Political Weekly* 2000; 35(35/36): 3106-3120.

Hirway I. Selective Development and Widening Disparities in Gujarat. *Economic and Political Weekly* 1995; 30 (40/41): 2603-2618.

Kannan K P. and G Raveendran. Growth sans Employment: A Quarter Century of Jobless Growth in India's Organised Manufacturing. *Economic and Political Weekly* 2009; 44(10): 80-91.

Lalitha N. Employment Trends in the Manufacturing Sector of Gujarat. Gujarat Institute of Development Research, 1999; Ahmedabad, April.

Mehta G S. Rajasthan Spinning and Weaving Mills keen to invest Rs 400 crore in Gujarat. *The Economic Times,* 5 September, 2012.

Streefkerk H. Thirty Years of Industrial Labour in South Gujarat: Trends and Significance. *Economic and Political Weekly* 2001; 36(26): 2398-2411.

Unni J, Lalitha N and Rani U. Economic Reforms and Productivity Trends in Indian Manufacturing. *Economic and Political Weekly* 2001; 36(41): 3914-3922.

7

Growth with Limited Outcomes: Poverty and Inequality in Gujarat

Nidhi Mittal

Section 1: Introduction

Gujarat has achieved a lot in terms of growth of the economy but nearly a third of its population still lives below the poverty line. In spite of massive efforts, poverty eradication still remains the key challenge for policy makers. The main focus in Gujarat is on increasing the economic growth so that its trickle down effect can help reduce poverty. There are some studies that are examining the growth performance of the state and the nature of change in poverty in Gujarat. What is missing in most of these studies is a detailed analysis of growth and poverty at the regional level as well as at the level of the social groups. Gujarat is a state with very unique geographical and social features. Within the state, there are some regions that lag behind others on behalf of their geography (e.g., dry areas), social exclusion (e.g., tribal areas) or natural disasters (e.g., drought). For these diverse regions, state level economic and social policies may not work. According to the United Nations Development Programme (UNDP), economic growth will not reduce poverty unless it is inclusive and action is taken at the local level, i.e., in villages, towns and regions and all groups of people contribute to and share the benefits of development. In this context, it would be interesting and useful to understand the dynamics of economic growth, poverty and inequality at a more disaggregated level. It will help in identifying target regions and groups in the state where a specifically-focused policy is needed.

In this paper, an attempt has been made to analyse the performance of Gujarat with respect to economic growth, poverty and inequality using the NSSO regions of Gujarat as the unit of analysis. This paper also analyses the performance of Gujarat in comparison to the all India rate of growth as well as to three other states; Haryana, Maharashtra and Tamil Nadu. The analysis is done for aggregate as well as for the rural and urban areas of the states and NSSO regions. The paper will also analyse these variables with respect to the social groups in Gujarat. For this, it relies on unit level data from three National Sample Survey Organization (NSSO) Consumer Expenditure Surveys (Schedule 1.0); 50th round, 61st round and 66th round conducted in 1993-94, 2004-05 and 2009-10 and the poverty lines as per the Tendulkar Committee. Accordingly, the period of study is divided into two sub-periods, 1993-05 and 2005-10. The first sub-period relates to the phase of liberalization while in the other sub-period Gujarat is said to have taken the leap.

The paper is organized as follows. Section 1 introduces issues to be focused on in the paper and gives the framework of the paper. It also presents the data source, methodology and concepts used in the paper. Section 2 explores trends in growth, poverty and inequality for all India and across four states between 1993-94, 2004-05 and 2009-10. Section 3 examines the nature of change in growth, poverty and inequality across the NSSO regions of Gujarat and section 4 does that for the social groups in Gujarat. Finally, Section 5 highlights the key results obtained and gives concluding remarks with some comments on policy implications.

Vibrant Gujarat

Gujarat is located on the western tip of India divided into 26 districts and 226 talukas with Gandhinagar as its capital (Tapi is the 26th district of Gujarat formed out of Surat district in the year 2007 but in NSSO data, it is analysed as a part of Surat). It is a fast-growing state and in fact is one of the fastest growing states in India especially since the economic reforms in the beginning of the 1990's (Dholakia, 2007). Its performance has always been better than the all India in terms of economic growth (Dholakia, 2000). The people of Gujarat are considered very entrepreneurial in nature and the government response is very fast, bringing Gujarat to the forefront of development. The Government of Gujarat is actively promoting the industry and is creating an investor-friendly environment in Gujarat by giving fiscal and financial incentives and building an impressive modern infrastructure. Geographically also, Gujarat has a very strategic location including one third of the coastline of the country which is the longest coastline in the country and better access to oil and natural gas (Socio-Economic Review 2010-11, Dholakia 2007).

NSSO Regions

The NSSO divides each state into several sub-regions. The bases of division are the different agricultural and climatic conditions in the given state and therefore these are called agro-climatic regions. A region is basically a group of contiguous districts having some similar geographical features like cropping pattern and population density. The natural ecosystem of Gujarat ranges from deserts, scrublands, grasslands, deciduous forests and wetlands to mangroves, coral reefs, estuaries and gulfs. Gujarat used to be the only exception where for region formation some districts are subdivided on the basis of location of dry areas and distribution of tribal population. But in the 66th round 5 regions were formed out of complete districts. As a whole, NSS has formed 5 regions in Gujarat.

1.2 Data and Methodological Issues

NSSO Consumption Expenditure Surveys

Estimates of growth, poverty and inequality are based on consumption expenditure data from large-scale quinquennial household surveys of the National Sample Survey Organization (NSSO). 50th, 61st and 66th rounds of NSSO are comparable to each other but 55th round is not comparable with any of these rounds due to use of mixed reference period. In the 55th round, information on food items is taken for two recall periods of 7 days and 30 days from the same households and these 7 days food questions are said to have contaminated the data (Himanshu, 2007). Therefore, we made use of unit level data from three Consumption Expenditure Surveys (Schedule 1.0) (i) NSSO, 50th round conducted in 1993-94, (ii) NSSO, 61st round conducted in 2004-05 and, (ii) NSSO, 66th round conducted in 2009-10.

The Tendulkar Committee Report: Poverty Line Used

According to new methodology suggested by the Tendulkar Committee report, poverty lines are not calculated via calorie norm (2100 calorie for urban and 2400 for rural per day). Poverty lines will now be calculated on the basis of Mixed Reference Period (MRP) instead of using Uniform Reference Period (URP). It will also incorporate private expenditure on health and education. In this study, MRP data has been used for estimation.

Inter Temporal Comparison: Price Effect

For inter temporal comparison, the data series has to be corrected to take into account the change in prices over the period. This paper uses the CPIAL (Consumer Price Index for Agricultural Labour) and CPIIW (Consumer Price Index for Industrial Workers) for rural and urban monthly per capita expenditure. 2009-10 is taken as the base year (base 1) and values for 1993-94 and 2004-05 are corrected accordingly.

Gujarat Regions: Compatibility between the Rounds

In Gujarat, the number of regions is the same across the rounds, i.e., 5 but the composition differs. In the 66th round, five regions are South Eastern, Plains Northern, Dry Areas, Kutch and Saurashtra. In the 50th and 61st rounds, the five regions were Eastern, Plains Northern, Plains Southern, Dry Areas and Saurashtra. To make the regions compatible with the 66th round; Eastern and Plains Southern have been merged to make South Eastern in 50th and 61st round. Similarly in the 61th round, Dry Areas and Kutch have been separated. In the 50th round separation is not possible because of unavailability of data at the district level.

Social Groups in Gujarat

In the 50th round, NSSO has divided all the households into three categories, i.e., scheduled tribe-1, scheduled caste-2 and others-9. However, in the 61st and 66th round, NSSO has created four social groups which are scheduled tribe-1, scheduled caste-2, other backward class-3 and others-9. To make the groups compatible backward classes have been merged with others in the last two rounds.

Section 2: Dynamics of Economic Growth, Poverty and Inequality: Inter-state and All-India

It is well known that India has adopted a major set of economic policy reforms in 1991 that unleashed high economic growth in India. However, individual states experienced different rates of growth and different outcomes. This section analyses trends and pattern of growth, poverty and inequality in Gujarat in comparison with three other states; Haryana, Maharashtra and Tamil Nadu as well as to all India rates of growth.

2.1 Growth in Average Monthly Per Capita Expenditure across States of India between 1993-94 and 2009-10

Over the 11 year period, from 1993-94 and 2004-05, aggregate average monthly per capita expenditure for all India has grown at the rate of 1.38 per cent per annum but during the 5 year period from 2004-05 and 2009-10 the all India growth rate has been 2.41 per cent per annum while in Gujarat it has grown at the rate of 1.81 per cent per annum in the first period and even better growth at the rate of 2.54 per cent per annum in the second period (see annexure Table 7.1). The performance of the competing states like Maharashtra and Tamil Nadu has comparatively improved in the second period and are doing better than Gujarat in growth terms. In Haryana, the growth rate has decreased from 2.26 per cent per annum in the first period to only 1.22 per cent per annum in the second period but still in absolute terms its average monthly per capita expenditure has been the highest. In the rural sector, average monthly per capita expenditure has grown at a faster rate in the second period for all India as well as for Gujarat, Maharashtra and Tamil Nadu while in Haryana the growth rate in the second period has been negative but again its average monthly per capita expenditure is comparatively higher than other states (Figure 7.1). However, Gujarat is again behind Maharashtra and Tamil Nadu in terms of growth rate but

Figure 7.1: Average Monthly Per Capita Expenditure across States: 1993-2012

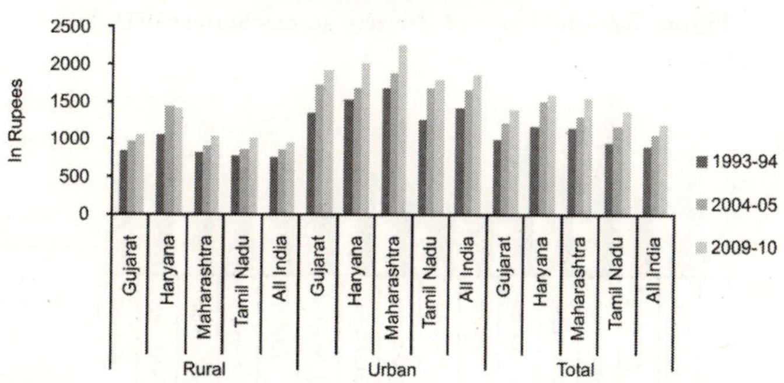

Source: Computed by Author from NSS CES 50th, 61st and 66th Round Unit Level Data, Using MRP.

not in absolute terms. Interestingly, in urban India, growth rate in the second period has impressively improved for all India as well as for Haryana and Maharashtra while for Gujarat and Tamil Nadu, per annum rate of growth has declined in the second period. Here, one can note that overall, the states are performing comparatively well in the second period but the performance of urban areas is better than their rural counterpart except in Tamil Nadu where the urban sector is deteriorating.

2.2 Incidence of Poverty across States of India between 1993-94 and 2009-10

At the all India level, the incidence of poverty between 1993-94 and 2004-05 and between 2004-05 and 2009-10 fell at the rate of 0.72 per cent per annum and 1.56 per cent per annum in aggregate, by 0.77 per cent per annum and 1.70 per cent per annum in rural and by 0.54 per cent and 0.96 per cent in the urban sector (see annexure Table 7.2). The extent of decline varies considerably across the states for total population as well as for the rural and urban areas. In Gujarat, Haryana, Maharashtra and Tamil Nadu, the incidence of poverty has decreased in both periods across sectors with much better performance in the second period except in Haryana (see Figure 7.2). In Haryana, fall in poverty in the first period was more and in fact in the urban Haryana there is an increase in poverty rate by 0.12 per cent per annum in the second period. But still poverty ratios in Haryana are the lowest throughout the rounds. Maharashtra is showing the largest decline rate in the incidence of poverty overall as well as in both the sectors. However, overall one can note that the extent of decline in the rural areas is more than the urban areas especially in the second period.

Figure 7.2: Incidence of Poverty across States: 1993-2010

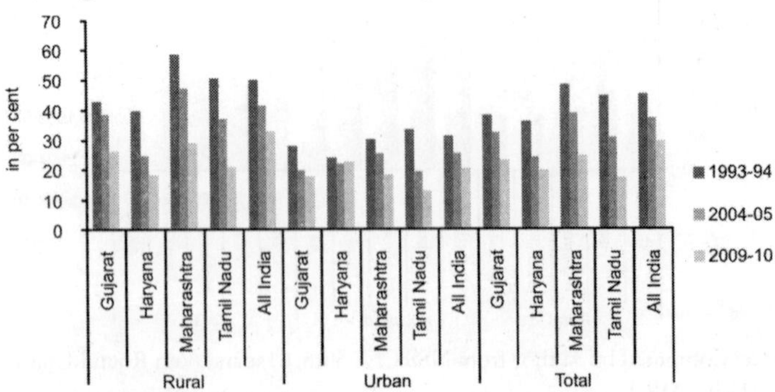

Source: Same as figure 7.1.

2.3 Inequality across States of India between 1993-94 and 2009-10

Gini coefficients of the distribution of consumption expenditure are used to measure inequality. Estimates shows that at the all India level Gini coefficient has increased throughout the sectors between the two time periods but the rate of growth has decreased in the second period (see annexure Table 7.3). In Gujarat also Gini coefficients are increasing except in rural Gujarat where there are signs of decreasing inequality in the second period (see Figure 7.3). Overall, in the first period, Gini coefficient has increased throughout the sectors except in rural Tamil Nadu. In the second period, rural sector, Gini coefficients of all states are showing a decrease in inequality while in the urban counterpart the Gini coefficients are showing an increase in inequality in all states except in Tamil Nadu where the inequality is declining. It can be noted that in the first period the extent of increase in inequality was more in urban areas than the rural counterpart and in the second period also most of the decline in Gini was reported in the rural sector showing declining inequality in the rural sector.

Figure 7.3: Gini Coefficient across States: 1993-2010

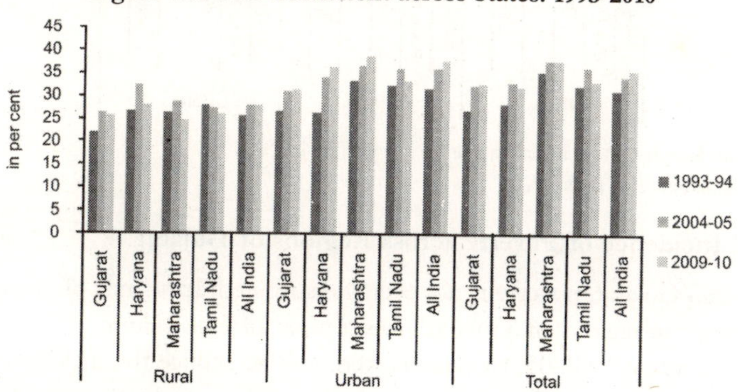

Source: Same as Figure 7.1

Section 3: Dynamics of Growth, Poverty and Inequality in Regions of Gujarat

3.1 Growth in Average Monthly Per Capita Expenditure across Regions of Gujarat

This section looks at the growth situation in Gujarat more closely by looking at the NSS regions of Gujarat. Across the regions also there are wide differences (see Figure 7.4). In the first period, growth rate in dry parts has been negative in aggregate and in rural areas while in the urban area there has been a negligible growth of only 0.22 per cent per annum but in the second period, it has shown an impressive growth especially in the urban sector. Saurashtra was also growing at the rate more than the state average in the second period for aggregate as well as across sectors (see annexure Table 7.4). In Northern Gujarat (excluding dry parts) and Southern Gujarat, monthly per capita expenditure is increasing over the rounds while urban Kutch is performing exceptionally well in the second period growing at 9.04 per cent per annum.

Figure 7.4: Average Monthly Per Capita Expenditure across Regions of Gujarat: 1993-2010

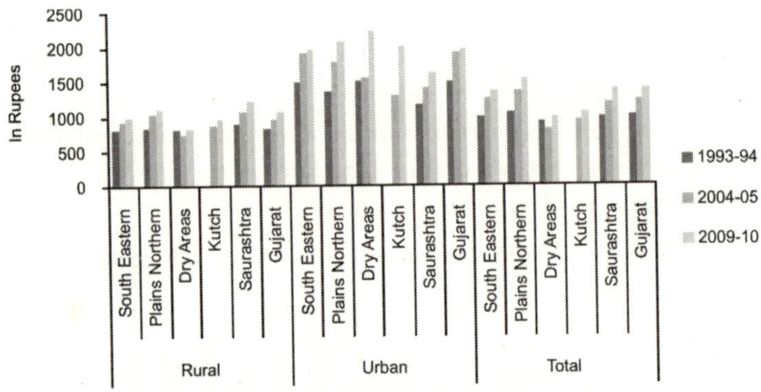

Note: Kutch was included in the Dry region in 1993-94.
Source: Same as figure 7.1.

3.2 Incidence of Poverty across Regions of Gujarat

Within Gujarat, poverty is not evenly distributed. Incidence of poverty across the regions of Gujarat gives a more diverse picture (see Figure 7.5). During 1993-05, all regions were able to reduce the incidence of poverty except southern region and dry parts in rural Gujarat and dry parts in total. During 2005-10, all regions have improved their performance significantly, decreasing the poverty incidence by even more rates except in urban dry parts where poverty is in fact increasing (see annexure Table 7.5). Only the urban areas of Southern and Saurashtra region were not able to increase the rate of poverty reduction in the second period leading to slower poverty reduction in urban Gujarat in the second period. In absolute terms also dry parts have the highest incidence of poverty across sectors.

Figure 7.5: Incidence of Poverty across Regions of Gujarat: 1993-2010

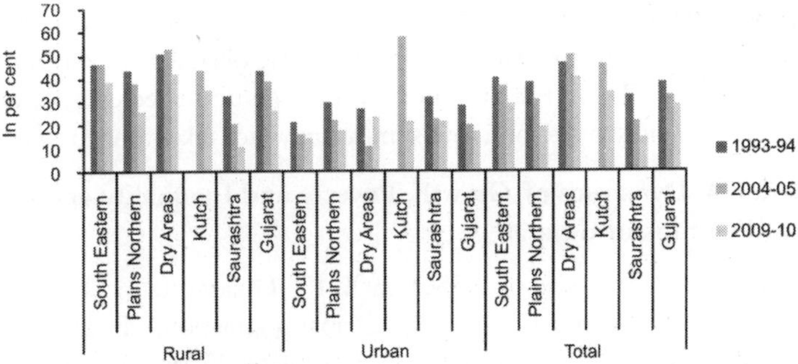

Note: Same as Figure 7.4.
Source: Same as Figure 7.1.

3.3 Inequality across Regions of Gujarat

During 1993-05, inequality has increased in Gujarat and its regions except in dry parts of Gujarat where inequality has shown a decline throughout the sectors (see Figure 7.6). In the second period, inequality has risen in aggregate except in the northern region (excluding dry parts) and Kutch where inequality has lowered. In rural Gujarat, overall Gini has decreased at the rate of 0.15 per cent per annum in the second period which was contributed by a decrease in inequality in the northern region, dry parts and Kutch region, while in the urban counterpart Gini coefficients have

Figure 7.6: Gini Coefficient across Regions of Gujarat: 1993-2010

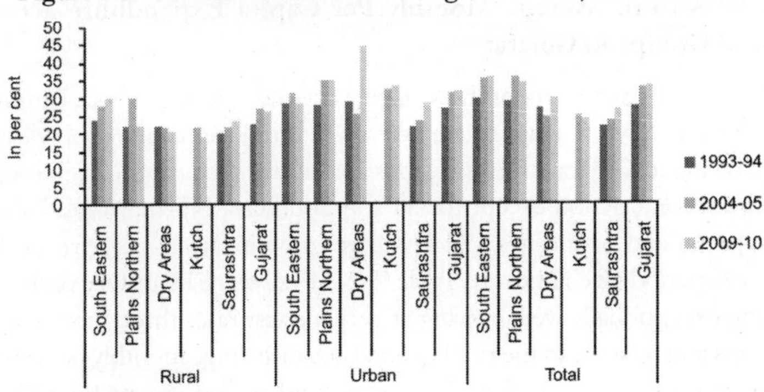

Note: Same as Figure 7.4.
Source: Same as Figure 7.1.

increased in the second period except in Southern region (see annexure Table 7.6). It can be seen that there is a sharp increase in inequality in the first period; however, in the second period, there are signs of decrease in inequality although at varying rates thus making overall inequality lower during 2005-10. This is a fairly important and significant decrease because Gini coefficient is said to be a robust measure which takes time to change.

Section 4: Dynamics of Growth, Poverty and Inequality across Social Groups in Gujarat

According to 66th round of NSSO (2009-10), Gujarat state's population is constituted of about 17 per cent of tribal population, 11 per cent of scheduled caste and 72 per cent others. Out of 17 per cent of tribal population maximum tribals live in South Eastern region (86.5%), followed by Plains Northern (10.3%) and Dry areas (2.1%) and Saurashtra region (1.2%). Moreover, out of 26 districts, 12 are so-called tribal dominated districts. These include all the districts of the South Eastern region including Dahod, Panchmahal, Vadodara, Narmada, Bharuch, Tapi, Surat, Navsari, Valsad and Dangs; one district from Plains Northern region named Sabarkantha and one district from Dry areas named Banaskantha. The main focus here is on scheduled tribes category as scheduled tribes are considered the most vulnerable category of population and Gujarat has a sizeable population of tribals. Therefore, there is a need to analyse the variables for the social groups separately. This section tries to analyse the nature of economic growth, poverty and inequality among the socio-economic groups in Gujarat.

4.1 Growth in Average Monthly Per Capita Expenditure across Social Groups in Gujarat

Estimates of average monthly per capita expenditure across social groups in Gujarat shows that aggregate average monthly per capita expenditure is growing in Gujarat and its regions for all the socio-economic groups in the second period except for ST's in Southern, Northern (excluding dry parts) and Saurashtra region where growth rate is negative in the second period (see annexure Table 7.4). However, ST's in Dry parts are doing exceptionally well growing at very highest rates throughout social groups and regions. In the rural Gujarat, again average monthly per capita expenditure is growing for all in the second period except for ST's in Northern region (excluding dry parts) and Saurashtra region. In fact, average monthly per capita expenditure trend for ST's in Northern region (excluding Dry parts) of the rural sector is very interesting. The average monthly per capita expenditure was Rs.582 in 1993-94 which shot up to Rs. 2396 in 2004-05 and again came down to as low as Rs. 953 in 2009-10 showing an increase of about 14 per cent per annum in the first period and a decline of about 17 per cent per annum in the next five years. In the urban sector, average monthly per capita expenditure of ST's and SC's is declining in Gujarat as well as in its regions in the second period, except for SC's in Saurashtra region (figures for Dry areas and Kutch are not available for analysis). As more than 86 per cent ST's belong to the Southern region it can be said that the condition of tribal group is worsening as average monthly per capita expenditure is showing either a marginal increase or a decrease in the second period. In absolute terms also the average monthly per capita expenditure among ST's in Southern region is lowest throughout the sectors.

4.2 Incidence of Poverty across Social Groups in Gujarat

The incidence of poverty in aggregate is showing a decline in both periods across the socio-economic groups and in almost all the regions with few exceptions. However, the tribal community bears a comparatively high incidence of poverty (see annexure Table 7.5). The incidence of rural poverty in the state was 43.29 per cent, 39.09 per cent and 26.63 per cent in 1993-94, 2004-05 and 2009-10. Against this incidence, rural poverty among tribal population in the state was as high as 53.24 per cent, 57.07 per cent and 48.57 per cent in 1993-94, 2004-05 and 2009-10. In the urban sector also, poverty ratios among ST's are high but still the difference is comparatively lower than the rural sector. Regionwise also, the poverty scenario for ST's is no better than the state. Looking at the change between periods, shows that in the Northern (excluding Dry parts) and Saurashtra region the incidence of poverty among ST's has increased during the second period and in Gujarat and other regions there is negligible decrease in poverty rates. In the rural sector, again there is a decline in poverty especially in the second period except for Northern region (excluding Dry parts) and Saurashtra region. In fact, the incidence of rural poverty among ST's in the Northern region shows a distinct pattern. In 1993-94, the head count ratio was as high as 92.66 per cent which shot down to zero per cent in 2004-05 and again went up to 26.52 per cent in 2009-10 showing a decline of 8.42 per cent per annum in first period and an increase of 5.30 per cent per annum in the next five years. This result shows a positive relationship between economic growth and poverty reduction as both variables show similar movement. In the urban regions of Gujarat, the incidence of poverty is showing a mixed trend. If we look at the poverty situation in absolute terms, ST's are bearing highest poverty incidence throughout sectors, regions and social groups rural-urban comparison shows that the socio-economic groups in the rural sector are better off than those in the urban sector as in the urban sector poverty is increasing for comparatively more regions and social groups and if decreasing, the rate of decrease is lower than the rural counterpart.

4.3 Inequality across Social Groups in Gujarat

Gini coefficients in the first period are showing increasing inequality for all social groups and regions with few exceptions, however in the second period, inequality has started decreasing (see annexure Table 7.6). But the spatial pattern of urban and rural poverty is quite different. In the rural sector, inequality among ST's is decreasing in the second period in Gujarat and its regions with the exception of Northern region (excluding Dry parts) though the rate of increase is only 0.45 per cent per annum. Urban Gujarat and its regions are again showing decreasing inequality among ST's in second period. Comparatively, the rural sector is performing better than the urban sector as in the rural sector, inequality is declining for more social groups and regions and the rate of decline is also comparatively high. However, in the urban sector Gini coefficients decline if any, is negligible. Moreover, the overall decline in inequality for the tribal population is more as compared to the non-tribal population.

Section 5: Summary and Conclusion

This study contributes to the ongoing debate in Gujarat on the impact of the recent growth experienced by Gujarat on poverty and income distribution. It also explores the spatial as well as social differences in growth, poverty and inequality in Gujarat.

The study finds that there has been an increase in the growth rate of monthly average per capita expenditure; however, this growth has not been uniform across states, geographic regions, sectors as well as social groups. It can be clearly seen that the urban sector is performing much better than the rural sector and is contributing to all India increase in average per capita expenditure.

The analysis of change of poverty ratios shows that, there has been a decline in the incidence of poverty in almost all states, regions, social groups and across rural and urban areas. However, one can note that poverty is decreasing more significantly in the rural areas than the urban areas especially in the second period, showing that poverty is more of an urban problem than a rural one. Kundu (2000) explained that the phenomenon of urban poverty being higher than the corresponding rural figures can be explained in terms of the high rate of immigration from other states, as well as migration from within the state, from the drought-prone areas, particularly in urban centres and their absorption in low paid casual jobs.

The analysis of change of inequality shows that the Gini coefficient had increased between 1993-94 and 2004-05, in almost all the states as well as in most of the regions of Gujarat suggesting that inequality has risen during the period. However, in the second period, there are signs of decreasing inequality. In general, rural areas are performing better than their urban counterpart especially in the second period, as most of the decline in the Gini figures was reported in the rural sector, although there are a few exceptions.

Gujarat lagged behind its competing states like Maharashtra and Tamil Nadu in terms of economic growth, poverty reduction as well as decrease in inequality. With respect to growth in GDP, Gujarat is always said to be a high performing state but with respect to growth in consumption expenditure it's an average performing state as depicted by the paper. Hirway and Shah (2011) in their study have observed that rapid growth in the state has not been shared by labour as gross domestic product (GDP) growth has been achieved by adopting highly capital-intensive measures. It has resulted in the state slipping in poverty reduction compared to other states and is also leading to high inequalities of income. In this scenario, promoting labour-intensive techniques can contribute towards equitable growth. To compete with these states and to achieve higher long-term growth along with significant reduction in poverty, Gujarat needs to modify its growth process and initiate more policy reforms in the future.

Analysis at the regional level indicates that regional disparities are more intense than disparities at the state level. Within a state, different regions are experiencing different outcomes. The level of economic growth, poverty reduction as well as decrease in inequality varies significantly across the regions of state. Dubey (2009) also found that Gujarat has a fairly high level of regional disparities in all three indicators; mean per capita expenditure, Gini coefficient and Head Count Ratio and explained that it may be on account of high variation in the physical features of the state. This increased variability in growth experience could be the reflection of the very characteristics of growth that has been initiated in Gujarat since 1990s. All regions do not stand an equal chance to become a beneficiary of this growth. Rather, regions or areas having relatively more conducive characteristics for growth have greater chances to gain from this growth and the so-called difficult and disadvantaged areas as well as tribal regions in Gujarat are left behind which are now affecting the overall performance of the state. Hirway (1995), has also mentioned that Gujarat has gone for the policy of selective development; 'Hi-tech industrialization in few well-endowed areas coupled with neglect of the relatively backward areas'; which has lead to stark regional disparities in levels of development and poverty in Gujarat.

The analysis of social groups in Gujarat shows that the condition of tribes is worsening as more than 86 per cent tribals lives in Southern region where the growth rate of average monthly per capita expenditure is showing either a marginal increase or a decrease in the second period. In absolute terms also the average monthly per capita expenditure among ST's in Southern region is lowest throughout the sectors. The incidence of poverty among tribes is also comparatively high. In fact, in Northern region (excluding Dry parts) and Saurashtra region incidence of poverty among ST's has increased during the second period. Estimates of growth and poverty for ST's in Northern region (excluding Dry parts) of the rural sector are quite interesting and are showing a positive relationship between economic growth and poverty reduction as both variables are moving in the same direction. Estimates shows that average monthly per capita expenditure which was Rs. 582 in 1993-94 shot up to Rs. 2396 in 2004-05 and again came down to as low as Rs. 953 in 2009-10 while head count ratio in 1993-94 was as high as 92.66 per cent which shot down to 0 per cent (zero) in 2004-05 and again went up to 26.52 per cent in 2009-10. The analysis of change of inequality among social groups in Gujarat shows that the Gini coefficient had decreased for ST's in the second period, and the overall decline in inequality for the tribal population is more as compared to the non-tribal population. This finding that inequality has sharply decreased within the last decade suggests that the forces that decrease inequality in the current growth processes are now getting strong and the need is to strengthen them if we wish to achieve more equitable and balanced growth outcomes in future.

There are a number of lessons that can be derived from the current study and are all relevant for the analytical as well as policy perspective. In view of intense disparity at the regional level, it can be misleading to design strategies on the basis of policy recommendations emerging from state level analysis. The scenario can be entirely different once the analysis is done at the micro-level. This demands that policies should be designed and implemented at the regional rather than state level. All the regions and socio-economic groups should be included to ensure the 'inclusiveness' of economic growth. As an initiative towards inclusive growth, Gujarat has already launched programs like Vanbandhu Kalyan Yojana for tribal areas and Sagarkhedu Sarvangi Vikas Yojana for the development of coastal areas and has also tried to decentralize the decision-making process for effective grass roots planning. But still no big changes are visible in the poverty situation of the state. It clearly signifies the need to identify and design more specifically targeted policies and programs that are needed to complement existing growth policies. The policies must be enabled to judiciously allocate the precious resources among all the sectors, regions and socio-economic groups.

BIBLIOGRAPHY

Dholakia RH. Liberalisation in Gujarat- Review of Recent Experience. *Economic and Political Weekly* 2000; 35(35/36): 3121-3124.

Dholakia RH. Sources of Economic Growth and Acceleration in Gujarat. *Economic and Political Weekly* 2007; 42(9): 770-778.

Dubey A. Intra-state Disparities in Gujarat, Haryana, Kerala, Orissa and Punjab. *Economic and Political Weekly* 2009; 44(26/27): 224-230.

Government of Gujarat. *Socio-Economic Review 2010-11 Gujarat State*. Budget Publication No. 34, February 2011. Gandhinagar: Directorate of Economics and Statistics, Government of Gujarat.

Himanshu. Recent Trends in Poverty and Inequality: Some Preliminary Results. *Economic and Political Weekly* 2007; 42(5): 497-508.

Hirway I and Shah N. Labour and Employment under Globalisation: The Case of Gujarat. *Economic and Political Weekly* 2011; 46(22): 57-65.

Hirway I. Selective Development and Widening Disparities in Gujarat. *Economic and Political Weekly* 1995; 30(41/42): 2603-2618.

Kundu A. Globalising Gujarat- Urbanisation, Employment and Poverty. *Economic and Political Weekly* 2000; 35(35-36): 3172-3181.

National Sample Survey Organization. *Level and Pattern of Consumer Expenditure 1993-94*. Report No. 402, May 1996. New Delhi: National Sample Survey Organisation, Department of Statistics, Government of India.

National Sample Survey Organization. *Level and Pattern of Consumer Expenditure 2004-05*. Report No. 508(61/1.0/1), December 2006. New Delhi: National Sample Survey Organisation, Department of Statistics, Government of India.

National Sample Survey Organization. *Level and Pattern of Consumer Expenditure 2009-10*. Report No. 538(66/1.0/1), December 2011. New Delhi: National Sample Survey Organisation, Department of Statistics, Government of India.

Planning Commission. *Press Note on Poverty Estimates, 2009-10*. 19th March 2012. New Delhi: Planning Commission, Government of India.

Planning Commission. *Report of the Expert Group to Review the Methodology for Estimation of Poverty*. 27th November 2009. New Delhi: Planning Commission, Government of India.

8

Galloping Growth Stagnant Employment: Mapping Regional and Social Differences

Ruchika Rani and Kalaiyarasan A.

The paper tries to understand the dynamics of the process that has brought about significant changes in the status of labour and employment in Gujarat. Gujarat is seen as a model state which has been in the forefront in adopting structural reforms and new development strategy initiated in the early 90s and has witnessed significant growth in the 1990s and 2000s. The Gujarat model of development has generated much debate from the critics as well as the proponent of the new development strategy. Therefore, to analyse the outcomes of the way the Gujarat model of growth and development has shaped the state's socio-economic structure has wider implication for the country at large.

Employment outcomes in Gujarat has attracted much attention of scholars in the last decade. Bagchi, Das and Chattopadhyay (2005) suggest that Gujarat experienced rapid economic growth mainly due to the high growth of income in manufacturing and services sector but Gujarat did not experience any structural transformation in employment. Agriculture sector still absorbs a significant section of labour because the development happening in Gujarat is capital-intensive in nature and state has witnessed falling employment per unit of capital. Hirway and Shah (2011a) suggest that benefits of growth were expected to trickle down, through the labour market functioning, but that has not happened in the state. On the contrary, it has been argued by Dholakia and Sapre (2011), that labour in Gujarat has actually significantly benefited from high economic growth and productivity gains. The state has done better than many other states in the level of employment and wages. Indira Hirway and Neha Shah (2011 b) in response to the Dholakia and Sapre comments argue that the ultimate goal of growth should not only be the growth of state domestic product but also the well-being of people and the employment which got generated from the growth momentum is not 'decent work'. They argue that the overall structure of employment has not shifted significantly from primary to non-primary sector and the growth in the non-primary sector has failed to generate adequate employment in this sector

In view of this ongoing debate in literature, it would be of great interest to see if the structural shift in employment has happened and how this shift relates with the patterns of growth. Has the high growth in the state been able to generate employment at commensurate rate? Is this employment growth evenly distributed across subregions, sectors, and the rural and urban areas of the state? How inclusive is this growth? How have the different social groups and religious minorities benefited from the growth?

In order to answer these questions sectorwise employment pattern and growth have been examined to see the structure and sources of employment. The pattern of employment has also been examined across geographical sectors, industrial sectors, gender and various social groups. The pattern of employment has been analysed with the help of NSSO quinquennial rounds of 1993-94 (50th round), 1999-00 (55th round) 2004-05 (61st round) and 2009-10 (66th round), Employment Unemployment Situation in India.

Movement of Income and Employment

It was expected that the structural reforms and the associated development strategy followed by the state would bring in changes not only in the structure of income but also in the workforce, shifting from low productivity and traditional sectors to high productivity and modern sectors. However, as shown in the Table 8.1 (see annexure), the shift as conceived by Arthur Lewis is far from reality. For instance, for 2009-10, the agricultural allied sector which is the source of employment for about 53 per cent of the workforce, contributes only 12 per cent to the state income. In other words, 88 per cent of the state income comes from the non-agriculture sectors while these sectors provide employment to only about 47 per cent of the workforce. Similarly, between 1993-94 and 2004-05, the decline in income share of agriculture was 6 per cent where as the decline in workforce dependent on agriculture was just about by 2 per cent. Moreover, during this period, the state economy elevated to a higher trajectory of growth. In other states, the nature of shift in employment has been different from Gujarat. In Maharashtra for example, the shift in employment has been proportional to the changes in the structure of growth between 1993-94 and 2009-10 (Table 8.1)

In addition to the above trend, the distribution of net employment generated between the years 1993-94 to 2009-10, endorses the fact that the new employment has come largely from agriculture and services. As shown in the Table 8.2 (see annexure), nearly 50 per cent net employment generated in Gujarat in the last two decades has come from service sector and followed by 30 per cent in agriculture itself. Interestingly, for India, the net additional employment has come predominantly from services and construction rather than agriculture. In fact, agriculture contributed just 2 per cent to the net national employment for this entire period. Even in the rural India, only service and construction sectors contributed to the employment generation. This may indicate a trend towards rural non-farm employment generation due to successive government policies or low growth in agriculture or by both. However, in contrast to the all India trend, for rural Gujarat, more than 70 per cent employment generated in this period has come from agriculture, and 25 per cent from service sector. How productive and remunerative this employment has been, is something that needs further probing. The literature suggests, that the high workforce dependency on agriculture and low income generation in this sector reflects the differences in productivity. However, there are others (Dholakia, 2011), who argue that the very notion of looking at structural change in employment across sectors is problematic and there is a possibility of change in the structures of employment within sectors, from low productive activities to more productive and modern activities.

Work Participation Rate

In this section, we examined the work participation for rural and urban areas for both Gujarat as well as all-India. Work Participation Rate (WPR) provides an idea about the participation of population in economic activities. The Table 8.3 (see annexure) provides a comprehensive view of the trend in the given period. The participation rates in rural Gujarat increased in 2004-05 before declining significantly in 2009-10. Though this decline occurred for both rural males and females; the decline for rural female is quite significant as it declined from 43 per cent in 2004-05, to 32 per cent in 2009-10. But there was substantial improvement in WPR between 1993-94 and 2004-05 for both rural and urban, males and females. However, there was an overall decline in WPR for sectors, males and females for both Gujarat and all India between 2004-05 and 2009-10. As this peculiar trend is not just confined to Gujarat, it has now generated a major debate in the academic circles. Some scholars (Chandrashekar 2011 and Rangarajan 2011) attribute this trend to the increased participation of the young population in education and the possible underestimation of the employment of women. However, what is agreed among all is, that there has been a decline in the workforce, and substantial shift in workforce from formal or secure employment to informal or insecure employment indicating casualization of labour. These aspects of employment have been strongly reinforced in the case of Gujarat. These aspects are discussed in detail in the following sections.

Employment Growth

In Gujarat, the employment growth stood at only 1.7 per cent for the entire period under study against impressive high growth of GSDP in the same period. During this period, growth rate of employment for rural Gujarat and rural India have been the same, while urban Gujarat performed slightly well than its counterpart for all India (Table 8.4 in annexure).

The growth rate of employment in Gujarat during 1993-94 to 2004-05 is 2.43 per cent compared to 2.08 per cent at all India level. At India level, the industrial growth is highest 4.07 per cent followed by services sector 3.31 per cent. Within services, the growth rate is highest in banking, insurance and real estate followed by transport, storage and communication and trade, hotels and restaurants. Gujarat has seen a lower growth rate in employment in both the industry and the service sector than the national average despite witnessing a higher GDP growth rate in these sectors. However, in Haryana, despite having low GDP growth in industrial sector, it has double employment growth in industrial sector than in Gujarat. Employment growth in both Maharashtra and Gujarat moved in same line (Table 8.5 in annexure).

However, the recent 66th NSS round (2009-10) shows that employment growth has declined in many sectors and has been negative in certain key sectors like agriculture and manufacturing in comparison to the trend that prevailed between 1993-94 and 2004-05. The Compound Annual Growth Rate (CAGR) for the period of 1993-94 to 2004-05 in Gujarat was 2.43 per cent per annum, but this came down to near zero in the latter half of the decade (2004-05 to 2009-10). Moreover, the key sectors, agriculture and manufacturing, witnessed negative growth rates at -1.59 and -2.23 per cent per annum respectively. However, agriculture and manufacturing sectors in Gujarat have done extremely well in terms of GDP growth in this period (Table 8.5 in annexure). Employment grew at a significant rate only in the service and construction sectors in Gujarat (Table 8.4 in annexure). During the latter half of the decade, total employment in All India and Maharashtra grew at similar negative rate, while in Haryana and Gujarat, it remained almost stagnant and in Tamil Nadu, employment increased comparatively faster at around 1 percent. But what is important to notice is the sectoral differences in growth rates across states. Industrial sector in Gujarat and Maharashtra has negative employment growth, while Tamil Nadu, Haryana and India has positive growth rate. In services sector, Gujarat is performing very well compared to all other states and India. Service sector employment at in all three states grew at similar to national average.

In order to identify the sectors that have grown within services, based on a study by Rani (2008) we categorized the service sector into two groups, on the basis of skill and capital requirements. Services 1 are largely low productive services, whereas services II consist of more modern, skilled and capital-intensive services. As shown in the Table 8.6 in annexure, both, service I and service II grew significantly at the rate of 3.61 per cent and 7.07 per cent respectively for the period between 2004-05 and 2009-10.

Furthermore, the sectors that witnessed growth have exhibited a certain pattern. As seen from Table 8.6 in annexure, the increased growth has largely come from self employed and causal labour. The construction sector which is the main driver of employment growth in the latter half of 2000s grew nearly at the rate of 6 per cent and this growth of employment is largely attributed to casual employment. Regular employment in construction sector has been negative. A similar trend prevails in service sector, where large share of growth has come from the causal and self employment.

Employment Growth in the Manufacturing sector

In India as for Gujarat, the 1980s were a decade of job loss in organized manufacturing.[1] The first half the 1990s, show significant efforts at liberalization in India and at the state level and investment boom in this period, saw high growth rates of gross value added and employment in organized manufacturing increased both in India and in Gujarat. However, as the growth momentum fizzled out from the latter half of the 1990s, employment declined again to the levels of early 1990s. From 2004 onwards, employment is the organized sector has increased significantly both in India and Gujarat and this holds a ray of hope for the organized manufacturing sector employment.

Within the manufacturing sector, the organized employment constitutes 31 per cent of manufacturing employment in 2005-06 as against 19 per cent in India. Between 2000 and 2006, the unorganized manufacturing workforce grew at 4.47 per cent in Gujarat. For most of the early years of this decade, the organized manufacturing saw a fall in employment. The total manufacturing sector saw a rise in employment in this period, on account of the unorganized manufacturing sector which constitutes the bulk of the manufacturing employment in India as well as Gujarat.

As pointed out in this paper, the latter half of the 2000s saw a negative growth in employment in the manufacturing sector (at -2.6 per cent between 2004-05 and 2009-10). This happened in spite of the high growth rate of employment in the organized sector in this period. This leads us to conclude that the negative employment witnessed in the manufacturing sector in the latter half of the 2000s has happened on account of the unorganized manufacturing sector. No latter rounds have been conducted on the unorganized sector enterprises after the 62nd round (2005-06). However, as Hirway (2011) has shown in her study, 45 per cent of the diamond industry workers in Gujarat lost their jobs owing to the global financial crisis in 2009. The gems and jewels sector is the highest contributor to employment (30 per cent) in unorganized manufacturing sector in Gujarat.

Employment Growth across Sectors and Gender in Gujarat

The percentage of the workforce employed in rural Gujarat has fallen from 75 per cent in 1993-94 to 66 per cent in 2009-10. This is mainly accounted for by a fall in female workforce. Throughout the period of study, the growth of employment in the urban sector has been higher than the rural sector in Gujarat (Table 8.7).

Between 1993-94 to 1999-00, employment in rural area grew marginally faster than urban area. Industrial employment growth is negative for both rural and urban areas. Growth rate of agriculture workforce in urban area is faster than rural area especially for males while the service sector grew comparatively faster in rural areas, except for banking and insurance.

Between 1999-00 to 2004-05, the total employment growth rate in urban Gujarat was much higher than rural Gujarat. This period witnessed a much higher growth in urban Gujarat mainly on account of the industrial sector (especially manufacturing) and had grown much faster for the female workforce. The service sector has also grown much faster in rural areas compared to urban areas. (Table 8.7 in annexure).

Between 2004-05 to 2009-10, as mentioned earlier, the growth rate is almost stagnant for Gujarat but across rural and urban areas, the employment is mainly decreased in the rural areas especially for females. For females in rural areas, the employment growth rate is negative for all the three sectors. However, for males it is positive for only agriculture and transport, storage and communication and the decrease in industry and service sector is much lesser than for the females. In urban areas, the growth rate is 4.98 per cent. It is comparatively higher for males 5.22 per cent and for females it is 3.92 per cent. For females, the employment growth rate is negative in both agriculture and industry and for the service sector it is even greater than the growth rate of males in the service sector. Within services, the employment growth rate is higher in banking, insurance and real estate and community, social and personal services for both males and females (Table 8.7 in annexure).

Nature of Employment Growth

Over the last two decades, the nature of employment growth in India has witnessed a significant change. During 1993-94 to 2004-05, the employment growth at all India level was derived by growth in self employed and regular employee, while in post 2005, the increase in casual workers has emerged as the main driver of employment growth. Noticeably, the casualisation is more prominent in urban area, where the number of casual workers has grown at a very high rate as compared to the rural area. At regional level, the story is different. Though, nature of employment growth in Haryana and Tamil Nadu has changed in line with national trend, Gujarat and Maharashtra has shown different trend. In both these states, the casual workers have witnessed an absolute decline in post 2005 as compared to a very high growth of casualisation in Tamil Nadu and Haryana. However, the rural urban breakup shows an interesting story for Gujarat, Tamil Nadu and Haryana. These three states have witnessed a very high growth of casual workers in urban area after witnessing a decline in casualisation in pre 2005. This trend of re-casualisation marks a U turn in wrong direction (Table 8.8 in annexure).

After seeing the nature of employment growth how these changes in growth affect the share of each type of employment in total employment in Gujarat. The proportion of casual employment for Gujarat has been declining over the period, in comparison to all India figure. However, this must be seen in the context of the already existing high levels of casual employment in Gujarat than the rest of the country. As much as 37 of the workforce were causal workers in Gujarat in 1993-94 against 32 per cent in India. This has come down to 30.5 per cent in Gujarat while in India it has increased to 33.5 per cent by 2009-10 (Table 8.9 in annexure).

However, this decrease in proportion of casual employment in Gujarat is taken by increase in proportion of self employment, which may or may not be better in terms of quality of work. There is no substantial change in the structure of employment, though there is a marginal increase in the proportion of regular employment. Regular employment which is a marker of better quality of employment has been stable throughout the period, for rural Gujarat as well as rural India. However, for urban area in Gujarat, there was marginal increase for the period of 1993-94 to 2004-05 followed by a decline in the latter period. For all India, the figures were slightly better off (Table 8.9 in annexure).

The above trend in the structure of the status of employment reflects the base effect as the initial share for casual in the total employment for Gujarat was high to start with. However, in terms of additional employment generated during the last two decades, there have been some changes in the rural Gujarat which is quite different from all India trend. For instance, the additional employment generated in rural Gujarat for the last two decade, nearly 90 per cent of it has come from self employment, for all India it is just 30 per cent, bulk of the rest of rural employment being from casual employment for rural India. This trend may indicate the predominant importance of agriculture and its vibrant high growth in the last decade for Gujarat (Table 8.10 in annexure).

Similarly, there is a significance difference between urban Gujarat and urban India in terms of status of additional employment generated during 1993-94 to 2009-10. As shown in the Table 8.10 in annexure, the additional employment generated in the last two decade in urban Gujarat has largely in the form of self employed and regular employment, where as for urban India, beside these forms, casualisation also took place. For instance, out of every 100 jobs generated in urban Gujarat, self employment accounts 49 and regular 42 and casual account just of 9. In Urban India, for the same categories, the figures are 38, 46 and 16 respectively. However, the increase in the share of self-employment is also no guarantee of prosperity, as the substantial increase has come from sectors with low intensity of capital and low productivity services.

Labour Productivity

Labour productivity has been calculated here using Net State Domestic Product (NSDP) at constant prices per (PS+SS) worker. Since the estimates of the Net State Domestic Product (NSDP) for the state are not available officially, we obtained them using the splicing method. The total workers provided by the NSSO unit level data have been used to arrive at the labour productivity.

The calculated labour productivity for the sectors provides an insight into the extent of different factors of production involved in the economy. Interestingly, labour productivity in the agricultural sector has significantly increased between 2004-05 and 2009-10 at the rate of 5.87 per annum in comparison to 2.66 per cent for the previous period. This growth in agricultural productivity may be attributed to the commercial and contract farming which involves production with larger capital intensity.

Similarly, all other sectors have also witnessed an increase in productivity, between 2004-05 and 2009-10 in comparison to 1993-94 and 2004-05. In line with the trend, the productivity in manufacturing, recorded a continuous growth since 1993 -94 onwards settling only at the highest in the recent period. The growth in manufacturing productivity was 9.75 per cent per annum between 2004-05 and 2009-10 as against 4.25 for the previous period. In a nutshell, the productivity of labour grew at a rate which was double than that of the earlier period. This is a clear reflection of rising capital intensity and falling employment per unit of capital in the state.

The productivity in the construction sector too witnessed a significant increase from 5 per cent to 8 per cent for the same period. However, the productivity in the service sector maintained a similar trend for the both periods.

Figure 8.1: Share of Employment across Sectors for Different Regions* in Gujarat

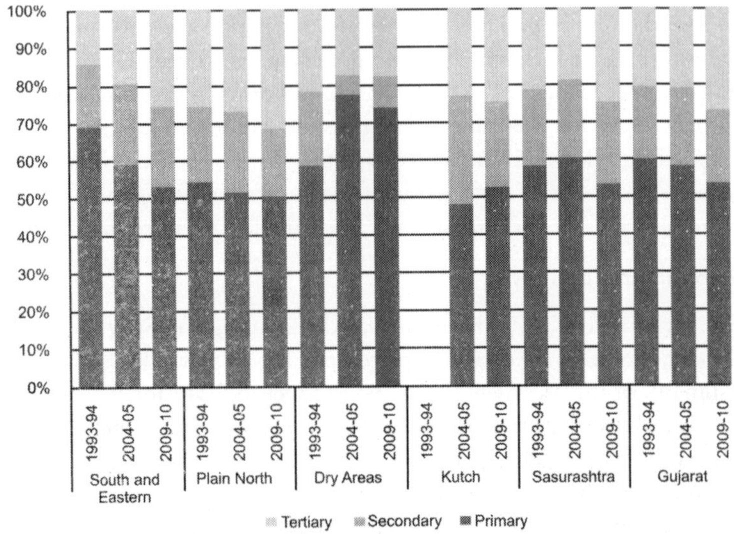

Source: Calculated from unit level data of various NSS rounds.
* Kutch was included in the Dry region in 1993-94.

Regional Employment Structures in Gujarat

The NSSO has classified Gujarat into five broad regions: South and South Eastern, Plain Northern, Dry Areas, Kutch and Saurashtra and this classification is based on the agro-climatic factors. It may be mentioned here that the NSS rounds (50th, 61st and 66th) have used, have different regional compositions. Unlike many other states, Gujarat displays considerable geographical heterogeneity in terms of agro meteorological and climatic conditions, and soil and water regimes. Therefore, to make the NSS regions meaningfully comparable for the successive rounds, become a daunting task. For instance, in 50th round (1993-94) and 61st round (2004-05), there were five regions namely Eastern, Plain Northern, Plain Southern, Dry Areas and Saurashtra.

However, the regions for 66th round (2009-10) are different, where NSSO merged Eastern and Plain Southern region in to one but both regions exhibit different structure in terms of geography and economy. The Eastern region is populated with tribal population and economically backward as inferred from the indicators of industrial development.

Therefore, some authors (Patel, 1991), demarcate Gujarat into just two regions, one as the heartland of Gujarat and the other as the periphery. The heartland endows a well-developed resource base including the fertile land and rivers canals and rainfall, the well irrigated areas comprise the districts of Gandhinagar, Ahemadabad, Kheda, Vadodara, Bharuch, Surat and Valsad. The region is also known as the Golden Corridor of Gujarat. This is the region which exhibits a high level industrial development and occupational diversification as compared to the other regions in the state (Kundu, 2000).

The other broader region is the periphery encircling the heartland and consists of Saurashtra and Kutch in the west and North East, and dry areas like Sabarkantha, Banakantha, Mahasana, Panchmahals and Dangs respectively in North and North-east and the South of Gujarat. Within these regions, one finds desert, semi-desert areas of the North, the saline coastal area of Saurashtra and the Eastern tribal belt. However, within the periphery, there are some areas like Kutch and Jamnagar which are agriculturally and industrially more prosperous (Streefkerk, 2001).

In spite of different classification of regions in Gujarat, by different scholars, the NSS regions still captures the broad trend of regional economic structure. As shown in the Table in 8.12 annexure, the share of employment in total employment for different regions for 2009-10 is the following: Southern region accounts 36 per cent, Northern region accounts 31 per cent followed by Saurashtra 24 per cent and Dry and Kutch 6 and 3 per cent respectively.

Aggregate employment growth for different regions has also been uneven. For instance, as shown in the Table 8.13, in the last five years, except Northern region and Dry region, all the other regions witnessed negative growth rate. Similarly, construction and service sectors have been major drivers of growth in employment. Particularly, regions of Saurashtra (26 per cent per annum) and Kutch (25 per cent per annum) have witnessed a phenomenal growth employment in construction sectors.

However, as mentioned elsewhere, the regions like Dry areas, Kutch and Saurashtra lag behind the other regions. For instance, in Dry region, employment share of secondary sector to total employment has come down from 19 per cent in 2003-04 to 5 per cent in 2004-05, and increased marginally up to 8 per cent in 2009-10. One may attribute this drastic decline to the Kutch region being included in the Dry region. However, the fact remains that more than 70 per cent workforce still depends on agriculture and allied sector in the region as against the state average of 53 per cent. Similarly, there is a decline in industrial employment in the Plain Northern region; it declined from 21 per cent in 2004-05 to 18 per cent in 2009-10. Besides, the reduction in dependency of workforce on agriculture has been stagnant for the region. Similarly, for the Kutch region, there is a rise in workforce dependency on agriculture and allied sector between 2004-05 and 2009-10. And also, the share of industrial employment has declined for the region from 28 per cent in 2004-05 to 22 per cent in 2009-10. The share of industrial employment for the Saurashtra region has been stagnant throughout the period.

In line with the above trend, in the sectoral share of employment for different regions, the employment status also exhibits the disparity in quality of employment for difference regions. For instance, in Dry region, the share of regular employment which is a measure of quality, has come down from 11 per cent in 2004-05 to 8 per cent in 2009-10 and the corresponding figures for the same for the state are 17 per cent in 2004-

Figure 8.2: Employment Status across Regions in Gujarat

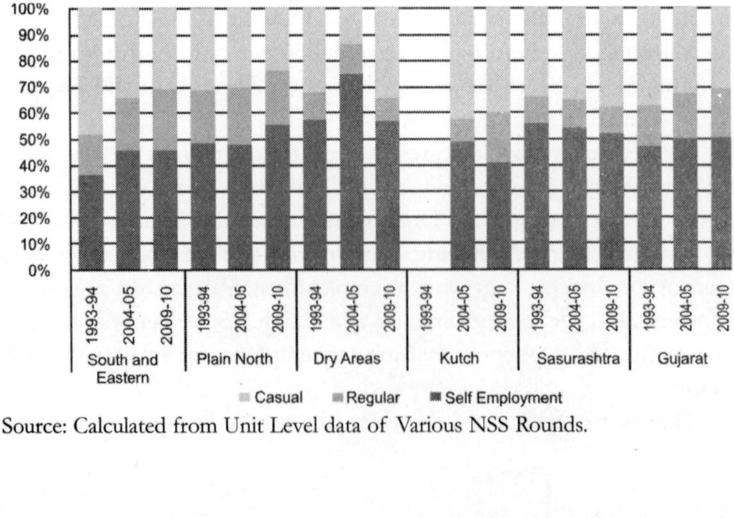

Source: Calculated from Unit Level data of Various NSS Rounds.

05 and 18 per cent in 2009-10. Similarly, except Kutch, other regions like Saurashtra and Plain North have witnessed stagnancy in regular employment. Besides, in some regions the causalization of employment is higher. The decline in the share of regular employment for Dry region was compensated only by causal employment. The share of employment for the region in 2004-05, was 13 per cent whereas in 2009-10, it had gone up to 34 per cent. A similar trend prevails for the Saurashtra region too. It has increased from 35 per cent in 2004-05 to 37 per cent. In totality, it appears that the increase in the status of employment has come either from the self-employment or the casual employment.

Employment across Social Groups

As mentioned earlier, Gujarat has an impressive record in many of the growth indicators settling itself on the above national average. However, there is now a growing concern among the academicians and policy-makers so as to see whether this growth is inclusive in nature or not. The debate has pushed the goal of inclusiveness to the centre of the growth strategy. It is to see whether such high growth has yielded benefits to all including the poor, social groups like the SCs, STs, OBCs, religious

Figure 8.3: Share of Employment across Sectors for Different Social and Religious Groups

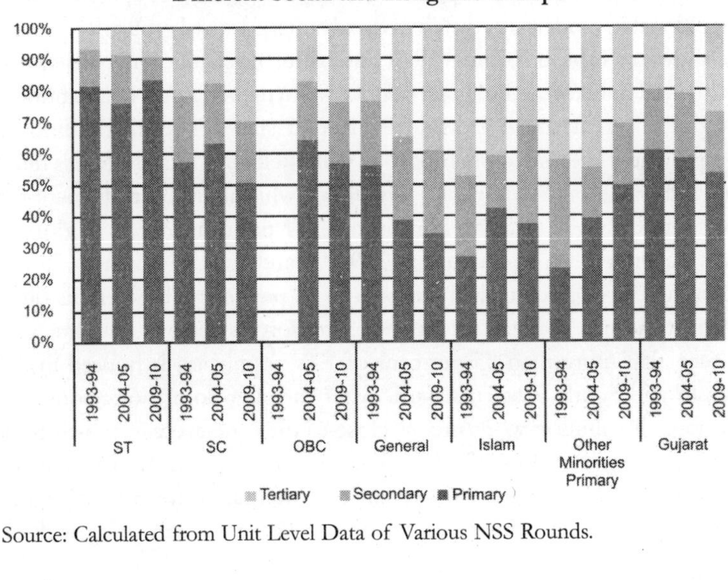

Source: Calculated from Unit Level Data of Various NSS Rounds.

minorities and other excluded groups. The Planning Commission defines inclusive growth as the one that brings down incidence of poverty, improvement in health outcomes, access to education and better opportunities for both wage employment and livelihoods.[2] An approach to twelfth five year plan, Planning Commission (2011). However, among all the indicators of inclusiveness, employment is taken here as an indicator to measure whether the high growth in the state has brought about any gainful regular employment for different socially marginalized and religious disadvantaged groups or not.

The share of employment in total employment as per the latest NSS round is the followings: as shown in the Table 8.16 in annexure, General category accounts 33 per cent, while it is 38 per cent for OBC, followed by STs 18 per cent, and SCs 10 per cent. Similarly, as argued elsewhere, aggregate employment growth has been negative for all the groups except General and STs, while for STs, it is stagnant and for General it is marginally positive in the second of last decade. However, as shown in the Table 8.17 in annexure, interestingly it was only STs which was witnessing positive growth in employment in agriculture while rest of the groups facing negative employment growth. Service and construction have been drivers for employment growth for the all the groups except STs.

It is expected that the growth induced change in the structure of economy, opens up the possibility of changing occupation from traditional to modern for different disadvantaged social groups. However, as shown in Table 8.18 and 8.19 of annexure, the change and consequent structural transformation in terms of employment has not been uniform across different social groups in different states. The distribution of employment across sectors for the STs and Religious Minorities has tilted towards traditional sectors like agriculture, while it has been stagnant for SCs and OBCs in Gujarat. For instance, 81 per cent of STs workforce was dependent on agriculture in 1993-94 and it came down to 76 per cent in 2004-05, but against went up to 83 per cent. This trend is quite against the state average moment of workforce structure. And it is also a fact, that more than 85 per cent of STs population is housed in the South and South Eastern region. After merging both the regions, the average distribution workforce is close to the state average, which is 46 per cent for agriculture, 23 per cent for industry and 31 per cent for service. Therefore, there is less chance of pull factor for bringing more STs population in primary sector due to better growth or agriculture prosperity. If it is so, it should have been reflected in others group's workforce distribution as well. Similarly, for other minorities, workforce dependency on agriculture was 23 per cent in 1993-94, while it went up 50 per cent in 2009-10. For SCs and the OBCs, the trend has been stagnant and nothing much significant occurred in the distribution of workforce.

A similar trend prevails in the distribution of employment status among the social groups as well. Here, as shown in the Table 8.20 in annexure, higher share in the regular salaried employment is being considered as a measure of quality of employment. Therefore, the fewer shares in the regular employment can be attributed to exclusive nature of growth or non-participation of certain social groups in the growth process. The performance of STs is very dismal. For instance, the contribution of regular employment to total employment of STs was just 7 per cent in 1993-94, and it increased marginally up to 9 per cent in 2004-05, and again came down to 7 per cent in 2009-10. Similarly for Muslims, it was 15 per cent in 1993-94, it increased to 17 per cent in 2004 05, and again came down to 14 per cent in 2009-10. Interestingly, for OBCs, the share of regular employment in its total employment was fewer and next to STs in the state. The SCs has been relatively better off in terms of the share of regular employment in its total employment. It is also to be noted here that the third largest population in the state is of STs. And its dismal performance in all the employment indicators is something that pushes one to rethink about the growth strategy in the state and its nature of inclusiveness.

Figure 8.4: Employment Status across Social and Religious Groups

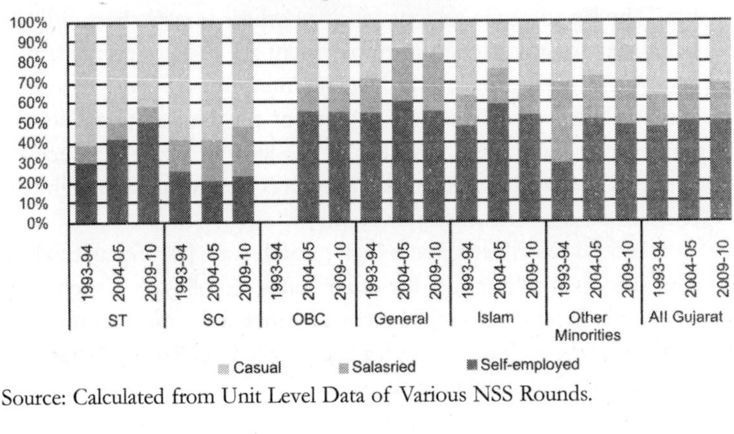

Source: Calculated from Unit Level Data of Various NSS Rounds.

Conclusion

Gujarat has been consistently maintaining an impressive growth in income in the last decade. This growth however, is not reflected in the employment outcomes. The conclusions of the paper are the following: First, the structural changes in the sources of GDP are not reflected in changes in the structure of employment. There is mismatch or disproportionality between the sources of income and employment across sectors. The analysis clearly establishes the fact that 88 per cent of the state income comes from non-agriculture sectors providing employment to only about 47 per cent of workforce. The shift to non-farm employment has not occurred in the rural Gujarat, whereas, there has been a substantial shift towards non-farm employment in rural India.

The stagnancy in the employment growth rates, while seen throughout India, is even more pronounced in the high growth state of Gujarat. Gujarat has seen high growth rates in all the three sectors, agriculture, manufacturing and services in the last five years. However, agriculture and industry have experienced negative growth in employment in this period. Whatever growth occurred in this period, has been on account of causal and self-employment, suggesting an increasing trend towards informalization in employment in the state.

Gujarat has also enjoyed a continuous and significant growth in labour productivity, however, the gains in productivity have not been passed on to the workers, either in terms of a rise in wages or gainful regular employment. The impact of wages has been highlighted by Hirway (2011).

The changes in employment are not evenly distributed across all regions. The lag of some regions vis-a-vis others is very sharp. Finally, the beneficiary of this growth in employment are also not evenly spread out across all social groups and religious minorities. Socially marginal groups like ST's, are increasingly dependent on the traditional sectors without regular gainful employment in modern and high productivity sectors. The non-inclusive nature of growth is clearly highlighted by the experiences of the state in employment.

It is indeed worrisome that a high growth state like Gujarat, which is being seen as a role model for other states to follow has such poor results to offer in terms of employment. Decent employment is important not only from the welfare aspect for the people but also for sustainable growth and political stability in the state.

NOTES

1. See paper on manufacturing in this book.

BIBLIOGRAPHY

Bagchi AK, et al. Growth and Structural Change in the Economy of Gujarat, 1970-2000. *Economic and Political Weekly* 2005; 40(28): 3039-3047.

Chandrashekar CP. Latest Employment trends from the NSSO. *Macroscan*, 2011. http://www.macroscan.org/fet/jul11/fet140711NSSO.html. (2011, accessed on 12 March 2012).

Dholakia HR and Spare AA. Gujarat's Growth Story. *Economic and Political Weekly* 2011; 46(32): 122- 124.

Dholakia RH. Liberalisation in Gujarat – Review of Recent Experience. *Economic and Political Weekly* 2000; 35(35/36): 3121-3124.

Directorate of Economics and Statistics. *Socio-Economic Review* 2010; Gujarat.

Hirway I and Shah N. Labour and Employment under Globalisation: The Case of Gujarat. *Economic and Political Weekly* 2011; 46(22): 57-65.

Hirway I. Dynamics of Development in Gujarat: Some Issues. *Economic and Political Weekly* 2000; 35(35/36): 3106-3120.

Hirway I. Selective Development and Widening Disparities in Gujarat. *Economic and Political Weekly* 1995; 30(40/41): 2603-2618.

Kundu A. Globalising Gujarat-Urbanisation, Employment and Poverty. *Economic and Political Weekly* 2000; 35(35/36): 3172-3182.

Mathur N and Kashyap SP. Agriculture in Gujarat: Problems and Prospects. *Economic and Political Weekly* 2000; 35(35/36): 3137-3146.

National Sample Survey Organization. *Employment and Unemployment Situation in India 1993-94*. New Delhi: National Sample Survey Organisation, Department of Statistics, Government of India.

National Sample Survey Organization. *Employment and Unemployment Situation in India 2004-05*. New Delhi: National Sample Survey Organisation, Department of Statistics, Government of India.

National Sample Survey Organization. *Employment and Unemployment Situation in India 2009-10*. New Delhi: National Sample Survey Organisation, Department of Statistics, Government of India.

Planning Commission. *Faster, Sustainable and More Inclusive Growth: An Approach to Twelfth Five-Year Plan,* 2011, New Delhi: Planning Commission, Government of India.

Rangarajan C, Kaul PI and Seema. Where is the Missing Labour force? *Economic and Political Weekly* 2011; 46(39): 68-72.

Streefkerk H. Thirty years of Industrial labour in South Gujarat: Trends and Significance. *Economic and Political Weekly* 2001; 36(26): 2308-2411.

9

An Analysis of State of Education in Gujarat

Sourindra Ghosh

1. Introduction

The current discourse regarding Gujarat is predominated by its success story in economic front, be it in terms of its phenomenal Gross State Domestic Product (GSDP) growth rate or its high rate of industrialization as compared to the rest of the states of India. From a marginally lower growth rate than the national average in the 1980's, it registered much higher growth rates in both the decades of 1990's and 2000, as compared to the country as a whole. In fact, Figure 9.1 shows that the divergence of Gujarat's GSDP growth rate from India's GDP growth rate has widened significantly during those three decades.

Figure 9.1: GDP/DSDP Growth Rates

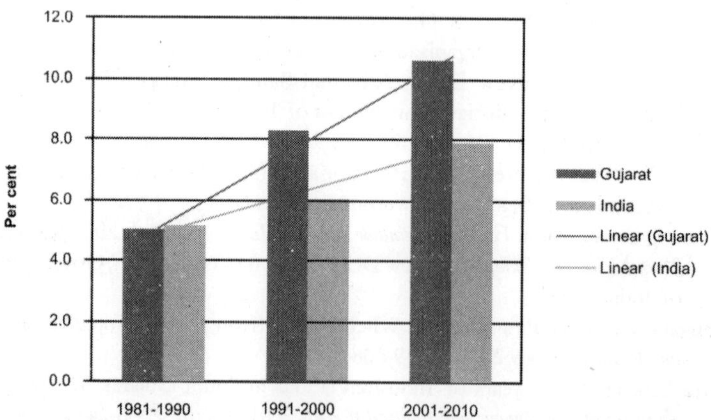

Source: CSO

But the question, that how much socially inclusive that growth or development trajectory of Gujarat is has been by and large remained unasked amid such celebrations. Has its high growth rate 'trickled down' to all the sections of the people? Has it resulted in better quality of life for the larger section of the population, or for the socio-economically weaker sections of 'lower castes', women and religious minorities?

Education is one such many socio-economic parameters which capture that quality aspect of human life. In this paper, we will critically examine Gujarat's performance in education sector during the last decade. In our cross-sectional analysis, we will compare our findings on Gujarat with the all India levels, as well as with the economically comparable states of Haryana, Maharashtra and Tamil Nadu. We will largely use NSSO 55th Round (1999-2000) and NSSO 64th Round (2007-08) data for our analysis. NSSO 55th Round is a quinquennial large sample round; hence broad estimates of education without much disaggregation will produce fairly accurate estimates (we won't use much disaggregation for NSSO 55th Round data). NSSO 64th Round is an education specific survey; so we will use this data more freely for our analysis at various disaggregated levels.

The paper is divided into eight sections. After this introductory section, Section 2 evaluates Gujarat's performance regarding certain key education indicators across regions and over time. Section 3 analyses those key indicators at a further disaggregated level by gender, caste and religion. We will restrict our analysis only across regions in this section. Section 4 will briefly discuss Gujarat's access to education at household level and compare it with the regions that we have previously decided upon. Section 5 will briefly deal with specifically higher education and technical education. Section 6 will discuss the pattern of state government expenditure in education sector. Section 7 will discuss the role of the private sector in education. We will end with some concluding remarks in Section 8.

2. Key Education Indicators: Gujarat's Performance Over Time

In this section, we would briefly evaluate Gujarat's performance in terms of some key educational indicators. We would make a comparison between NSSO 55th Round (1999-2000) and NSSO 64th Round (2007-08), and across the states of Tamil Nadu, Maharashtra and Haryana.

2.1 Literacy

Literacy rate is one of the basic indicators of education outcomes. Though literacy rate of Gujarat is higher than the all India average, in its comparison with economically similar performing states, Gujarat does not fare much better. Literacy rate in Gujarat is lower than that of Maharashtra and Tamil Nadu. However, it has a higher literacy rate as compared to Haryana.

Literacy rate of Gujarat increased to 75.2 per cent in 2007-08 (NSSO 64th Round) from 69.4 per cent in 1999-2000 (NSSO 55th Round) for individuals of age 6 years and above; in comparison, India's literacy rate improved to 72 per cent from 62.1 per cent in that same time period of that same age group. It is evident that the improvement of Gujarat in literacy rates is sluggish as compared to the all India scenario. Ranking all the states and Union Territories (UTs)[1] in terms of literacy rate for NSSO 55th and 64th Rounds reveals that Gujarat has slipped in position for age group of 6 years and above, whereas it has maintained its position for 6-14 years age group. For the 15 major states[2], Gujarat's ranking in terms of literacy rate has deteriorated for both 6 years and above and 6-14 years age group. This is shown in Table 9.1 in annexure.

2.2 Current Attendance

Another way of looking into educational performance is the participation of the populace in educational institutions. As compared to the all India average, Gujarat has a lower percentage of persons who are currently attending any educational institution. The same is also low as compared to that of Tamil Nadu, Maharashtra and Haryana.

To analyse Gujarat's performance over time in this regard as compared to the national scenario, we have ranked the states in terms of proportion of the people who are currently attending any educational institution. Among all the states and UTs, Gujarat's rank has deteriorated from 21st position in NSSO 55th Round to the 26th in NSSO 64th Round, for the age group of 6-14 years, i.e. what is generally considered as school going age for children. In that same age group, Gujarat's rank has deteriorated among 15 major states as well. The same is the case for age group of 6-29 years. The detailed illustration is given in Table 9.2 in annexure.

Thus between the time period 1999-2000 (NSSO 55th Round) and 2007-08 (NSSO 64th Round), Gujarat's educational status has certainly deteriorated in comparison with the other states of the country. As compared to the states of our comparison, Gujarat has been more often than not worse-off with respect to those indicators.

3. Social Inclusion: Literacy and Attendance Disparity by Gender, Caste and Religion

Degree of uniformity of any social good or service across various groups and communities is an important indicator of social inclusion. In this section, we will disaggregate the literacy and attendance data by gender, caste and religion to understand how inclusive the system of education in Gujarat is, as compared to the national picture and other states.

3.1 Gender

There are many facets of gender inequality that are intricately linked with the educational attainment of women (Sen 2001). So, gender inequality in education is linked to inequality in other spheres of women's lives. In Gujarat, male literacy rate stands at 84.75 per cent as compared to 64.8 per cent for the females. The difference is thus of 20 percentage points, which is higher than the gap in literacy rate between male and female at the national level. This gap is also higher in Gujarat in comparison with similar states like Haryana, Maharashtra and Tamil Nadu. This is enumerated in Table 9.3 in annexure.

We will repeat the same exercise for people who are currently attending any educational institution while focusing only in the school going age for children, i.e., 6-14 year age group. Gender gap in Gujarat is higher, both in absolute terms as well as relative to other states/all India level, in the 11-14 year age group (above primary-education age group) than in 6-10 year age group (primary-education age group). For 6-10 year age group, gender-gap in Gujarat is higher than Maharashtra and Tamil Nadu, while it is lower than that of Haryana; in 11-14 year age group, it is higher than all those states. In both the age groups, gender gap is higher in Gujarat than the national average. This is enumerated in Table 9.4 in annexure.

3.2 Caste

In a society stratified with caste hierarchies, socio-economic disparities are visible across caste groups. And extent of such disparity is an indicator of social inclusion, or the lack of it. Overall in India, the 'General' social category—or the so-called 'upper-castes'—has higher literacy rate as compared to the other social groups, such as the Scheduled Tribes (ST), Scheduled Castes (SC) and the Other Backward Classes (OBC), combined. However, in Gujarat the disparity between literacy rate of the General category and the overall literacy rate—measured in terms of difference in percentage point between literacy rate of the General category and the overall literacy rate—is higher than the national average; it is also higher than our states of comparison, viz. Haryana, Maharashtra and, though marginally, Tamil Nadu. This is shown in Table 9.5 in annexure.

We will repeat the same exercise, as we did with gender, for percentage of people who are currently attending any educational institution while focusing only in the school going age for children, i.e., 6-14 year age group. Caste gap, measured in terms of difference in percentage points between General category and total, is higher in Gujarat, both in absolute terms as well as relative to other states/all India level, in the 11-14 year age-group (above primary education age group) than in 6-10 year age group (primary education age group). For both 6-10 year age group and 11-14 year age group, caste gap in Gujarat is higher than all the states under comparison and the national average. This is enumerated in Table 9.6 in annexure.

3.3 Religion—Status of the Muslims

In recent times, the Muslim minority question in Gujarat has been one of the burning issues of our national discourse. In that light, it demands a special attention while analysing the status of Muslim education in Gujarat. For that purpose, alongside a cross sectional analysis with the national scenario, as we have done with gender and caste, we would additionally investigate how status of Muslim education in Gujarat has changed over time. NSSO 55th Round, as we have mentioned earlier, is not an education specific survey. It might produce wrong estimates for religionwise disaggregation of education data owing to sampling issues. Thus, for comparison over time, we would use Census 2001 data and compare it with NSSO 64th Round.

Table 9.7 in annexure compares Muslim literacy rates with overall literacy rates for states of Gujarat, Haryana, Maharashtra and Tamil Nadu, along with the all India levels. Overall, Muslim literacy rate in Gujarat is better than the all India Muslim literacy rate, while among our states of comparison it is lower than Maharashtra and Tamil Nadu. Actually,

Muslim literacy rates of Maharashtra and Tamil Nadu is higher than their respective overall literacy rates, which is reflected in negative values in the fourth column of Table 9.7 in annexure. Gujarat's Muslim literacy rate relative to its overall literacy rate is higher than Haryana, while it is lower than that of Maharashtra and Tamil Nadu. The same is higher in Gujarat compared to the all India situation.

It is interesting to note that, though overall Muslim literacy in Gujarat is higher than the national average, in its rural region literacy rate of non upper caste Muslims (i.e. combined SC, STs and OBC Muslims) is lower than the corresponding all India figure. This is shown in Table 9.8 in annexure.

As stated earlier, given the gravity of the Muslim debate regarding Gujarat, we would now briefly investigate the status of Muslim education in Gujarat over time. We would use literacy rates to make that comparison. The Census measures literacy rates in terms of the percentage of persons aged 7 years and above, who can read and write (the Census definition of literacy is thus comparable with NSSO definition). According to Census, in 2001 Muslim literacy rate in Gujarat was 73.5 per cent which was higher than its overall literacy rate of 69.1 per cent. In 2007-08, according to NSSO 64th Round figures, Muslim literacy rate in Gujarat increased marginally, to 74.3 per cent resulting in a worsening off of Muslim literacy rate compared to Gujarat's overall literacy rate of 74 per cent at that time. Thus, Gujarat's Muslim literacy rate relative to its overall literacy rate experienced a decline in 2007-08 compared to 2001. This is shown in Table 9.9 in annexure.

Table 9.10 in annexure, compares percentage of Muslims who are currently attending any educational institution with that of the overall population, while focusing only on the school going age for children, i.e. 6-14 year age group. At the all India level, percentage of Muslims in that age group currently attending any educational institution is lower than that of the overall percentage in that same age group. However, the gap is much higher in Gujarat as compared to that of all India level for the above primary age group (i.e., 11-14 years). It is also higher than that in Maharashtra and Tamil Nadu, while it is lower than that in Haryana. For primary age group (i.e., 6-10 years), the gap is higher in Gujarat as compared to Maharashtra and Tamil Nadu, while it is lower than Haryana and the national level as well.

In this section, we thus find that social disparities, be it in terms of gender, caste or religion, is more often than not higher in Gujarat regarding education outcomes, participation and access, as compared to our states of comparison, as well as all India levels. It is also quite shocking to note that gender disparity in Gujarat has been found to be even higher than Haryana, which is known for its gender disparity. From our analysis above, it seems that the problem in Gujarat is much bigger at the above primary stage.

4. Access—Distance of Educational Institution from Residence

Physical access to education is one of the major supply side factors that affect educational outcomes and participation. NSSO records distance of each household from nearest school (primary, upper primary and secondary), which would give us an idea about physical access of households, and individuals, to education.

In rural Gujarat, lesser percentage of households, as compared to all India levels and our comparable states of Haryana, Maharashtra and Tamil Nadu, are at a distance of less than 2 km from nearest upper primary and secondary schools; a greater percentage of households, compared to all India and those comparable states, are at a distance of more than 5 km from nearest upper primary and secondary schools. Thus, in rural Gujarat, access to upper primary and secondary schools is less in comparison with all India situation and those states under comparison. Access to primary schools in rural Gujarat, however, is more or less same in such comparison. This is depicted in Table 9.11 in annexure.

For urban Gujarat, however, the situation is just the opposite. In such a comparison with those regions/states as well as national situation, access to primary, upper primary as well as secondary school is better in urban Gujarat. This is depicted in Table 9.12 in annexure.

Access to social amenities/infrastructure has been observed to vary across caste groups. This is because of 'ghettoization' of the lower caste houses, typically confining them to the locations with lesser social-economic facilities of day-to-day life. Table 9.13 in annexure shows percentage of households which are less than 2 km distance from nearest school by caste groups. There are greater percentages of General or 'upper caste' households in Gujarat in this category, as compared to the all India levels, for each of the three school types. This is in sync with our finding in the previous section that disparity between the 'upper castes' and rest of the population in terms of education outcomes and participation is higher in Gujarat as compared to other regions under comparison, including that of all India levels.

5. Higher & Technical Education

While the above sections shows Gujarat's less than satisfactory performance in the education sector, we have so far not dealt specifically with higher education and professional/technical education. Any discussion on education will remain incomplete without touching upon those subjects.

Percentage of persons who are currently attending any educational institution by different age groups is shown in Table 9.14 in annexure. It shows, that for higher age groups in Gujarat, percentage of persons who are currently going to any educational institutions is low as compared to all India average as well as our states of comparison.

Table 9.15 in annexure, shows percentage distribution of all persons (all ages) as per their highest education level attended. Though, there is nothing much to choose between Gujarat and all India scenario, but in respect to our states of comparison, Gujarat has much less percentage of people in higher education groups. However, we must bear in mind two issues. First of all, these results may have been influenced by demographic age bias, if it is present. Secondly, of course, it is influenced not only by the dynamics of current period but also by the past regimes, their policies and outcomes.

So, to solve those issues, we present in Table 9.16 in annexure, the percentage of persons belonging to different education groups among 'relevant' age groups. Thus, for formal education till middle school education level, we look into the age group of 4-13 years of age and calculate the percentage of individuals in that age group who has attained that education level. Similarly, for graduate/postgraduate, we consider the age group 19-29 years. We see that, Gujarat has considerably less percentage of people in higher education groups as compared to our states of comparison and, though by a small margin, to the all India scenario as well.

For technical/professional education, one would have thought that Gujarat might have a different story to tell. Table 9.17 in annexure, shows the percentage distribution of persons in age group 17-29 years who are currently attending any education institution by type of education, viz., general, professional/technical and vocational education. It shows that, there is virtually no difference between Gujarat and the all India situation, while for Maharashtra and especially Tamil Nadu, much higher percentage of persons in this age group is attending professional/technical courses.

Thus, even in higher education, Gujarat's performance is worse than the all India situation as well as in respect to our states of comparison. For technical/professional education, Gujarat's story is not any different from the all India picture while states like Maharashtra and Tamil Nadu are giving huge emphasis on technical/professional education.

6. State Expenditure

The role of state policy must have had serious implication for such deterioration of the education sector in Gujarat; and more so education being primarily a state subject. Figure 9.2 shows Developmental Expenditure (Revenue+Capital) as a proportion of Total Expenditure (Revenue+Capital)[3], taking three year averages. After liberalization in 1990, Developmental Expenditure as a proportion of Total Expenditure, of all states combined, has declined consistently till 2003-04. After that, it started improving, though it never recovered to the initial level of 1991-92. The other states also followed the similar pattern (Haryana having dissimilar pattern till 1999-00), and roughly at same levels as compared with the all states combined figures. In contrast, Gujarat's Developmental Expenditure as a proportion of Total Expenditure was more or less constant during the 1990's. In 1999-2000, the proportion was much higher (more than 10 percentage points) for Gujarat as compared to all the states in our comparison, as well as the all states combined figures. However, after 1999-2000, proportion of Developmental Expenditure to Total Expenditure in Gujarat started to decline rapidly and came down to the level of the states in our comparison, as well as all states combined level, by 2003-04. Thus, as compared to all the states taken together, as well as the states of Haryana, Tamil Nadu and Maharashtra individually, Gujarat's Developmental Expenditure as a proportion of Total Expenditure has declined more rapidly during the period 1999-2000 to 2003-04. Though after 2003-04, it started improving, and so did the other states, it never came back to the level of 1999-2000. This being the direction of state policy of Gujarat, the same can be seen for spending in the education sector. Figure 9.3 shows, expenditure on education[4] as a proportion of total expenditure. For all the states, overall,

Figure 9.2: Share of Developmental Expenditure to Total Expenditure(%)

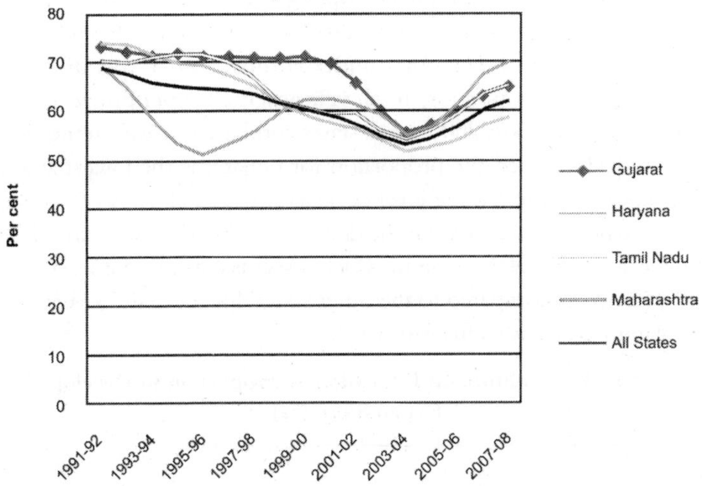

Source: RBI, Handbook of Statistics on State Government Finances.

Figure 9.3: Share of Expenditure on Education to Total Expenditure (%)

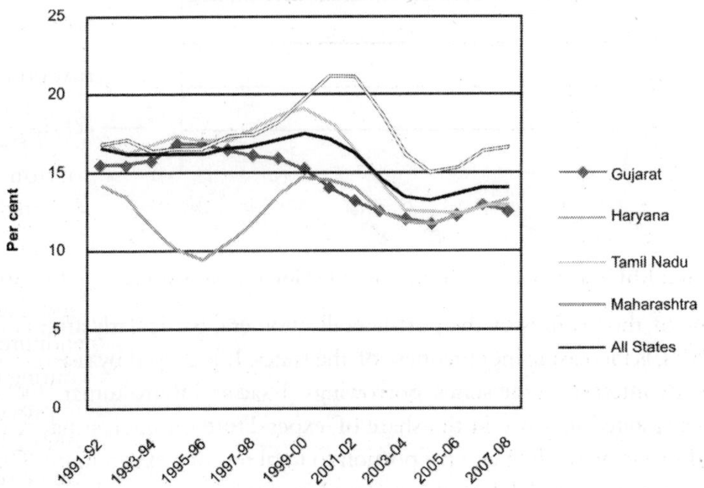

Source: RBI, Handbook of Statistics on State Government Finances.

the decade of 2000, is a period of decline in that proportion. However, the proportion for Gujarat came down below the level of an average state (i.e. for all states combined) during the end of 1990's and has remained below ever since. It was also lower than the other states (at almost same level of Haryana) under comparison. Expenditure on education, as a proportion to developmental expenditure is also consistently falling post 2000 for all states combined, as well in the states under study. However, the proportion for Gujarat is the lowest among those states (at almost same level of Haryana) and all states combined figures, particularly throughout the decade of 2000 (Figure 9.3a). This is definitely a state level decision by which it seems education is a sector of lesser priority, as compared to the other states, for the state government of Gujarat particularly after late 1990's.

Figure 9.3a: Expenditure on Education as Proportion to Development Expenditure (%)

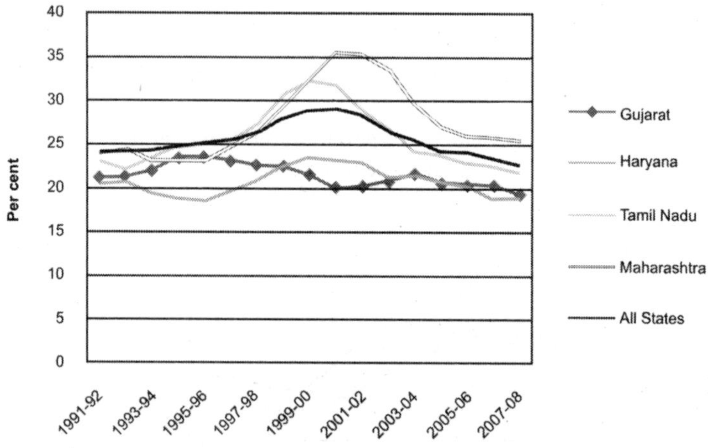

Source: RBI, Handbook of Statistics on State Government Finances.

One of the features of the post-liberalization era, particularly after late-1990's, is increasing indebtedness of the states. It is caused by rise of the rate of interest on the states' borrowings (Issac and Ramakumar, 2006). This resulted in a rise in the share of expenditure on interest payment and servicing of debt as a proportion to total revenue expenditure. This is shown in Figure 9.4. For all states combined, it has consistently increased during the 1990's till 2003-04, after which it has started to decline, though it still remained higher than the 1990's and pre-1990's. This had severely limited the states' capacity to spend in the developmantal sector, of which education is one of the components. Figure 9.4a and 9.4b shows, the relationship between expenditure on interest payment and servicing of debt and developmental expenditure. The proportion of developmental expenditure to total expenditure (revenue+capital) is measured in primary axis. The inverse of expenditure on interest payment/debt servicing as proportion to total revenue expenditure is measured in the secondary axis.

However, there is a variation in the story of Gujarat. Throughout the 1990's, interest payment and servicing of debt as a proportion to total revenue expenditure has almost remained constant, or has increased only marginally, which is reflected in a stable proportion of developmental expenditure in 1990's for Gujarat. In 1999-00, the proportion of interest payment and servicing of debt was lower in Gujarat than an average state. However, after 1999-00, proportion of interest payment and servicing of debt started increasing rapidly for Gujarat and in 2005-06 (three year average), it stood at around 27 per cent, which was much higher than an average state. During that period, we had observed deterioration—and at a much rapid rate than an average indian state—of relative spending in developmental sector as a whole, and on education in particular. Moreover, it is that period roughly where we have seen, in earlier sections, deterioration of education indicators for Gujarat vis-a-vis the other states of the country.

Figure 9.2, has indicated an improvement in the share of Developmental Expenditure in Total Expenditure post 2003-04, for all states combined as well as for Gujarat. We had noted earlier, that the increase was a minor one; but still, it's an increase nonetheless and hence demand some attention.

This increase, albeit a minor one, has been brought about by a decrease in relative expenditure on interest payment and servicing of debt during that same corresponding period, which is shown in Figure 9.4. Fiscal Regulation and Budget Management (FRBM) Act, 2003 which came into force in July 2004 was an exercise, among other things, of limiting fiscal deficit as a proportion to GDP—a typical neo-liberal phenomenon. The Twelfth Finance Commission (2005-10) laid out the conditions for debt-relief of the states by the centre, which among many other things, was the implementation of FRBM Act by the states (Chowdhury and Dasgupta, 2012). It was adopted by most of the states;

Figure 9.4: Revenue Expenditure: Share of Expenditure on Interest Payment to Total Expenditure (%)

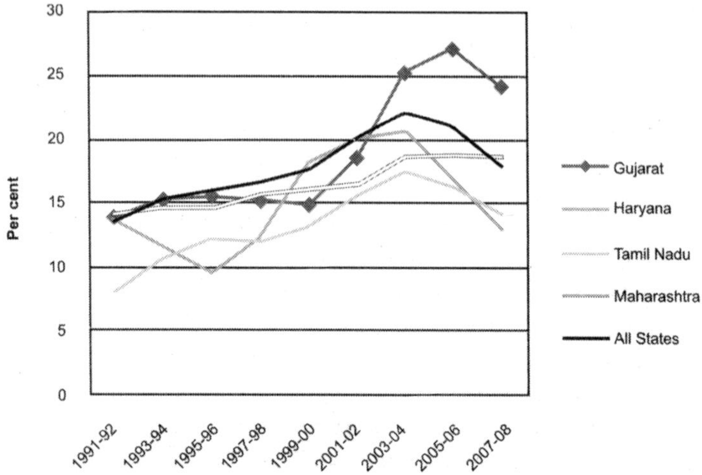

Source: RBI, Handbook of Statistics on State Government Finances.

Figure 9.4a: Gujarat: Relation Between Developmental Expenditure & Expenditure on Interest Payment/Debt Servicing

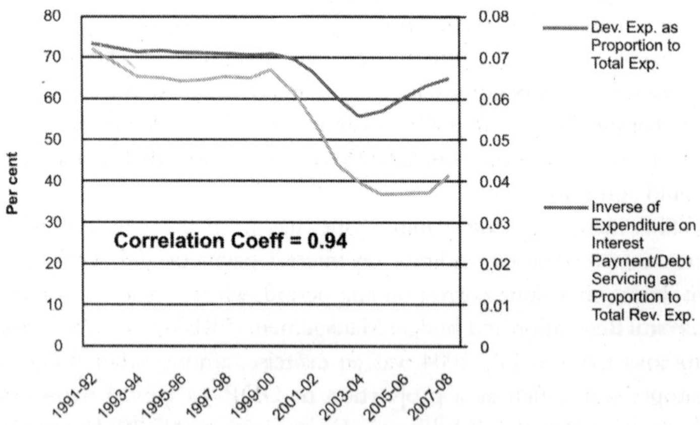

Source: RBI, Handbook of Statistics on State Government Finances.

Figure 9.4b: All States : Relation Between Developmental Expenditure & Expenditure on Interest Payment/Debt Servicing

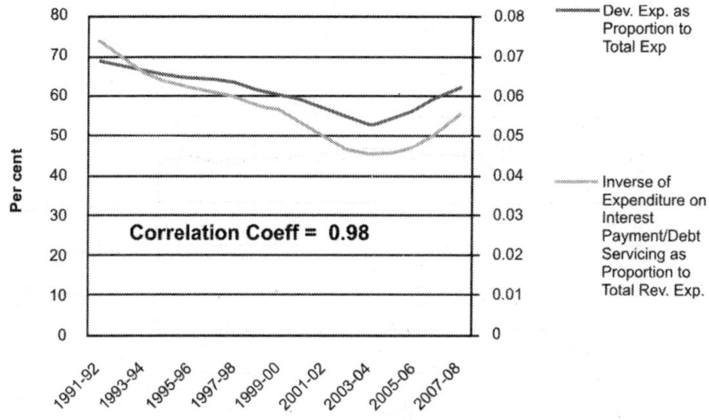

Source: RBI, Handbook of Statistics on State Government Finances.

Gujarat passed its state FRBM Act in 2005. The reduction in relative expenditure on interest payment and servicing of debt by the states has occurred due to this particular policy decision by the state governments ('imposed' by the central government). However, the acceptance of FRBM Act, though has reduced relative expenditure on interest payment and servicing of debt, has also restricted fical deficit as a proportion of GSDP. That has typically restricted developmental expenditure of the states. Figure 9.5 shows, for all the states combined, overall post 1990, developmental expenditure as a proportion to GDP has fallen; and even after reduction of relative expenditure on interest payment and servicing of debt, it hasn't improved. For Gujarat, developmental expenditure as a proportion to GSDP has fallen at a much rapid rate compared to the combined figures, and it has come below the level of the combined-state figures in 2003-04. Spending on education as a proportion to GDP/GSDP has also consistently decreased post 1999-00, for both at the combined state level as well as for Gujarat. It is shown in Figure 9.6. Moreover, Figure 9.6 reveals that, Gujarat's expenditure on education as a proportion to its GSDP fell below the combined states level after 2000-01, and is falling at a higher rate since then, which also explains deterioration of educational performance of Gujarat as compared to the other states.

Figure 9.5: Share of Developmental Expenditure to GSDP (%)

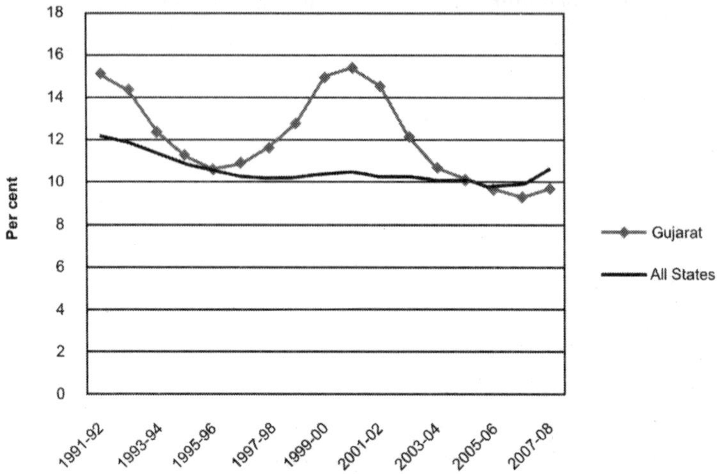

Source: RBI, Handbook of Statistics on State Government Finances, and CSO,

Figure 9.6: Share of Expenditure on Education to GSDP

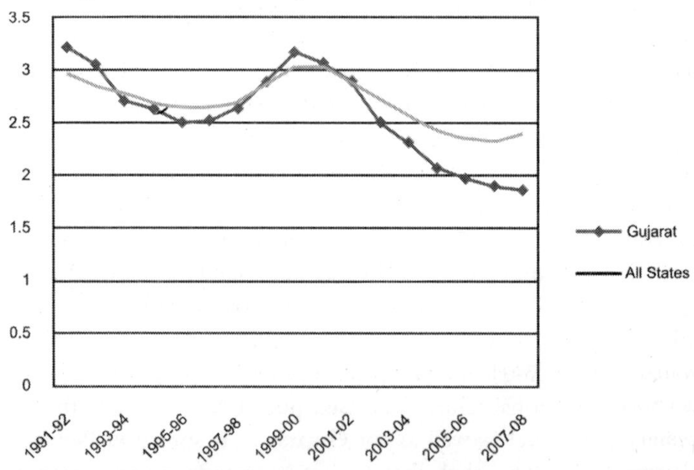

Source: RBI, Handbook of Statistics on State Government Finances, and CSO.

To sum it up, there has been a general phenomenon of decreasing share of developmental expenditure in total expenditure in general, and on education in particular, post 1990 till 2003-04. However, particularly during 1999-00 to 2003-04, the rate of that fall is higher in Gujarat as compared to all the states taken together. This is one of the reasons for why Gujarat has fared even worse than the other states of the country–which is a state level decision that within given resources how much will be allocated to different sectors. The declining share of developmental expenditure in total expenditure in general, and on education in particular, was due to increase in expenditure on interest payment and servicing of debt as a proportion to total expenditure during the post-liberalization era, which in Gujarat's case has increased massively from 1999-00 till 2005-06.

However, post 2003-04, for all states combined, expenditure on interest payment and servicing of debt as a proportion to total revenue expenditure came down, which resulted in minor improvement in relative expenditure in the developmental sector. For Gujarat, it happened post 2005-06. It took place by debt waiver of the states by the centre with the condition of implementing FRBM Act. This, though reduced relative expenditure on interest payment and servicing of debt, has put further restriction on the states on spending in the development sector. As a result (which was again a policy choice of the state government though 'imposed' by the centre), the general post 1999-00, trend of declining Developmental Expenditure in general, and on education in particular, as a proportion to GDP continued. Moreover, the decline was at a higher rate in Gujarat compared to the all states combined figures, for both developmental expenditure and expenditure on education. Moreover, Gujarat's expenditure on education as a proportion to its GSDP has fallen below the combined states level in 2000-01, and is falling at a higher rate since then. Hence, it is no surprise that Gujarat's educational indicators would deteriorate during this time period.

7. Private Education

Privatized education system is seen as an alternative to state funded education, a panacea to the failure and 'limitations' of the state. So it is necessary to investigate the role the private sector—or private schools—is playing in Gujarat in the context of weaker state support as compared to the all India situation. In this section, we will analyse the issue by taking into account persons (5-29 years age) who are currently attending any educational institution at primary level and above.

Table 9.18 in annexure shows, the percentage of persons (5-29 years age) currently attending any educational institution by type of institution.

There are two important observations that one can highlight from it.

Firstly, overall, proportion of people going to government institutions or institutions run by local bodies is almost the same for Gujarat as well as the all India levels. Which means, the impact of relative greater neglect of education sector by the state in Gujarat (as compared to all India situation) is definitely not mitigated by the private education sector of Gujarat. Moreover, there is considerable rural-urban disparity in this issue as well, with much greater percentage of the persons in rural Gujarat dependent on public education as compared to the rural all India situation. Which means, the state neglect of education sector has a much larger impact in rural Gujarat in comparison with rural India taken as a whole. However, in urban Gujarat there are less proportion of people dependent upon public education in comparison with urban India taken as a whole.

The second obeservation that one can highlight is that in Gujarat, particularly in the urban areas, there are significantly larger proportion of people dependent on government-aided private institutions as compared to the all India situation. In fact, in Gujarat, more proportion of people is currently attending in government-aided private institutions than un-aided private institutions. This may indicate that the Gujarat government is more inclined, as compared to other states in general, to promote private initiatives in education sector.

Expanding our previous observation, regarding the possiblity of private sector as an agency with ability to mitigate the impact of neglect of education sector by the state, we further disaggregate our analysis by economic status. We will investigate about the type of educational institution the persons, belonging to poorest 20 per cent and richest 20 per cent of the households (rural and urban separately), are currently attending.

Table 9.19 in annexure shows, that persons belonging to poorer households depend much more on public education than their richer counterparts, for both in Gujarat as well as India as a whole. We had previously observed, that in rural Gujarat, much greater percentage of the persons are dependent on public education as compared to the rural all India, whereas in urban Gujarat there are somewhat less proportion of people dependent upon public education in comparison with urban India taken as a whole. However, Table 19 in annexure shows that the persons belonging to poorest 20 per cent household in urban Gujarat is significantly more dependent on public education than their urban all India counterparts.

This disproves any possibility of the claim that the neglect of the education sector by the state in Gujarat, relative to the all India situation, is balanced by the better performance of the private sector in the state compared to the all India situation. That might have been the case if there were more proportion of people in Gujarat, compared to the all India situation, currently attending private education institutions; on the contrary, the situation is just the opposite, except for rich urban Gujratis.

Why the private sector has not been able to take up the stead of the public sector is also quite evident. Table 9.20 in annexure shows, average per head total expenditure on education incurred by persons who are currently attending any educational institution, by different types of educational institutions, both in Rupee terms as well as expressed as a percentage of expenditure (average) in government educational institutions. It must be noted, that average per head expense on education is lower in Gujarat than that of the all India levels.

One of the factors that influence choice regarding type of educational institution is affordability. High cost of private education relative to public education means a vast section of population will always remain outside the domain of private education sector. In Gujarat, particularly in the urban areas, the cost (i.e., average per head total expense on education) of private education relative to public education is much higher than the corresponding all India levels. This indicates why in Gujarat, except its rich urban sections, greater percentage of persons are more dependent on public education than their all India counterparts. It also indicates that Gujarat government's greater inclination, as compared to other states in general, to promote private initiatives in education sector, as we had tentatively inferred previously, is accompanied by less regulation of the private sector in education. This approach certainly leaves lesser scope for the private sector to balance the neglect and the failures of the state regarding education sector.

8. Conclusion

The big mismatch between Gujarat's phenomenal growth story and its poor performance in key social sector such as education is actually a part of the phenomenal growth story of Gujarat. The neo-liberal growth trajectory, which has ensured higher growth rate in the condition of retreating developmental role of the state, induces such 'disparities'. There are strong indications that regarding certain basic educational outcome and participation parameters, Gujarat has slipped from its previous position, during the period of our study, in comparison with other states of India. That expectedly coincided with the retreating social role of the government of Gujarat, championing the neo-liberal economic trajectory of the country. With narrowing social role of the government, and hence the crunch in resource allocation in key sectors, the deprived sections—the 'lower castes', minorities, women—suffered the most; where resource is scarce, proportionately more of it goes in hands of the socially powerful sections. Thus, due to the process of the growth trajectory and a diminishing social role of the government (which that very growth process demands), the benefit of such high growth rates concentrated only in the hands of the few. Only an alternative economic system based on the principles of egalitarianism and an equitable socio-economic order can address these issues.

NOTES

1. Jharkhand, Chhattisgarh and Uttaranchal were excluded in analysis of NSSO 64th Round data as they were not present in the 55th Round.
2. Andhra Pradesh, Assam, Bihar, Gujarat, Haryana, Karnataka, Kerala, Madhya Pradesh, Maharashtra, Orissa, Punjab, Rajasthan, Tamil Nadu, Uttar Pradesh and West Bengal.
3. In Capital Expenditure, Public Accounts is not considered.
4. It includes expenditure on sports, art and culture.

BIBLIOGRAPHY

Chowdhury S and Dasgupta Z. Fiscal Problem in West Bengal - Towards an Explanation. *Economic and Political Weekly* 2012; 47(13): 57-64.

Isaac MT and Ramakumar R. Why Do the States Not Spend? An Exploration of the Phenomenon of Cash Surpluses and the FRBM Legislation. *Economic and Political Weekly 2006;* 41(48): 4965-4976.

Sen AK. The Many Faces of Gender Inequality. *Frontline* 2001; 18(22).

10

Rich State with Poor Health: Disappointing Status of Public Health in Gujarat

Sandeep Sharma

Introduction

The state of Gujarat has been the front runner in the overall economic development of the country. But whether this impressive growth has transformed to overall socio-economic development especially in case of health of the people is something that needs to be understood. The limited evidence on the progress of health sector in Gujarat suggests that progress has not been so significant. Ghosh and Chandrasekhar (2011) and Mahadevia (2000), have raised serious doubts about the model of development adopted by Gujarat when it comes to progress in the health sector of the state. The criticisms range from low progress in health outcomes to lower budgetary allocation by state on health sector.

This study looks at the progress in health achievement in the state of Gujarat. The focus of this study is twofolds, it analyses the role of state in provision of health care and for that we have evaluated the state's health care expenditure from 1990 onwards. And it also looks at the health outcomes at the state level. This study gives special focus on distribution of health outcomes across different social groups in the state and how it fares as compared to the other states.

The findings of this study clearly show that progress in health outcomes has not been satisfactory as the state was found lacking in numerous aspects. Decline in infant mortality rate (IMR) from 1990 to 2009-2010 in Gujarat has been lower than the national average and far lower than the states such as Maharashtra and Tamil Nadu. The relative rank of the state has not changed across major states and it has remained stagnant at the middle level during the same period. Although, there has been a decline in IMR in the state but rural urban gap as well as gender differences still persists and over time we don't see much decline in this difference.

Social gaps in health outcomes are also quite significant in the state. Analysis of IMR, under 5 mortality (U5MR) and children nutrition status show a higher social gaps persisting in the state compared to national average and it shows an increasing trend over time between 1998-99 and 2005-06. We see a similar pattern in use of vital health services such as antenatal care services.

Health expenditure of the state also shows the lack of commitment of the government to improve health status of the citizen. Health expenditure as a share of total expenditure of the state is lower than the all state average for the time period 1990 to 2010. And it is much lower than the other developed states such as Tamil Nadu and Maharasthra. Even in the case of per capita health expenditure, the state's figure has been lower than that of Tamil Nadu and Maharashtra and across major states the rank of the state has been at the lower side. Health expenditure as a share of Net State Domestic Product (NSDP) for Gujarat has been dismal, the share has been lower than the all state average. For the year 2005-06 to 2009-2010, Gujarat was ranked fourth from below in terms of health expenditure as a share of NSDP. The lacklustre performance of health budget of the state is also reflected in the lower utilization of government health services.

These findings corroborate to the fact that economic growth of the state has not lead to improvement in health sector in the state. The development policy of the state has been geared more towards the economic growth with the assumption that growth will lead improvement in human development what Dreaze and Sen (1996), have termed the 'growth led security'. This analysis clearly show, that this is not the case as still the vulnerable section of the society in the state have health indices worse than the national average. The role of state in promotion of health is also questionable as revealed by relatively lower allocation for health services in the budget of the state government.

Health Profile of Gujarat

Life expectancy for male in Gujarat stands at 63 for male and 65 for female for the year 2002-2006. The corresponding figures at the national level stand at 63 and 64. The life expectancy in Gujarat is very close to the national average but in comparison to other developed states like Tamil Nadu, Gujarat and Haryana we can see that it is lacking behind. Maternal Mortality Rate (MMR) which is a very sensitive indicator of development is 160 for the state and it is well below the national average of 254 but again if we compare with the averages of other developed states, mortality rate is quite high in the state, for instance the MMR in Tamil Nadu is 111. In case of IMR and U5MR, Gujarat show a slightly higher incidence compared to the national average, IMR in Gujarat is 63 compared to 57 at the national level and U5MR is 77 compared to 74 at the national level. Across all the four developed state of the country, Gujarat's performance has been worst for both the indicators. In case of undernutrition of children, again incidence in Gujarat has been above the national average and across the selected states it has been the worst performing state. Gujarat has done better than the national average in case of vaccination of children and antenatal care but again across the developed states it's performance has been worst (Table 10.1 in Annexure).

It is important to see, how Gujarat has fared in improvement of health indicators over time. In this regard, we have analysed the IMR data from 1990 onwards. IMR is one of the most frequently used indicators of health. Reduction in IMR requires an improvement in overall socio-economic environment and adequate health facilities (Claeson et. al, 2000), which is possible through better health access as well as improved socio-economic conditions at the household level. Thus, IMR has a very important position in overall health development. Infants of age 0 to 12 months are most sensitive to the provision of clean water, good food, suitable housing and clothing, quality health care, the education of their parents and close attention to their essential needs. IMR summarizes in itself a variety of information, such as the quality of the food and water available, the quality of housing and clothing, the quality of the health care and the quality of the education in a population group. Figure 10.1 shows the trend in IMR it clearly points out the relative improvement in IMR in Gujarat, Tamil Nadu, Maharashtra, Haryana and all India. IMR in Gujarat have come down from 77 to 44 per 1000 birth between 1990 and 2010. In 1990, the national average was 80, and it has come down to 51. IMR in Gujarat has been quite near the national average, whereas Maharashtra and Tamil Nadu have shown much lesser level of IMR for the given time period.

Figure 10.1: Trend in IMR for Gujarat, Selected States and All India

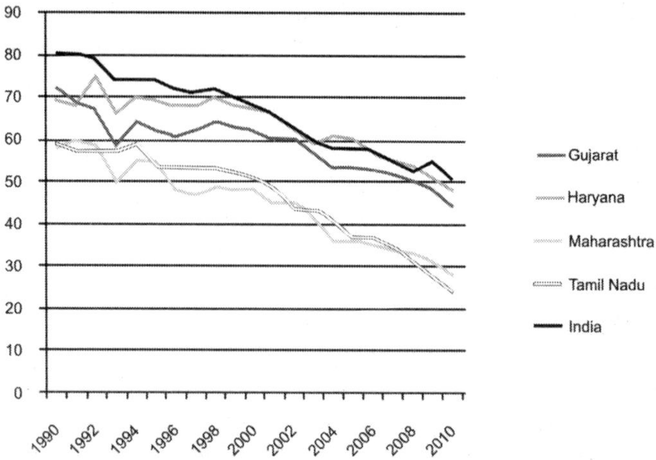

Source: SRS Bulletin Various Years.

In order to capture the magnitude of decline we calculated the annual average growth rate from 1990 to 2010 (Table 10.2 in Annexure). The trend rate for Gujarat for the time period is –1.68 per cent whereas the corresponding figure at the national level is –2.39 per cent. It clearly indicates the pace of decline in Gujarat has been slow. Infact, if we take into account the 15 major states of the country Gujarat is ranked 10th, just ahead of states such as Assam, Bihar, Haryana, Andhra and Kerala. But we have to keep in mind that Kerala already had very a low level of IMR in 1990 so slow rate of decline is understandable. But in case of Tamil Nadu and Maharashtra, both the states had lower level of IMR in 1990 as compared to Gujarat, even then the rate of decline is much higher than Gujarat at –3.37 per cent and –3.61 per cent respectively.

Decline in IMR in Gujarat has not been so significant and it's effect can be seen in the relative rank of the state over time. Rank of Gujarat has remained same for the state in comparison to the major states in India between 1990 to 2010. The average IMR for the period 1990 to 1994 and 2005-2010 placed Gujarat in 7th position.

Improvement in IMR in Gujarat has also been challenged on the basis of widening disparity between rural and urban areas (Ghosh and Chandrasekhar, 2011). The rural disadvantage in case of IMR compared to the urban areas have been well established in literature (Shastry, 1997). The rural disadvantage can be attributed to lower socio-economic development in rural areas and also the dearth of health infrastructure in these areas. Higher IMR in rural areas do indicate not only the lack of socio-economic development but it also signifies the limited avaibility of the health facilities in the far-flung rural areas. In order to measure disparity between rural and urban areas we took rural urban ratios in IMR.

Rural Urban Gap = Rural IMR/ Urban IMR

Ratio greater than 1 will indicate higher disadvantage for rural child compared to the children in urban areas whereas ratio less than 1 will indicate otherwise. It is presumed that with time the ratio will come down since the level of IMR in urban areas is lower than the rural areas so their pace of decline will be slower whereas in rural areas due to higher level of IMR rate of decline will be faster and in the process there will be a convergence between two regions.

The rural-urban gap at all India level has increased between 1990 and 2004 but in the time period 2005-2010, we see a decline (Table 10.3 in Annexure). In Gujarat, we see increase between 1990-94 to 1995-99 and again in 2000-2004. Between 2000-2004 and 2005-2010, we don't see any change in ratio for Gujarat clearly indicating that decline in IMR in the state has not been able to bridge the gap between rural and urban areas. Till 2000-2004, the rural-urban gap in the state was lower than the national average but in 2005-2010, it exceeds the national average.In 1990-94, the ratio was 1.40 much lower than the national average of 1.66 and it was ranked third in terms of lower rural urban gap but in 2005-2010, it is ranked at 14th position with the ratio of 1.68 which stood higher than the national average of 1.62. It clearly indicates, the rural disadvantage in reduction of IMR in the state. Tamil Nadu, Kerala and Haryana have shown relatively lower ratio in 2005-2010.

Gender differential in IMR is another important aspect that gives reflection of nature of IMR decline. In order to measure gender disparity we have taken female-male ratio of IMR.

Gender Disparity Ratio = Female IMR/Male IMR

Ratio greater than 1 will indicate higher disadvantage for female child compared to the male child whereas the ratio less than 1 will indicate otherwise.

For the period 1990-94, Gujarat's disparity was 1.01 indicating higher female IMR compared to males (Table 10.4 in Annexure). And this ratio was same as the national average and across states it was ranked sixth. In 1995-99, the disparity ratio for Gujarat was 1.08 greater than the national average of 1.03. In 2000-2004, we see an increase in disparity ratio to 1.11 much higher than the national average of 1.05. In 2005-2010, the ratio is 1.06 higher than the national average of 1.05. Across state, it is ranked fourth in terms of high gender disparity for the same period. In all the time periods, ratio higher than 1 indicate the female disadvantage of IMR in Gujarat. The gender disparity in Gujarat is comparable to underdeveloped states such as Bihar and Uttar Pradesh which clearly indicates lack of focus on girl child in the state. Although, states such as, Kerala and Tamil Nadu have also shown higher gender disparity ratio but we have to take into account the low level of IMR in these states and where mortality is mostly confined to neonatal mortality which are difficult to control.

Social Group Inequality in Health in Gujarat

Social inequality in health can be broadly defined as inequality in health that results due to the differences in the socio-economic conditions. Income is the most commonly used socio-economic determinant of health although other factors such as sex, race, and place of residence also play a very important role in promotion of health. In this section, we will look at the health inequality based on caste. Although, inequality based on income plays an important role in understanding health inequality and there is a wide range of literature that has documented inequality based on economic status, however inequality based on caste groups is an area that still deserves much more attention as it has been observed that caste based inequality in health is one of the significant hindrance in overall improvement in health status of the country (National Human Development Report, 2011). So, the social group such as caste becomes an important unit of analysis.

Work of Joe et. al (2008), have looked extensively in inequality in health based upon economic status or the wealth index of the household. They used the third round of National Family Health Survey (NFHS) data to analyse health inequality across states in India. In order to measure health inequality, they constructed concentration index[1] of different health variables such as under-five mortalities, immunization status and nutritional performance (stunting and underweight) of the child population in different states. Their analysis clearly portrays Gujarat as one of the states that had very high health inequality in all the health indicators.

This analysis looks at the inequality in health across social groups; here we look at the difference in health between scheduled castes (SC), scheduled tribes (ST) and others or those who fall under upper castes or others using the NFHS data for two years 1998-99 and 2005-2006. NFHS also gives information on one more social group, i.e., the other backward classes (OBC), but in this analysis we have not included them. SCs and STs are deprived section of the society and to measure how their performance varies with others we have calculated disparity ratio. Thorat and Mahamallick (2006) used similar measure to understand disparity across social groups in human development.

Disparity ratio = Health SC/Health others

or

Disparity ratio = Health ST/Health others

Different health variables used in the analysis are IMR, U5MR, undernutrition, child immunization and antenatal coverage of pregnant mothers. The analysis is based for two time periods 1998-99 and 2005-2006. While interpreting the ratio, we have to keep in mind that in case of negative indicators such as mortality and undernutrition value more than 1 will indicate social disparity towards SCs and STs and less than 1 will indicate higher disadvantage for others. In case of utilization of essential health services, this ratio has to be interpreted in reverse order as value more than 1 will indicate higher use of health services by SCs and STs and value less than 1 indicates the opposite.

The level of IMR was below the national average for the 1998-99, even across social groups we see a similar trend as IMR for SCs and STs was below the national average of the same social group. But in 2005-06, there is a shift in the picture as IMR in the state is above the national average. If we look across the social groups, SCs and STs in Gujarat show higher IMR compared to the national average of the same social group. But in case of others, it is less than the national average, clearly indicating that the declines in these indicators was more prevalent in the other castes (Table 10.5 in Annexure).

Disparity ratio for IMR across social group in 1998-99 showed relatively higher ratio for SCs compared to others at 1.48 and it was higher than the national average of 1.34. In fact, the disparity ratio was placed third next to Punjab and Andhra Pradesh in terms of disparity between SCs and others. In case of STs and others, ratio was relatively less at 1.11 and it was below the national average of 1.36. Out of eleven states, disparity ratio for STs and others Gujarat was ranked ninth. If we look at the change over times there has been an increase in the ratio in case of STs and others whereas SCs and others have shown decline in Gujarat. In 2005-2006, the disparity ratio for STs and others stood at 1.81 much higher than the national average of 1.27 and it is the highest disparity if we make comparison across major states. In case of SCs and others, in 2005-2006, the disparity ratio stands at 1.38 slightly higher than the national average of 1.36 (Table 10.10 in Annexure).

The trend in U5MR also show a similar trend as IMR, the level of U5MR in Gujarat was below the national average for the 1998-99, even across social groups we see a similar trend as U5MR for SCs and STs was below the national average of the same social group. But in 2005-06 there is a shift as U5MR in the state is above the national average. If we look across the social groups, SCs and STs in Gujarat show higher U5MR compared to the national average of the same social group. But in case of others, it is less than the national average it clearly indicates the decline in these indicators was more prevalent among others or the general castes (Table 10.6 in Annexure).

Social disparity in case of SCs and others, at 1.75, was third highest in Gujarat after Andhra Pradesh and Punjab in 1998-99, and it was higher than the national average of 1.44 for U5MR. Disparity in case of STs and others, in 1998-99, was relatively lower in 1998-99 at 1.35 compared to 1.53 as the national average and it was ranked eight across the major states. In 2005-2006, although there has been a decline in disparity ratio for SCs, and others but still it was higher than the national average for Gujarat. Across states, it is ranked second after Rajasthan in terms of high disparity between SCs and others. In case of STs and others, there has been increase in disparity ratio for the later period, with a disparity ratio of 2.08 which is much higher than the national average of 1.62. Across states, disparity ratio for STs and others is second next to Orissa. These findings clearly elabourate the extent of caste based inequality in Gujarat (Table 10.11 in Annexure).

Child undernutrition is a primary cause of ill health and premature mortality among children. Stunting is a widely used indicator of child undernutriton as it reflects the long-term deprivation of child. Incidence of undernutrition in state of Gujarat for the year 1998-99 was lower than the national average. Even across social groups, we see a similar picture as undernutrion for SCs, STs and others were lower than the national average (Table 10.7 in Annexure). In 2005-2006, we don't see this trend as undernutrition in the state is higher than the national average. Across caste groups, SCs of Gujarat and national average show similar incidence whereas in case of STs, it is higher than the national average whereas in case of others it is lower than the national average (Table 10.7 in Annexure). If we look at the disparity ratios, it has come down in Gujarat both for SCs and others and STs and others over time. In 1998-99, disparity ratio of SCs and others and STs and others was higher than the national average whereas in 2005-2006, SCs and others shows higher disparity compared to the national average but in case of STs and others, it is lower than the national average. If we compare disparity ratios of the Gujarat with other states it comes in the middle position for both the time periods. So, even though there has been decline in disparity within the state but its performance vis-a-vis other states has not changed much (Table 10.12 in Annexure).

Immunization of children in Gujarat has been above the national average for both the time periods. But overall share of immunized children has come down from 53 per cent to 45 per cent. Six states in the country have shown decline between 1998-99 and 2005-2006, and Gujarat is one of them. Across social groups, immunization coverage has been higher than the national average for both the time periods with an exception of others in 2005-2006, where it shows lower figure than the national average (Table 10.8 in Annexure).In case of disparity ratios both in case SCs and others and STs and Others, there has been improvement over time (Table 10.13 in Annexure). And in both time periods, it has fared better than the national average. Across states also Gujarat has fared well specially in 2005-2006, both in case of SCs and others, as well as STs and others, where it is placed at third and second position respectively in terms of better performance.

Antenatal care coverage in Gujarat has shown slight improvement from 86 per cent to 87 per cent between 1998-99 and 2005-2006. Both at the state level as well as across social group utilization of antenatal services have been better than the national average for both the time periods (Table 10.9 in Annexure). Across social groups, there has been marginal increase for SCs from 84 per cent to 85 per cent and in case of

STs, there have been reduction from 78 per cent to 74 per cent. This stagnation in growth of SCs and STs can also be seen at the disparity ratios there has been a decline in ratio for both STs and others as well SCs and others between 1998-99 and 2005-2006. Only five states have shown decline in disparity ratios for SCs and others and Gujarat is one among them whereas in case of STs and others, apart from Gujarat only three states have shown decline. Disparity ratio for STs and others is 0.78 in Gujarat in 2005-2006, which is lower than the national average of 0.83. The stagnation is also visible in relatively lower rank of Gujarat compared to other states in terms of low disparity ratio. In case of SCs and others, it was ranked in the middle in 1998-99, whereas in 2005-2006, it's position has deteriorated to the bottom three. In case of STs and others, it was placed fourth in 1998-99 but in 2005-2006, it is placed in eighth position (Table 10.14 in Annexure).

Health Expenditure and Utilization of Health Services in Gujarat

Health expenditure is one of the prime mechanisms to enable higher levels of health achievement as well as increasing overall access to health service. Health falls in the concurrent list, which means that both centre as well as state has a responsibility towards health sector allocation. Kaur and Mishra (2002), point out that the share of state is more than 80 per cent of the total allocation, which means that the state has a major responsibility in the health sector development of this country.

Health expenditure (Revenue+Capital) in the state of Gujarat has increased at an absolute level. In 1990-95, per capita health expenditure stood at Rs. 113 but in 2005-2010 it increased to Rs. 266. But overall rank of the state has deteriorated over time. It was ranked 9th in 1990-95 and showed considerable improvement in 1995-2000, as it reached fourth position but in 2000-2005, it was placed nineth again and in 2005-2010, it was placed 11th across the major states of India. The year 2005-2010, also includes the expenditure under the national rural health mission (National Rural Health Mission).[2] NRHM has categorized states into two groups: focus states and non-focus states. All eight North Eastern states are focus states and 10 large and financially weak states (Berman and Ahuja, 2008). Although Gujarat does not fall under focus state but other developed states of the country like Tamil Nadu has done much better in terms of health expenditure and it is ranked second after Kerala in 2005-2010. Haryana the other developed state of the country is ranked seventh in 2005-2010, Maharashtra is placed at eighth position (Table 10.15 in Annexure).

Per capita health expenditure gives a broad pattern of health expenditure but does not say much about the intent of government on what priority they give to health sector in their budgetary allocations. Share of health expenditure out of total expenditure enables us to understand the health expenditure performance and whether there has been any provision to protect this sector. Health expenditure comes under development expenditure as a broad category and it is listed under social sector.

Health expenditure in Gujarat as a share of total expenditure has reduced from 4.25 per cent in 1990-95 to 0.77 per cent in 2005-2010. Although this declining trend is not exceptional to Gujarat as we see similar trend across all the major states of the country. But one thing to be noticed is the share of health expenditure in the state has been lower than the all state average in all the time periods. In 1990-95 the share of Gujarat was 4.25 per cent whereas at the all state level it was 5.03 per cent. In 2005-2010 for Gujarat it was 0.77 per cent whereas at the all state level it was 0.95 per cent. In 2005-2010 Gujarat was ranked fourth from below and in the preceding period it was second from below clearly highlighting the fact, that health expenditure in the state has not received much attention even though the state is going through high level of economic growth. Other developed states such as Maharashtra and Tamil Nadu have spent much higher share compared to Gujarat. But Gujarat has been slightly better than Haryana in all the time periods (Table 10.16 in Annexure).

Income both at household level as well as at the state level influences the level of health expenditure. In fact, this route of economic growth leading to higher allocation of health expenditure is one of the main arguments in favour of growth leading to positive health outcome (Human Development Report, 1996). But does economic growth facilitates higher resources for health at the state level needs to be proved further as there are numerous examples of state like, Kerala or country like Sri Lanka where in spite of low economic growth government proceeded with strong social welfare programmes and high level of health expenditure.

To understand this relationship between economic growth and health expenditure, we looked at the health expenditure as a share of Net State

Domestic Product (NSDP). There has been a decline in share of health expenditure out of NSDP in Gujarat from 1990-95 to 2005-2010, as it has come down from 0.85 per cent to 0.73 per cent. It was ranked 12th in 1990-95 as well as in 2005-2010. If we take into account the other developed states, it has done better than Haryana and Maharashtra. But it has not been lower than the Tamil Nadu in all the four subperiods we have taken for analysis. In 2005-2010, Tamil Nadu's share stood at 0.97 per cent compared to 0.73 per cent of Gujarat. In 1990-95 Tamil Nadu's share was 1.07 per cent compared to 0.85 per cent in Gujarat. If we compare with average share of all the major states again Gujarat has been lower for all the sub periods of analysis (Table 10.17 in Annexure).

Health expenditure at the state level has a direct consequence on the availability of health services at the household level. Even the out-of-pocket health expenditure to a great extent depends upon the level of health expenditure by the government. If we look at the average expenditure a household pays in government health facility for hospitalization we see an increase in case of Gujarat between 1995-96 and 2004 from Rs. 1465 to Rs. 2253 in rural areas and Rs. 1897 to Rs. 4185 in urban areas. Although this level of expenditure has been lower than the lower national average but if we compare with a state like Tamil Nadu we do see a contrasting picture, for instance in 2004 the average health expenditure in Tamil Nadu was merely Rs. 934 in rural areas and in urban area it was Rs. 1666 (Table 10.18 in Annexure).

Availability and quality of health services to a great extent determine the choice of health services in India, where the health services is a mix of public and private health providers. Over time, there has been a prominence of private sector in health in India and one of the prime reason being the gradual withdrawal of the government from the health sector. Low health care allocation by the government has made the quality of health services in government institutions deplorable and it has led to increase in use of private facilities. Health utilization pattern in Gujarat has been highly privatized, in 1995-96, 32 per cent of those went for hospitalization preferred going to government health facility whereas at the national level the corresponding figure stood at 45 per cent. In 2005-2006, 31 per cent of the total hospitalization cases have gone for government facility and the national figure is 42 per cent. In urban areas, 37 per cent went for government institutions in 1995-96, but it came down to 26 per cent in 2004. The utilization rate of government services even in urban areas was lower than the national average for both the time periods.

Utilization pattern across the income groups in selected states of India clearly show that, it is the poor who are more dependent on the government health facilities (Table 10.19 in Annexure). In rural areas of Gujarat, at the lowest income group there has not been any change in use of government health services between 1995-96 and 2004. But as we go up in income quintile, the share of persons going to government health facility show a decreasing trend. Overall in rural areas apart from Tamil Nadu, we see a decline in use of government facility. In Tamil Nadu, the average use of government health facility has remained unchanged at 41 per cent in rural areas. In urban areas we see a decline in use of government health facility across the income quintiles in Gujarat and it is true for all the developed states barring Tamil Nadu. In Tamil Nadu, we see an increase in use of government health facility in all the income groups leaving the richest quintile. Tamil Nadu has higher share of people going to government health facility for both in rural and urban areas if we compare it with other developed states of the country. We have already seen that health expenses in Tamil Nadu is one of the cheapest and that might be the reason for such a high use of government health facility in the state. And this to a great extent explains the proactive role played by the state government of Tamil Nadu in enabling universal access to health services.

Conclusion

This study looked at the health sector development in the state of Gujarat. This study indicates that mere economic growth is not sufficient for improvement in health. As it was revealed in this study, high level of growth in the state does not necessarily lead to progress in health sector. Cross sectional analysis as well as trend analysis of different health outcomes, clearly points to the fact, that the progress of state in health sector has not been so impressive. Rate of reduction in IMR for Gujarat has been lower than the national average and there has been considerable gap in IMR between rural and urban areas and also there has been higher mortality of girl child compared to boy child in the state. Progress in basic health indicators such as IMR, U5MR and child undernutrition in the state has been questionable. Comparisons with other developed states clearly show that states like, Maharashtra and Tamil Nadu have fared much better than Gujarat. And to couple with it there exists a significant social gap in health outcomes of the state.

Trend in health expenditure also show a dismal picture for Gujarat as it was found lacking in per capita health expenditure as well as health expenditure as a share of total expenditure and NSDP. On the other hand, state like Tamil Nadu has done relatively much better than Gujarat. And this can be seen in utilization pattern of government health services. As the states are gradually falling into the grip of privatization including Gujarat, Tamil Nadu has come out as an exception as there has been increase in use of government health facility and cost of health services also has been very low in the state. It clearly indicates that health policy of Gujarat is tuned more towards ensuring more private participation in health service provision. But given the fact that advances in basic health indicators have been below the satisfaction level there is a strong need to relook at the health policies of the state and there is a very urgent need for strong state intervention in health sector of the state.

NOTES

1. Concentration index is used to measure health inequality across the quintiles of wealth index.
2. In April 2005, the prime minister launched NRHM, committing the national government to increased and more effective health spending. Over 60 per cent of all central government health allocation is now routed through NRHM. Most NRHM funds are routed through state health societies, which have been restructured to incorporate a number of earlier programme specific societies (Berman and Ahuja, 2008).

BIBLIOGRAPHY

Berman P and Ahuja R. Government Health Spending in India. *Economic and Political Weekly* 2008; 43(26/27): 209-216.

Central Statistical Organisation. *National Accounts Statistics.* 2012. New Delhi: Ministry of Planning and Programme Implementation.

Claeson M, et al. Reducing Child Mortality in India in the New Millennium. *Bulletin of World Health Organisation* 2000; 78(10): 48-54.

Dreze J and Sen A. *Hunger and Public Action.* Oxford: Clerendon Press, 1989.

Ghosh J and Chandrasekhar CP. Health Outcomes across the Major Indian States. Online referencing http://www.macroscan.org/ (2010, accessed on 10 April 2012).

Government of India. *National Human Development Report: Towards Social Exclusion.* 2011. New Delhi: Planning Commission, Government of India.

International Institute for Population Science (IIPS). *National Family Health Survey (MCH and Family Planning)*. 1995. Bombay: International Institute for Population Science.

International Institute for Population Science (IIPS). *National Family Health Survey (MCH and Family Planning)*. 1999. Bombay: International Institute for Population Science.

International Institute for Population Sciences (IIPS) and Macro International. *National Family Health Survey (NFHS-3), 2005–06: India*. 2007, Mumbai: International Institute for Population Science.

International Institute for. Population Sciences (IIPS) and Macro International. *National Family Health Survey (NFHS-3), India, 2005-06: Punjab*. 2008, Mumbai: International Institute for Population Science.

Joe W, et al. Health Inequality in India: Evidence from NFHS 3. *Economic and Political Weekly* 2008; 43(31): 41-48.

Kaur B and Misra S. *Social Sector Expenditure and Attainments: An Analysis of Indian States*, Occasional Papers 24(1/2). Reserve Bank of India, Mumbai, 2003.

Mahadevia D. Health for All in Gujarat is it Achievable?. *Economic and Political Weekly* 2010; 35(35/36): 3193-3204.

Ministry of Health and Family Welfare. *Selected Health Parameter: A Comparative Analysis Across the National Sample Survey Organization, 42nd, 52nd and 60th Round.* 2007. New Delhi: Ministry of Health and Family Welfare.

National Sample Survey Organization. *Morbidity and Treatment of Ailments, NSS Fifty-Second Round, July 1995-June 1996*. 1998. New Delhi: Department of Statistics, Government of India.

National Sample Survey Organization. *Survey on Morbidity, Health Care and the Condition of the Aged, NSS Sixtieth Round, January- June 2004*. 2006. New Delhi: Department of Statistics, Government of India.

Reserve Bank of India. RBI Bulletin, Various Issues. Mumbai: RBI.

Thorat S and Mahamallik M. Human Development and the Status of Social Group in Gujarat. *Working Paper* No 6, Indian Institute of Dalit Studies, New Delhi, 2006.

United Nation Development Programme. *Human Development Report.* 1996. New York: Oxford University Press.

Annexures

Table 2.1: GDP Growth Rate by Basic Economic Activities and Their Contribution to GDP Growth

	Gujarat				*India*			
	1980-2010	*1980-90*	*1990-2000*	*2000-10*	*1980-2010*	*1980-90*	*1990-2000*	*2000-10*
Agriculture	2.85 (7.8)	-0.84 (12.8)	4.44 (3.2)	7.64 (10.3)	2.86 (10.6)	2.93 (22.5)	3.15 (13.4)	2.96 (6.8)
Industry	8.02 (42.8)	7.88 (39.1)	9.89 (49)	11.01 (41.1)	6.7 (27.5)	6.88 (30.3)	6.56 (24.7)	8.65 (27.3)
Manufacturing	8.26 (31)	8.57 (29.6)	10.81 (36.9)	11.14 (29)	6.89 (16.6)	7.3 (18.8)	7.21 (14.9)	8.77 (16.5)
Services	8.02 (49.4)	7.55 (48.1)	8.82 (47.8)	11.01 (48.6)	7.71 (61.9)	6.65 (47.2)	8.04 (61.9)	9.52 (65.8)
Transport, Storage & Communication	9.35 (10.3)	11.52 (10.2)	10.45 (8.5)	12.29 (10.5)	9.08 (13.9)	7.38 (7.5)	8.2 (9.7)	13.39 (17)
Trade, Hotels and Restaurants	8.14 (19.2)	5.72 (14.9)	8.73 (12.1)	14.36 (21.5)	7.58 (16.8)	6.02 (12.9)	8.63 (18)	9.23 (17.4)
Banking & Insurance	11.04 (7.9)	14.1 (7.8)	9.9 (9.1)	12.57 (7.9)	11.61 (9.3)	12.89 (5.9)	12.09 (10)	12.51 (10.5)
Real Eestate and Business Services	4.46 (4.5)	3.1 (5)	4.1 (4.6)	7.93 (4)	5.29 (7.6)	3.62 (5.8)	4.5 (6.3)	8.69 (8.3)
Public Administration	5.94 (2.8)	7.96 (5.1)	9.55 (5.9)	5.42 (1.7)	6.03 (6.2)	7.98 (8.4)	6.26 (7.8)	6.03 (5.4)
Other Services	6.8 (4.6)	5.37 (5.1)	8.58 (7.6)	5.12 (2.9)	6.87 (8.1)	5.25 (6.7)	7.47 (10.1)	6.88 (7.3)
Gross Domestic Product	**6.77**	**5.05**	**8.3**	**10.5**	**6.12**	**5.41**	**6.21**	**8**

Note: GDP at 1999-00 constant prices. Figures in parenthesis show contribution to GDP.
Source: Central Statistical Organization.

Table 2.2: GDP Growth Rate by Basic Economic Activities and Their Contribution to GDP Growth

	Maharashtra				*Tamil Nadu*			
	1980-2010	*1980-90*	*1990-2000*	*2000-10*	*1980-2010*	*1980-90*	*1990-2000*	*2000-10*
Agriculture	3.93 (8.1)	3.13 (19.3)	4.35 (9.2)	4.75 (6.9)	2.75 (6.7)	3.4 (19.4)	2.95 (9.7)	2.8 (1.9)
Industry	6.32 (26.4)	6.1 (30.9)	6.66 (25.8)	10.83 (27)	5.69 (25.6)	4.73 (27.4)	6.01 (25.5)	7.55 (22.8)
Manufacturing	6.69 (19.8)	6.36 (21.6)	7.11 (18.8)	11.05 (20.8)	4.84 (16.2)	4.4 (18.8)	5.22 (14.1)	7.64 (15.4)
Services	8.48 (65.5)	6.76 (49.8)	8.55 (65.1)	10.61 (66.1)	7.86 (67.7)	6.56 (53.3)	8.95 (64.8)	10.23 (75.3)
Transport, Storage & Communication	8.11 (9.6)	7 (8)	9.36 (10.3)	9.42 (8.6)	8.09 (12.8)	6.93 (8.5)	8.85 (11.6)	10.72 (14.6)
Trade, Hotels and Restaurants	7.62 (19.7)	5.69 (14.2)	7.75 (14.2)	12.54 (22.4)	7.66 (19.1)	5.69 (12)	9.29 (19.2)	10.55 (21.1)
Banking & Insurance	12.38 (16.6)	10.8 (8.5)	11.16 (19)	13.57 (17.5)	11.61 (10.5)	11 (5.8)	13.97 (11.7)	11.46 (11.9)
Real Estate and Business Services	5.26 (9.4)	3.17 (7)	3.99 (6.4)	9.9 (10)	7.36 (10.9)	5.73 (9.3)	5.26 (6.3)	12.59 (14)
Public Administration	6.39 (4.6)	7.39 (4.8)	7.59 (6.5)	7.82 (4)	6.83 (4.6)	8.79 (6.1)	7.42 (6.8)	4.83 (3.3)
Other Services	7.08 (5.6)	6.79 (7.3)	7.23 (8.7)	5.34 (3.6)	5.75 (9.9)	4.86 (11.5)	7.14 (9.2)	8.1 (10.4)
Gross Domestic Product	**6.96**	**5.64**	**7.12**	**10**	**6.2**	**5.18**	**6.64**	**8.49**

Note: Same as Table 2.1

Source: Same as Table 2.1

Table 2.3: GDP Growth Rate by Basic Economic Activities and Their Contribution to GDP Growth

	Haryana			
	1980-2010	*1980-90*	*1990-2000*	*2000-10*
Agriculture	3.16 (12.5)	3.77 (28.1)	1.87 (13.7)	3.27 (7.5)
Industry	7.35 (28.8)	9.54 (33.1)	6.12 (31.4)	8.93 (27.8)
Manufacturing	7.47 (18.8)	11.34 (27.1)	6.77 (23.7)	7.77 (16)
Services	8.88 (58.8)	7.69 (38.8)	7.58 (55)	12.25 (64.7)
Transport, Storage & Communication	10.15 (11.1)	7.67 (5.9)	7.14 (9.7)	13.84 (12.7)
Trade, Hotels and Restaurants	9.28 (21.9)	8.11 (13.6)	8.2 (19.5)	12.32 (24.1)
Banking & Insurance	11.96 (5.6)	12.85 (3.2)	13.03 (7.5)	13.72 (6)
Real Estate and Business Services	7.76 (11.1)	4.56 (5.2)	4.08 (5.5)	14.54 (13.6)
Public Administration	6.39 (2.7)	9.24 (4.2)	6.71 (4.6)	6.35 (2.2)
Other Services	5.78 (6.4)	5.25 (6.7)	5.6 (8.2)	8.29 (6.3)
Gross Domestic Product	**6.47**	**6.2**	**4.94**	**9.17**

Note: Same as Table 2.1
Source: Same as Table 2.1

Table 2.4: Comparison of Structure of Economy

	Gujarat				*India*			
	1980-81	*1990-91*	*2000-01*	*2009-10*	*1980-81*	*1990-91*	*2000-01*	*2009-10*
Agriculture	37.3	25.2	15.0	12.1	38.1	30.9	23.9	14.5
Industry	30.4	37.5	40.3	40.7	25.9	30.0	25.8	28.3
Manufacturing	22.0	29.6	29.4	27.4	17.7	21.1	15.3	16.1
Registered	16.5	22.7	20.1	21.6	10.0	13.0	10.0	10.9
Unregistered	5.6	6.9	9.3	5.8	7.6	8.1	5.3	5.2
Services	32.3	37.2	44.7	47.2	36.0	39.1	50.3	57.2
Transport, Storage & Communication	5.0	6.4	7.6	9.3	2.8	5.3	8.0	10.1
Trade, Hotels and Restaurants	9.5	10.4	13.4	18.1	12.0	12.5	14.3	16.2
Banking & Insurance	3.5	7.3	5.7	7.0	6.0	5.0	7.5	7.8
Real Estate and Business Services	6.8	5.5	6.7	5.1	4.7	5.3	6.7	9.5
Public Administration	2.6	2.7	4.4	2.8	5.8	5.7	8.3	6.2
Other Services	4.9	5.0	7.0	4.6	4.7	5.3	8.0	7.5

Note: GDP at 1999-00 constant prices.
Source: Central Statistical Organization.

Table 2.5: Comparison of Structure of Economy

	Maharashtra				*Tamil Nadu*			
	1980-81	*1990-91*	*2000-01*	*2009-10*	*1980-81*	*1990-91*	*2000-01*	*2009-10*
Agriculture	26.7	21.4	15.3	8.4	24.3	21.6	16.7	8.5
Industry	36.0	36.3	27.6	29.9	35.0	35.1	30.5	28.1
Manufacturing	27.6	28.4	19.1	21.5	27.2	25.0	20.1	18.4
Registered	19.5	21.6	13.7	16.0	15.2	16.9	13.2	11.9
Unregistered	8.1	6.9	5.4	5.5	12.0	8.1	6.9	6.5
Services	37.2	42.3	57.1	61.7	40.7	43.3	52.8	63.4
Transport, Storage & Communication	5.8	6.4	9.4	7.5	7.2	7.2	9.1	9.8
Trade, Hotels and Restaurants	11.6	11.9	14.3	18.6	15.4	15.1	15.3	17.9
Banking & Insurance	5.0	8.7	10.8	13.7	3.0	5.3	6.6	9.1
Real Estate and Business Services	5.2	3.9	10.1	11.9	5.6	5.9	6.7	13.6
Public Administration	2.9	3.0	4.8	4.8	3.6	4.3	5.5	3.9
Other Services	6.8	8.3	7.7	5.3	5.8	5.4	9.6	9.0

Note: Same as Table 2.4.
Source: Same as Table 2.4.

Table 2.6: Comparison of Structure of Economy

	Haryana			
	1980-81	*1990-91*	*2000-01*	*2009-10*
Agriculture	53.4	44.9	30.4	15.9
Industry	19.8	24.4	27.9	30.6
Manufacturing	14.5	20.4	19.9	19.5
Registered	10.6	12.0	14.7	13.6
Unregistered	4.0	8.4	5.3	6.0
Services	26.8	30.7	41.7	53.4
Transport, Storage & Communication	3.4	4.1	6.9	9.1
Trade, Hotels and Restaurants	11.6	14.0	14.7	20.5
Banking & Insurance	1.7	3.0	3.6	4.5
Real Estate and Business Services	3.7	3.1	6.7	11.4
Public Administration	2.3	2.8	3.1	2.3
Other Services	4.1	3.7	6.7	5.6

Note: Same as Table 2.4.
Source: Same as Table 2.4.

Table 3.1: Industrial Investment Proposals – State wise August 1991 – December 2011

Name of the State/UTs	Total Investment (Rs. Crore)	% Share	INDUSTRIAL ENTREPRENEUR MEMORANDUM (IEMs)						LETTERS OF INTENT (LOIs)+DIRECT INDUSTRIAL LICENCES (DILs)					
			Numbers Filed	% Share	Proposed Investment (Rs. Cr)	% Share	Proposed Emp. (Nos)	% Share	Numbers Granted	% Share	Proposed Investment (Rs. Cr)	% Share	Proposed Emp. (Nos)	% Share
Orissa	1365495	14.9	1730	1.96	1360051	15.07	732257	3.55	39	0.86	5444	3.97	11882	1.23
Chhattisgarh	1147911	12.53	2881	3.27	1147346	12.71	803939	3.9	31	0.69	565	0.41	3816	0.39
Gujarat	1040590	11.36	10406	11.81	1013056	11.23	1994854	9.67	471	10.43	27534	20.07	77760	8.04
Maharashtra	877197	9.57	16141	18.32	858216	9.51	4137369	20.05	603	13.36	18981	13.83	140147	14.49
Andhra Pradesh	793573	8.66	6772	7.69	777638	8.62	1304763	6.32	552	12.23	15935	11.61	100959	10.44
Karnataka	693396	7.57	3819	4.33	681698	7.55	1007657	4.88	295	6.53	11698	8.53	83598	8.65
Madhya Pradesh	679808	7.42	3592	4.08	676534	7.5	1011426	4.9	147	3.26	3274	2.39	31682	3.28
West Bengal	640967	7	4886	5.55	636812	7.06	1007127	4.88	102	2.26	4155	3.03	20706	2.14
Jharkhand	433958	4.74	1050	1.19	433484	4.8	389168	1.89	18	0.4	474	0.35	2368	0.24
Tamil Nadu	387285	4.23	7294	8.28	372957	4.13	2185656	10.59	874	19.36	14328	10.44	151559	15.67
Uttar Pradesh	259219	2.83	6988	7.93	249262	2.76	1854587	8.99	378	8.37	9957	7.26	102504	10.6
Rajasthan	158705	1.73	3573	4.06	157019	1.74	682851	3.31	105	2.33	1686	1.23	17915	1.85
Bihar	152259	1.66	404	0.46	150797	1.67	86853	0.42	33	0.73	1462	1.07	13674	1.41
Punjab	121101	1.32	3194	3.63	112748	1.25	741875	3.6	268	5.94	8353	6.09	86170	8.91
Haryana	99832	1.09	4256	4.83	95284	1.06	683903	3.31	253	5.6	4548	3.31	64539	6.67
Uttrakhand	67401	0.74	2112	2.4	66840	0.74	410201	1.99	36	0.8	561	0.41	8722	0.9
Himachal Pradesh	34341	0.37	996	1.13	33841	0.37	185313	0.9	36	0.8	500	0.36	6537	0.68
Assam	32436	0.35	632	0.72	30001	0.33	92009	0.45	13	0.29	2435	1.77	4606	0.48
Kerala	17750	0.19	638	0.72	14884	0.16	106653	0.52	76	1.68	2866	2.09	14918	1.54
Nagaland	16363	0.18	16	0.02	16363	0.18	302751	1.47	1	0.02	0	0	0	0
Jammu & Kashmir	15909	0.17	678	0.77	15833	0.18	129254	0.63	7	0.16	76	0.06	2074	0.21
Meghalaya	14645	0.16	295	0.33	14638	0.16	38221	0.19	3	0.07	7	0.01	207	0.02
Goa	13964	0.15	756	0.86	13796	0.15	84387	0.41	37	0.82	168	0.12	3526	0.36
Delhi	7419	0.08	574	0.65	7389	0.08	54396	0.26	21	0.47	30	0.02	1652	0.17
Sikkim	4710	0.05	104	0.12	4705	0.05	21156	0.1	1	0.02	5	0	204	0.02
Arunachal Pradesh	3790	0.04	58	0.07	3789	0.04	9527	0.05	4	0.09	1	0	522	0.05
Tripura	2525	0.03	42	0.05	2525	0.03	5297	0.03	0	0	0	0	0	0
Manipur	33	0	6	0.01	33	0	937	0	0	0	0	0	0	0
Mizoram	27	0	1	0	27	0	293	0	0	0	0	0	0	0
Location in More Than One State	419	0	0	0	0	0	0	0	27	0.6	419	0.31	3803	0.39
Total	**9161992**	**100**	**88102**	**100**	**9024775**	**100**	**20630891**	**100**	**4515**	**100**	**137217**	**100**	**966947**	**100**

Source: Secretariat for Industrial Assistance Statistics, January 2012, Department of Industrial Policy and Promotion, Ministry of Commerce, GOI.

Table 3.2: Statewise Break-up of IEMs Implemented

(From August 1991-December 2011)

State	*IEMs*		*Investment (Rs. Crore)*	
	Number	*Per cent*	*Number*	*Per cent*
Andaman & Nicobar Islands	1	0.01	0	0
Andhra Pradesh	985	10.28	24280	7.37
Arunachal Pradesh	4	0.04	9	0.00
Assam	125	1.31	1630	0.50
Bihar	15	0.16	168	0.05
Chandigarh	4	0.04	258	0.08
Chhattisgarh	81	0.85	3126	0.95
Dadra & Nagar Haveli	114	1.19	2061	0.63
Daman & Diu	110	1.15	2426	0.74
Delhi	51	0.53	646	0.20
Goa	123	1.28	890	0.27
Gujarat	1606	16.77	87035	26.43
Haryana	462	4.82	17797	5.41
Himachal Pradesh	93	0.97	1912	0.58
Jammu & Kashmir	23	0.24	2117	0.64
Jharkhand	73	0.76	2485	0.75
Karnataka	274	2.86	12884	3.91
Kerala	81	0.85	1019	0.31
Lakshadweep	0	0.00	0	0.00
Madhya Pradesh	396	4.13	22657	6.88
Maharashtra	1652	17.25	42372	12.87
Manipur	1	0.01	13	0.00
Meghalaya	28	0.29	124	0.04
Mizoram	0	0.00	0	0.00
Nagaland	0	0.00	0	0.00
Orissa	85	0.89	2109	0.64
Pondicherry	55	0.57	364	0.11
Punjab	326	3.40	6879	2.09
Rajasthan	453	4.73	15198	4.62
Sikkim	23	0.24	15	0.00
Tamil Nadu	585	6.11	15440	4.69
Tripura	6	0.06	253	0.08
Uttar Pradesh	631	6.59	25993	7.89
Uttaranchal	366	3.82	4904	1.49
West Bengal	746	7.79	32186	9.78
Total	**9578**	**100**	**329250**	**100**

Note: IEM – Industrial Entrepreneur Memorandum.

Source: Calculated from Secretariat for Industrial Assistance Statistics, Department of Industrial Policy and Promotion, Ministry of Commerce, GOI.

Table 3.3: Industries Group-wise Analysis of LOI+LOP+IEM Commissioned During 01/01/1983 to 31/03/2010. (Investment Rs. in Crore) (As 30/04/2010)

Industry Group	*Project*		*Investment*		*Employment*	
	Number	*Per cent*	*Amount*	*Per cent*	*Number*	*Per cent*
Metallurgical Industry	311	5.78	13688	8.07	40920	4.51
Industrial Machinery	119	2.21	781	0.46	16022	1.77
Transport Equipment	23	0.43	1575	0.93	11295	1.24
Other Engineering	395	7.34	13734	8.1	74828	8.25
Electrical Tele & Electronics	323	6	4642	2.74	76366	8.41
Food Processing	314	5.83	3692	2.18	54196	5.97
Textiles	1157	21.49	17431	10.28	209190	23.05
Chemicals & Petrochemicals	1576	29.27	71519	42.19	240875	26.54
Drugs & Pharmaceuticals	373	6.93	3544	2.09	44831	4.94
Glass, Ceramic & Cement	311	5.78	10424	6.15	52652	5.8
Infrastructure Projects	31	0.58	4792	2.83	4353	0.48
Others	451	8.38	23690	13.98	82007	9.04
Total	**5384**	**100**	**169512**	**100**	**907535**	**100**

Note: IEM – Industrial Entrepreneur Memorandum, LOI – Letter of Intent, & LOP – Letter of Permission for 100% Export Oriented Units.
Source: Industries in Gujarat, Statistical Information 2010, Government of Gujarat.

Table 3.4: Industries Groupwise Analysis of LOI+LOP+IEM under Implementation As on 31/04/2010. (Investment in Rs. Crore)

Industry Group	*Project*		*Investment*		*Employment*	
	Number	*Per cent*	*Amount*	*Per cent*	*Number*	*Per cent*
Metallurgical Industry	141	5.68	19949	3.97	31205	5.96
Industrial Machinery	22	0.89	539	0.11	2863	0.55
Transport Equipment	16	0.64	4954	0.99	4794	0.91
Other Engineering	206	8.3	42721	8.5	39315	7.5
Electrical Tele & Electronics	143	5.76	20190	4.02	21836	4.17
Food Processing	146	5.88	4551	0.91	19513	3.72
Textiles	390	15.71	7742	1.54	57049	10.89
Chemicals & Petrochemicals	722	29.08	123439	24.55	118447	22.61
Drugs & Pharmaceuticals	69	2.78	1179	0.23	6779	1.29
Glass, Ceramic & Cement	177	7.13	44617	8.87	49307	9.41
Infrastructure Projects	80	3.22	188996	37.59	112823	21.53
Others	371	14.94	43877	8.73	60006	11.45
Total	**2483**	**100**	**502754**	**100**	**523937**	**100**

Note: IEM – Industrial Entrepreneur Memorandum, LOI – Letter of Intent, & LOP -- Letter of Permission for 100% Export Oriented Units.
Source: Industries in Gujarat, Statistical Information 2010, Government of Gujarat.

Table 3.5: Districtwise Projects under Implementation in Gujarat (IEM+LOI+LOP) (As on March 31, 2010) (Investment in Rs. Crore)

District	*Project*		*Investment*		*Employment*	
	Number	*Per cent*	*Number*	*Per cent*	*Number*	*Per cent*
Ahmedabad	225	9.06	46672	9.28	121904	23.27
Anand	17	0.68	339	0.07	2031	0.39
Bharuch	365	14.70	67997	13.52	83983	16.03
Dahod	0	0	0	0	0	0
Dang	0	0	0	0	0	0
Godhra	84	3.38	2767	0.55	9337	1.78
Kheda	14	0.56	951	0.19	2177	0.42
Narmada	3	0.12	315	0.06	214	0.04
Navsari	17	0.68	96	0.02	4027	0.77
Surat	545	21.95	54012	10.74	54797	10.46
Vadodara	185	7.45	10713	2.13	21179	4.04
Valsad	205	8.26	3459	0.69	18063	3.45
Banaskantha	14	0.56	24684	4.91	4214	0.80
Gandhinagar	41	1.65	1554	0.31	6930	1.32
Mehsana	60	2.42	2270	0.45	9630	1.84
Patan	7	0.28	4185	0.83	438	0.08
Sabarkantha	21	0.85	308	0.06	3644	0.70
Amreli	16	0.64	16436	3.27	2864	0.55
Bhavnagar	33	1.33	5830	1.16	5598	1.07
Jamnagar	54	2.17	70083	13.94	26163	4.99
Junagadh	23	0.93	21340	4.24	7413	1.41
Porbandar	6	0.24	2713	0.54	1289	0.25
Rajkot	92	3.71	2739	0.54	17280	3.30
Surendranagar	13	0.52	187	0.04	9588	1.83
Kutch	442	17.80	162204	32.26	111174	21.22
Total	**2483**	**100**	**502754**	**100**	**523937**	**100**

Note: IEM–Industrial Entrepreneur Memorandum, LOI–Letter of Intent & LOP–Letter of Permission for 100% Export Oriented Units.

Source: Industries in Gujarat, Statistical Information 2010, Government of Gujarat.

Table 4.1: Traffic Handled at Indian Ports, Values in Millions Tons

Year	*Major Ports* *1*	*Non-major Ports* *2*	*Total* *3*	*% Share of Non-major Ports* *4=2/3*
1990-91	152.85	12.78	165.63	7.72
2001-02	287.56	95.52	383.08	24.93
2002-03	313.45	108.30	421.75	25.68
2003-04	344.80	118.86	463.66	25.64
2004-05	383.60	137.50	521.10	26.39
2005-06	423.57	150.12	573.69	26.17
2006-07	463.84	185.54	649.38	28.57
2007-08	519.31	203.62	722.93	28.17
2008-09	530.80	213.22	744.02	28.66
2009-10	561.09	288.94	850.03	33.99
2010-11	569.90	314.64	884.54	35.57

Source: Compiled from Annual Report of Ministry of Shipping, Government of India, Various Issues, Available at: http://shipping.gov.in/index1.php?lang=1&level=0&linkid=12&lid=55

Table 4.2: Private Investment in Infrastructure Sector of Gujarat

	Completed Project		*EOI Letter Issues*		*Bedding Stage*		*Construction*		*Pipeline*		*Total*	
	No.	*In (Cr)*	*No.*	*In (Cr)*	*No.*	*In (Cr)*	*No.*	*In (Cr)*	*No.*	*In (Cr)*	*No.*	*In (Cr)*
Port	16	15542	5	2900	7	5479	8	11701	6	3525	42	39147
Power	4	7600	0	0	0		0		12	24245	16	31845
Road	18	2081	1	1020	5	2269	4	2620	2	150	30	8140
Road-Transport	0		3	400	1	250	2	250	3	200	9	1100
Railway	0		1	499	0				2	312	3	811
Water	0		0	0	1	700			3	150	4	850
IT	4		0	0					0		4	0
Aviation	0		0	0					1	2500	1	2500
Urban-Development	0		3	17			1	500	3	500	7	1017
ULB Urban	1	485	1	50					9	242	11	777
Others	0		0	0					8	13800	8	13800
Total	**43**	**25708**	**14**	**4886**	**14**	**8698**	**15**	**15071**	**49**	**45624**	**135**	**99987**

Source: Gujarat Infrastructure Development Board, Available at: http://www.gidb.org/cms.aspx?content_id=135

Table 4.3: Share of Maritime States in Total Traffic Handled at Non-major Ports

Year	*Gujarat*	*Maharashtra*	*Andhra Pradesh*	*Goa*	*Tamil Nadu*	*Karnataka*	*Others*
2001-02	83.3	5.2	5.9	3.0	0.6	0.8	1.3
2002-03	75.3	8.0	9.5	5.1	0.6	0.6	1.0
2003-04	73.5	8.7	8.4	7.1	0.6	1.0	0.7
2004-05	70.2	8.9	11.0	6.0	0.6	2.6	0.8
2005-06	69.0	7.4	11.8	7.8	0.5	2.7	0.8
2006-07	71.0	6.3	10.1	7.7	0.4	3.5	1.0
2007-08	72.9	5.5	9.3	6.2	0.4	4.3	1.3
2008-09	71.7	4.9	13.9	5.6	0.4	2.3	1.2
2009-10	71.2	4.2	15.1	4.8	0.4	3.0	1.4
2010-11	73.4	4.7	13.5	4.6	0.5	1.0	2.2

Source: Basic Ports Statistics of India, Ministry of Shipping, GOI, various Issues, available at: http://shipping.gov.in/index1.php?lang=1&level=0&linkid=12&lid=55

Table 4.4: Total Road Length in Selected Indian States

				Per cent Share of Surfaced Road		
State		*1999*	*2008*	*1999*	*2008*	*Growth from 1999 to 2008*
Haryana	Total	28416	29726			4.61
	Surfaced	25790	27030	90.76	90.93	4.81
Gujarat	Total	92043	143630			56.05
	Surfaced	81385	132321	88.42	92.13	62.59
Tamil Nadu	Total	145062	181213			24.92
	Surfaced	109972	178045	75.81	98.25	61.9
Maharashtra	Total	236340	223322			-5.51
	Surfaced	183020	147446	77.44	66.02	-19.44

Source: Basic Road Statistics of India, Ministry of Road Transport and Highways, GOI, Various Issues

Table 4.5: Connectivity Status in Gujarat

	1000 & Above	*500-999*	*250-499*	*Below 250*	*Total*
Total Number of Habitations	9941	9101	7948	7197	**34187**
Connected Habitations on 25-12-2000	9499	7036	5422	4810	**26767**
Unconnected Habitations as on 25-12-2000	442	2065	2526	2387	**7420**
No. of Connected During 2000-2010	438	2022	844	736	**4040**
Balance to be Connected as on 1-04-2010	4	43	1682	1651	**3380**
% of Unconnected Habitations in 2010	0.04	0.47	21.16	22.94	**9.89**

Source: Road and Building Department, Government of Gujarat, Available at: http://www.rnbgujarat.org/panchayat1.htm

Table 4.6: Installed Power Generations Capacity and Compound Annual Growth Rate (CAGR) of Selected Indian States

	Installed Power Generation Growth Rate		*Share of Hydro*		*Share of Thermal*		*Share of RES*		*Share of Total Private*		*Total*	
	2001-2006	*2007-2011*	*2001-02*	*2010-11*	*2001-02*	*2010-11*	*2001-02*	*2010-11*	*2001-02*	*2010-11*	*2001-02*	*2010-11*
Gujarat	2.17	12.87	7.49	5.89	90.22	78.85	2.29	15.26	36.16	54.75	7300.4	13110.2
State	5.23	0.56	7.49	5.89	56.11	39.13	0.24	0.23			4660.6	5931.9
Private	-4.04	33.24	0	0	34.11	39.72	2.05	15.03			2639.8	7178
Haryana	7.19	14.68	44.41	19.97	55.59	77.64	0	2.39	0	0.81	2627.44	4429.3
State	7.12	14.53	44.41	19.97	55.59	77.64	0	1.58			2620.38	4393.5
Private	0	50.06	0	0	0	0	0	0.81			7.06	35.8
Maharashtra	1.48	6.93	21.91	19.38	76.24	64.28	1.85	16.34	25.01	35.32	12994	17193.2
State	1.47	2.08	18.47	16.78	56.46	46.34	0.05	1.57			9743.57	11121.1
Private	1.51	20.2	3.44	2.6	19.78	17.94	1.8	14.77			3250.4	6072.1
Tamil Nadu	7.33	7.4	29.44	16.85	58.28	36.99	12.27	46.16	22.94	54.7	6776.01	12592.8
State	6.39	-3.75	29.44	16.85	47.33	27.74	0.29	0.71			5221.55	5705
Private	10.3	25.05	0	0	10.95	9.25	11.99	45.45			1554.46	6887.8
All India	4.64	7.88	24.8	21.64	71.05	64.98	4.16	13.38	10.43	21.17	103134	173626
State	3.48	3.81	21.69	15.7	37.92	30.06	0.06	1.73			61541.6	82452.6
Private	5.24	27.41	0.55	0.82	8.56	11.46	1.32	8.9			10752	36761.2
Central	6.66	5.92	2.56	5.12	24.57	23.47	2.77	2.75			30840.5	54412.6

Note: * Where MW stands for Megawatt and RES stands for Renewable Energy Resource

Source: Annual Reports of Ministry of Power, GOI and Annual Report 2011-12 on the Working of State Power Uutilities and Electricity Department, (Power and Energy Division) Planning Commission, GOI, October 2011.

Table 4.7: Yearwise Installed Capacity Addition of Wind Power (MW)

States	*up to 2005-06*	*2006-07*	*2007-08*	*2008-09*	*2009-10*	*2010-11*	**Total**
Andhra	126.04	0.8	-	-	13.6	63.4	**203.84**
Gujarat	345.755	328.95	580.13	313.605	296.15	312.175	**2176.8**
Karnataka	578.37	264.75	187	322.35	154.4	257.05	**1763.9**
Kerala	2.35	-	8.7	18.6	1.5	4.8	**35.95**
Madhya	39.14	17.45	69.25	25.1	16.6	46.5	**214.04**
Maharashtra	996.705	483.6	276.08	181.075	134.1	232.8	**2304.4**
Rajasthan	359.895	111.75	70.45	199.6	350	436.7	**1528.4**
Tamil	2890.855	570.46	392.65	423.675	598.3	991.225	**5867.2**
West Bengal		1.25	0.5	-	-	-	**1.75**
Others	1.3	-	-	-	-		**1.3**
All India	5341.66	1778.26	1584.3	1484.005	1564.7	2344.65	**14097**

Source: Report on Assessment of Investment Climate for Wind Power Development in India, prepared by ENERGY for Indian Renewable Energy Development Agency (IREDA), New Delhi, September 2011.

Table 4.8: Gross Generation of Electricity of State Electricity Boards (in MKWH) and Compound Annual Growth Rate (CAGR)

	Gross Generation			*CAGR*	
States	*2001-02*	*2006-07*	*2010-11*	*2001-11*	*2006-11*
Gujarat	33501	44352.9	61827.88	7.05	8.66
State	26076	29568.5	33523.98	2.83	3.19
Private	7423	14784.4	28303.9	16.03	17.63
Private Share	22.16	33.33	45.78		
Haryana	5308	14141.7	15560.53	12.69	2.42
State	5308	10780.5	15560.53	12.69	9.61
Private	0	0	0	0.00	0.00
Private Share	0	0	0		
Maharashtra	62800	68962.9	65790.57	0.52	-1.17
State	49018	51494.9	47504.41	-0.35	-2.00
Private	13896	17468	18286.16	3.10	1.15
Private Share	22.13	25.33	27.79		
Tamil Nadu	28743	40734.2	32565.71	1.40	-5.44
State	25547	29510	25478.54	-0.03	-3.61
Private	3196	11224.2	7087.17	9.25	-10.86
Private Share	11.12	27.55	21.76		

Source: Same as Table 4.6

Table 4.9: CPP Exports and Total Industrial Energy for Selected States, 2004

States	*CPP Export (GWh)*	*% of Export*	*CPP Industrial*	*Utility Industrial*	*Total Industrial*	*CPP% Total*
Gujarat	609	10.90%	14380	15293	30282	49.50%
Tamil Nadu	1097	19.70%	7541	15262	23899	36.10%
Maharashtra	130	2.30%	9585	19962	29678	32.70%
All India	5567	100.00%	96677	124572	226816	45.10%

Note: *Where CPP stands for Captive Power Plants and GWH stands for Gigawatt Hour
Source: Hansen, 2008.

Table 4.10: Consumer Categorywise Tariff (in Paisa/KWH)

States	*Domestic*	*Commer-cial*	*Agricul-ture*	*Industry*	*Railway*	*Outside State*	*Average*
Consumer Categorywise Average Tariff for 2007-08 (in Paisa/KWH)							
Gujarat	305.31	487.82	119.52	458	501.7	473.02	337.31
Haryana	343.14	442.06	37.72	431.34	425.89	0	274.73
Maharashtra	308	620.95	173	443.44	464	0	361.81
Tamil Nadu	153.07	606.3	0.04	455.01	0	446.93	296.66
All India	242.23	494.34	77.57	416.41	437.45	484.29	306.46
Consumer Categorywise Average Tariff for 2008-09 (in Paisa/KWH)							
Gujarat	379.45	563.91	197.49	537.72	585.69	706.55	417.84
Haryana	338.17	439.79	40.18	429.68	431.69	0	323.02
Maharashtra	345.23	692.1	194.08	445.99	491	0	403.69
Tamil Nadu	165.17	616.23	0.04	457.9	0	372.31	290.69
All India	252.96	509.88	94.73	432.74	481.02	547.71	325.76
Consumer Categorywise Average Tariff for 2009-10 (in Paisa/KWH)							
Gujarat	374.23	562.58	176.92	527.47	579	494.04	405.71
Haryana	326.65	417.67	35.84	424.67	424.41	0	337.9
Maharashtra	401.7	673.98	196.98	481.97	542	0	432.3
Tamil Nadu	172.52	606.45	0.03	473.52	0	190.62	290.18
All India	275.82	525.76	100.97	449.99	498.48	392.39	333.44
Consumer Categorywise Average Tariff for 2010-11 (in Paisa/KWH)							
Gujarat	372.35	564.8	176.45	527.47	571	372.7	394.82
Haryana	338.68	425.43	35.03	428.56	418.89	0	336.12
Maharashtra	417.77	700.96	204.86	490.25	564	0	447.45
Tamil Nadu	177.55	662.31	0.04	502.55	0	308.22	330.86
All India	300.49	560.23	123.49	477.82	523.72	437.65	357.33

Note: * Where KWH stands for Kilowatt Hour
Source: Annual Report 2011-12 on the Working of State Power Utilities and Electricity Department, (Power and Energy Division) Planning Commission, GOI, October 2011.

Table 4.11: Per Capita Consumption of Electricity (in KWH)

States	*2001-02*	*2002-03*	*2003-04*	*2004-05*	*2005-06*	*2006-07*	*2007-08*	*2008-09*	*2009-10*	CAGR
Gujarat	1094.23	1192.9	1175.2	1298.8	1283.77	1330.8	1486.31	1457.29	1615.24	4.99
Haryana	924.37	997.08	923.83	950.69	1090.39	1208.2	1295.58	1278.85	1222.21	3.55
Maharashtra	851.24	848.02	878.57	879.09	934.43	975.43	1019.91	969.4	1028.22	2.39
Tamil Nadu	782.12	815.26	866.43	918.08	976.81	1079.9	1144.94	1134.48	1131.58	4.73
All India	559.18	566.69	592	612.5	631.41	671.89	717.13	733.54	778.71	4.23

Source: Annual Reports of Ministry of Power, GOI and Annual Report 2011-12 on the Working of State Power Utilities and Electricity Department, (Power and Energy Division) Planning Commission, GOI, October 2011.

Table 4.12: Commercial Profit/Loss (with Subsidy) in Rs. Crores

States	*2001-02*	*2002-03*	*2003-04*	*2004-05*	*2006-07*	*2007-08*	*2008-09*	*2009-10*	*2010-11*
Gujarat	188	101	-343	649	124	150	385	513	642
Haryana	-919	-5	187	-392	-822.6	-1381.52	-1674.92	-1797.09	-2024.25
Maharashtra	-451	-368	415	2209	40.12	-1381.16	-622.97	164.95	149.54
Tamil Nadu	-4457	700	-494	-139	-3512.08	-7768.39	-9680.25	-8871.65	-8143.91
All India	-16725	-4846	-2268	-3438	-16665.7	-29494.82	-35437.14	-41401.12	-37835.91

Source: Annual Reports of Ministry of Power, GOI and Annual Report 2011-12 on the Working of State Power Utilities and Electricity Department, (Power and Energy Division) Planning Commission, GOI, October 2011.

Table 4.13: Total Subsidy for Agriculture and Domestic Consumers (in Rs. Crores)

	2007-08		*2008-09*		*2009-10*		*2010-11*	
States	*Agricul-ture*	*Domes-tic*	*Agricul-ture*	*Domes-tic*	*Agricul-ture*	*Domes-tic*	*Agricul-ture*	*Domest-tic*
Gujarat	3049	451.12	3128	485.4	3390	410.64	3451	356.1
Haryana	3122	416.62	3699	773.02	4980	1096.46	4224	1174.9
Maharashtra	2928	975.05	3259	1117.05	3749	765.76	3654	651.5
Tamil Nadu	4422	3125.8	5458	4332.46	6136	5014.36	5924	5477.36

Source: Annual Report of the Working of State Power Utilities & Electricity Department, Planning Commission, GOI, October 2011.

Table 5.1: Pattern of land Utilization: Gujarat & India

		Not Available for Cultivation	*AUNAU**	*BUW**	*Culturable Waste Land*	*Fallow Lands Other than Current Fallows*	*De facto CPR**	*De facto CPR Minus Forest*	*Land under Productive Agricultural Use*	*Total Cultivable Land*	*Net Area Sown*
India	TE 1990-91	13.4	7.0	6.5	4.9	3.3	35.3	13.2	51.3	59.5	46.01
	TE 2001-02	13.6	7.7	6.0	4.5	3.3	35.2	12.6	51.2	59.0	50.50
	TE 2008-09	14.1	8.5	5.6	4.3	3.4	35.0	12.2	50.9	58.6	51.75
Gujarat	TE 1990-91	19.9	5.9	14.0	10.3	0.3	25.0	15.1	55.2	65.8	46.60
	TE 2001-02	19.5	6.0	13.8	10.6	0.1	25.1	15.2	55.0	65.7	46.20
	TE 2008-09	19.9	6.2	13.8	10.5	0.1	24.9	15.1	55.2	65.8	41.65

Source: Calculated from Directorate of Economics and Statistics, Department of Agriculture and Cooperation.

Note: * AUNAV – Area Under Non-Agricultural Use
* BUW – Barren and Unculturable Waste.
* CPR – Common Property Revenue

Table 5.2: Share of Net Irrigated Area by sources: Gujarat & India

	Canals				*Wells*				*Share of*
	Govt.	*Pvt.*	*Total*	*Tanks*	*Tube-wells*	*Other Wells*	*Total well*	*Other Source*	*NSA irrigated*
Gujarat									
TE 2001-02	13.92	0.00	13.92	0.52	33.10	52.06	85.2	0.40	27.62
TE 2008-09	18.62	0.00	18.62	0.94	26.73	51.30	78.0	2.41	35.34
India									
TE 2001-02	28.30	0.36	28.66	4.23	40.01	21.11	61.1	5.98	40.06
TE 2008-09	26.25	0.34	26.58	3.19	40.79	19.84	60.6	9.60	65.14

Source: Calculated from Directorate of Economics and Statistics, Department of Agriculture and Cooperation.

Table 5.3: Annaul Growth Rates of Agriculture and Allied Sector in Gujarat and India

	% share to Total output of agriculture & Allied			*Simple Growth rate*	
	TE 1992-93	*TE 2001-02*	*TE 2008-09*	*TE 1992- to TE 2001-02*	*TE 2001- to TE 2008-09*
Gujarat					
Total Cereal	12.2	9.3	7.8	5.3	5.3
Total Pulses	4.0	2.1	1.8	6.2	6.2
TOTAL FOOD GRAIN	16.2	11.3	9.7	5.5	5.5
Total Oilseed	15.6	13.5	14.8	11.1	11.1
Total Fibre	5.3	5.2	13.3	45.0	45.0
Total Condiments & Spices	1.6	1.2	2.2	29.9	29.9
Total Fruits & Vegetables	5.9	7.9	11.1	18.5	18.5
Total Value of Agriculture	64.9	59.3	62.6	10.2	10.2
Value of Milk	14.6	19.2	19.0	8.7	8.7
Total Value of Livestock	17.2	22.8	22.8	9.0	9.0
Total Output of Agriculture & Allied	100.0	100.0	100.0	8.9	8.9
India					
Total Cereal	22.7	21.0	18.9	2.2	1.2
Total Pulses	3.6	2.8	2.6	0.1	1.7
TOTAL FOOD GRAIN	26.3	23.9	21.6	1.9	1.2
Total Oilseed	6.7	5.5	6.2	.7	5.0
Total Fibre	2.3	1.8	2.9	.2	14.3
Total Condiments & Spices	1.6	1.9	2.1	6.5	4.4
Total Fruits & Vegetables	12.3	15.6	15.9	7.0	3.3

Total Value of Agriculture	65.2	63.5	61.9	2.9	2.5
Value of Milk	14.0	15.8	16.5	5.1	3.7
Total Value of Livestock	20.9	22.5	24.3	4.4	4.3
Total output of agriculture & allied	100.0	100.0	100.0	3.3	2.9

Source: Calculated from CSO

Table 5.4: Value of Incremental Output from Major Components of Agriculture & Allied Sector in Gujarat (in Lakh Rs and constant prices of 2005)

Items	*TE 1992-93 to TE 2001-02*	*TE 2001-02 to TE 2008-09*	*Items*	*TE 1992-93 to TE 2001-02*	*TE 2001-02 to TE 2008-09*
Total Output of Agriculture & Allied	406583	2022417	Cotton	23069	530647
Total Value of Agriculture	82965	1371353	Value of Milk	209168	377059
Total Fibre	18166	530169	Total Fruits & Vegetables	88900	330669
Total Value of Livestock	251506	463271	Groundnut	21097	300207
Total Oilseed	-4307	339420	Wheat	-11784	151138
TOTAL FOOD GRAIN	-90302	141127	Total Condiments & Spices	-6871	78268
Total Cereal	-46178	111683	Paddy	31318	35939
Total Pulses	-44604	29433	Sugarcane & gur	44730	-36916

Source: Calculated from CSO

Table 5.5: Share of Area under Major Foodgrain & Non-Food Crops

	TE 1990-91	*TE 2001-02*	*TE 2008-09*
India			
Total Foodgrain	69.0	65.1	63.6
Total Non- foodgrain	19.4	20.5	22.3
Gujarat			
Total Foodgrain	48.5	36.4	35.2
Total Non- foodgrain	35.9	42.8	43.7

Source: Calculated from Ministry of Agriculture, Govt. of India.

Table 5.6: Share of Area under Major Crops as Percentage of Total Cropped Area Gujarat

	Rice	*Wheat*	*Jowar*	*Bajra*	*Maize*	*Tur*	*Gram*	*Groundnut*	*Cotton*	*Tobacco*
TE 1990-91	6.2	6.2	7.0	15.4	3.7	3.9	1.1	19.4	11.3	0.0
TE 2001-02	6.5	4.1	2.4	10.9	4.4	3.4	0.5	17.4	15.8	1.1
TE 2008-09	6.1	9.6	1.2	7.1	3.6	2.2	1.6	15.6	19.9	0.4

Source : Calculated from Ministry of Agriculture, Govt. of India.

Table 5.7: Share of Area under Different Crop Groups to Total Cropped Area

	Total Cereal	*Total Pulses*	*Total Food Grain*	*Total and vege-tables*	*Total Food*	*Total Oil-seeds Crops*	*Total Condi-ments & Spices*	*Total Fiber*	*Fodder Crops*	*Total Non-food*	*Total Area sown*
GUJARAT											
TE 1990-91	35.7	8.9	44.0	1.7	50.1	22.6	1.6	11.0	12.2	49.9	100.0
TE 2001-02	29.1	7.3	36.4	2.8	42.9	27.0	1.8	15.9	10.9	57.1	100.0
TE 2009-10	28.0	6.9	34.6	3.8	43.1	24.5	2.7	20.8	7.7	56.7	100.0
INDIA											
TE 1990-91	57.0	13.0	70.0	3.5	76.5	13.3	1.3	4.8	4.7	23.5	100.0
TE 2001-02	54.2	11.8	65.1	4.5	74.6	12.4	1.6	5.3	5.0	25.4	100.0
TE 2009-10	51.6	12.5	63.2	5.2	73.4	13.8	1.7	5.5	4.2	26.5	100.0

Source: Directorate of Economics and Statistics, Department of Agriculture and Cooperation

Table 5.8: Share of Production of Major Crops of Gujarat to All India Total

	Rice	*Wheat*	*Total Major Coarse Cereal #*	*Total Cereals*	*Total Pulses*	*Total Foodgrains*	*Ground-nut*	*Total Oilseeds*	*Cotton*
TE 1990-91	0.4	0.8	2.4	1.0	1.5	1.0	21.9	12.0	15.9
TE 2001-02	0.3	0.4	2.1	0.7	1.0	0.7	21.9	12.2	16.5
TE 2008-09	0.5	1.3	1.5	1.0	1.5	1.0	36.8	14.2	32.7

Source: Calculated from Ministry of Agriculture, Govt. of India.
Total coarse Cereal in Gujarat includes only Jowar, Bajra & Maize

Table 5.9: Coefficient of Variation of Production

	Cotton			*Total Foodgrain*		
	1996-97 to 1999-00	*2000-01 to 2003-04*	*2004-05 to 2007-08*	*1996-97 to 1999-00*	*2000-01 to 2003-04*	*2004-05 to 2007-08*
Gujarat	26.2	59.7	25.5	14.6	39.7	18.9
Karnataka	18.7	52.7	14.8	9.6	25.3	15.2
All India	11.9	21.5	20.3	3.7	9.1	6.4

Source: Calculated from Ministry of Agriculture, Govt. of India.

Table 5.10: Yield of Major Crops

	Rice	Wheat	Total Coarse Cereals	Total Cereals	Total Pulses	Total Food grains	Ground nut	Total Oil-seeds	Cotton
GUJARAT									
TE 1990-91	1531	2127	915	1214	633	1098	977	843	243
TE 2001-02	1282	2208	1061	1267	480	1109	736	851	174
TE 2008-09	1781	2664	1195	1817	763	1609	1390	1358	551
INDIA									
TE 1990-91	1725	2216	879	1532	575	1353	989	779	226
TE 2001-02	1988	2750	1064	1917	596	1688	957	859	200
TE 2008-09	2145	2710	1262	2046	611	1842	1163	1012	430

Source: Ministry of Agriculture, Govt. of India.

Table 5.11: Growth Rates of Yield of the Major Crops

	Rice	Wheat	Total Coarse Cereals	Total Cereals	Total Pulses	Total Food Grains	Ground nut	Total Oil-Seeds	Cotton
GUJARAT									
TE 1990-91 to 2001-02	-16.26	3.82	15.93	4.32	-24.21	0.99	-24.69	1.03	-28.67
TE 2001-02 to 2008-09	38.86	20.64	12.65	43.47	58.89	45.07	88.86	59.48	217.08
INDIA									
TE 1990-91 to 2001-02	15.29	24.10	21.07	25.13	3.55	24.73	-3.24	10.23	-11.49
TE 2001-02 to 2008-09	7.88	-1.45	18.58	6.77	2.64	9.10	21.53	17.90	114.81

Source: Calculated from Ministry of Agriculture, Govt. of India.

Table 5.12: Changes of Percentage Shares of Number and Area of Operational Holdings Across Farm Size Categories between 1995-96 and 2005-06

Size of Holding (in ha.)	*Gujarat*		*India*	
	1995-96	*2004-05*	*1995-96*	*2004-05*
	N(umber	*Area*	*Number*	*Area*
Below 0.5	4.78	0.53	2.99	1.53
0.5 - 1.0	1.89	1.51	0.19	1.48
1.0 - 2.0	0.89	3.41	-0.21	2.10
2.0 - 3.0	-1.07	1.63	-0.84	0.31
3.0 - 4.0	-1.30	0.27	-0.57	-0.22
4.0 - 5.0	-1.28	-0.60	-0.44	-0.49
5.0 - 7.5	-1.92	-2.02	-0.50	-0.86
7.5 - 10.0	-1.05	-2.18	-0.27	-0.89
10.0 - 20.0	-0.95	-3.60	-0.29	-1.88
20.0 & ABOVE	0.00	1.04	-0.07	-1.09

Source: Calculated from Agricultural Census.

Table 5.13: Percentage of Number and Area of Operational Holdings Cultivated by Scheduled Caste Households to Total Households

Size Categories	*Gujarat*		*India*	
	Number	*Area*	*Number*	*Area*
1995-96				
Marginal	5.3	5.3	13.0	12.0
Small	4.6	4.5	9.5	9.6
Semi-Medium	3.9	3.8	7.8	7.8
Medium	2.8	2.7	6.3	6.3
Large	1.8	2.1	6.4	6.2
2005-06				
Marginal	4.0	4.0	17.2	16.0
Small	3.5	3.4	11.3	11.0
Semi-Medium	3.1	3.0	7.1	6.9
Medium	2.7	2.6	4.6	4.5
Large	2.4	2.7	4.0	3.7

Source: Calculated from Agricultural Census

Table 5.14: Percentage of Number and Area of Operational Holdings Cultivated by Scheduled Tribe Households to Total Households

Size Categories	*Gujarat*		*India*	
	Number	*Area*	*Number*	*Area*
1995-96				
Marginal	12.8	12.2	6.1	7.6
Small	10.8	10.7	10.8	10.8
Semi-Medium	10.5	10.4	12.5	12.3
Medium	8.9	8.7	12.7	12.6
Large	6.8	6.5	9.6	8.5
2005-06				
Marginal	11.8	11.0	6.1	7.7
Small	10.0	9.9	11.1	11.2
Semi-Medium	10.0	10.0	12.0	12.0
Medium	9.0	8.9	12.0	12.0
Large	7.8	7.8	10.2	9.8

Source: Calculated from Agricultural Census.

Table 5.15: Participation in Cotton Cultivation across Farm-size Classes in Gujarat

Classes	*Percentage of Irrigated Cotton Area*	*Percentage of Unirrigated Cotton Area*	*Percentage Total Cotton Area*	*% of Holdings Cultivating Cotton*
1995-96				
Marginal	9.87	8.58	9.00	9.52
Small	16.25	12.38	13.44	19.82
Semimedium	18.01	15.28	15.98	27.47
Medium	20.42	19.36	19.59	37.72
Large	22.53	23.47	23.33	48.39
2005-06				
Marginal	15.68	13.55	14.41	11.86
Small	24.59	18.81	20.80	24.51
Semimedium	26.32	21.65	23.16	31.43
Medium	27.28	24.80	25.51	38.07
Large	26.00	25.22	25.39	41.59

Source: Calculated from Agricultural Census.

Table 5.16: Participation in Groundnut Cultivation across Farm-size Classes in Gujarat

Classes	*Percentage of Irrigated Groundnut Area*	*Percentage of Unirrigated Groundnut Area*	*Percentage Total Groundnut Area*	*% of Holdings Cultivating Groundnut*
1995-96				
Marginal	2.30	16.73	12.01	10.85
Small	4.96	28.13	21.74	26.92
Semimedium	5.59	25.45	20.36	28.78
Medium	6.98	22.20	18.88	30.28
Large	5.58	14.22	12.93	25.15
2005-06				
Marginal	5.79	19.85	14.20	10.23
Small	12.04	29.64	23.57	26.02
Semimedium	12.03	24.66	20.57	26.18
Medium	12.72	18.47	16.83	24.74
Large	17.86	13.31	14.31	20.36

Source: Calculated from Agricultural Census.

Table 5.17: Participation in Vegetables Cultivation across Farm-size Classes in Gujarat (2005-06)

Classes	*Percentage of Irrigated Vegetable Area*	*Percentage of Unirrigated Vegetable Area*	*Percentage Total Vegetable Area*	*% of Holdings Cultivating Vegetable*
Marginal	2.95	1.27	1.95	2.03
Small	2.67	1.15	1.68	2.26
Semimedium	2.57	1.45	1.81	2.98
Medium	2.49	1.95	2.10	4.56
Large	2.59	2.44	2.47	6.54
All Classes	2.61	1.67	1.96	2.70

Source: Calculated from Agricultural Census.

Table 5.18: Participation in Fruits Cultivation across Farm-size Classes in Gujarat (2005-06)

Classes	*Percentage of Irrigated Fruit Area*	*Percentage of Unirrigated Fruit Area*	*Percentage Total Fruit Area*	*% of Holdings Cultivating Fruit*
Marginal	3.08	0.44	1.50	1.49
Small	2.94	0.32	1.22	1.51
Semimedium	2.46	0.27	0.98	1.43
Medium	2.59	0.24	0.91	1.60
Large	1.96	1.31	1.46	1.35
All Classes	2.63	0.40	1.09	1.49

Source: Calculated from Agricultural Census.

Table 5.19: Landlessness in India and Gujarat

State/Country	*Does not Own any land*	*Does not Cultivate any land*
	NSSO 50th Round 1993-94	
Gujarat	6.2%	46.3%
India	6.1%	38.7%
	NSSO 66th Round 2009-10	
Gujarat	3.4%	42.9%
India	5.3%	45.4%

Source: NSSO 60th & 66th rounds, Consumption Expenditure

Table 5.20: Landlessness in Gujarat Across Regions

	No Cultivated land		
Regions/State	*2004-05*	*2009-10*	*Total*
Tribal Area	145326 23.9%	188170 29.1%	608547 100.0%
North Gujarat	912150 50.3%	744942 40.1%	1815198 100.0%
Canal Districts	1195504 52.9%	957116 43.2%	2258640 100.0%
Saurashtra and Kutch	1083951 56.7%	937405 50.0%	1912621 100.0%
Gujarat	3336931 50.6%	2827633 42.9%	6595006 100.0%

Source: NSSO 66th round, 2009-10.

Table 5.21: Relationship between Landlessness and Poverty in Gujarat

	MPCE quartile classes			
Categories by Land Cultivated	*1 (lowest)*	*2*	*3*	*4 (highest)*
2004-05				
Landless	21.65%	35.33%	10.62%	32.40%
Marginal	35.70%	26.75%	24.10%	13.45%
Large	0.00%	22.46%	31.53%	46.01%
2009-10				
Landless	40.90%	29.49%	2.99%	26.62%
Marginal	24.83%	29.02%	25.91%	20.24%
Large	0.13%	13.71%	6.61%	79.55%

Source: NSSO 66th round, 2009-10.

Table 5.22: Relationship between Landlessness and Poverty in Gujarat

	MPCE quartile classes			
Categories by Land Cultivated	*1 (lowest)*	*2*	*3*	*4 (highest)*
2004-05				
Landless	27.92%	26.38%	13.95%	31.74%
Marginal	27.68%	26.65%	24.70%	20.97%
Large	6.91%	11.29%	25.08%	56.73%
2009-10				
Landless	42.7%	29.1%	10.0%	18.2%
Marginal	36.6%	27.5%	21.1%	14.9%
Large	10.4%	18.9%	20.7%	50.0%

Source: NSSO 66th round, 2009-10.

Table 6.1: Sectoral Shares in GSDP/GDP and Employment

	GSDP/GDP			*Employment*		
	1993-94	*2004-05*	*2009-10*	*1993-94*	*2004-05*	*2009-10*
			Gujarat			
Agriculture	22.4	16.1	12.1	60.7	58.2	53.4
Industry	38.8	40.0	40.7	19.0	20.5	19.6
Manufacturing	29.6	29.4	27.4	14.7	15.7	13.9
Services	38.8	43.9	47.2	20.3	21.3	27.0
			India			
Agriculture	31.0	18.9	14.5	64.9	58.5	53.2
Industry	26.3	28.1	28.3	14.7	18.1	21.5
Manufacturing	21.1	15.3	16.1	10.4	11.7	11
Services	42.8	53.0	57.2	20.5	23.4	25.3

Source: Central Statistical Organization and NSSO Reports (50th, 61st and 66th Rounds) on Employment and Unemployment Situation in India.

Table 6.2: Share of Selected States in India's Manufacturing GVA, Employment, Fixed Capital and Number of Factories (Percentage) and Their Respective Growth Rates

	Share in GVA				*Growth Rate of GVA*			
	1980s	*1990s*	*2000s*	*All Years*	*1980s*	*1990s*	*2000s*	*All Years*
Gujarat	7.78	11.57	14.19	10.96	13.07	12.89	13.95	11.56
Haryana	2.96	3.42	4.31	3.51	8.7	11.22	11.2	9.77
Maharashtra	20.34	22.34	21.33	21.33	8.85	8.29	15.81	8.15
Tamil Nadu	9.45	10.49	9.5	9.84	10.12	6.2	10.71	7.8
India					7.65	8.73	13.41	7.78
	Share in Employment				*Growth Rate of Employment*			
	1980s	*1990s*	*2000s*	*All Years*	*1980s*	*1990s*	*2000s*	*All Years*
Gujarat	8.54	8.97	9.34	8.92	-1.20	3.24	5.55	1.71
Haryana	2.72	3.35	4.19	3.36	2.65	4.90	8.23	3.65
Maharashtra	15.61	15.45	13.99	15.09	-1.91	2.17	2.57	0.65
Tamil Nadu	9.04	12.8	15.21	12.14	2.36	3.23	6.92	4.01
India					-0.11	1.88	4.56	1.24
	Share in Net Capital Stock				*Growth Rate of Net Capital Stock*			
	1980s	*1990s*	*2000s*	*All Years*	*1980s*	*1990s*	*2000s*	*All Years*
Gujarat	6.15	12.18	17.03	11.41	14.16	18.70	6.79	15.38
Haryana	2.03	2.71	3.52	2.70	17.70	14.05	7.35	12.82
Maharashtra	14.56	17.75	17.87	16.65	13.94	11.96	6.16	10.72
Tamil Nadu	7.25	9.05	9.82	8.63	13.94	12.41	7.56	11.26
India					10.55	11.25	6.27	9.42

	Share in Number of Factories				*Growth Rate of No. of Factories*			
	1980s	*1990s*	*2000s*	*All Years*	*1980s*	*1990s*	*2000s*	*All Years*
Gujarat	9.91	10.25	10.24	10.12	0.52	4.04	0.96	1.90
Haryana	2.74	2.96	3.37	3	3.23	3.67	0.28	2.81
Maharashtra	14.67	14.48	13.47	14.26	-0.04	2.87	0.40	1.26
Tamil Nadu	11.06	14.45	15.38	13.5	3.47	3.88	1.90	3.53
India					0.98	2.24	1.97	1.70

Source: Own calculations from State Level Data, Annual Survey of Industry, 1980-81 to 2007-08.

Table 6.3: Growth Rate of Employment by Type between 2000 and 2008

	Total Employment	*Workers*	*Directly Employed Workers*	*Contract Workers*
Gujarat	5.55	6.24	4.36	10.29 (37 per cent)
Haryana	8.23	9.63	4.53	18.36 (48 per cent)
Maharashtra	2.57	2.84	-1.00	14.26 (36 per cent)
Tamil Nadu	6.92	11.29	9.15	17.22 (30 per cent)
India	4.56	4.78	2.52	11.67 (31 per cent)

Source: Own Calculations from State Level Data, Annual Survey of Industry, 2000-01 to 2007-08. Figures in parenthesis show the per cent of contractual workers in total workers in 2007-08.

Table 6.4: Employment Elasticity

	1980-81 to 2007-08	*1980s*	*1990s*	*2000s*
Gujarat	0.16	-0.04	0.25	0.40
Haryana	0.38	0.31	0.36	0.68
Maharashtra	0.09	-0.19	0.30	0.19
Tamil Nadu	0.52	0.24	0.51	0.67
India	0.17	-0.001	0.23	0.37

Source: Own Calculations from State Level Data, Annual Survey of Industry, 1980-81 to 2007-08.

Table 6.5: Capital Intensity, Labour Productivity and Capital Productivity Levels and Growth Rates

	Capital Intensity				*Growth Rate of Capital Intensity*			
	1980-81 to 2007-08	*1980s*	*1990s*	*2000s*	*1980-81 to 2007-08*	*1980s*	*1990s*	*2000s*
Gujarat	6.01	1.23	5.69	12.38	13.44	15.55	14.98	1.18
Haryana	3.26	1.26	3.3	5.71	8.84	14.66	8.72	-0.81
Maharashtra	4.73	1.61	4.69	8.7	10.01	16.16	9.58	3.5
Tamil Nadu	2.76	1.33	2.87	4.4	6.97	11.31	8.89	0.6
India	3.98	1.65	4.07	6.78	8.07	10.67	9.2	1.63

	Labour Productivity				*Growth Rate of Labour Productivity*			
	1980-81 to 2007-08	*1980s*	*1990s*	*2000s*	*1980-81 to 2007-08*	*1980s*	*1990s*	*2000s*
Gujarat	1.73	0.64	1.62	3.23	9.69	14.45	9.35	7.96
Haryana	1.33	0.72	1.28	2.16	5.91	5.9	6.02	3.47
Maharashtra	1.91	0.89	1.8	3.32	7.45	10.97	5.99	12.91
Tamil Nadu	0.98	0.7	1.01	1.31	3.64	7.58	2.87	3.55
India	1.29	0.67	1.25	2.13	6.45	7.77	6.73	8.52
	Capital Productivity				*Growth Rate of Capital Productivity*			
	1980-81 to 2007-08	*1980s*	*1990s*	*2000s*	*1980-81 to 2007-08*	*1980s*	*1990s*	*2000s*
Gujarat	0.37	0.52	0.3	0.26	-3.31	-0.96	-4.89	6.71
Haryana	0.47	0.63	0.39	0.38	-2.7	-7.65	-2.49	4.32
Maharashtra	0.46	0.58	0.39	0.38	-2.32	-4.47	-3.27	9.09
Tamil Nadu	0.41	0.54	0.36	0.3	-3.12	-3.35	-5.53	2.93
India	0.35	0.41	0.31	0.31	-1.5	-2.62	-2.26	6.78

Source: Own Calculations from State Level Data, Annual Survey of Industry, 1980-81 to 2007-08.

Table 6.6: Growth Rate of Wages per Employee and per Worker

	Growth Rate of Wages of All Employees			
	1980s	*1990s*	*2000s*	*All Years*
Gujarat	3.37	3.70	1.48	4.10
Haryana	2.04	4.12	0.01	3.89
Maharashtra	6.13	1.52	2.20	3.48
Tamil Nadu	2.11	1.92	0.18	1.34
India	3.17	1.54	3.78	2.22
	Growth Rate of per Worker Wages			
	1980s	*1990s*	*2000s*	*All Years*
Gujarat	3.69	1.12	1.32	1.04
Haryana	2.29	0.71	-0.66	1.71
Maharashtra	5.30	-0.41	0.13	1.03
Tamil Nadu	2.06	-1.14	0.47	-0.44
India	3.29	0.07	-0.09	0.74

Source: Own Calculations from State Level Data, Annual Survey of Industry, 1980-81 to 2007-08.

Table 6.7: Sectoral Share of Gujarat in India's Total GVA, Capital and Employment (Percentage)

	GVA			*Employment*			*Fixed Capital*		
	1980s	*1990s*	*2000s*	*1980s*	*1990s*	*2000s*	*1980s*	*1990s*	*2000s*
All Industries	7.78	11.57	14.19	8.54	8.97	9.34	6.37	13.96	18.65
Food and Beverages (15)	6.08	5.40	5.93	6.12	5.11	5.15	8.72	6.46	5.75
Tobacco (16)	3.52	2.14	3.14	2.83	1.37	1.06	5.16	4.34	4.67
Textiles (17)	18.42	12.75	14.40	15.67	12.71	12.15	21.47	16.01	17.20
Wearing Apparel (18)	10.61	3.56	2.87	12.58	5.08	2.24	12.38	4.72	2.77
Leather and Fur (19)	1.28	0.88	0.51	1.21	1.02	0.43	2.74	1.31	0.57
Wood Products (20)	3.46	3.51	10.29	11.93	4.07	9.41	2.90	3.35	7.36
Paper Products (21)	5.96	6.79	8.64	8.20	8.26	10.27	4.86	6.05	10.74
Publishing (22)	5.00	5.51	5.24	4.97	5.17	4.55	5.38	5.65	4.41
Refined Petroleum (23)	15.07	29.27	29.94	2.81	7.29	17.55	3.27	15.64	44.51
Chemical Products (24)	7.38	27.19	30.18	6.50	21.53	22.42	4.03	34.13	34.86
Rubber and Plastic (25)	5.95	8.46	9.01	9.21	10.13	9.20	8.54	9.71	12.18
Mineral Products (26)	8.31	10.88	13.71	13.14	12.45	11.52	9.08	11.39	15.46
Basic Metals (27)	2.87	5.13	6.31	5.00	5.54	6.42	1.58	7.89	9.37
Fabricated Metals (28)	6.86	7.78	11.73	8.38	9.13	9.25	7.34	7.95	13.09
Machinery Equipment (29)	9.14	10.38	10.72	11.37	12.95	14.55	10.37	12.31	11.57
Office A/C (30)	6.67	4.46	0.16	5.97	7.43	0.51	9.44	2.58	0.46
Electrical Machinery (31)	6.24	5.80	6.11	9.84	7.69	8.33	5.59	6.37	7.74
Radio, TV (32)	2.08	4.62	8.59	2.47	3.99	5.57	2.47	9.00	15.20
Medical, Optical (33)	0.25	6.55	5.56	0.51	6.59	8.63	0.17	5.28	6.34
Motor Vehicles (34)	1.01	0.96	1.37	2.67	2.69	2.76	1.88	1.13	2.45
Transport Equipment (35)	1.44	2.94	3.31	2.13	4.26	4.92	1.47	2.60	4.44
Furniture, Gems, Jewels (36)	2.20	7.46	16.69	3.99	14.07	20.81	3.03	10.33	13.66
Recycling (37)			25.98			23.73			21.32

Source: Own Calculations from State Level Data, Annual Survey of Industry, 1980-81 to 2007-08.

Table 6.8: Sectoral Contribution to GVA and Employment and Respective Growth Rate in Gujarat (Percentage)

	Sectoral Contribution						*Growth Rate*					
	GVA			*Employment*			*GVA*			*Employment*		
	1980s	*1990s*	*2000s*	*1980s*	*1990s*	*2000s*	*1980s*	*1990s*	*2000s*	*1980s*	*1990s*	*2000s*
All Industry	100	100	100	100	100	100	13.1	12.9	14.0	-1.2	3.2	5.5
Food Beverages	8.4	4.8	3.7	12.2	9.3	9.0	8.3	9.3	6.1	-4.1	4.7	3.3
Tobacco	0.7	0.3	0.4	1.8	0.9	0.6	0.9	18.0	3.5	-2.7	-4.6	-2.5
Textiles	37.1	11.7	7.5	37.5	23.8	20.6	-1.4	5.7	5.7	-4.9	0.2	3.7
Wearing Apparel	0.8	0.6	0.4	1.5	1.5	1.2	19.5	1.6	9.4	13.3	-0.7	10.7
Leather,Fur	0.2	0.1	0.0	0.2	0.2	0.1	15.5	11.3	1.1	0.8	1.3	-5.3
Wood	0.2	0.1	0.2	1.4	0.4	0.7	2.6	7.7	15.0	-15.8	3.1	5.6
Paper	1.7	1.2	1.1	1.9	1.9	2.4	7.8	7.2	5.9	0.5	2.7	3.3
Publishing	1.3	0.8	0.5	1.4	1.1	0.7	2.9	6.9	8.4	-0.1	-3.3	7.5
Refined Petroleum	5.6	9.1	22.8	0.3	0.7	1.8	68.5	27.0	38.4	33.6	7.2	28.9
Chemical Products	11.0	45.0	37.4	6.1	22.1	23.0	47.1	18.3	6.1	9.4	8.0	1.5
Rubber and Plastic	2.4	2.4	2.0	2.3	3.3	3.5	20.9	6.4	5.2	6.9	5.9	3.5
Mineral Products	5.8	4.8	5.1	9.6	8.1	8.0	9.4	8.9	15.2	0.9	1.1	6.5
Basic Metals	5.1	5.5	6.4	5.4	5.1	5.0	7.0	14.4	23.3	2.2	4.6	12.5
Fabricated Metal	2.6	1.9	2.4	3.1	3.5	4.1	11.7	2.1	34.5	4.2	2.3	13.6
Machinery Equipment	10.4	6.1	4.3	9.0	9.1	8.4	8.0	6.7	15.3	1.5	1.7	5.6
Office A/C	0.6	0.2	0.0	0.3	0.2	0.0	28.7	10.7		9.9	5.2	
Electrical Machinery	3.9	2.3	1.6	3.4	2.8	2.7	9.5	8.9	13.8	-2.3	3.7	7.0
Radio, TV	0.5	0.9	1.2	0.4	0.8	0.8	28.0	13.5	-3.3	11.8	2.1	4.4
Medical, Optical	0.0	0.5	0.4	0.0	0.6	0.7		2.5	19.3		8.5	5.8
Motor Vehicles	0.6	0.4	0.6	0.9	0.9	1.1	-1.6	3.2	38.4	-1.4	9.2	12.0
Transport Equipment	0.7	0.8	0.6	1.2	2.0	1.2	11.6	11.8	24.9	3.2	11.1	-2.0
Gems, Jewels	0.2	0.6	1.6	0.3	1.8	4.4	16.9	17.0	24.9	7.6	7.9	21.2

Source: Own Calculations from State Level Data, Annual Survey of Industry, 1980-81 to 2007-08.,

Table 6.9: Share of Districts in Manufacturing Activity (Percentage) and Growth Rate between 2000-01 and 2005-06

	GVA Share		*Growth Rate of GVA*	*Employment Share*		*Growth Rate of Employment*	*Fixed Capital*		*Growth Rate of Fixed Capital*	*No. of Units*		*Growth Rate of Number Factory of Units*
	2001	*2006*		*2001*	*2006*		*2001*	*2006*		*2001*	*2006*	
Jamnagar	3.22	22.52	76.71	2.23	3.31	10.58	8.78	27.74	38.38	1.8	1.95	-2.36
Vadodara	16.06	21.34	26.74	13.65	11.05	-2.03	18.61	12.38	1.34	12.82	9.79	-8.96
Surat	27.14	17.7	9.92	16.57	19.16	5.21	22.18	23.58	11.31	12.08	14.01	-1.04
Kutch	3.31	7.97	42.71	1.49	4.47	27.34	0.81	5.8	62.99	0.97	1.29	1.68
Bharuch	15.63	6.67	0.99	7.21	5.4	-3.52	19.53	9.24	-5.33	4.99	3.65	-9.74
Ahmedabad	11.01	6.18	6.66	20.67	16.96	-1.76	9.26	5.39	-1.32	25.95	25.27	-4.43
Valsad	9.46	3.21	-3.58	9.71	8.65	-0.14	4.36	3.53	5.4	8.98	9.37	-3.11
Rajkot	1.72	2.11	24.73	4.96	5.49	4.28	1.13	1.26	12.44	8.87	9.69	-2.2
Gandhinagar	2.78	2.03	12.41	4.06	4.96	6.4	3.48	2.32	1.35	4.41	4.9	-1.9
Total of 9 Districts	**90.33**	**89.73**		**80.54**	**79.45**		**88.14**	**91.24**		**80.88**	**79.92**	
Gujarat			**19.73**			**2.19**			**9.95**			**-3.92**

Note: Growth Rate is Calculated by Compound Annual Growth Rate

Source: Calculated from Unit Level Data, Annual Survey of Industry - 2000-01 and 2005-06.

Table 6.10: Concentration of Manufacturing Activity in Districts

	Herfindahl–Hirschman Index			
	Employment		*GVA*	
	2000-01	*2005-06*	*2000-01*	*2005-06*
Gujarat	11.39	10.10	11.48	14.53
Haryana	18.85	20.61	23.20	28.81
Maharashtra	11.93	12.25	13.64	18.32
Tamil Nadu	8.57	8.91	10.00	10.50
	Employment		*GVA*	
	2000-01	*2005-06*	*2000-01*	*2005-06*
Gujarat	0.63	0.59	0.61	0.71
Haryana	0.63	0.65	0.72	0.77
Maharashtra	0.71	0.72	0.78	0.82
Tamil Nadu	0.66	0.59	0.62	0.67

Source: Calculated from Unit Level Data, Annual Survey of Industry 2000-01 and 2005-06.

Table 6.11: Presence of Manufacturing Activity in Rural Areas (Percentage)

		GVA	*Total Output*	*Employment*	*Land Assets*	*Fixed Assets*	*No. of Units*
Gujarat	2000-01	56.0	57.8	40.6	44.7	65.7	29.2
	2005-06	51.9	56.8	42.0	48.5	72.0	33.4
Haryana	2000-01	24.5	23.2	26.1	22.8	24.7	22.9
	2005-06	25.0	27.7	30.0	24.5	27.1	29.9
Maharashtra	2000-01	46.9	43.3	37.2	32.9	53.8	24.6
	2005-06	54.8	45.6	42.7	42.5	59.7	29.7
Tamil Nadu	2000-01	46.2	46.1	50.3	38.9	58.7	43.1
	2005-06	49.9	45.5	52.0	38.3	53.7	44.7
India	2000-01	43.0	43.4	37.9	35.5	52.6	33.8
	2005-06	45.6	43.4	41.7	37.7	53.3	39.1

Source: Calculated from Unit Level Data, Annual Survey of Industry 2000-01 and 2005-06.

Table 6.12: Growth Rate of Number of Enterprises and Workforce in Unorganized Manufacturing between 2000-01 and 2005-06

	Growth Rate of Number of Enterprises				*Growth Rate of Workers*			
	OAME	*NDME*	*DME*	*All*	*OAME*	*NDME*	*DME*	*All*
				RURAL				
Gujarat	4.46	6.52	-5.71	4.09	5.06	3.49	-0.63	3.36
Haryana	2.63	8.02	20.52	3.52	1.59	8.60	13.91	4.71
Maharashtra	-4.15	4.03	-1.38	-3.60	-5.20	2.75	-3.31	-4.13
Tamil Nadu	-0.90	6.64	8.19	0.11	-2.62	8.95	8.33	1.30
All India	0.09	3.43	2.13	0.32	-1.23	4.28	0.99	-0.41
				URBAN				
Gujarat	6.40	-7.12	7.40	3.61	6.05	-7.46	11.40	5.13
Haryana	0.90	7.09	8.93	3.58	1.11	9.90	5.77	5.71
Maharashtra	-0.78	-0.45	3.88	-0.02	-2.46	-0.36	6.35	1.84
Tamil Nadu	-0.75	-3.73	-3.16	-1.53	-0.32	-4.58	-2.84	-2.19
All India	-0.58	-1.08	0.65	-0.58	-0.85	-1.32	2.01	-0.15
				ALL				
Gujarat	5.35	-5.04	4.51	3.83	5.51	-6.07	8.04	4.47
Haryana	1.96	7.34	10.95	3.55	1.39	9.59	8.18	5.29
Maharashtra	-2.87	0.48	2.99	-1.88	-4.10	0.22	4.40	-0.48
Tamil Nadu	-0.84	-0.03	1.30	-0.61	-1.70	0.30	1.70	-0.43
All India	-0.07	0.68	1.23	0.05	-1.14	0.77	1.56	-0.32

Source: Own Calculations, NSS Reports, 56th and 62nd Round, Employment and Unemployment Situation in India.

Table 6.13: Percentage of Female Workers in Unorganized Workforce

	Rural		*Urban*		*All*	
	2000-01	*2005-06*	*2000-01*	*2005-06*	*2000-01*	*2005-06*
Gujarat	22.0	25.2	11.5	16.4	15.5	19.5
Haryana	14.6	21.6	10.8	9.3	12.4	14.4
Maharashtra	28.0	32.9	19.5	16.9	23.0	22.4
Tamil Nadu	53.4	56.2	35.3	40.7	44.1	48.9
All India	38.7	43.9	24.6	27.3	33.7	38.0

Source: NSS Reports, 56th and 62nd Round, Employment and Unemployment Situation in India.

Table 7.1: Average Monthly Per Capita Expenditure: Statewise

States	*MPCE*			*CAGR (% per annum)*	
	1993-94	*2004-05*	*2009-10*	*1993-05*	*2005-10*
			RURAL		
Gujarat	838.2	962.5	1065.4	1.27	2.05
Haryana	1051.0	1436.8	1423.3	2.88	-0.19
Maharashtra	814.2	917.9	1048.4	1.10	2.69
Tamil Nadu	774.2	859.5	1017.1	0.95	3.42
All India	752.8	864.5	953.0	1.27	1.97
			URBAN		
Gujarat	1353.5	1722.6	1914.2	2.22	2.13
Haryana	1535.6	1690.7	2008.2	0.88	3.50
Maharashtra	1689.0	1889.9	2251.4	1.03	3.56
Tamil Nadu	1264.8	1690.3	1794.5	2.67	1.20
All India	1405.6	1648.6	1856.0	1.46	2.40
			TOTAL		
Gujarat	1005.5	1224.6	1388.2	1.81	2.54
Haryana	1176.0	1504.4	1598.4	2.26	1.22
Maharashtra	1140.0	1309.7	1549.6	1.27	3.42
Tamil Nadu	947.1	1179.0	1363.3	2.01	2.95
All India	914.6	1063.1	1197.3	1.38	2.41

Source: Calculated from the Unit Level Data of NSSO 50th, 61st and 66th Round, Consumption Expenditure Survey (using Mixed Reference Period).

Table 7.2: Incidence of Poverty: Statewise

States	*HCR*			*Changes in Poverty (% per annum)*	
	1993-94	*2004-05*	*2009-10*	*1993-05*	*2005-10*
			RURAL		
Gujarat	43.29	39.09	26.63	-0.38	-2.49
Haryana	40.27	24.82	18.55	-1.40	-1.25
Maharashtra	59.36	47.88	29.51	-1.04	-3.67
Tamil Nadu	51.18	37.54	21.17	-1.24	-3.27
All India	50.24	41.77	33.25	-0.77	-1.70
			URBAN		
Gujarat	28.15	20.05	17.66	-0.74	-0.48
Haryana	24.17	22.39	23.00	-0.16	0.12
Maharashtra	30.49	25.62	18.27	-0.44	-1.47
Tamil Nadu	33.76	19.74	12.75	-1.27	-1.40
All India	31.57	25.64	20.85	-0.54	-0.96
			TOTAL		
Gujarat	38.37	32.53	23.22	-0.53	-1.86
Haryana	36.12	24.18	19.88	-1.09	-0.86
Maharashtra	48.60	38.91	24.83	-0.88	-2.82
Tamil Nadu	45.04	30.69	17.42	-1.30	-2.65
All India	45.61	37.68	29.90	-0.72	-1.56

Source: Same as Table 7.1.

Table 7.3: Gini Coefficient: Statewise

States	*Gini Ratios (in percentage)*			*Changes in Gini (% per annum)*	
	1993-94	*2004-05*	*2009-10*	*1993-05*	*2005-10*
			RURAL		
Gujarat	22.22	26.63	25.87	0.40	-0.15
Haryana	26.85	32.54	28.23	0.52	-0.86
Maharashtra	26.56	28.75	24.91	0.20	-0.77
Tamil Nadu	28.13	27.59	26.22	-0.05	-0.27
All India	25.83	28.08	28.32	0.21	0.05
			URBAN		
Gujarat	26.86	31.26	31.51	0.40	0.05
Haryana	26.63	34.13	36.55	0.68	0.48
Maharashtra	33.48	36.89	38.93	0.31	0.41
Tamil Nadu	32.72	36.43	33.50	0.34	-0.59
All India	31.87	36.43	38.05	0.41	0.32
			TOTAL		
Gujarat	27.11	32.43	32.90	0.48	0.09
Haryana	28.50	33.38	32.20	0.44	-0.24
Maharashtra	35.70	38.09	38.02	0.22	-0.01
Tamil Nadu	32.68	36.59	33.71	0.36	-0.58
All India	31.72	34.65	35.77	0.27	0.22

Source: Same as Table 7.1.

Table 7.4: Average Monthly Per Capita Expenditure: Regionwise and Social Groupwise

Regions/States	*Social Group*	*MPCE*			*CAGR (% per annum)*	
		1993-94	*2004-05*	*2009-10*	*1993-05*	*2005-10*
			RURAL			
South Eastern	ST	756.7	762.7	793.6	0.07	0.80
	SC	718.1	851.5	922.9	1.56	1.62
	OTH.	992.1	1075.6	1430.3	0.74	5.87
	Total	819.9	918.4	996.3	1.04	1.64
Plains Northern	ST	581.7	2396.3	952.6	13.74	-16.85
	SC	724.2	907.4	1343.7	2.07	8.17
	OTH.	855.5	1048.1	1052.9	1.86	0.09
	Total	834.2	1032.2	1086.9	1.95	1.04
Dry Areas	ST	603.6	444.7	735.7	-2.74	10.59
	SC	726.2	590.5	771.5	-1.86	5.49
	OTH.	838.2	824.1	860.6	-0.15	0.87
	Total	806.9	756.3	839.6	-0.59	2.11
Kutch	ST	-	-	-	-	-
	SC	-	645.8	898.4	-	6.82
	OTH.	-	910.9	1007.6	-	2.04
	Total	-	876.1	968.4	-	2.02

Saurashtra	ST	628.1	1722.4	1007.0	9.60	-10.18
	SC	802.6	799.7	1023.8	-0.03	5.07
	OTH.	906.6	1107.8	1260.4	1.84	2.61
	Total	892.5	1071.9	1229.0	1.68	2.77
Gujarat	ST	745.8	766.39	809.74	0.25	1.11
	SC	735.1	822.57	1074.21	1.03	5.48
	OTH.	889.0	1044.18	1169.89	1.47	2.30
	Total	838.2	962.49	1065.40	1.27	2.05
			URBAN			
South Eastern	ST	1215.8	1617.7	1414.3	2.63	-2.65
	SC	933.1	1658.5	1489.6	5.37	-2.13
	OTH.	1646.9	1973.7	2025.4	1.66	0.52
	Total	1500.7	1911.3	1941.6	2.22	0.32
Plains Northern	ST	1057.6	2018.7	1774.4	6.05	-2.55
	SC	1107.1	1252.8	1176.0	1.13	-1.26
	OTH.	1414.9	1827.9	2184.7	2.36	3.63
	Total	1367.1	1773.1	2057.0	2.39	3.01
Dry Areas	ST	1084.3	-	4292.2	-	-
	SC	1008.5	-	735.1	-	-
	OTH.	1495.0	1511.5	1948.0	0.10	5.21
	Total	1475.4	1511.5	2177.8	0.22	7.58
Kutch	ST	-	-	-	-	-
	SC	-	-	2230.0	-	-
	OTH.	-	1300.8	1953.1	-	8.47
	Total	-	1300.8	2004.8	-	9.04
Saurashtra	ST	1005.3	2379.8	1031.9	8.15	-15.39
	SC	908.9	1152.0	1201.7	2.18	0.85
	OTH.	1194.2	1403.4	1659.8	1.48	3.41
	Total	1169.8	1394.7	1628.0	1.61	3.14
Gujarat	ST	1182.41	1714.75	1662.15	3.44	-0.62
	SC	1022.69	1426.71	1311.12	3.07	-1.68
	OTH.	1405.73	1753.87	1989.34	2.03	2.55
	Total	1353.51	1722.58	1914.17	2.22	2.13
			TOTAL			
South Eastern	ST	791.7	830.5	821.4	0.43	-0.22
	SC	772.0	1191.0	1257.3	4.02	1.09
	OTH.	1293.4	1483.0	1810.6	1.25	4.07
	Total	989.8	1243.9	1366.3	2.10	1.89
Plains Northern	ST	735.7	2110.4	1037.4	10.05	-13.24
	SC	903.6	1024.5	1275.2	1.15	4.48
	OTH.	1090.1	1412.1	1610.9	2.38	2.67
	Total	1060.0	1367.8	1532.3	2.34	2.30
Dry Areas	ST	652.7	444.7	1477.9	-3.43	27.15
	SC	732.9	590.5	770.6	-1.94	5.47
	OTH.	975.0	882.3	991.1	-0.90	2.35
	Total	922.6	807.2	989.4	-1.21	4.15

Kutch	ST	-	-	-	-	-
	SC	-	645.8	957.6	-	8.20
	OTH.	-	973.8	1104.2	-	2.54
	Total	-	937.0	1053.6	-	2.37
Saurashtra	ST	690.6	1894.0	1017.0	9.60	-11.69
	SC	840.1	868.0	1061.0	0.30	4.10
	OTH.	1013.1	1220.2	1413.0	1.71	2.98
	Total	994.0	1187.8	1374.6	1.63	2.96
Gujarat	ST	784.19	853.51	859.55	0.77	0.14
	SC	822.38	1003.40	1154.97	1.83	2.85
	OTH.	1087.03	1328.91	1549.00	1.84	3.11
	Total	1005.54	1224.61	1388.24	1.81	2.54

Note: Kutch was included in the Dry region in 1993-94 and no observations are available for Scheduled Tribes in Kutch in all rounds; for Scheduled castes in Urban Kutch in 2004-05 and for Scheduled Tribes and Scheduled castes in urban Dry areas in 2004-05.
Source: Same as Table 7.1.

Table 7.5: Incidence of Poverty: Regionwise and Social Groupwise

Regions/States	*Social Group*	*1993-94*	*HCR* *2004-05*	*2009-10*	*Change (% per annum)* *1993-05*	*2005-10*
			RURAL			
South Eastern	ST	50.89	56.28	50.98	0.49	-1.06
	SC	54.08	44.22	17.90	-0.90	-5.26
	OTH.	34.36	37.94	17.08	0.32	-4.17
	Total	46.51	46.65	38.99	0.01	-1.53
Plains Northern	ST	92.66	0.00	26.52	-8.42	5.30
	SC	54.12	46.11	0.65	-0.73	-9.09
	OTH.	40.99	36.67	21.75	-0.39	-2.98
	Total	43.66	38.03	19.05	-0.51	-3.80
Dry Areas	ST	90.48	90.69	54.08	0.02	-7.32
	SC	60.26	70.20	31.23	0.90	-7.79
	OTH.	46.09	44.85	43.76	-0.11	-0.22
	Total	50.58	52.75	42.34	0.20	-2.08
Kutch	ST	-	-	-	-	-
	SC	-	82.90	28.00	-	-10.98
	OTH.	-	37.50	39.00	-	0.30
	Total	-	43.46	35.05	-	-1.68
Saurashtra	ST	63.36	0.00	40.58	-5.76	8.12
	SC	60.24	46.10	29.22	-1.29	-3.38
	OTH.	29.65	16.85	8.01	-1.16	-1.77
	Total	32.90	20.66	10.90	-1.11	-1.95
Gujarat	ST	53.24	57.07	48.57	0.35	-1.70
	SC	56.60	49.26	17.91	-0.67	-6.27
	OTH.	37.40	32.04	19.16	-0.49	-2.58
	Total	43.29	39.09	26.63	-0.38	-2.49

			URBAN			
South Eastern	ST	29.80	36.58	37.10	0.62	0.11
	SC	54.55	11.98	21.94	-3.87	1.99
	OTH.	14.45	14.79	12.13	0.03	-0.53
	Total	21.34	16.22	14.31	-0.47	-0.38
Plains Northern	ST	36.55	11.71	10.72	-2.26	-0.20
	SC	43.17	22.10	28.91	-1.92	1.36
	OTH.	27.64	22.14	16.54	-0.50	-1.12
	Total	29.92	21.93	17.97	-0.73	-0.79
Dry Areas	ST	0.00	-	0.00	-	-
	SC	32.33	-	87.12	-	-
	OTH.	27.68	11.15	24.69	-1.50	2.71
	Total	27.24	11.15	23.90	-1.46	2.55
Kutch	ST	-	-	-	-	-
	SC	-	-	35.86	-	-
	OTH.	-	57.49	18.25	-	-7.85
	Total	-	57.49	21.54	-	-7.19
Saurashtra	ST	59.89	4.71	69.15	-5.02	12.89
	SC	60.24	30.58	48.98	-2.70	3.68
	OTH.	28.94	21.77	19.69	-0.65	-0.42
	Total	31.69	22.18	21.81	-0.86	-0.07
Gujarat	ST	31.00	31.17	32.19	0.02	0.20
	SC	49.26	18.73	29.41	-2.78	2.14
	OTH.	25.25	19.69	15.90	-0.51	-0.76
	Total	28.15	20.05	17.66	-0.74	-0.48
			TOTAL			
South Eastern	ST	49.28	54.72	50.36	0.49	-0.87
	SC	54.20	30.65	20.28	-2.14	-2.07
	OTH.	25.20	27.44	13.92	0.20	-2.70
	Total	40.23	36.67	29.33	-0.32	-1.47
Plains Northern	ST	74.50	8.87	24.89	-5.97	3.20
	SC	48.99	37.96	12.19	-1.00	-5.15
	OTH.	35.39	29.89	19.18	-0.50	-2.14
	Total	37.84	30.74	18.55	-0.65	-2.44
Dry Areas	ST	81.24	90.69	42.79	0.86	-9.58
	SC	59.59	70.20	32.65	0.96	-7.51
	OTH.	42.25	42.00	41.47	-0.02	-0.11
	Total	46.55	49.95	40.28	0.31	-1.93
Kutch	ST	-	-	-	-	-
	SC	-	82.90	28.35	-	-10.91
	OTH.	-	40.73	36.88	-	-0.77
	Total	-	45.47	33.93	-	-2.31
Saurashtra	ST	62.79	1.23	52.09	-5.60	10.17
	SC	60.24	43.09	33.35	-1.56	-1.95
	OTH.	29.39	18.72	12.47	-0.97	-1.25
	Total	32.46	21.21	14.88	-1.02	-1.27

Gujarat	ST	51.29	54.69	47.61	0.31	-1.42
	SC	54.38	40.12	21.83	-1.30	-3.66
	OTH.	32.74	27.08	17.65	-0.51	-1.89
	Total	38.37	32.53	23.22	-0.53	-1.86

Note: Same as Table 7.4.
Source: Same as Table 7.1.

Table 7.6: Gini Coefficient: Regionwise and Social Groupwise

Regions/States	*Social Group*	*Gini Ratios (in percentage)* 1993-94	2004-05	2009-10	*Change (% per annum)* 1993-05	2005-10
			RURAL			
South Eastern	ST	21.03	23.21	20.80	0.20	-0.48
	SC	23.21	20.97	16.94	-0.20	-0.81
	OTH.	25.78	29.56	36.66	0.34	1.42
	Total	23.80	27.82	29.85	0.37	0.40
Plains Northern	ST	6.19	18.01	20.26	1.07	0.45
	SC	18.85	23.92	19.56	0.46	-0.87
	OTH.	22.29	30.32	21.36	0.73	-1.79
	Total	22.11	29.73	21.99	0.69	-1.55
Dry Areas	ST	9.42	28.11	10.80	1.70	-3.46
	SC	22.44	15.78	13.37	-0.61	-0.48
	OTH.	21.39	17.38	21.72	-0.36	0.87
	Total	21.76	21.33	20.34	-0.04	-0.20
Kutch	ST	-	-	-	-	-
	SC	-	12.88	12.72	-	-0.03
	OTH.	-	21.51	21.21	-	-0.06
	Total	-	21.52	19.03	-	-0.50
Saurashtra	ST	19.68	27.61	23.85	0.72	-0.75
	SC	22.95	14.07	22.84	-0.81	1.75
	OTH.	18.92	21.11	22.80	0.20	0.34
	Total	19.59	21.46	23.10	0.17	0.33
Gujarat	ST	20.91	25.53	20.92	0.42	-0.92
	SC	22.07	20.66	22.19	-0.13	0.31
	OTH.	21.97	26.45	26.18	0.41	-0.06
	Total	22.22	26.63	25.87	0.40	-0.15
			URBAN			
South Eastern	ST	25.70	43.88	24.34	1.65	-3.91
	SC	25.44	23.19	26.34	-0.20	0.63
	OTH.	26.40	29.80	27.64	0.31	-0.43
	Total	28.08	31.02	28.02	0.27	-0.60
Plains Northern	ST	20.62	32.58	31.80	1.09	-0.16
	SC	23.52	24.19	23.28	0.06	-0.18
	OTH.	27.78	34.81	33.84	0.64	-0.19
	Total	27.63	34.44	34.54	0.62	0.02

Dry Areas	ST	3.97	-	32.78	-	-
	SC	14.83	-	6.35	-	-
	OTH.	28.50	24.92	41.92	-0.33	3.40
	Total	28.36	24.92	44.48	-0.31	3.91
Kutch	ST	-	-	-	-	-
	SC	-	-	26.40	-	-
	OTH.	-	31.82	33.43	-	0.32
	Total	-	31.82	33.01	-	0.24
Saurashtra	ST	28.19	23.56	22.56	-0.42	-0.20
	SC	12.99	20.90	23.12	0.72	0.44
	OTH.	21.43	22.96	27.89	0.14	0.99
	Total	21.33	23.19	27.97	0.17	0.96
Gujarat	ST	25.00	42.95	33.51	1.63	-1.89
	SC	22.79	25.05	26.39	0.21	0.27
	OTH.	26.73	31.00	31.17	0.39	0.03
	Total	26.86	31.26	31.51	0.40	0.05
			TOTAL			
South Eastern	ST	22.55	27.59	22.21	0.46	-1.08
	SC	24.73	28.78	27.24	0.37	-0.31
	OTH.	29.56	34.05	33.15	0.41	-0.18
	Total	29.31	35.13	35.49	0.53	0.07
Plains Northern	ST	19.88	29.93	24.78	0.91	-1.03
	SC	24.23	25.58	21.63	0.12	-0.79
	OTH.	28.66	36.00	35.17	0.67	-0.16
	Total	28.37	35.31	33.88	0.63	-0.29
Dry Areas	ST	13.85	28.11	47.27	1.30	3.83
	SC	22.56	15.78	13.30	-0.62	-0.50
	OTH.	27.04	20.62	29.04	-0.58	1.69
	Total	26.82	23.98	29.58	-0.26	1.12
Kutch	ST	-	-	-	-	-
	SC	-	12.88	17.34	-	0.89
	OTH.	-	24.75	25.72	-	0.20
	Total	-	24.67	23.72	-	-0.19
Saurashtra	ST	23.71	29.58	23.70	0.53	-1.18
	SC	20.26	17.87	23.31	-0.22	1.09
	OTH.	21.35	22.83	26.12	0.13	0.66
	Total	21.62	23.30	26.24	0.15	0.59
Gujarat	ST	22.53	30.54	23.92	0.73	-1.32
	SC	23.89	26.59	24.34	0.25	-0.45
	OTH.	27.15	31.83	32.78	0.43	0.19
	Total	27.11	32.43	32.90	0.48	0.09

Note: Same as Table 7.4.

Source: Same as Table 7.1.

Table 8.1: Sectoral Shares in GDP and Employment (UPSS-NIC)

	GDP			*Employment*		
Sectors	*1993-94*	*2004-05*	*2009-10*	*1993-94*	*2004-05*	*2009-10*
		GUJARAT				
Agriculture	22.4	16.1	12.1	60.7	58.2	53.4
Industry	38.8	40.0	40.7	19.0	20.5	19.6
Services	38.8	43.9	47.2	20.3	21.3	27.0
		MAHARASHTRA				
Agriculture	19.5	10.6	8.4	61.2	55.7	52.4
Industry	33.4	29.7	29.9	14.9	17.3	17.1
Services	47.1	59.7	61.7	23.9	26.9	30.5
		TAMIL NADU				
Agriculture	24.1	11.1	8.5	53.6	46.4	44.6
Industry	34.4	31.6	28.1	22.3	26.4	27.9
Services	41.5	57.2	63.4	24.0	27.3	27.5
		HARYANA				
Agriculture	42.2	21.8	15.9	56.9	52.1	44.4
Industry	26.5	33.1	30.6	15.4	21.5	27.2
Services	31.3	45.2	53.4	27.7	26.4	28.4
		INDIA				
Agriculture	31.0	18.9	14.5	64.9	58.5	53.2
Industry	26.3	28.1	28.3	14.7	18.1	21.5
Services	42.8	53.0	57.2	20.5	23.4	25.3

Source: Calculated from CSO and Unit Level Data of Various NSS Rounds.

Table 8.2: Distribution of Additional Net Employment Generated

Distribution of Additional Net Employment Generated Between 1993-94 to 2009-10

	Gujarat			*India*		
	Rural	*Urban*	*Total*	*Rural*	*Urban*	*Total*
Agriculture	76	2	30	7	-3	3
Manufacturing	-17	28	11	9	21	14
Construction	17	7	11	51	19	38
Service	24	64	48	34	64	46
Total	100	100	100	100	100	100

Source: Calculated from Unit Level Data of NSSO, 50th and 66th Rounds, Employment Unemployment Situation in India.

Table 8.3: Work Participation Rate for Gujarat and All India (PS+SS)

		Gujarat			*India*		
Year	*Sector*	*Male*	*Female*	*Total*	*Male*	*Female*	*Total*
1993-94	Rural	57.4	39.6	48.8	55.3	32.8	44.4
	Urban	53.5	14.2	34.7	52.1	15.5	34.7
	Total	55.4	26.9	41.8	53.7	24.1	39.5
1999-00	Rural	58.4	41.3	49.9	53.1	29.9	41.7
	Urban	53.6	13.5	34.5	51.8	13.9	33.7
	Total	56.8	32.6	45.0	52.7	25.9	39.7
2004-05	Rural	59.3	42.7	51.3	54.6	32.7	43.9
	Urban	57.8	15.1	36.4	54.9	16.6	36.5
	Total	58.6	28.9	43.9	54.7	24.7	40.2
2009-10	Rural	58.5	32.0	45.9	54.7	26.1	40.8
	Urban	56.3	14.3	37.0	54.3	13.8	35.0
	Total	57.4	23.2	41.5	54.5	19.9	37.9

Source: Same as Table 8.2.

Table 8.4: Employment Growth Rate (CAGR)

	Gujarat											
	1993-94 to 1999-00			*1999-2000 to 2004-05*			*2004-05 to 2009-10*			*1993-94 to 2009-10*		
	Rural	*Urban*	*Total*	*Rural*	*Urban*	*Total*	*Rural*	*Urban*	*Total*	*Rural*	*Urban*	*Total*
Agriculture	3.2	5.8	3.3	4.4	2.9	0.5	-1.7	1.5	-1.6	0.9	0.9	0.9
Manufacturing	-2.5	-2.2	-2.4	3.4	2.1	9.9	-7.9	0.1	-2.6	-2.0	3.2	1.2
Construction	5.1	5.8	5.4	3.7	2.7	1.7	6.1	5.3	5.7	4.9	3.6	4.3
Service	4.4	3.4	3.7	4.2	0.6	1.9	-2.3	8.7	4.9	2.2	4.1	3.5
Total	2.9	2.1	2.7	1.5	3.9	2.1	-2.0	5.0	0.1	0.9	3.6	1.7
	All India											
	1993-94 to 1999-00			*1999-2000 to 2004-05*			*2004-05 to 2009-10*			*1993-94 to 2009-10*		
	Rural	*Urban*	*Total*	*Rural*	*Urban*	*Total*	*Rural*	*Urban*	*Total*	*Rural*	*Urban*	*Total*
Agriculture	1.3	-1.6	1.2	1.0	1.1	1.0	-2.3	-1.6	-2.3	0.1	-0.8	0.1
Manufacturing	1.1	1.0	1.1	5.1	5.0	5.1	-2.8	0.1	-1.4	1.1	2.0	1.5
Construction	7.9	6.9	7.5	10.5	3.0	7.8	12.9	6.4	11.0	10.3	5.5	8.7
Service	3.0	3.9	3.5	4.2	2.1	3.0	0.4	1.8	1.2	2.6	2.7	2.7
Total	1.7	2.8	1.9	2.1	2.8	2.2	-1.0	1.5	-0.4	1.0	2.4	1.3

Source: Calculated from Unit Level Data of NSSO, 50th, 61st and 66th Rounds, Employment Unemployment Situation in India.

Table 8.5: Comparison of GDP and Employment Growth Rate

	GDP		*Employment*	
Gujarat				
	1993-94 to 2004-05	*2004-05 to 2009-10*	*1993-94 to 2004-05*	*2004-05 to 2009-10*
Agriculture	1.61	3.19	2.03	-1.59
Industry	6.20	10.14	3.14	-0.79
Manufacturing	6.02	9.60	3.00	-2.23
Services	8.02	11.93	2.88	4.91
Transport, Storage & Communication	11.86	13.69	4.50	6.63
Trade, Hotels & Restaurants	8.63	13.93	5.85	2.29
Banking, Insurance & Real Estate	5.54	11.05	6.18	13.81
Community Social and Personal Services	7.33	7.36	-1.14	5.62
Total	5.97	9.91	2.43	0.10
Maharashtra				
	GDP		*Employment*	
Agriculture	2.36	5.59	1.56	-1.66
Industry	3.59	11.80	3.85	-0.71
Manufacturing	3.70	10.57	3.25	-1.59
Services	7.24	11.61	3.55	2.07
Transport, Storage & Communication	8.30	9.53	4.89	2.03
Trade, Hotels & Restaurants	6.64	12.88	5.21	0.52
Banking, Insurance & Real Estate	7.01	12.99	7.07	7.69
Community Social and Personal Services	6.56	8.41	0.67	1.95
Total	5.31	11.11	2.43	-0.44
Tamil Nadu				
	GDP		*Employment*	
Agriculture	-0.63	3.33	-1.40	0.14
Industry	4.35	6.53	1.42	2.08
Manufacturing	3.20	7.33	0.76	-1.80
Services	7.48	11.96	1.07	1.12
Transport, Storage & Communication	8.75	10.95	1.73	6.36
Trade, Hotels & Restaurants	6.78	10.29	2.53	0.83
Banking, Insurance & Real Estate	8.44	15.43	5.83	2.57
Community Social and Personal Services	6.13	9.66	-1.78	-2.28
Total	4.97	9.43	-0.09	0.93

Haryana				
	GDP		*Employment*	
Agriculture	1.88	3.72	2.08	-3.11
Industry	7.61	7.87	6.06	4.88
Manufacturing	7.24	7.48	6.12	3.72
Services	10.65	13.49	2.43	1.55
Transport, Storage & Communication	13.24	12.08	3.22	0.29
Trade, Hotels & Restaurants	10.90	14.77	5.67	-0.75
Banking, Insurance & Real Estate	11.02	14.71	10.73	9.48
Community Social and Personal Services	6.24	10.17	-1.53	3.39
Total	6.81	9.80	2.89	0.06
India				
	GDP		*Employment*	
Agriculture	2.12	3.21	1.12	-2.28
Industry	6.05	8.87	4.07	3.05
Manufacturing	6.02	9.62	3.17	-1.64
Services	8.21	10.30	3.31	1.18
Transport, Storage & Communication	10.51	12.74	5.13	2.09
Trade, Hotels & Restaurants	8.17	9.08	5.13	0.65
Banking, Insurance & Real Estate	7.75	12.15	6.89	5.62
Community Social and Personal Services	7.39	8.01	0.34	0.42
Total	6.05	8.68	2.08	-0.41

Source: Same as Table 8.4.

Table 8.6: Employment Growth across Sectors by Status (Percentage Per Annum) for 2004-05 to 2009-10

Status	*Primary*	*Manufacturing*	*Construction*	*Service I*	*Service II*
Self-employed	-0.68	-1.98	8.87	3.40	5.73
Regular	-3.38	-2.58	-8.34	1.39	6.77
Casual	-2.91	-3.64	5.85	11.34	13.28
Total	-1.59	-2.61	5.72	3.61	7.07

Source: Same as Table 8.4.

Table 8.7: Employment Growth Rate by UPSS-NIC, Sector & Gender

	Gujarat								
1993-94 to 1999-00	*Rural*			*Urban*			*Total*		
	Male	*Female*	*Total*	*Male*	*Female*	*Total*	*Male*	*Female*	*Total*
Agriculture	2.36	4.00	3.11	9.37	-0.57	4.89	2.60	3.85	3.17
Industry	0.01	-0.62	-0.10	-0.37	-0.80	-0.42	-0.19	-0.70	-0.27
Manufacturing	-1.07	-6.56	-1.94	-1.77	-2.34	-1.84	-1.45	-4.52	-1.88
Services	4.61	3.23	4.41	3.35	3.07	3.29	3.79	3.12	3.67
Trade, Hotels & Restaurants	7.38	12.49	8.10	8.97	10.60	9.15	8.48	11.29	8.82
Transport, Storage & Communication	10.33	0	10.73	2.78	16.15	3.27	5.86	21.88	6.27
Banking, Insurance & Real estate	-2.41	0	-2.41	10.48	24.72	11.69	7.04	24.72	8.17
Community Social and Personal Services	-0.63	-2.52	-1.06	-5.13	-0.51	-3.51	-3.36	-1.03	-2.64
Total	2.30	3.73	2.87	2.23	1.40	2.07	2.28	3.41	2.67
1999-00 to 2004-05	*Rural*			*Urban*			*Total*		
	Male	*Female*	*Total*	*Male*	*Female*	*Total*	*Male*	*Female*	*Total*
Agriculture	1.10	0.59	0.86	-7.66	0.35	-4.38	0.78	0.58	0.69
Industry	2.40	9.38	3.79	9.35	16.49	10.35	6.33	12.66	7.39
Manufacturing	1.74	15.79	4.08	11.67	20.30	12.89	7.57	18.23	9.17
Services	3.94	5.73	4.20	1.16	-1.72	0.63	2.21	0.63	1.94
Trade, Hotels & Restaurants	6.02	0.61	5.23	1.64	-4.25	1.01	3.03	-2.29	2.39
Transport, Storage & Communication	4.55	-39.33	4.13	1.71	-22.14	0.88	3.08	-25.15	2.43
Banking, Insurance & Real Estate	4.78	0	6.15	4.42	-6.12	3.34	4.49	-2.73	3.84
Community Social and Personal Services	0.45	10.19	2.88	-1.48	0.45	-0.71	-0.62	3.22	0.69
Total	1.71	1.25	1.53	3.94	3.95	3.94	2.42	1.62	2.14

2004-05 to 2009-10	*Rural*			*Urban*			*Total*		
	Male	*Female*	*Total*	*Male*	*Female*	*Total*	*Male*	*Female*	*Total*
Agriculture	0.84	-4.98	-1.69	5.51	-3.89	1.52	0.98	-4.95	-1.59
Industry	-0.96	-14.15	-3.44	1.35	-1.69	0.87	0.48	-6.98	-0.79
Manufacturing	-4.66	-22.18	-7.57	0.51	-0.39	0.36	-1.16	-7.40	-2.23
Services	-1.37	-8.46	-2.33	8.38	10.04	8.67	4.95	4.73	4.91
Trade, Hotels & Restaurants	-4.17	-12.54	-5.09	5.94	1.58	5.58	2.89	-3.64	2.29
Transport, Storage & Communication	3.58	108.47	4.52	8.57	9.55	8.59	6.18	37.38	6.63
Banking, Insurance & Real Estate	-6.28	-100.00	-7.49	15.84	28.95	17.06	12.78	24.47	13.81
Community Social and Personal Services	-2.35	-9.97	-4.41	10.65	11.37	10.95	5.48	5.84	5.62
Total	0.23	-5.63	-1.96	5.22	3.92	4.98	2.00	-3.98	0.10
1993-94 to 2009-10	*Rural*			*Urban*			*Total*		
	Male	*Female*	*Total*	*Male*	*Female*	*Total*	*Male*	*Female*	*Total*
Agriculture	1.49	0.06	0.89	2.58	-1.33	0.86	1.52	0.01	0.89
Industry	0.44	-2.18	0.03	3.12	4.01	3.24	2.02	1.21	1.90
Manufacturing	-1.35	-5.63	-1.93	2.98	4.88	3.26	1.37	1.10	1.33
Services	2.50	0.17	2.19	4.20	3.65	4.09	3.65	2.83	3.51
Trade, Hotels & Restaurants	3.22	0.42	2.92	5.69	2.95	5.44	4.99	2.15	4.72
Transport, Storage & Communication	6.37	0.00	6.68	4.21	0.65	4.14	5.08	8.65	5.16
Banking, Insurance & Real Estate	-1.47	0.00	-1.47	10.17	15.32	10.62	7.99	15.32	8.51
Community Social and Personal Services	-0.84	-1.20	-0.92	0.72	3.37	1.70	0.19	2.40	0.92
Total	1.47	-0.05	0.92	3.69	2.97	3.55	2.24	0.49	1.69

Source: Calculated from Unit Level Data of NSSO, 50th, 55th, 61st and 66th Rounds, Employment Unemployment Situation in India.

Table 8.8: Employment Growth across Sectors by Nature of Employment

	1993-94 to 2004-05														
	Gujarat			*Maharashtra*			*Tamil Nadu*			*Haryana*			*India*		
	Rural	*Urban*	*Total*	*Rural*	*Urban*	*Total*	*Rural*	*Urban*	*Total*	*Rural*	*Urban*	*Total*	*Rural*	*Urban*	*Total*
Self-employed	2.84	3.67	3.02	2.40	3.99	2.80	-0.47	2.15	0.28	3.14	3.06	3.13	2.21	3.43	2.41
Regular Employees	2.82	3.77	3.47	2.34	3.05	2.86	0.33	2.75	1.90	6.82	2.57	4.53	2.70	2.79	2.75
Casual Workers	1.39	-1.10	1.08	1.21	4.60	1.66	-1.14	-3.30	-1.49	1.14	-3.59	0.48	1.10	0.94	1.08
Total	2.24	2.89	2.41	1.89	3.63	2.43	-0.72	1.22	-0.12	3.13	2.11	2.89	1.86	2.76	2.05
	2004-05 to 2009-10														
	Gujarat			*Maharashtra*			*Tamil Nadu*			*Haryana*			*India*		
	Rural	*Urban*	*Total*	*Rural*	*Urban*	*Total*	*Rural*	*Urban*	*Total*	*Rural*	*Urban*	*Total*	*Rural*	*Urban*	*Total*
Self-employed	-1.33	5.54	0.36	-2.30	-1.32	-2.03	-5.43	-0.39	-3.70	-3.49	-1.91	-3.20	-3.05	-0.50	-2.58
Regular Employees	-3.28	3.24	1.43	-4.08	4.55	2.61	-1.56	1.66	0.68	2.07	8.55	5.37	-0.42	2.47	1.40
Casual Workers	-2.60	8.60	-1.07	0.30	-3.60	-0.28	3.28	15.53	5.46	2.62	15.04	4.28	2.30	4.66	2.58
Total	-1.96	4.98	0.10	-1.34	1.28	-0.44	-0.60	3.72	0.93	-1.43	4.54	0.06	-0.98	1.52	-0.41

Source: Same as Table 8.4.

Table 8.9: Employment Status for Rural and Urban Sectors

Year	*Sector*	*Gujarat* *Self-employed*	*Regular*	*Casual*	*All India* *Self-employed*	*Regular*	*Casual*
1993-94	Rural	50.2	6.7	43.1	58.0	6.4	35.6
	Urban	38.3	40.9	20.8	42.3	39.4	18.3
	Total	**47.2**	**15.4**	**37.4**	**54.7**	**13.2**	**32.0**
2004-05	Rural	53.6	7.1	39.3	60.2	7.1	32.8
	Urban	41.7	44.9	13.5	45.4	39.5	15.0
	Total	**50.4**	**17.3**	**32.4**	**56.9**	**14.3**	**28.9**
2009-10	Rural	55.3	6.7	38.0	54.2	7.3	38.6
	Urban	42.8	41.3	16.0	41.1	41.4	17.5
	Total	**51.0**	**18.4**	**30.5**	**51.0**	**15.6**	**33.5**

Source: Same as Table 8.4.

Table 8.10: Distribution of Additional Net Employment Generated Distribution of Additional Net Employment Generated between 1993-94 to 2009-10 by Status

	Gujarat			*India*		
	Rural	*Urban*	*Total*	*Rural*	*Urban*	*Total*
Self-employed	88	49	64	31	38	34
Regular	6	42	28	12	46	26
Casual	6	9	8	57	16	40
Total	100	100	100	100	100	100

Source: Same as Table 8.4.

Table 8.11: Labour Productivity (NSDP Per PS+SS Workers) in Various Sectors (Rs. in 1999-2000 Constant Prices)

	1993-94	*2004-05*	*2009-10*	*CAGR for 1993-94*	*CAGR for 2004-05*
Primary	13973	18169	24162	2.66	5.87
Manufacturing	67242	101985	162377	4.25	9.75
Construction	52293	85075	124397	4.99	7.90
Service	68483	121171	160771	5.87	5.82
Total	50333	56649	86144	5.04	8.74

Source: Same as Table 8.4.

Table 8.12: Share of Employment for Regions

	Share of Employment for Regions		
	1993-94	*2004-05*	*2009-10*
Southern	34.2	43.5	36.0
Northen	31.4	24.0	31.1
Dry	11.6	6.0	6.4
Kutch		3.2	2.7
Saurashtra	22.8	23.4	23.8
Gujarat	100.0	100.0	100.0

Source: Same as Table 8.4.

Table 8.13: Employment Growth for Different Regions

	Agriculture		*Manu-facturing*		*Construction*		*Service*		*Total*	
	1993-94 to 2004-05	*2004-05 to 2009-10*	*1993-94 to 2004-05*	*2004-05 to 2009-10*	*1993-94 to 2004-05*	*2004-05 to 2009-10*	*1993-94 to 2004-05*	*2004-05 to 2009-10*	*1993-94 to 2004-05*	*2004-05 to 2009-10*
Southern	3.49	-5.68	7.64	-3.28	8.22	-5.46	8.87	1.95	5.18	-3.59
Northern	-0.51	4.81	-0.06	0.72	3.68	6.81	0.46	8.78	-0.03	5.41
Dry	1.75	0.50	-1.41	13.30	-10.54	6.77	-0.85	1.69	0.34	1.40
Kutch		-1.67		-16.29		25.08		-1.87		-3.43
Saurashtra	3.28	-1.86	3.04	-4.02	3.31	26.26	1.83	5.87	2.94	0.50
Gujarat	2.26	-1.59	3.34	-2.61	4.08	5.72	-18.09	4.91	2.69	0.10

Source: Same as Table 8.4.

Table 8.14: Employment Structures for Different Regions

	South and Eastern			*North*			*Dry Areas*			*Kutch*			*Saurashtra*			*Gujarat*		
	1993-94	*2004-05*	*2009-10*	*1994-94*	*2004-05*	*2009-10*	*1993-94*	*2004-05*	*2009-10*	*1993-94*	*2004-05*	*2009-10*	*1993-94*	*2004-05*	*2009-10*	*1993-94*	*2004-05*	*2009-10*
Primary	68.9	59.0	52.9	54.0	51.5	50.0	58.4	77.3	73.9		48.2	52.7	58.1	60.0	53.3	59.9	58.2	53.4
Secondary	16.9	21.4	21.1	20.1	21.4	18.2	19.6	5.1	8.2		28.7	22.3	20.5	20.7	21.8	19.3	20.5	19.6
Tertiary	14.2	19.6	26.0	25.8	27.1	31.8	22.0	17.6	17.9		23.1	25.0	21.4	19.2	24.9	20.9	21.3	27.0

Source: Calculated from Unit Level Data of NSSO, 50th, 61st and 66th Rounds, Employment Unemployment Situation in India.

Table 8.15: Distribution for Employment Status for Different Regions

	South and eastern			*North*			*Dry Areas*			*Kutch*			*Saurashtra*			*Gujarat*		
	1993-94	*2004-05*	*2009-10*	*1994-94*	*2004-05*	*2009-10*	*1993-94*	*2004-05*	*2009-10*	*1993-94*	*2004-05*	*2009-10*	*1993-94*	*2004-05*	*2009-10*	*1993-94*	*2004-05*	*2009-10*
Self-employment	36.3	45.9	46.1	48.8	48.3	55.6	57.3	75.1	57.0		49.2	40.9	55.9	54.8	52.1	47.2	50.4	51.0
Regular	16.0	20.0	23.3	20.4	21.7	20.9	10.7	11.4	8.8		8.8	19.6	10.7	10.2	10.3	15.4	17.3	18.4
Casual	47.8	34.1	30.6	30.9	30.1	23.5	32.0	13.4	34.2		42.0	39.4	33.5	35.0	37.6	37.4	32.4	30.5

Source: Same as Table 8.4.

Table 8.16: Share of Employment by Social Groups

	1993-94	*2004-05*	*2009-10*
ST	18.7	17.5	18.0
SC	10.8	12.1	10.6
OBC	0.0	39.2	38.6
Others	70.4	31.2	32.9
Gujarat	100.0	100.0	100.0

Source: Same as Table 8.4.

Table 8.17: Employment Growth by Social Groups

	Agriculture		*Manu-facturing*		*Construction*		*Service*		*Total*	
	1993-94 to 2004-05	*2004-05 to 2009-10*	*1993-94 to 2004-05*	*2004-05 to 2009-10*	*1993-94 to 2004-05*	*2004-05 to 2009-10*	*1993-94 to 2004-05*	*2004-05 to 2009-10*	*1993-94 to 2004-05*	*2004-05 to 2009-10*
ST	1.32	2.40	1.97	-10.67	8.34	-15.52	4.55	2.15	2.00	0.59
SC	4.86	-6.86	3.05	-8.70	1.84	14.38	1.81	7.87	3.84	-2.61
OBC		-2.81		-2.95		13.44		6.63		-0.27
Others	-8.76	-1.26	-2.44	-0.05	-6.30	8.53	-1.55	3.49	-5.33	1.08
Gujarat	2.26	-1.67	3.34	-2.67	4.08	5.72	3.20	4.89	2.69	0.04

Source: Same as Table 8.4.

Table 8.18: Percentage Distribution of Workers by UPSS-NIC & Social Groups

	Maharashtra				*Tamil Nadu*				*Haryana*			
1993-94	*ST*	*SC*	*OBC*	*Others*	*ST*	*SC*	*OBC*	*Others*	*ST*	*SC*	*OBC*	*Others*
Agriculture	59.2	58.6		61.2	73.8	47.0		53.6	53.4	57.7		56.9
Industry	22.0	15.2		14.9	12.7	25.5		22.4	21.5	13.6		15.4
Manufacturing	12.3	11.5		10.8	8.4	21.0		17.9	8.0	9.6		9.2
Services	18.8	26.2		23.9	13.5	27.5		24.0	25.1	28.7		27.7
Trade, Hotels & Restaurants	4.0	9.0		8.0	2.9	10.8		8.8	6.3	9.4		8.6
Transport, Storage & Communication	4.1	3.7		3.5	3.5	3.8		3.7	3.2	5.0		4.5
Banking, Insurance & Real Estate	0.5	2.0		1.7	0.5	1.7		1.4	0.1	0.9		0.7
Community Social and Personal Services	10.2	11.5		10.7	6.5	11.2		10.1	15.5	13.4		13.9
2004-05	ST	SC	OBC	Others	ST	SC	OBC	Others	ST	SC	OBC	Others
Agriculture	80.3	51.0	62.4	46.5	56.5	61.8	43.2	8.7	54.9	47.6	48.6	57.0
Industry	8.1	23.1	15.7	18.6	16.4	19.9	28.6	21.9	29.2	27.8	25.7	15.2
Manufacturing	4.5	13.5	10.2	14.1	13.5	12.8	21.8	19.1	24.2	9.7	15.1	13.0
Services	11.6	25.9	22.0	34.8	27.0	18.3	28.1	69.4	15.9	24.6	25.7	27.9
Trade, Hotels & Restaurants	4.3	8.6	7.8	15.5	15.7	5.8	13.0	23.5	13.2	10.3	10.2	13.2
Transport, Storage & Communication	3.6	4.4	3.6	5.5	3.4	3.3	4.7	7.9	0.0	3.0	6.9	4.0
Banking, Insurance & Real Estate	0.5	1.7	1.7	4.7	1.7	1.1	2.4	21.4	2.3	0.9	1.2	2.2
Community Social and Personal Services	3.2	11.1	8.9	9.1	6.3	8.2	8.1	16.6	0.4	10.4	7.4	8.4
2009-10	ST	SC	OBC	Others	ST	SC	OBC	Others	ST	SC	OBC	Others
Agriculture	74.0	50.1	58.6	42.8	71.9	59.1	41.5	9.8	33.5	36.8	41.1	51.6
Industry	12.6	19.2	15.4	18.9	7.8	22.6	29.7	26.1	16.3	38.9	29.1	18.6
Manufacturing	4.9	9.2	9.7	14.5	4.9	9.8	19.2	20.2	6.8	16.1	18.4	13.0
Services	18.2	40.3	31.9	46.5	23.3	21.7	34.1	85.1	54.4	31.1	37.3	36.0
Trade, Hotels & Restaurants	3.7	8.4	10.6	14.9	8.6	6.2	13.0	16.0	44.0	9.4	11.0	11.9
Transport, Storage & Communication	1.9	5.9	4.4	6.1	3.0	5.8	5.8	6.2	0.0	2.5	6.4	5.0
Banking, Insurance & Real estate	1.0	3.3	2.5	6 6	0.0	1.3	2.9	18.6	0.0	1.3	2.9	3.0
Community Social and Personal Services	6.8	13.2	8.5	10.6	8.6	5.0	7.1	23.3	6.2	11.0	9.6	9.9

Source: Same as Table 8.4.

Table 8.19: Employment Structure for Different Social and Religious Groups

	ST			*SC*			*OBC*			*General*			*Islam*			*Other Minorities*			*Gujarat*		
	1993-94	*2004-05*	*2009-10*	*1993-94*	*2004-05*	*2009-10*	*1993-94*	*2004-05*	*2009-10*	*1993-94*	*2004-05*	*2009-10*	*1993-94*	*2004-05*	*2009-10*	*1993-94*	*2004-05*	*2009-10*	*1993-94*	*2004-05*	*2009-10*
Primary	81.5	76.2	83.3	57.3	63.2	50.6		64.3	56.5	55.7	38.5	34.3	26.8	42.5	37.0	23.2	39.0	49.8	60.7	58.2	53.4
Secondary	11.8	15.2	7.4	21.0	18.9	19.7		18.6	19.5	20.6	26.4	26.3	25.9	16.8	31.3	34.4	16.3	19.3	19.0	20.5	19.6
Tertiary	6.7	8.6	9.3	21.7	17.8	29.7		17.2	24.0	23.7	35.1	39.4	47.3	40.7	31.7	42.4	44.7	30.9	20.3	21.3	27.0
	100.0	100.0	100.0	100.0	100.0	100.0		100.0	100.0	100.0	100.0	100.0	100.0	100.0	100.0	100.0	100.0	100.0	100.0	100.0	100.0

Source: Same as Table 8.4.

Table 8.20: Distribution of Employment Status for Different Social and Religious Groups

	ST			*SC*			*OBC*			*General*			*Islam*			*Other Minorities*			*Gujarat*		
	1993-94	*2004-05*	*2009-10*	*1993-94*	*2004-05*	*2009-10*	*1993-94*	*2004-05*	*2009-10*	*1993-94*	*2004-05*	*2009-10*	*1993-94*	*2004-05*	*2009-10*	*1993-94*	*2004-05*	*2009-10*	*1993-94*	*2004-05*	*2009-10*
Selfemployed	30.8	41.6	50.2	25.3	21.1	23.3		55.2	55.1	54.9	60.5	55.5	47.9	59.0	53.9	29.5	51.4	48.8	47.4	50.4	51.0
Salaried	7.7	9.4	7.8	16.5	20.5	24.9		12.4	13.1	17.3	26.5	28.4	15.6	17.5	14.0	40.5	21.0	21.8	15.4	17.3	18.4
Casual	61.4	49.0	41.9	58.2	58.4	51.8		32.3	31.8	27.8	13.0	16.1	36.5	23.5	32.1	30.0	27.6	29.4	37.4	32.4	30.6
	100.0	100.0	100.0	100.0	100.0	100.0		100.0	100.0	100.0	100.0	100.0	100.0	100.0	100.0	100.0	100.0	100.0	100.2	100.0	100.0

Source: Same as Table 8.4.

Table 9.1: Rank of Gujarat—Literacy Rate

	6 years and above		*6-14 years of age*	
	All States/ UTs	*Major 15 States*	*All States/ UTs*	*Major 15 States*
NSSO 55th Rnd	19	5	19	5
NSSO 64th Rnd	21	7	19	7

Source: Calculated from the Unit Level Data of NSSO 55th Round, Employment & Unemployment Situation in India Survey and NSSO 64th Round, Participation and Expenditure in Education Survey.

Table 9.2: Rank of Gujarat – Percentage of Persons Currently Attending any Education Institution

	6 -29 years of age		*6-14 years of age*	
	All States/ UTs	*Major 15 States*	*All States/ UTs*	*Major 15 States*
NSSO 55th Rnd	23	9	21	6
NSSO 64th Rnd	30	14	26	10

Source: Calculated from the Unit Level Data of NSSO 64th Round, Participation and Expenditure in Education Survey.

Table 9.3: Literacy Rate (6+ years age) by Gender (%) – NSSO 64th Round

	Female	*Male*	*Gender Gap (% points)*
Gujarat	64.80	84.75	20.0
Haryana	63.24	83.03	19.8
Maharashtra	73.61	88.24	14.6
Tamil Nadu	72.74	88.17	15.4
India	62.80	80.66	17.9

Source: Same as Table 9.2..

Table 9.4: Currently Attending by Gender (%) – NSSO 64th Round

	6-10 years			*11-14 years*		
	Male	*Female*	*Gender-gap*	*Male*	*Female*	*Gender Gap*
Gujarat	93.79	91.06	2.73	85.44	72.14	13.3
Haryana	93.24	89.07	4.17	93.31	84.34	8.97
Maharashtra	94.93	93.99	0.94	89.4	89.46	-0.06
Tamil Nadu	98.25	99.72	-1.47	94.8	96.04	-1.24
India	90.73	88.27	2.46	86.36	81.02	5.34

Source: Same as Table 9.2.

Table 9.5: Literacy Rate (6+ years age) by Caste (%) - NSSO 64th Round

	ST	*SC*	*OBC*	*General*	*Total*	*Total General Gap*
Gujarat	62.34	74.57	70.27	87.98	75.24	12.7
Haryana	60.16	63.84	73.32	79.26	73.84	5.4
Maharashtra	62.03	78.08	81.1	85.78	81.12	4.7
Tamil Nadu	54.84	72.87	81.96	92.8	80.33	12.5
India	60.98	64.04	70.63	82.3	71.99	10.3

Source: Same as Table 9.2.

Table 9.6: Persons Currently Attending by Caste (%) – NSSO 64th Round

	6-10 years						*11-14 years*					
	ST	*SC*	*OBC*	*General*	*Total*	*Total-General-Gap*	*ST*	*SC*	*OBC*	*General*	*Total*	*Total-General-Gap*
Gujarat	86.8	95.9	91.5	97.2	92.5	4.7	76.0	81.8	75.1	87.5	79.3	8.1
Haryana	-	88.9	89.6	94.7	91.5	3.2	-	86.4	85.1	93.8	89.2	4.6
Maharashtra	81.5	94.9	95.5	96.8	94.5	2.3	73.8	88.6	92.2	91.0	89.4	1.5
Tamil Nadu	100.0	98.8	99.0	98.8	99.0	-0.1	83.6	94.0	95.8	100.0	95.4	4.6
India	86.0	87.1	89.2	93.8	89.6	4.2	77.2	80.1	84.3	88.2	83.9	4.3

Source: Same as Table 9.2.

Table 9.7: Muslim vs. Overall Literacy (6+ years age) Rate (%) – NSSO 64th Round

	Muslim	*Total*	*Total-Muslim Gap*
Gujarat	74.45	75.24	0.79
Haryana	59.39	73.84	14.45
Maharashtra	81.51	81.12	-0.39
Tamil Nadu	87.84	80.33	-7.51
India	67.84	71.99	4.15

Source: Same as Table 9.2.

Table 9.8: Literacy Rate (6+ years age) of SC, STs and OBC Muslims – NSSO 64th Round

	Rural	*Urban*	*Total*
Gujarat	57.38	80.67	67.44
India	59.71	71.97	63.85

Source: Same as Table 9.2.

Table 9.9: Literacy Rate in Gujarat (7+ yrs age)

	2001 (Census)	*2007-08 (NSSO 64th Round)*
Muslim	73.5	74.3
Total	69.1	74.9

Source: Calculated from the Unit Level Data of NSSO 64th Round, Participation and Expenditure in Education Survey, and Census 2001 as reported in Sachar Committee Report.

Table 9.10: Persons Currently Attending Schools by Religion (%) – NSSO 64th Round

	6-10 years			*11-14 years*		
	Muslim	*Total*	*Total-Muslim Gap*	*Muslim*	*Total*	*Total-Muslim Gap*
Gujarat	89.1	92.5	3.4	60.4	79.3	19.0
Haryana	81.6	91.5	9.9	59.0	89.2	30.2
Maharashtra	94.1	94.5	0.4	78.9	89.4	10.6
Tamil Nadu	99.4	99.0	-0.4	93.9	95.4	1.5
India	83.6	89.6	6.0	71.6	83.9	12.2

Source: Same as Table 9.2.

Table 9.11: Percentage of Households by Distance of Nearest School from Residence (Rural)–NSSO 64th Round

	Primary			*Upper Primary*			*Secondary*		
	Less than 2 km	*2-5 km*	*More than 5 km*	*Less than 2 km*	*2-5 km*	*More than 5 km*	*Less than 2 km*	*2-5 km*	*More than 5 km*
Gujarat	99.12	0.88	0.00	76.30	19.21	4.49	42.12	37.99	19.89
Haryana	99.82	0.18	0.00	96.30	3.28	0.43	77.30	15.52	7.18
Maharashtra	98.73	1.08	0.19	79.56	16.64	3.79	61.85	24.62	13.53
Tamil Nadu	99.04	0.96	0.00	78.47	18.26	3.28	44.34	36.61	19.05
India	98.39	1.48	0.13	78.86	18.05	3.08	47.40	35.52	17.08

Source: Same as Table 9.2.

Table 9.12: Percentage of Households by Distance of Nearest School from Residence (Urban) – NSSO 64th Round

	Primary			*Upper Primary*			*Secondary*		
	Less than 2 km	*2-5 km*	*More than 5 km*	*Less than 2 km*	*2-5 km*	*More than 5 km*	*Less than 2 km*	*2-5 km*	*More than 5 km*
Gujarat	99.96	0.03	0.00	97.75	2.25	0.00	94.75	4.74	0.52
Haryana	99.76	0.25	0.00	98.55	1.46	0.00	91.60	8.06	0.34
Maharashtra	98.52	1.28	0.19	95.74	3.72	0.55	88.43	9.63	1.94
Tamil Nadu	98.26	1.73	0.01	95.01	4.80	0.19	89.55	9.91	0.54
India	99.00	0.96	0.05	96.59	3.24	0.17	90.80	8.16	1.05

Source: Same as Table 9.2.

Table 9.13: Percentage of Households Less Than 2 km Distance from Nearest School by Caste – NSSO 64th Round

	Primary		*Upper Primary*		*Secondary*	
	Gujarat	*India*	*Gujarat*	*India*	*Gujarat*	*India*
ST	97.66	97	70.2	69.94	46.87	38.67
SC	99.66	98.85	90.79	83.28	67.87	58.26
OBC	99.61	98.78	81.16	84.51	52.55	56.77
General	99.96	98.56	93.18	87.57	80.16	70.94
Total	99.45	98.57	84.68	83.91	62.7	59.74
Total Gen-Gap	0.51	-0.01	8.50	3.66	17.46	11.20

Source: Same as Table 9.2.

Table 9.14: Percentage of Persons Currently Attending Any Education Institution by Age Group

Age Group	*Gujarat*	*Haryana*	*Maharashtra*	*Tamil Nadu*	*India*
5-14	85.5	89.0	89.8	97.2	85.2
15-20	31.9	46.2	47.7	46.9	42.3
21-29	2.6	4.6	6.8	3.8	4.9
Total	46.5	51.8	51.4	52.7	51.9

Source: Same as Table 9.2.

Table 9.15: Percentage of Persons by Different Education Groups

Education Level	*Gujarat*	*Haryana*	*Maharashtra*	*Tamil Nadu*	*India*
No formal Education	32.6	34.2	27.0	25.8	36.3
Formal Education till Middle	50.0	42.4	47.2	51.6	46.5
Sec/HS/Diploma	13.5	18.7	19.6	17.4	13.1
Graduate/PG	3.9	4.6	6.2	5.3	4.2
Total	100.0	100.0	100.0	100.0	100.0

Source: Same as Table 9.2.

Table 9.16: Percentage of Persons Belonging to Different Education Groups by Age Groups

Education Level	*Gujarat*	*Haryana*	*Maharashtra*	*Tamil Nadu*	*India*
Formal Education till Middle (4-13 year)	80.8	81.7	80.8	88.9	78.0
Sec/HS/Diploma(14-19 year)	25.8	32.4	34.0	46.9	26.5
Graduate/PG (19-29 year)	7.8	10.9	11.7	11.0	8.7

Source: Same as Table 9.2.

Table 9.17: Percentage of Persons Currently Attending Any Education Institution (17-29 years) by Type of Education

	Gujarat	*Haryana*	*Maharashtra*	*Tamil Nadu*	*India*
General	83.5	90.4	77.9	63.6	84.1
Professional/Technical	14.3	7.3	20.7	31.8	14.2
Vocational	2.2	2.3	1.4	4.6	1.7
Total	100.0	100.0	100.0	100.0	100.0

Source: Same as Table 9.2.

Table 9.18: Persons (5-29 years) Currently Attending Education Institution by Institution Type (%)–NSSO 64th Round

	All India			*Gujarat*		
	Rural	*Urban*	*Total*	*Rural*	*Urban*	*Total*
Government	71.3	39.4	63.0	81.9	33.3	63.7
Local Body	5.1	3.6	4.7	4.5	7.1	5.4
Private Aided	9.0	21.7	12.4	9.3	33.5	18.3
Private Unaided	14.2	34.2	19.4	4.3	25.3	12.2
Not Known	0.4	1.1	0.6	0.1	0.9	0.4
Total	100.0	100.0	100.0	100.0	100.0	100.0

Source: Same as Table 9.2.

Table 9.19: Persons (5-29 years) Currently Attending Different Types of Educational Institution by Economic Status (%)–NSSO 64th Round

	Rural				*Urban*			
	All India		*Gujarat*		*All India*		*Gujarat*	
	Poorest 20%	*Richest 20%*	*Poorest 20%*	*Richest 20%*	*Poorest 20%*	*Richest 20%*	*Poorest 20%*	*Richest 20%*
Government	83.1	48.3	89.1	65.1	53.8	21.3	59.4	15.5
Local Body	4.9	3.9	6.8	1.9	6.0	1.1	20.5	1.4
Private Aided	4.5	18.9	2.3	21.3	17.1	23.1	15.1	44.0
Private Unaided	7.1	28.3	1.8	11.5	22.3	53.2	4.8	35.1
Not Known	0.4	0.7	0.0	0.2	0.8	1.4	0.2	4.0
Total	100.0	100.0	100.0	100.0	100.0	100.0	100.0	100.0

Source: Same as Table 9.2.

Table 9.20: Average Total Expenses on Education Per-Head (Currently Attending Persons) by Type of Education Institution – NSSO 64th Round

	Rural				*Urban*			
	All India		*Gujarat*		*All India*		*Gujarat*	
	Rs.	%	*Rs.*	%	*Rs.*	%	*Rs.*	%
Government	1037	100	984	100	3473	100	2815	100
Local Body	691	67	501	51	2382	69	1548	55
Private Aided	4001	386	3509	357	7504	216	7569	269
Private Unaided	4722	455	5015	510	10061	290	8037	286
Not Known	3649	352	360	37	7583	218	11346	403
Total	1820	176	1370	139	6607	190	5710	203

Source: Same as Table 9.2.

Table 10.1: Selected Health Indicators of Gujarat and Other Developed States and All India

	Gujarat	*Tamil Nadu*	*Maharashtra*	*Haryana*	*India*
Male Life Expectancy 2002-06	62.9	65	66	65.9	62.6
Female Life Expectancy 2002-06	65.2	67.4	68.4	66.3	64.2
Maternal Mortality Ratio 2004-06	160	111	130	186	254
IMR *	62.8	37.7	45.3	44.2	57
U5MR*	77	45	53.4	58.8	74.3
Children Who are Undernourished (Stunting) *	49.20	31.1	44.00	43.30	45.8
Vaccination*	45.2	80.9	58.8	65.3	43.5
Antenatal Care*	87.4	89.9	92.7	98.9	77.2

* For the year 2005-2006

Source: Selected Socio Indicators, Central Statistical Organization and National Family Health Survey 3, (2005-2006), IIPS.

Table 10.2: Rate of Decline in IMR across Major States and All India (1990 to 2010)

State	*Initial Level in 1990*	*IMR in 2010*	*#Rate of Decline*	*Rank IMR 1990-94*	*Rank IMR 2005-2010*
Andhra	70	46	-1.64	6	8
Assam	76	58	-1.27	11	12
Bihar	75	48	-1.56	9.5	10
Gujarat	72	44	-1.68	7	7
Haryana	69	48	-1.55	8	9
Karnataka	70	38	-2.67	9.5	6
Kerala	17	13	-1.57	1	1
MP	111	62	-2.67	14	15
Maharashtra	58	28	-3.37	3	3
Orissa	122	61	-3.18	15	14
Punjab	61	34	-3.18	2	5
Rajasthan	84	55	-1.81	12	11
Tamil Nadu	59	24	-3.61	4	2
UP	99	61	-2.14	13	13
WB	63	31	-3.68	5	4
India	80	47	-2.39		

Note: # Rate of decline was calculated using the following formula of trend growth rate
log y = a + bt
Where y = IMR and t = years
Source: Sample Registration System Bulletin, GOI for Various Years.

Table 10.3: Rural Urban Gap in IMR

	1990-94	*1995-99*	*2000-2004*	*2005-2010*
Andhra	1.46	1.90	1.92	1.60
Assam	1.50	1.93	2.04	1.71
Bihar	1.49	1.30	1.25	1.34
Gujarat	1.40	1.50	1.68	1.68
Haryana	1.31	1.17	1.32	1.36
Karnataka	1.83	2.37	2.31	1.48
Kerala	1.24	0.92	1.24	1.28
MP	1.72	1.74	1.62	1.55
Maharasthra	1.72	1.80	1.65	1.65
Orissa	1.69	1.56	1.52	1.44
Punjab	1.51	1.43	1.49	1.34
Rajasthan	1.57	1.46	*1.51*	*1.82*
Tamil Nadu	1.60	1.47	1.49	1.18
UP	1.42	1.34	1.40	1.42
WB	1.63	1.35	1.42	1.31
India	1.66	1.69	1.70	1.62

Source: Sample Registration System Bulletin for Various Years, GOI.

Table 10.4: Gender Disparity Ratio in Infant Mortality Rate across Major States in India

	1990-94	*1995-99*	*2000-2004*	*2005-2010*
Andhra	0.88	0.99	0.99	1.05
Assam	0.90	0.96	1.01	1.06
Bihar	1.02	1.00	1.09	1.06
Gujarat	1.01	1.08	1.11	1.06
Haryana	1.12	1.18	1.20	1.06
Karnataka	0.88	0.97	0.92	1.05
Kerala	0.74	0.98	0.92	1.14
MP	0.98	0.99	1.07	1.04
Maharasthra	1.00	1.04	1.18	1.05
Orissa	0.97	0.98	0.97	1.02
Punjab	1.18	1.16	1.42	1.12
Rajasthan	1.03	1.09	1.08	1.07
Tamil Nadu	1.00	1.09	1.01	1.06
UP	1.10	1.10	1.08	1.06
WB	0.99	0.84	0.88	1.06
India	1.01	1.03	1.05	1.05

Source: Sample Registration System bulletin for various years, GOI.

Table 10.5: IMR across Social Groups in Major States of India

	1998-99				*2005-2006*			
State	*SC*	*ST*	*Others*	*All*	*SC*	*ST*	*Others*	*All*
Andhra Pradesh	95	104	47	71	88.1	94.1	54	68.4
Assam	45	59	68	62	*81.7*	59	74	70.9
Bihar	86	82	61	76	71		82.2	65
Gujarat	80	60	54	64	65.4	86	47.3	62.8
Haryana	68		57	59	53.3		36.1	44.2
Karnataka	70	85	56	62	57.2	45.8	43.5	53
Kerala			21	21			19.9	17.7
Madhya Pradesh	102	101	72	93	81.9	95.6	66.8	81.9
Maharashtra	53	74	49	53	45.2	51.4	40.5	45.3
Orissa	84	99	79	90	73.7	78.7	53.1	67.7
Punjab	74		44	57	46.2		44.1	44.9
Rajasthan	99	95	82	88	96.4	73.2	58.1	72.7
Tamil Nadu	42		52.7*	51	37.4		38.2*	37.7
Uttar Pradesh	110	*83*	82	95	90.7		71.4	83
West Bengal	55	*85*	45	51	38.8		56.6	52.1
India	83	84.2	61.8	73	66.4	62.1	48.9	57

Note: *Others for Tamil Nadu include only OBC due to relatively low sample of others in the state.
Source: National Family and Health Survey 2 (1998-99) and National Family and Health Survey 3 (2005-2006), IIPS.

Table 10.6: U5MR across Social Groups in Major States of India

	1998-99				*2005-2006*			
	SC	*ST*	*Others*	*All*	*SC*	*ST*	*Others*	*All*
Andhra Pradesh	122.4	115.9	64.7	91.3	96.1	112	63.2	78.7
Assam	56.3	73.5	86.9	79.5	110.7	83.2	100.9	95.2
Bihar	133.8	116.6	89.3	110.2	113.1		108.9	95
Gujarat	123	94.6	70.3	90.7	86.6	115.8	55.7	77
Haryana	92.1		74.8	79.1	73.9		49.7	58.8
Karnataka	104.6	120.6	69.8	83.3	65.4	*77.9*	60.4	66.2
Kerala			23.9	26			20.7	19.5
Madhya Pradesh	156	179.6	94.8	144.7	110.1	140.7	79.9	108.2
Maharashtra	66.1	92.3	65.9	69.9	50.2	69.8	47.4	53.4
Orissa	122.7	138.4	92.9	115.7	91.8	136.3	64.2	94.7
Punjab	94.6		51.4	69.9	61.5		50.5	54.6
Rajasthan	140.7	155	109.3	124.9	123.1	113.8	69.9	93.3
Tamil Nadu	63.3		63	64.5	48.3		44.6*	45
Uttar Pradesh	158.1	124.5	112.1	132.1	135.1		87.7	112.3
West Bengal	81.5	100.1	63.4	71	46.6		70.4	65.4
India	119.3	126.6	82.6	101.4	88.1	95.7	59.2	74.3

Note: *Others for Tamil Nadu include only OBC due to relatively low sample of others in the state.
Source: National Family and Health Survey 2 (1998-99) and National Family and Health Survey 3 (2005-2006), IIPS.

Table 10.7: Undernutrition (Stunting) of Children across Social Groups in Major States of India

	1998-99				*2005-2006*			
	SC	*ST*	*Others*	*All*	*SC*	*ST*	*Others*	*All*
Andhra Pradesh	42.7	42.7	32.3	38.6	47.7	54.9	36.3	38.40
Assam	45.1	42.6	31.7	50.2	***53.3***	38.1	47.4	41.10
Bihar	57.6	56.4	45.1	53.7	68.7		47.7	50.10
Gujarat	48.9	46.9	37.8	43.6	54.5	60.9	39	49.20
Haryana	56.3		44.6	50	53.4		39.7	43.30
Karnataka	43.7	41.2	35	36.6	48.9	51	35.3	42.40
Kerala	38.2		17.7	21.9	33.7		20.2	26.50
Madhya Pradesh	52.7	59.9	37.2	51	56.7	56.4	38.4	46.50
Maharashtra	43.7	57.1	35.0		55.2	57.8	42.5	44.00
Orissa	50.7	49.4	32.4	44	49.7	57.2	33.6	43.90
Punjab	49.6		43.1	39.2	44.5		30	34.70
Rajasthan	55	60	48.3	52	48.2	48.8	37.3	40.10
Tamil Nadu	41.2		25.1*	29.4	39.7		28.2*	31.1
Uttar Pradesh	63.1	69.3	50.3	55.5	59.7	68.5	48.3	52.40
West Bengal	45.6	46.6	40.1	41.5	44.7	58.6	43.5	41.8
India	51.7	52.8	40.7	45.5	53.9	53.9	40.7	45.8

Note: *Others for Tamil Nadu include only OBC due to relatively low sample of others in the state.
Source: National Family and Health Survey 2 (1998-99) and National Family and Health Survey 3 (2005-2006), IIPS.

Table 10.8: Child Immunization across Social Groups in Major States of India

	1998-99				*2005-2006*			
	SC	*ST*	*Others*	*All*	*SC*	*ST*	*Others*	*All*
Andhra Pradesh	60.7		62.3	58.7	44.3	26.7	58.2	45
Assam	20.4	14.4	18.2	17	31.3	36.1	27.6	31.4
Bihar	9.5	38.1	15.3	16.8	11.7		5.8	32.8
Gujarat	52.8	40.6	61.6	53	51.2	39.5	48.6	45.2
Haryana	56.4		67.7	62.7	66.9		71.2	65.3
Karnataka	55.2	***31.5***	63.2	60	56	39.7	75.4	55
Kerala			83.5	79.7			69.9	75.3
Madhya Pradesh	17.9	11.1	40.1	22.4	40.5	22.3	62.4	40.3
Maharashtra	79.8	62.2	78.5	78.4	59	39.3	62.5	58.8
Orissa	44.5	26.4	49.3	43.7	59.5	30.4	58	51.8
Punjab	54.6		82.3	72.1	47.6		70.1	60.1
Rajasthan	13.4	10.3	22.8	17.3	35.8	***3.3***	40	26.5
Tamil Nadu	84.2		90.6*	88.8	72.3		84.6*	80.9
Uttar Pradesh	21.7	***14.1***	24.7	21.2	15.9		30	23
West Bengal	50.9		40.4	43.8	61.4		65.3	64.3
India	40	26.4	46.8	42	39.7	31.3	53.8	43.5

Note: *Others for Tamil Nadu includes only OBC due to relatively low sample of others in the state.
Source: National Family and Health Survey 2 (1998-99) and National Family and Health Survey 3 (2005-2006), IIPS.

Table 10.9: Mother's Antenatal Care across Social Groups in Major States of India

	1998-99				*2005-2006*			
	SC	*ST*	*Others*	*All*	*SC*	*ST*	*Others*	*All*
Andhra Pradesh	91.9	74.1	97.1	92.7	97.1	82.9	98.3	94.8
Assam	75.5	52.6	59.1	61.1	78.6	63.2	68.2	72.2
Bihar	29.3	30.3	50.2	37.5	21.1		51.9	34.3
Gujarat	84.4	77.8	93.1	86.4	85.3	73.9	95.3	87.4
Haryana	45.1		61.1	58.1	91.1		89.7	89.9
Karnataka	82.4	71.8	89	86.3	85.9	82.1	94.4	90.6
Kerala	100	100	99.7	99.7	100		99.8	99.9
Madhya Pradesh	62.5	44.3	78.8	61.5	82.4	63.8	89.9	79.7
Maharashtra	88.6		93.4	79.7	93.5	83.8	92.7	92.7
Orissa	82.3	63	85.2	100	87.2	77.9	93.2	87.3
Punjab	66.2		81.4	74	84.7		93.1	90.3
Rajasthan	41.9	42.1	51.9	47.5	74.2	69.3	77.8	74.9
Tamil Nadu	98.9		98.8*	98.8	98		99.2	98.9
Uttar Pradesh	30.2	21.9	44.2	36.1	61	27.3	72	66.5
West Bengal	94.3	88.4	88.9	90.5	96.5	79.5	91.8	92.3
India	61.8	56.9	72.1	66	74.1	70.6	84.8	77.2

Note: *Others for Tamil Nadu include only OBC due to relatively low sample of others in the state.
Source: National Family and Health Survey 2 (1998-99) and National Family and Health Survey 3 (2005-2006), IIPS.

Table 10.10: Disparity Ratio for IMR**

	1998-99		*2005-2006*	
	SC/Others	*ST/Others*	*SC/Others*	*ST/Others*
Andhra Pradesh	2.02	2.21	1.63	1.74
Assam	0.66	0.87	1.10	0.80
Bihar	1.41	1.34	0.86	
Gujarat	1.48	1.11	1.38	1.82
Haryana#	1.19	0.00	1.48	
Karnataka	1.25	1.52	1.31	1.05
Madhya Pradesh	1.42	1.40	1.23	1.43
Maharashtra	1.08	1.51	1.12	1.27
Orissa	1.06	1.25	1.39	1.48
Punjab#	1.68		1.05	
Rajasthan	1.21	1.16	1.66	1.26
Tamil Nadu#	0.80		0.98*	
Uttar Pradesh	1.34	1.01	1.27	
West Bengal	1.22	1.89	0.69	
India	1.34	1.36	1.36	1.27

Note: *Others for Tamil Nadu include only OBC due to relatively low sample of others in the state.
**Information for state of Kerala is not given due to fewer sample size across social group.
No STs population.
Source: National Family and Health Survey 2 (1998-99) and National Family and Health Survey 3 (2005-2006), IIPS.

Table 10.11: Disparity Ratio for U5MR**

	1998-99		*2005-2006*	
	SC/Others	*ST/Others*	*SC/Others*	*ST/Others*
West Bengal	1.22	1.89	0.69	
Andhra Pradesh	1.89	1.79	1.52	1.77
Assam	0.65	0.85	1.10	0.82
Bihar	1.50	1.31	1.04	
Gujarat	1.75	1.35	1.55	2.08
Haryana#	1.23		1.49	
Karnataka	1.50	1.73	1.08	1.29
Madhya Pradesh	1.65	1.89	1.38	1.76
Maharashtra	1.00	1.40	1.06	1.47
Orissa	1.32	1.49	1.43	2.12
Punjab#	1.84		1.22	
Rajasthan	1.29	1.42	1.76	1.63
Tamil Nadu*	1.00		1.08	
Uttar Pradesh	1.41	1.11	1.54	
West Bengal	1.29	1.58	0.66	
India	1.44	1.53	1.49	1.62

Note: *Others for Tamil Nadu include only OBC due to relatively low sample of others in the state.
**Information for state of Kerala is not given due to fewer sample size across social group.
No STs population.
Source: National Family and Health Survey 2 (1998-99) and National Family and Health Survey 3 (2005-2006), IIPS.

Table 10.12: Disparity Ratio for Child Undernutrition

	1998-99		*2005-2006*	
	SC/Others	*ST/Others*	*SC/Others*	*ST/Others*
Andhra Pradesh	1.31	1.51	1.32	1.32
Assam	1.12	0.80	1.42	1.34
Bihar	1.44		1.28	1.25
Gujarat	1.40	1.56	1.29	1.24
Haryana#	1.35		1.26	
Karnataka	1.39	1.44	1.25	1.18
Kerala	1.67		2.16	
Madhya Pradesh	1.48	1.47	1.42	1.61
Maharashtra	1.30	1.36	1.25	1.63
Orissa	1.48	1.70	1.56	1.52
Punjab#	1.48		1.15	
Rajasthan	1.29	1.31	1.14	1.24
Tamil Nadu*	1.64		1.41	
Uttar Pradesh	1.24	1.42	1.25	1.38
West Bengal	1.03	1.35	1.14	1.16
India	1.32	1.32	1.27	1.30

Note: *Others for Tamil Nadu include only OBC due to relatively low sample of others in the state.
No STs population.
Source: National Family and Health Survey 2 (1998-99) and National Family and Health Survey 3 (2005-2006), IIPS.

Table 10.13: Social Disparity in Child Immunization**

	1998-99		*2005-2006*	
	SC/Others	*ST/Others*	*SC/Others*	*ST/Others*
Andhra Pradesh	0.97	0.00	0.76	0.46
Assam	1.12	0.79	1.13	1.31
Bihar	0.62	2.49	2.02	
Gujarat	0.86	0.66	1.05	0.81
Haryana#	0.83	0.00	0.94	0.00
Karnataka	0.87	0.50	0.74	0.53
Madhya Pradesh	0.45	0.28	0.65	0.36
Maharashtra	1.02	0.79	0.94	0.63
Orissa	0.90	0.54	1.03	0.52
Punjab#	0.66		0.68	
Rajasthan	0.59	0.45	0.90	0.08
Tamil Nadu	0.93		0.85	
Uttar Pradesh	0.88	0.57	0.53	0.00
West Bengal	1.26	0.00	0.94	0.00
India	0.85	0.56	0.74	0.58

Note: *Others for Tamil Nadu include only OBC due to relatively low sample of others in the state.
**Information for state of Kerala is not given due to fewer sample size across social group.
No STs population.
Source:National Family and Health Survey 2 (1998-99) and National Family and Health Survey 3 (2005-2006), IIPS.

Table 10.14: Social Disparity in Antenatal Services

	1998-99		*2005-2006*	
	SC/Others	*ST/Others*	*SC/Others*	*ST/Others*
Gujarat	1.40	1.56	1.29	1.24
Andhra Pradesh	0.95	0.76	0.99	0.84
Assam	1.28	0.89	1.15	0.93
Bihar	0.58	0.60	0.41	0.00
Gujarat	0.91	0.84	0.90	0.78
Haryana#	0.74	0.00	1.02	0.00
Karnataka	0.93	0.81	0.91	0.87
Kerala	1.00	1.00	1.00	
Madhya Pradesh	0.79	0.56	0.92	0.71
Maharashtra	0.95	0.00	1.01	0.90
Orissa	0.97	0.74	0.94	0.84
Punjab#	0.81	0.00	0.91	0.00
Rajasthan	0.81	0.81	0.95	0.89
Tamil Nadu	1.00		0.99	
Uttar Pradesh	0.68	0.50	0.85	0.38
West Bengal	1.06	0.99	1.05	0.87
India	0.86	0.79	0.87	0.83

Note: *Others for Tamil Nadu include only OBC due to relatively low sample of others in the state.
No STs population.
Source: National Family and Health Survey 2 (1998-99) and National Family and Health Survey 3 (2005-2006), IIPS.

Table 10.15 :Per Capita Health Expenditure in Gujarat and Other Major States of India

	*Per Capita Health Expenditure***				*Rank of the State*			
State	*1990-91 to 1994-1995*	*1995-96 to 1999-2000*	*2000-01 to 2004-2005*	*2005-06 to 2009-2010**	*1990-91 to 1994-1995*	*1995-96 to 1999-2000*	*2000-01 to 2004-2005*	*2005-06 to 2009-2010**
Andhra	113.0	133.3	166.4	224.2	10	10	5	14
Assam	131.8	121.3	132.2	377.3	4	12	11	3
Bihar	106.7	98.5	85.7	155.1	13	14	15	15
Gujarat	118.6	159.6	145.8	265.6	9	4	9	11
Haryana	119.0	136.5	138.2	322.6	8	7	10	7
Karnataka	123.1	152.5	171.7	343.1	7	6	4	4
Kerala	159.5	183.7	228.2	438.4	2	2	2	1
Maharasthra	126.3	136.0	166.3	309.11	6	8	6	8
MP	111.2	130.8	113.2	242.0	12	11	13	13
Orissa	100.7	106.3	125.9	250.9	14	13	12	12
Punjab	173.8	195.6	229.5	324.0	1	1	1	6
Rajasthan	126.8	159.0	158.7	332.0	5	5	8	5
Tamil Nadu	149.5	175.6	181.0	382.7	3	3	3	2
UP	99.5	93.5	95.0	281.9	15	15	14	9
WB	112.9	133.8	162.8	277.4	11	9	7	10

Note: *Post NRHM period
**Health expenditures are in constant 1999-2000 prices.
Source: Reserve Bank of India Bulletin for various years and National Rural Health Mission (Online), available at http://www.mohfw.nic.in/NRHM.htm> Accessed on 10th March, 2012.

Table 10.16: Health Expenditure as a Share of Total Expenditure

State	*1990-91 to 1994-95*	*1995-96 to 1999-2000*	*2000-01 to 2004-05*	*2005-06 to 2009-2010*
Andhra	4.77	4.76	2.27	1.20
Assam	5.09	4.81	2.94	0.58
Bihar	5.60	5.45	2.86	1.01
Gujarat	4.25	4.39	2.02	0.77
Haryana	3.06	3.08	1.76	0.67
Karnataka	5.07	5.25	2.72	0.90
Kerala	5.66	5.29	3.17	1.36
MP	4.75	4.74	2.78	0.82
Maharashtra	4.36	3.95	2.95	1.13
Orissa	4.61	4.52	2.97	0.66
Punjab	4.15	4.33	2.92	0.94
Rajasthan	5.43	5.66	2.89	1.02
Tamil Nadu	5.33	5.50	2.78	0.82
UP	5.18	4.69	2.20	0.79
WB	6.57	5.96	2.84	1.02
All States	5.03	4.90	2.75	0.95

Source: Reserve Bank of India Bulletin for Various Years.

Table 10.17: Health Expenditure as a Share of NSDP

State	*1990-91 to 1994-95*	*1995-96 to 1999-2000*	*2000-01 to 2004-05*	*2005-06 to 2009-2010**
Assam	5.09	4.81	2.94	0.58
Andhra	0.95	0.94	0.92	1.01
Assam	1.10	0.98	1.00	1.92
Bihar	1.86	1.78	1.32	1.65
Gujarat	0.85	0.87	0.72	0.73
Haryana	0.61	0.63	0.50	0.58
Karnataka	1.02	0.99	0.94	0.98
Kerala	1.12	1.03	1.03	1.03
Maharasthra	0.74	0.64	0.69	0.66
MP	1.18	1.18	0.98	1.34
Orissa	1.13	1.08	1.11	1.09
Punjab	0.80	0.82	0.86	0.72
Rajasthan	1.20	1.21	1.14	1.49
Tamil Nadu	1.07	0.99	0.87	**0.97**
UP	1.16	0.98	0.96	1.77
WB	1.00	0.94	0.91	0.89
Average of Major States	1.02	0.95	0.89	1.04

Note: *Post NRHM period

Source: Central Statistical Organization, Reserve Bank of India Bulletin and National Rural Health Mission (Online) Available at <http://www.mohfw.nic.in/NRHM.htm> Accessed on 10th March, 2012.

Table 10.18: Average Expenditure for Hospitalization in Government Institutions in Selected States and All India (in Rs)

	Average Expenditure	
RURAL	*1995-96*	*2004*
Gujarat	1465	2,253
Haryana	2667	11,665
Maharashtra	1529	2,243
Tamil Nadu	751	637
India	2080	3,238
URBAN		
Gujarat	1897	4185
Haryana	8888	20,372
Maharashtra	1439	3,297
Tamil Nadu	934	1,666
India	2195	3,877

Source: Ministry for Health and Family Welfare, 2007.

Table 10.19: Quintilewise Utilization of Government Health Facility for Hospitalization in Selected States and All India

		Rural					*Urban*				
		Guj	*Har*	*Mah*	*TN*	*Ind*	*Guj*	*Har*	*Mah*	*TN*	*Ind*
Q1	1995-96	44	18	66	64	61	57	51	56	59	62
	2004	44	28	49	45	55	32	13	51	62	54
Q2	1995-96	43	48	41	55	58	42	31	52	44	52
	2004	51	24	34	51	50	36	27	23	46	44
Q3	1995-96	25	30	42	50	50	44	27	37	32	45
	2004	40	8	31	40	43	34	32	31	35	39
Q4	1995-96	35	31	24	34	42	33	17	22	26	37
	2004	18	23	21	42	37	16	28	20	25	30
Q5	1995-96	23	25	15	16	33	20	49	18	12	27
	2004	19	23	12	30	29	21	32	18	9	21
All	1995-96	32	31	31	41	45	37	37	37	36	43
	2004	31	21	29	41	42	26	29	29	37	38

Source: Calculated from the Unit Level Record of NSSO on 52nd and 60th Round on Morbidity and Health Care.

Contributors

Atul Sood is an Associate Professor, at the Centre for the Study of Regional Development, Jawaharlal Nehru University, New Delhi. He teaches political economy of regional development and his recent research publications are on political economy of green growth in India; health sector reforms and access to health services; politics of government finances and centre state financial relations; uneven regional development in India with special focus on employment and industrial development; and scope and potential of non-state regulation. Dr Sood has done numerous field based studies on Gujarat beginning with his first work on economic roots of social tensions, power and handloom sector, textile industry in Ahmadabad, salt manufacturing in Kutch and livelihood restoration after the earthquake.

Chinmoyee Mallik is a guest lecturer in the Department of Geography, Vidaysagar College, University of Kolkata, Kolkata. She is a PhD candidate at the Centre for the Study of Regional Development, Jawaharlal Nehru University and is interested in Land and Livelihoods issues in the Rural Peripheries of Mega Cities.

Gaurav Arya is working on social and economic implications of Power Sector Reforms in India. He has done his M.Phil from Jawaharlal Nehru University, New Delhi.

Kalaiyarasan A. is working on the nature of group inequalities in India, with particular emphasis on caste, and its linkages with social and economic capital. His M. Phil research was on SEZs in Tamil Nadu.

Nidhi Mittal is currently examining the patterns of poverty and inequality in India and its association with nature and characteristics of growth across various regions of India. She has completed her M.Phil from Jawaharlal Nehru University, New Delhi.

Pankaj Vashisht, is working on the issues related to Global Economic Integration and its implications for growth and income distribution. He has worked at the Indian Council for Research on International Economic Relations (ICRIER) and has numerous publications including book, chapters in edited books, journals articles, working papers and government reports. He has done M. Phil. in economics from Jawaharlal Nehru University, New Delhi.

Ruchika Rani is currently working with Education Department, Government of Haryana. She has completed her M. Phil from Jawaharlal Nehru University on *Employment and Poverty among Agricultural Workers* and has written on the subject in edited volumes. Her current research interest is on Determinants of Income and Consumption Inequality in India across the Indian States.

Sandeep Sharma, Associate Fellow at IIDS and currently pursuing research on Inequalities in Health in India. Earlier he had secured M. Phil Degree in Applied Economics from the Centre for Development Studies, Trivandrum. Before joining the IIDS he had worked as Research Associate with Punjab Government Reforms Commission. His area of research interest includes Public health, Health Economics and Social Exclusion and Discrimination.

Sangeeta Ghosh, is currently working on growth dynamics and employment and conditions of labour in the manufacturing sector in India. Her M. Phil work was focused on examining the linkages between the formal and the informal manufacturing sector in India. She has worked at Indian Institute of Foreign Trade, Confederation of Indian Industry and for Punjab Governance Reforms Commission.

Santosh Kumar Das, is specializing on issues of financial intermediation and integration in India and its implications for growth and distributive justice. He is pursuing his Ph.D. His M. Phil work was focused on examining growth, investment and profitability in manufacturing sector in India.

Sourindra Ghosh, is currently working with SEWA Bharat, Delhi. He has extensive experience in field based research and has published on educational outcomes, poverty and women's empowerment in

India. He has worked with Collaborative Research and Dissemination (CORD), National Commission for Minority Educational Institutions (NCMEI) and Centre for Budget and Governance Accountability (CBGA), New Delhi.

Sucharita Sen is an Associate Professor, Centre for the Study of Regional Development, School of Social Sciences, Jawaharlal Nehru University New Delhi. She is an Economic Geographer and her research interest revolves around the following themes: access to land and water, land dispossession in the peri-urban areas, rural livelihoods. She teaches Economic Geography, Agricultural Geography and Natural Resource in Agriculture with special reference to India.